MrExcel
LIBRARY

Excel 2013 Pivot Table Data Crunching

Bill Jelen

Michael Alexander

D0572469

que

800 East 96th Street,
Indianapolis, Indiana 46240
USA

Excel 2013 Pivot Table Data Crunching

ISBN-13: 978-0-7897-4875-1
ISBN-10: 0-7897-4875-4

Library of Congress Cataloging-in-Publication data is on file.

Printed in the United States of America

First Printing: January 2013

Trademarks

All terms mentioned in this book that are known to be trademarks or service marks have been appropriately capitalized. Que Publishing cannot attest to the accuracy of this information. Use of a term in this book should not be regarded as affecting the validity of any trademark or service mark.

Warning and Disclaimer

Bulk Sales   *5246 7254   8/13*

Que Publishing offers excellent discounts on this book when ordered in quantity for bulk purchases or special sales. For more information, please contact

> **U.S. Corporate and Government Sales**
>
> **1-800-382-3419**
>
> **corpsales@pearsontechgroup.com**

For sales outside of the U.S., please contact

> **International Sales**
>
> **international@pearsoned.com**

Editor-in-Chief
Greg Wiegand

Executive Editor
Loretta Yates

Development Editor
Charlotte Kughen

Managing Editor
Sandra Schroeder

Senior Project Editor
Tonya Simpson

Copy Editor
Bart Reed

Indexer
Lisa Stumpf

Proofreader
Debbie Williams

Technical Editor
Bob Umlas

Publishing Coordinator
Cindy Teeters

Book Designer
Anne Jones

Compositor
Bronkella Publishing

Contents

About the Authors

Bill Jelen, Excel MVP and the host of MrExcel.com, has been using spreadsheets since 1985, and he launched the MrExcel.com website in 1998. Bill was a regular guest on *Call for Help* with Leo Laporte and has produced more than 1,500 episodes of his daily video podcast, Learn Excel from MrExcel. He is the author of 38 books about Microsoft Excel and writes the monthly Excel column for *Strategic Finance* magazine and his Excel tips appear regularly in *CFO Excel Pro* newsletter and *CFO Magazine*. Before founding MrExcel.com, Bill Jelen spent 12 years in the trenches, working as a financial analyst for the finance, marketing, accounting, and operations departments of a $500 million public company. He lives near Akron, Ohio with his wife, Mary Ellen.

Mike Alexander is a Microsoft Certified Application Developer (MCAD) and author of several books on advanced business analysis with Microsoft Access and Excel. He has more than 15 years of experience consulting and developing Office solutions. Mike has been named a Microsoft MVP for his ongoing contributions to the Excel community. In his spare time, he runs a free tutorial site, www.datapigtechnologies.com, where he shares basic Access and Excel tips to the Office community.

Dedication

To everyone at Boca Raton Fire Department

—Bill Jelen

To my twelve fans at datapigtechnologies.com

—Mike Alexander

Acknowledgments

Mike Alexander is the funniest guy doing live Excel seminars. I appreciate him as a coauthor on all four editions of this book, which has earned the #1 spot on the Amazon Computer Book bestseller list (for 54 minutes one day in January). Rob Collie of PowerPivotPro.com keeps me up to speed on PowerPivot. At Microsoft, thanks to Scott Ruble and Diego Oppenheimer for always being willing to answer a quick question. At MrExcel.com, thanks to Tracy Syrstad, Wei Jiang, Scott Pearson, Tyler Nash, and an entire community of people passionate about Excel. Thanks to VoG, Richard Schollar, Jerry JS411, Daniel Nieves, and Cindy Kredo. Loretta Yates at Pearson Education is the best editor ever. Bob Umlas keeps us on our toes as tech editor. Finally, thanks to my wife, Mary Ellen, for her support during the writing process.

—Bill Jelen

Thanks to Bill Jelen for deciding to coauthor this book with me many editions ago. His knowledge of Excel still blows me away to this day. My deepest thanks to the professionals at Pearson Education for all the hours of work put into bringing this book to life. Thanks also to Bob Umlas, whose technical editing has helped us make numerous improvements to the examples and text in this book. Finally, a special thank-you goes to the wife and kids for putting up with all the time I spent locked away on this project.

—Mike Alexander

We Want to Hear from You!

As the reader of this book, *you* are our most important critic and commentator. We value your opinion and want to know what we're doing right, what we could do better, what areas you'd like to see us publish in, and any other words of wisdom you're willing to pass our way.

We welcome your comments. You can email or write to let us know what you did or didn't like about this book—as well as what we can do to make our books better.

Please note that we cannot help you with technical problems related to the topic of this book.

When you write, please be sure to include this book's title and author as well as your name and email address. We will carefully review your comments and share them with the author and editors who worked on the book.

Email: feedback@quepublishing.com

Mail: Que Publishing
         ATTN: Reader Feedback
         800 East 96th Street
         Indianapolis, IN 46240 USA

Reader Services

Visit our website and register this book at quepublishing.com/register for convenient access to any updates, downloads, or errata that might be available for this book.

The pivot table is the single most powerful command in all of Excel. Pivot tables came along during the 1990s when Microsoft and Lotus were locked in a bitter battle for dominance of the spreadsheet market. The race to continually add enhanced features to their respective products during the mid-1990s led to many incredible features, but none as powerful as the pivot table.

With a pivot table, you can take 1 million rows of transactional data and transform it into a summary report in seconds. If you can drag a mouse, you can create a pivot table. In addition to quickly summarizing and calculating data, pivot tables enable you to change your analysis on the fly by simply moving fields from one area of a report to another.

No other tool in Excel gives you the flexibility and analytical power of a pivot table.

What You Will Learn from This Book

It is widely agreed that close to 60 percent of Excel users leave 80 percent of Excel untouched. That is, most users do not tap into the full potential of Excel's built-in utilities. Of these utilities, the most prolific by far is the pivot table. Despite the fact that pivot tables have been a cornerstone of Excel for almost 20 years, they remain one of the most under-utilized tools in the entire Microsoft Office Suite. Having picked up this book, you are savvy enough to have heard of pivot tables or even have used them on occasion. You have a sense that pivot tables provide a power that you are not using, and you want to learn how to leverage that power to increase your productivity quickly.

Within the first two chapters, you will be able to create basic pivot tables, increase your productivity, and produce reports in minutes instead of hours. Within the first seven chapters, you will be able to output complex pivot reports with drill-down capabilities and accompanying charts. By the end of the book, you will be able to build a dynamic pivot table reporting system.

What Is New in Excel 2013's Pivot Tables

Luckily, Microsoft continues to invest heavily in Business Intelligence (BI), and pivot tables are the front end that let you access the new features. Some of the features added to Excel 2013 pivot tables include the following:

- Excel offers thumbnails for four possible pivot tables in the Data Analysis Lens. If you happen to need one of these pivot tables, it requires three mouse clicks.
- Excel offers thumbnails for ten recommended pivot tables when you choose Insert, Recommended Pivot Tables. If you are not sure how best to summarize your data, you'll find plenty of inspiration in this dialog.
- A new timeline slicer enables you to easily filter your pivot table by month, quarter, or year. Excel 2010 had added visual filters called *slicers*—the timeline in Excel 2013 extends slicers for date fields.
- All people using any version of Excel 2013 (except Excel RT on a tablet) can now jump through a few hoops to build a pivot table using data on multiple worksheets. This functionality replaces the need to join two worksheets using VLOOKUP.
- People using the client version of Office 365 or Excel Professional Plus can enable the PowerPivot add-in. PowerPivot provides drag-and-drop functionality to link tables, worksheets, SQL Server, and more. PowerPivot adds better calculated fields.
- PowerView enables you to animate your pivot tables in an ad-hoc query tool.

If you skipped Excel 2010, you missed these new features:

- New calculations for Rank, Percentage of Parent, and Running Percent of Total.
- Repeat Item Labels to fill in the blanks along the outer column fields in a pivot table.
- Slicers to create visual filters.

Skills Required to Use This Book

We have created a reference that is comprehensive enough for hard-core analysts yet relevant to casual users of Excel. The bulk of the book covers how to use pivot tables in the Excel user interface. Chapter 10, "Mashing up Data with PowerPivot," delves into the PowerPivot window. Chapter 14, "Advanced PivotTable Tips and Techniques," describes how to create pivot tables in Excel's powerful VBA macro language. This means that any user who has a firm grasp of the basics, such as preparing data, copying, pasting, and entering simple formulas, should not have a problem understanding the concepts in this book.

CASE STUDY: LIFE BEFORE PIVOT TABLES

Your manager asks you to create a one-page summary of a sales database. He would like to see total revenue by region and product. Suppose you do not know how to use pivot tables. You will have to use dozens of keystrokes or mouse clicks to complete this task.

First, you have to build the outline of the report:

1. Copy the Product column to a blank section of the worksheet.

2. Use Data, Remove Duplicates to eliminate the duplicates.

3. Delete the Product heading.

4. Copy the unique list of products and then use Paste Special Transpose to turn the list sideways.

5. Delete the vertical list of products.

6. Copy the Region column to a blank section of the worksheet.

7. Use Data, Remove Duplicates to remove the duplicates.

8. Delete the Region heading.

9. Cut and paste the products so they appear left of and below the regions.

At this point, I count 27 mouse clicks or keystrokes. You've built the shell of the final report, but there are no numbers inside yet, as shown in Figure I.1.

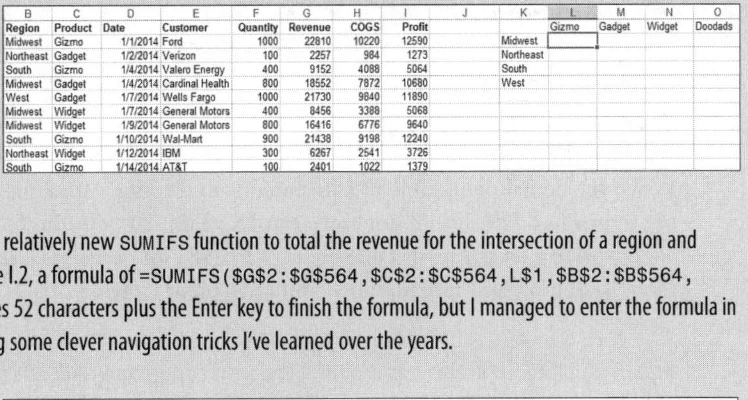

Figure I.1

It took 27 clicks to get to this point.

	B	C	D	E	F	G	H	I	J	K	L	M	N	O
	Region	Product	Date	Customer	Quantity	Revenue	COGS	Profit			Gizmo	Gadget	Widget	Doodads
	Midwest	Gizmo	1/1/2014	Ford	1000	22810	10220	12590		Midwest				
	Northeast	Gadget	1/2/2014	Verizon	100	2257	984	1273		Northeast				
	South	Gizmo	1/4/2014	Valero Energy	400	9152	4088	5064		South				
	Midwest	Gadget	1/4/2014	Cardinal Health	800	18552	7872	10680		West				
	West	Gadget	1/7/2014	Wells Fargo	1000	21730	9840	11890						
	Midwest	Widget	1/7/2014	General Motors	400	8456	3388	5068						
	Midwest	Widget	1/9/2014	General Motors	800	16416	6776	9640						
	South	Gizmo	1/10/2014	Wal-Mart	900	21438	9198	12240						
	Northeast	Widget	1/12/2014	IBM	300	6267	2541	3726						
	South	Gizmo	1/14/2014	AT&T	100	2401	1022	1379						

Next, you need to build the relatively new SUMIFS function to total the revenue for the intersection of a region and product. As shown in Figure I.2, a formula of =SUMIFS($G$2:$G$564,$C$2:$C$564,L$1,$B$2:$B$564, $K2) does the trick. It takes 52 characters plus the Enter key to finish the formula, but I managed to enter the formula in 36 clicks or keystrokes using some clever navigation tricks I've learned over the years.

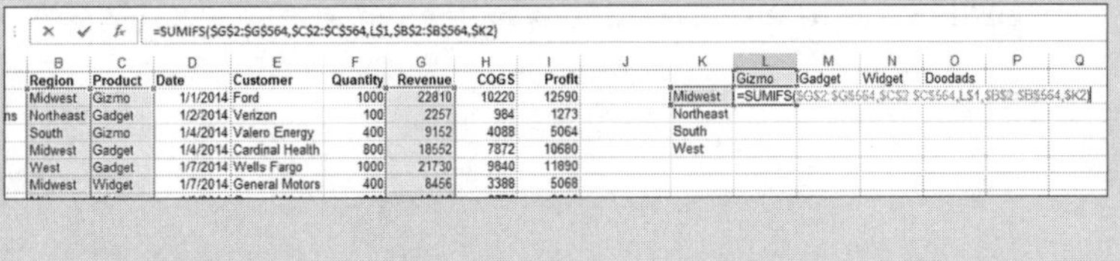

Figure I.2

If this was the year 2006, the SUMIFS function would have been an uglier SUMPRODUCT function.

		fx	=SUMIFS($G$2:$G$564,$C$2:$C$564,L$1,$B$2:$B$564,$K2)												
	B	C	D	E	F	G	H	I	J	K	L	M	N	O	P	Q
	Region	Product	Date	Customer	Quantity	Revenue	COGS	Profit			Gizmo	Gadget	Widget	Doodads
ns	Midwest	Gizmo	1/1/2014	Ford	1000	22810	10220	12590		Midwest	=SUMIFS($G$2:$G$564,$C$2:$C$564,L$1,$B$2:$B$564,$K2)	
	Northeast	Gadget	1/2/2014	Verizon	100	2257	984	1273		Northeast	
	South	Gizmo	1/4/2014	Valero Energy	400	9152	4088	5064		South	
	Midwest	Gadget	1/4/2014	Cardinal Health	800	18552	7872	10680		West	
	West	Gadget	1/7/2014	Wells Fargo	1000	21730	9840	11890			
	Midwest	Widget	1/7/2014	General Motors	400	8456	3388	5068			

Provided you are adept at using the fill handle, you need just two more mouse drags to copy the formula to the rest of the table.

Enter the heading "Total" in the total row and total column. You can do this in nine keystrokes, if you type the first heading, press Ctrl+Enter to stay in the same cell, then use Copy, select cell for second heading and Paste.

If you select K1:P6 and press Alt+Enter, you can add the total formulas in three keystrokes.

You have a nice summary report, as shown in Figure I.3. It took 77 clicks or keystrokes. If you could pull all this off in 5 or 10 minutes, you would probably be fairly proud of your Excel prowess—there were some good tricks among those 77 operations.

Figure I.3

A mere 77 operations later, you have a summary report.

	K	L	M	N	O	P
		Gizmo	Gadget	Widget	Doodads	Total
	Midwest	652651	544772	537965	6036	1741424
	Northeast	751724	714009	620019	38860	2124612
	South	918588	839551	844186	0	2602325
	West	70057	65382	75349	28663	239451
	Total	2393020	2163714	2077519	73559	6707812

Hand the report to your manager. Within a few minutes, your manager will come back with one of the following requests, which will certainly cause a lot of rework:

- Could you put products down the side and regions across the top?
- Could you show me the same report for only the manufacturing customers?
- Could you show profit instead of revenue?
- Could you copy this report for each of the customers?

Invention of the Pivot Table

When the actual pivot table was invented is in dispute. Although the Excel team coined the term *Pivot Table*, it did not appear in Excel until 1993. Pito Salas and his team at Lotus were working on the pivot table concept in 1986 and released Lotus Improv in 1991. Before then, Javelin offered functionality similar to pivot tables.

The core concept behind a pivot table is that the data, formulas, and data views are stored separately. Each column has a name, and you can group and rearrange the data by dragging field names to various positions on the report.

CASE STUDY: LIFE AFTER PIVOT TABLES

Say you need to produce the same report in the last case study but you want to use a pivot table. Excel 2013 offers you 10 thumbnails of recommended pivot tables to get you close to the goal. Follow these steps:

1. Click the Insert tab of the ribbon.

2. Click Recommended PivotTables. The first recommended item is Revenue by Region (see Figure I.4).

Figure I.4
The first recommended pivot table is as close as you will get to the required report.

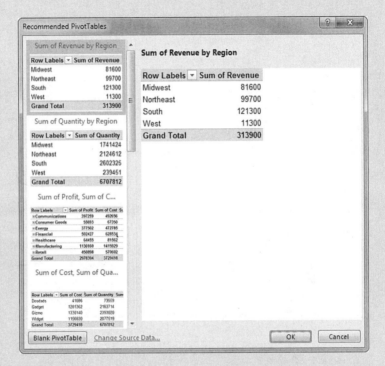

3. Click OK to accept the first pivot table.

4. Drag the Product field from the PivotTable Field List to the COLUMNS area (see Figure I.5).

Figure I.5
To finish the report, drag the Product heading to the COLUMNS area.

5. Unselect Field Headers on the right side of the ribbon.

After just five clicks of the mouse, you have the report shown in Figure I.6.

Figure I.6
It took five clicks to create this report.

	A	B	C	D	E	F
1						
2						
3	Sum of Revenue					
4		Doodads	Gadget	Gizmo	Widget	Grand Total
5	Midwest	300	24700	28200	28400	81600
6	Northeast	1800	32500	33300	32100	99700
7	South		37700	39500	44100	121300
8	West	1300	2900	3000	4100	11300
9	Grand Total	3400	97800	104000	108700	313900

In addition, when your manager comes back with one of the requests near the end of the prior case study, a pivot table makes it easy for you to make the changes. You find out about all of these methods in the chapters that follow, but here is a quick recap:

- Could you put products down the side and regions across the top? (10 seconds: drag Product to Rows and Region to Columns.)

- Could you show me the same report for only the Manufacturing customers? (15 seconds: select Insert Slicer, Sector, click OK, click Manufacturing.)

- Could you show profit instead of revenue? (10 seconds: uncheck Revenue, check Profit.)
- Could you copy this report for each of the customers? (30 seconds: move Customer to Report Filter, open the tiny drop-down next to the Options button, choose Show Report Filter Pages, click OK.)

Sample Files Used in This Book

All data files used throughout this book are available for download from `www.mrexcel.com/pivotbookdata2013.html`. You will find one Excel workbook per chapter and should be able to achieve the exact results shown in the figures in this book by starting with the raw data on the Data worksheet. If you simply want to work with the final pivot table, you can find it in the workbook as well.

Conventions Used in This Book

This book follows certain conventions:

- `Monospace`—Text messages you see onscreen or code appears in a monospace font.
- **Bold**—Text you type appears in a bold font.
- *Italic*—New and important terms appear in italics.
- Initial Caps—Tab names, dialog names, and dialog elements are presented with initial capital letters so you can identify them easily.

Referring to Versions

From 1997 through 2003, Microsoft released similar versions of Excel known as Excel 97, Excel 2000, Excel 2002/XP, and Excel 2003. This book refers to those versions as "legacy versions" of Excel.

Referring to Ribbon Commands

Office 2007 introduced a new interface called the ribbon. The ribbon is composed of several tabs labeled Home, Insert, Page Layout, and so on. When you click the Page Layout tab, you see the icons available on the Page Layout tab.

When the active cell is inside a pivot table, two new tabs appear on the ribbon. In the help files, Microsoft calls these tabs "PivotTable Tools | Analyze" and "PivotTable Tools | Design." For convenience, this book refers to these elements as the Analyze tab and the Design tab, respectively. The Slicer feature has a ribbon tab that Microsoft calls "Slicer Tools | Options." This book refers to this as the Slicer tab. Excel 2013 introduced the Timeline Tools | Options tab. This book calls this the Timeline tab.

In some cases, the ribbon icon leads to a drop-down with additional choices. In these cases, the book lists the hierarchy of ribbon, icon, menu choice, and submenu choice. For example, in Figure I.7, the shorthand specifies "select Design, Report Layout, Repeat All Item Labels."

Figure I.7
For shorthand, instructions might say to select Design, Report Layout, Repeat All Item Labels.

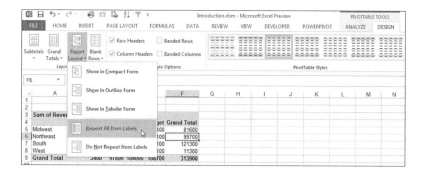

Special Elements

This book contains the following special elements:

CASE STUDY

Cast studies provide a real-world look at topics previously introduced in the chapter.

> **NOTE**
>
> Notes provide additional information outside the main thread of the chapter discussion that might be useful for you to know.

> **TIP**
>
> Tips provide quick workarounds and time-saving techniques to help you do your work more efficiently.

> **CAUTION**
>
> Cautions warn you about potential pitfalls you might encounter. Pay attention to Cautions because they alert you to problems that otherwise could cause you hours of frustration.

Pivot Table Fundamentals

1

What Is a Pivot Table?

Imagine that Excel is a large toolbox that contains different tools at your disposal. The pivot table is essentially one tool in your Excel toolbox. If a pivot table were indeed a physical tool that you could hold in your hand, a kaleidoscope would most accurately represent it.

When you look through a kaleidoscope at an object, you see that object in a different way. You can turn the kaleidoscope to move around the details of the object. The object itself doesn't change, and it's not connected to the kaleidoscope. The kaleidoscope is simply a tool you use to create a unique perspective on an ordinary object.

Think of a pivot table as a kaleidoscope that is pointed at your data set. When you look at your data set through a pivot table, you have the opportunity to see details in your data you might not have noticed before. Furthermore, you can turn your pivot table to see your data from different perspectives. The data set itself doesn't change, and it's not connected to the pivot table. The pivot table is simply a tool you are using to create a unique perspective on your data.

A pivot table enables you to create an interactive view of your data set, called a *pivot table report*. With a pivot table report, you can quickly and easily categorize your data into groups, summarize large amounts of data into meaningful information, and perform a variety of calculations in a fraction of the time it takes by hand. But the real power of a pivot table report is that you can interactively drag and drop fields within your report, dynamically changing your perspective and recalculating totals to fit your current view.

Why Should You Use a Pivot Table?

As a rule, what you do in Excel can be split into two categories: calculating data and shaping (formatting) data. Although many built-in tools and formulas facilitate both of these tasks, the pivot table is often the fastest and most efficient way to calculate and shape data.

Let's look at one simple scenario that illustrates this point. You have just given your manager some revenue information by month, and he has predictably asked for more information. He adds a note to the worksheet and emails it back to you. As you can see in Figure 1.1, he would like you to add a line that shows credits by month.

Figure 1.1
Your manager predictably changes his request after you provide the first pass of a report.

⊿	A	B	C	D	E	F	G	H
1		Jan	Feb	Mar	Apr	May	Jun	Jul
2	Revenues	66,427,076	68,619,453	69,444,496	67,669,316	69,572,075	67,196,220	66,884,7
3		Please add a "credits" line and show the amount of credits for each month

To meet this new requirement, you run a query from your legacy system that provides the needed data. As usual, the data is formatted specifically to make you suffer. Instead of data by month, the legacy system provides detailed transactional data by day, as shown in Figure 1.2.

Figure 1.2
The data from the legacy system is by day instead of by month.

⊿	A Document Number	B In Balance Date	C Credit Amount
1			
2	D29210	01/03/12	(34.54)
3	D15775	01/03/12	(313.64)
4	D46035	01/03/12	(389.04)
5	D45826	01/03/12	(111.56)
6	D69172	01/03/12	(1,630.25)
7	D25388	01/03/12	(3,146.22)
8	D49302	01/03/12	(1,217.37)
9	D91669	01/03/12	(197.44)
10	D14289	01/03/12	(33.75)
11	D38471	01/03/12	(6,759.20)
12	D18645	01/03/12	(214.54)
13	D63807	01/03/12	(19.58)
14	D77943	01/03/12	(136.17)
15	D37446	01/03/12	(128.36)

Your challenge is to calculate the total dollar amount of credits by month and shape the results into an extract that fits the format of the original report. The final extract should look like the data shown in Figure 1.3.

Figure 1.3
Your goal is to produce a summary by month and transpose the data to a horizontal format.

Jan	Feb	Mar	Apr	May	Jun	Jul
-3,695,319	-3,698,537	-3,833,977	-3,624,967	-3,800,526	-3,603,367	-3,746,754

Creating the extract manually would take 18 mouse clicks and three keystrokes:

- Format dates to month: three clicks
- Create subtotals: four clicks
- Extract subtotals: six clicks, three keystrokes
- Transpose vertical to horizontal: five clicks

In contrast, creating the extract with a pivot table would take nine mouse clicks:

- Create the pivot table report: five clicks
- Group dates into months: three clicks
- Transpose vertical to horizontal: one click

Both methods give you the same extract, which you can paste into the final report, as shown in Figure 1.4.

Figure 1.4
After adding credits to the report, you can calculate net revenue.

⊿	A	B	C	D	E	F	G	H
1		Jan	Feb	Mar	Apr	May	Jun	Jul
2	Revenues	66,427,076	68,619,453	69,444,496	67,669,316	69,572,075	67,196,220	66,884,77:
3	Credits	-3,695,319	-3,698,537	-3,833,977	-3,624,967	-3,800,526	-3,603,367	-3,746,754
4	Adjusted Revenues	62,731,757	64,920,916	65,610,519	64,044,349	65,771,549	63,592,853	63,138,01:

Using a pivot table to accomplish this task not only cuts down the number of actions by more than half, but also reduces the possibility of human error. Over and above that, using a pivot table allows for the quick-and-easy shaping and formatting of the data.

What this example shows is that using a pivot table is not just about calculating and summarizing your data. Pivot tables can often help you do a number of tasks faster and better than conventional functions and formulas. For example, you can use pivot tables to instantly transpose large groups of data vertically or horizontally. You can use pivot tables to quickly find and count the unique values in your data. You can also use pivot tables to prepare your data to be used in charts.

The bottom line is that pivot tables can help you dramatically increase your efficiency and decrease your errors on a number of tasks you might have to accomplish with Excel. Pivot tables can't do everything for you, but knowing how to use just the basics of pivot table functionality can take your data analysis and productivity to a new level.

When Should You Use a Pivot Table?

Large data sets, ever-changing impromptu data requests, and multilayered reporting are absolute productivity killers if you have to tackle them by hand. Going into hand-to-hand combat with one of these not only is time consuming, but also opens up the possibility of an untold number of errors in your analysis. So how do you recognize when to use a pivot table before it's too late?

Generally, a pivot table would serve you well in any of the following situations:

- You have a large amount of transactional data that has become increasingly difficult to analyze and summarize in a meaningful way.
- You need to find relationships and groupings within your data.
- You need to find a list of unique values for one field in your data.
- You need to find data trends using various time periods.
- You anticipate frequent requests for changes to your data analysis.
- You need to create subtotals that frequently include new additions.
- You need to organize your data into a format that's easy to chart.

The Anatomy of a Pivot Table

Because the anatomy of a pivot table is what gives it its flexibility and, indeed, its ultimate functionality, truly understanding pivot tables would be difficult without understanding their basic structure.

A pivot table is composed of four areas. The data you place in these areas defines both the utility and appearance of the pivot table. Keeping in mind that you will go through the process of creating a pivot table in the next chapter, let's prepare by taking a closer look at the four areas and the functionality around them.

Values Area

The *values area* is shown in Figure 1.5. It is a large rectangular area below and to the right of the headings. In this example, the values area contains a sum of the revenue field.

Figure 1.5
The heart of the pivot table is the values area. This area typically includes a total of one or more numeric fields.

	A	B	C	D	E	F
1	REGION	(All)				
2						
3	Sum of REVENUE	MONTH				
4	MODEL	January	February	March	April	May
5	2500P	$33,073	$29,104	$25,612	$22,538	$19,834
6	3002C	$35,880	$31,574	$27,786	$24,451	$21,517
7	3002P	$90,258	$79,427	$69,896	$61,508	$54,127
8	4055T	$13,250	$11,660	$10,261	$9,030	$7,946
9	4500C	$100,197	$88,173	$77,593	$68,281	$60,088

The values area is the area that calculates. This area is required to have at least one field and one calculation on that field in it. The data fields you drop here are those you want to measure or calculate. The values area might include Sum of Revenue, Count of Units, and Average of Price.

It is also possible to have the same field dropped in the values area twice, but with different calculations. A marketing manager might want to see Minimum of Price, Average Price, and Maximum of Price.

Rows Area

The *rows area* is shown in Figure 1.6. It is composed of the headings that go down the left side of the pivot table.

Figure 1.6
The headings down the left side of the pivot table make up the rows area of the pivot table.

	A	B	C	D	E	F
1	REGION	(All)				
2						
3	REVENUE	MONTH				
4	MODEL	January	February	March	April	May
5	2500P	$33,073	$29,104	$25,612	$22,538	$19,834
6	3002C	$35,880	$31,574	$27,785	$24,451	$21,517
7	3002P	$90,258	$79,427	$69,896	$61,508	$54,127
8	4055T	$13,250	$11,660	$10,261	$9,030	$7,946
9	4500C	$100,197	$88,173	$77,593	$68,281	$60,088

Dropping a field into the rows area displays the unique values from that field down the rows of the left side of the pivot table. The rows area typically has at least one field, although it is possible to have no fields. The example earlier in the chapter where you needed to produce a one-line report of credits is an example where there are no row fields.

The types of data fields you would drop here include those you want to group and categorize—for example, Products, Names, and Locations.

Columns Area

The *columns area* is composed of headings that stretch across the top of columns in the pivot table. In the pivot table in Figure 1.7, the month field is in the column area.

Figure 1.7
The columns area stretches across the top of the columns. In this example, it contains the unique list of months in your data set.

	A	B	C	D	E	F
1	REGION	(All)				
2						
3	Sum of REVENUE	MONTH				
4	MODEL	January	February	March	April	May
5	2500P	$33,073	$29,104	$25,612	$22,538	$19,834
6	3002C	$35,880	$31,574	$27,785	$24,451	$21,517
7	3002P	$90,258	$79,427	$69,896	$61,508	$54,127
8	4055T	$13,250	$11,660	$10,261	$9,030	$7,946
9	4500C	$100,197	$88,173	$77,593	$68,281	$60,088

Dropping fields into the columns area would display your items in column-oriented perspective. The columns area is ideal to show trending over time. The types of data fields you would drop here include those you want to trend or show side by side—for example, Months, Periods, and Years.

Filters Area

The *filters area* is an optional set of one or more drop-downs at the top of the pivot table. In Figure 1.8, the filter area contains the Region field, and the pivot table is set to show all regions.

Figure 1.8
Filter fields are great for quickly filtering a report. The Region drop-down in cell B1 enables you to print this report for one particular region manager.

	A	B	C	D	E	F
1	REGION	(All)				
2						
3	Sum of REVENUE	MONTH				
4	MODEL	January	February	March	April	May
5	2500P	$33,073	$29,104	$25,612	$22,538	$19,834
6	3002C	$35,880	$31,574	$27,785	$24,451	$21,517
7	3002P	$90,258	$79,427	$69,896	$61,508	$54,127
8	4055T	$13,250	$11,660	$10,261	$9,030	$7,946
9	4500C	$100,197	$88,173	$77,593	$68,281	$60,088
10						

Dropping fields into the filters area would enable you to filter the data items in your fields. The filters area is optional and comes in handy when you need to filter your results dynamically. The types of data fields you would drop here include those you want to isolate and focus on—for example, Regions, Line of Business, and Employees.

Pivot Tables Behind the Scenes

It's important to know that pivot tables do come with a few file space and memory implications for your system. To get an idea of what this means, let's look at what happens behind the scenes when you create a pivot table.

When you initiate the creation of a pivot table report, Excel takes a snapshot of your data set and stores it in a *pivot cache*, which is nothing more than a special memory subsystem where your data source is duplicated for quick access. Although the pivot cache is not a physical object you can see, you can think of it as a container that stores the snapshot of the data source.

CAUTION

Any changes you make to your data source are not picked up by your pivot table report until you take another snapshot of the data source or "refresh" the pivot cache. Refreshing is easy: Simply right-click the pivot table and click Refresh Data. You can also select the large Refresh button on the Options tab.

The benefit of working against the pivot cache and not your original data source is optimization. Any changes you make to the pivot table report, such as rearranging fields, adding new fields, or hiding items, are made rapidly and with minimal overhead.

Limitations of Pivot Table Reports

Before discussing the limitations of pivot table reports, we should note that, with Excel 2007, Microsoft introduced a dramatic increase in the number of rows and columns allowed in one worksheet. This increase in limits had a ripple effect on several of the tools and functions in Excel, forcing limitation increases in many areas, including pivot tables.

Table 1.1 highlights the changes in pivot table limits from Excel 2003 to Excel 2013. Whereas some of these limitations remain constant, others are highly dependent on available system memory.

Table 1.1   Pivot Table Limitations

Category	Excel 2002/2003	Excel 2007–2013
Number of Row Fields	Limited by available memory	1,048,576 (could be limited by available memory)
Number of Column Fields	256	16,384
Number of Page Fields	256	16,384
Number of Data Fields	256	16,384
Number of Unique Items in a Single Pivot Field	32,500	1,048,576 (could be limited by available memory)
Number of Calculated Items	Limited by available memory	Limited by available memory
Number of Pivot Table Reports on One Worksheet	Limited by available memory	Limited by available memory

A Word About Compatibility

If you are working in an environment where Excel 2003 is still being used, you should be aware of the compatibility issues between Excel 2003 and later versions of Excel. As you can imagine, the extraordinary increases in pivot table limitations lead to some serious compatibility questions. For instance, what if you create a pivot table that contains more than 256 column fields and more than 32,500 unique data items? How are users with previous versions of Excel affected? Luckily, Excel comes with some precautionary measures that can help you avoid compatibility issues.

The first precautionary measure is Compatibility mode. Compatibility mode is a state that Excel automatically enters when opening an .xls file. When Excel is in Compatibility mode, it artificially takes on the limitations of Excel 2003. This means while you are working with an .xls file, you cannot exceed any of the Excel 2003 pivot table limitations shown in Table 1.1. This effectively prevents you from unwittingly creating a pivot table that is not compatible with previous versions of Excel. If you want to get out of Compatibility mode, you have to save the .xls file as one of Excel's new file formats (.xlsx or .xlsm).

> **CAUTION**
>
> Beware of the Convert option found under the Info section of the File menu. Although this command is designed to convert a previous file from Excel 2003 to Excel 2013, it actually deletes the Excel 2003 copy of the file.

The second precautionary measure is Excel's Compatibility Checker. The Compatibility Checker is a built-in tool that checks for any compatibility issues when you try to save an Excel workbook as an .xls file. If your pivot table exceeds the bounds of Excel 2003 limitations, the Compatibility Checker alerts you with a dialog similar to the one shown in Figure 1.9.

Figure 1.9
The Compatibility Checker alerts you of any compatibility issues before you save to a previous version of Excel.

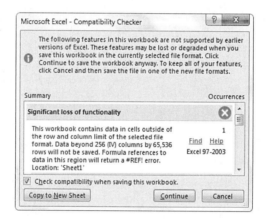

With this dialog, Excel gives you the option of saving your pivot data as hard values in the new .xls file. If you choose to do so, the data from your pivot table is saved as hard values, but the pivot table object and the pivot cache are lost.

> **NOTE**
>
> For information on Excel's compatibility tools, pick up Que Publishing's *Special Edition Using Microsoft Excel 2013*, by Bill Jelen.

Next Steps

In the next chapter, you learn how to prepare your data to be used by a pivot table. Chapter 2, "Creating a Basic Pivot Table," also walks through creating your first pivot table report using the Pivot Table Wizard.

Creating a Basic Pivot Table

2

Preparing Your Data for Pivot Table Reporting

When you have a family portrait taken, the photographer takes time to make sure that the lighting is right, the poses are natural, and everyone smiles his or her best smile. This preparation ensures that the resulting photo is effective in its purpose.

When you create a pivot table report, you're the photographer, taking a snapshot of your data. Taking time to make sure your data looks its best ensures that your pivot table report is effective in accomplishing the task at hand.

One of the benefits of working in a spreadsheet is that you have the flexibility of laying out your data to suit your needs. Indeed, the layout you choose depends heavily on the task at hand. However, many of the data layouts used for presentations are not appropriate when used as the source data for a pivot table report.

As you read the next section, which goes into preparing your data, keep in mind that pivot tables have only one hard rule pertaining to your data source: Your data source must have column headings, which are labels in the first row of your data describing the information in each column. If this is not the case, your pivot table report cannot be created.

However, just because your pivot table report is created successfully does not mean that it's effective. A host of things can go wrong as a result of bad data preparation—from inaccurate reporting to problems with grouping and sorting.

Let's look at a few of the steps you can take to ensure you end up with a viable pivot table report.

Ensure Your Data Is in a Tabular Layout

A perfect layout for the source data in a pivot table is a tabular layout. In tabular layout, there are no blank rows or columns. Every column has a heading. Every field has a value in every row. Columns do not contain repeating groups of data.

Figure 2.1 shows an example of data structured properly for a pivot table. There are headings for each column. Even though the values in D2:D6 are all the same model, the model number appears in each cell. Month data is organized down the page instead of across the columns.

Figure 2.1

This data is structured properly for use as a pivot table source.

	A	B	C	D	E	F
1	REGION	MARKET	STORE	MODEL	MONTH	REVENUE
2	North	Great Lakes	65061011	4055T	April	$2,354
3	North	Great Lakes	65061011	4055T	February	$3,040
4	North	Great Lakes	65061011	4055T	January	$3,454
5	North	Great Lakes	65061011	4055T	March	$2,675
6	North	Great Lakes	65061011	4055T	May	$2,071
7	North	New England	2105015	2500P	April	$11,851
8	North	New England	2105015	2500P	February	$15,304
9	North	New England	2105015	2500P	January	$17,391
10	North	New England	2105015	2500P	March	$13,468
11	North	New England	2105015	2500P	May	$10,429
12	North	New England	22022012	3002C	April	$256
13	North	New England	22022012	3002C	February	$330
14	North	New England	22022012	3002C	January	$375
15	North	New England	22022012	3002C	March	$300

Tabular layouts are *database centric*, meaning you would most commonly find these types of layouts in databases. These layouts are designed to store and maintain large amounts of data in a well-structured, scalable format.

> **TIP**
>
> You might work for a manager who demands that the column labels be split into two rows. For example, he might want the heading Gross Margin to be split with Gross in row 1 and Margin in row 2. Because pivot tables require a unique heading one row high, your manager's preference can be problematic. To overcome this problem, start typing your heading; for example, type **Gross**. Before leaving the cell, press Alt+Enter and then type **Margin**. The result is a single cell that contains two lines of data.

Avoid Storing Data in Section Headings

Examine the data in Figure 2.2. This spreadsheet shows a report of sales by month and model for the North region of a company. Because the data in rows 2 through 24 pertains to the North region, the author of the worksheet put a single cell with North in C1. This approach is effective for display of the data, but not effective when used as a pivot table data source.

Figure 2.2
Region and model data are not formatted properly in this data set.

	A	B	C
1			North
2	Model 2500P	January	33,073
3		February	35,880
4		March	90,258
5		April	13,250
6		May	100,197
7			
8	Model 3002P	January	29,104
9		February	31,574
10		March	79,427
11		April	11,660
12		May	88,173
13			
14	Model 4055T	January	35,880
15		February	25,612
16		March	27,785
17		April	69,896
18		May	10,261
19			
20	Model 4500T	January	33,073
21		February	25,612
22		March	27,785
23		April	69,896
24		May	10,261

Also in Figure 2.2, the author was very creative with the model information. The data in rows 2 through 6 applies to Model 2500P, so the author entered this value once in A2 and then applied a fancy vertical format combined with Merge Cells to create an interesting look for the report. Again, although this is a cool format, it is not useful for pivot table reporting.

Also, the worksheet in Figure 2.2 is missing column headings. You can guess that column A is Model, column B is Month, and column C is Sales, but for Excel to create a pivot table, this information must be included in the first row of the data.

Avoid Repeating Groups as Columns

The format shown in Figure 2.3 is common. A time dimension is presented across several columns. Although it is possible to create a pivot table from this data, this format is not ideal.

The problem is that the headings spread across the top of the table pull double duty as column labels and actual data values. In a pivot table, this format would force you to manage and maintain six fields, each representing a different month.

Figure 2.3
This matrix format is common but not effective for pivot tables. The Month field is spread across several columns of the report.

	A	B	C	D	E	F	G	H
1								
2	North	MODEL	JANUARY	FEBRUARY	MARCH	APRIL	MAY	JUNE
3		4054T	$2,789	$2,454	$2,160	$1,901	$1,673	$1,472
4		4500C	$32,605	$28,692	$25,249	$22,219	$19,553	$17,207
5		3002P	$52,437	$46,145	$40,607	$35,734	$31,446	$27,673
6		2500P	$17,391	$15,304	$13,468	$11,851	$10,429	$9,178
7		4055T	$2,468	$2,172	$1,911	$1,682	$1,480	$1,302
8		3002C	$375	$330	$290	$256	$225	$198

Eliminate Gaps and Blank Cells in Your Data Source

Delete all empty columns within your data source. An empty column in the middle of your data source causes your pivot table to fail on creation because the blank column, in most cases, does not have a column name.

Delete all empty rows within your data source. Empty rows may cause you to inadvertently leave out a large portion of your data range, making your pivot table report incomplete.

Fill in as many blank cells in your data source as possible. Although filling in cells is not required to create a workable pivot table, blank cells in and of themselves are generally errors waiting to happen. So a good practice is to represent missing values with some logical missing value code wherever possible.

> **NOTE**   Although this might seem like a step backward for those of you who are trying to create a nicely formatted report, it pays off in the end. When you are able to create a pivot table, there will be plenty of opportunities to apply some pleasant formatting. In Chapter 3, "Customizing a Pivot Table," you discover how to apply styles formatting to your pivot tables.

Apply Appropriate Type Formatting to Your Fields

Formatting your fields appropriately helps you avoid a whole host of possible issues, from inaccurate reporting to problems with grouping and sorting.

Make certain that any fields to be used in calculations are explicitly formatted as a number, currency, or any other format appropriate for use in mathematical functions. Fields containing dates should also be formatted as any one of the available date formats.

Summary of Good Data Source Design

The attributes of an effective tabular design are as follows:

- The first row of your data source is made up of field labels or headings that describe the information in each column.
- Each column in your data source represents a unique category of data.
- Each row in your data source represents individual items in each column.
- None of the column names in your data source double as data items that will be used as filters or query criteria (that is, names of months, dates, years, names of locations, or names of employees).

CASE STUDY: CLEANING UP DATA FOR PIVOT TABLE ANALYSIS

The worksheet shown in Figure 2.4 is a great-looking report. However, it cannot be effectively used as a data source for a pivot table. Can you identify the problems with this data set?

Figure 2.4
Someone spent a lot of time formatting this report to look good, but what problems prevent it from being used as a data source for a pivot table?

	A	B	C	D	E	F	G
1	Region	Market		Jan	Feb	Mar	Apr
2	Bar Equipment						
3	Midwest	Chicago		132	106	110	90
4		Kansas City		413	504	2,571	505
5		Omaha		332	543	372	424
6	North	Dakotas		130	136	106	90
7		Great Lakes		488	445	4,140	517
8							
9	Commercial Appliances						
10	Midwest	Chicago		780	76	851	76
11		Kansas City		3,352	76	8,442	2,831
12		Omaha		228	17,628	76	304
13	North	Dakotas		0	0	2,608	0
14		Great Lakes		990	76	11,435	76
15							
16	Concession Equipment						
17	Midwest	Chicago		808	0	3,912	0
18		Kansas City		824	1,761	11,181	1,616
19		Omaha		0	8,147	2,968	3,118
20	North	Dakotas		0	0	5,463	2,370
21		Great Lakes		751	808	13,814	1,632

■ The model information does not have its own column. Product Category information appears in the Region column. To correct this problem, insert a new column for Product Category and include the category name on every row.

■ There are blank columns and rows in the data. Column C should be deleted. The blank rows between models (such as rows 8 and 15) also should be deleted.

■ Blank cells present the data in an outline format. The person reading this worksheet would probably assume that cells A4:A5 fall into the Midwest region. These blank cells need to be filled in with the values from above.

> **TIP**
>
> Here's a trick for filling in the blank cells. Select the entire range of data. Then select the Home tab on the ribbon and choose the Find & Select icon from the Editing group. This brings up a menu from which you select Go To Special. In the Go To Special dialog, select Blanks. With all the blank cells selected, start a formula by typing the equal sign (=), press the up arrow on your keyboard, and then press Ctrl+Enter to fill this formula in all blank cells. Remember to copy and paste special values to convert the formulas to values.

■ The worksheet presents the data for each month in several columns (one column per month). Columns D through G need to be reformatted as two columns. Place the month name in one column and the units for that month in the next column. This step either requires a fair amount of copying and pasting or a few lines of VBA macro code.

TIP

For a great book on learning VBA macro programming, read Que Publishing's *VBA and Macros for Microsoft Excel 2013* by Bill Jelen and Tracy Syrstad.

After you make the four changes described here, the data is ready for use as a pivot table data source. As you can see in Figure 2.5, every column has a heading. There are no blank cells, rows, or columns in the data. The monthly data is now presented down column E instead of across several columns.

Figure 2.5
Although this data will take up six times as many rows, it is perfectly formatted for pivot table analysis.

	A	B	C	D	E
1	Product Category	Region	Market	Month	Units
2	Bar Equipment	Midwest	Chicago	Jan	132
3	Bar Equipment	Midwest	Kansas City	Jan	413
4	Bar Equipment	Midwest	Omaha	Jan	332
5	Bar Equipment	North	Dakotas	Jan	130
6	Bar Equipment	North	Great Lakes	Jan	488
7	Commercial Appliances	Midwest	Chicago	Jan	780
8	Commercial Appliances	Midwest	Kansas City	Jan	3,352
9	Commercial Appliances	Midwest	Omaha	Jan	228
10	Commercial Appliances	North	Dakotas	Jan	0
11	Commercial Appliances	North	Great Lakes	Jan	990
12	Concession Equipment	Midwest	Chicago	Jan	808
13	Concession Equipment	Midwest	Kansas City	Jan	824
14	Concession Equipment	Midwest	Omaha	Jan	0
15	Concession Equipment	North	Dakotas	Jan	0
16	Concession Equipment	North	Great Lakes	Jan	751
17	Bar Equipment	Midwest	Chicago	Feb	106
18	Bar Equipment	Midwest	Kansas City	Feb	504

Creating a Basic Pivot Table

Now that you have a good understanding of the importance of a well-structured data source, let's walk through creating a basic pivot table.

TIP

The sample data set used throughout this book is available for download at www.MrExcel.com/pivotbookdata2013.html.

To start, click any single cell in your data source. This ensures that the pivot table captures the range of your data source by default. Next, select the Insert tab and find the Tables group. In the Tables group, select PivotTable and then choose PivotTable from the drop-down list. Figure 2.6 demonstrates how to start a pivot table.

Choosing these options activates the Create PivotTable dialog, shown in Figure 2.7.

Figure 2.6
Start a pivot table by selecting PivotTable from the Insert tab.

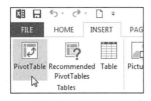

Figure 2.7
The Create PivotTable dialog.

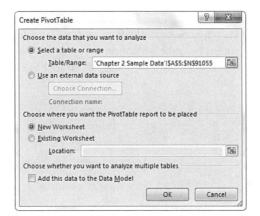

TIP

You can also press the hotkeys Alt+N+V to start a pivot table.

As you can see in Figure 2.7, the Create PivotTable dialog asks you only two fundamental questions: Where's the data that you want to analyze, and where do you want to put the pivot table?

■ **Choose the Data That You Want to Analyze**—In this section, you tell Excel where your data set is. You can specify a data set that is located within your workbook, or you can tell Excel to look for an external data set. As you can see in Figure 2.7, Excel is smart enough to read your data set and fill in the range for you. However, you always should take note of this to ensure you are capturing all your data.

■ **Choose Where You Want the PivotTable Report to Be Placed**—In this section, you tell Excel where you want your pivot table to be placed. This is set to New Worksheet by default, meaning your pivot table will be placed in a new worksheet within the current workbook. You will rarely change this setting because there are relatively few times you'll need your pivot table to be placed in a specific location.

> **NOTE**
>
> Note the presence of another option in the Create PivotTable dialog shown in Figure 2.7: the Add This to the Data Model option. You would select this option if you were trying to consolidate multiple data sources into one single pivot table. We cover this option in detail in Chapter 7, "Analyzing Disparate Data Sources with Pivot Tables," and in Chapter 10, "Mashing Up Data with PowerPivot." For now, we cover the steps to create a pivot table from a single source, which means you can ignore this particular option.

After you have answered the two questions in the Create PivotTable dialog, simply click the OK button. At this point, Excel adds a new worksheet that contains an empty pivot table report. Next to that is the PivotTable Field List dialog, illustrated in Figure 2.8. This dialog helps you build your pivot table.

Figure 2.8
You use the PivotTable Field List dialog to build your pivot table.

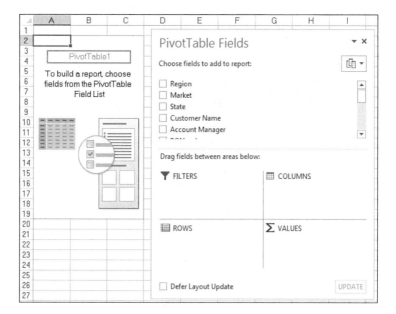

Finding the PivotTable Field List

The PivotTable Field List dialog is your main work area in Excel 2013. This is the place where you add fields and make changes to your pivot table report. By default, this dialog pops up when you place your cursor anywhere inside your pivot table. However, if you explicitly close this dialog, you override the default and essentially tell the dialog not to activate when you are in the pivot table.

If clicking on the pivot table does not activate the PivotTable Field List dialog, you can manually activate it by right-clicking anywhere inside the pivot table and selecting Show Field List. You can also click anywhere inside the pivot table and then choose the large Field List icon on the Analyze tab under PivotTable Tools in the ribbon.

Adding Fields to the Report

The idea here is to add the fields you need into the pivot table by using the four "drop zones" found in the PivotTable Field List: Filters, Columns, Rows, and Values. These drop zones, which correspond to the four areas of the pivot table, are used to populate your pivot table with data.

> **TIP**
>
> Review Chapter 1, "Pivot Table Fundamentals," for a refresher on the four areas of a pivot table.

- **Filters**—Adding a field to the Filters drop zone enables you to filter on its unique data items. In previous versions of Excel, this area was known as the Report Filters area.
- **Columns**—Adding a field into the Columns drop zone displays the unique values from that field across the top of the pivot table.
- **Rows**—Adding a field into the Rows drop zone displays the unique values from that field down the left side of the pivot table.
- **Values**—Adding a field into the Values drop zone includes that field in the values area of your pivot table, allowing you to perform a specified calculation using the values in the field.

Now let's pause a moment and go over some fundamentals of laying out your pivot table report. This is generally the point where most new users get stuck. How do you know which field goes where?

Before you start dropping fields into the various drop zones, ask yourself two questions: "What am I measuring?" and "How do I want to see it?" The answer to the first question tells you which fields in your data source you need to work with, and the answer to the second question tells you where to place the fields.

For your first pivot table report, you want to measure the dollar sales by region. This automatically tells you that you need to work with the Sale Amount field and the Region field. How do you want to see it? You want regions to go down the left side of the report and the sales amount to be calculated next to each region.

To achieve this effect, you need to add the Region field to the Rows drop zone and add the Sale Amount field to the Values drop zone.

Find the Region field in the field list and place a check in the check box next to it. As you can see in Figure 2.9, not only is the field automatically added to the Rows drop zone, but your pivot table is updated to show the unique region names.

Figure 2.9
Place a check next to the Region field to automatically add that field to your pivot table.

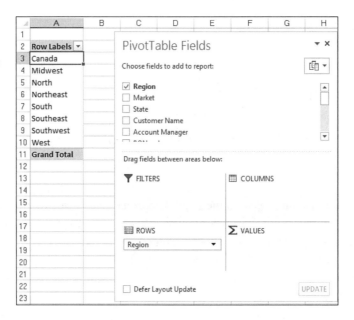

Now that you have regions in your pivot table, it's time to add in the dollar sales. To do that, simply find the Sale Amount field and place a check next to it. As Figure 2.10 illustrates, the Sale Amount field is automatically added to the Values drop zone, and your pivot table report now shows the total dollar sales for each region.

Figure 2.10
Place a check next to the Sale Amount field to add data to your pivot table report.

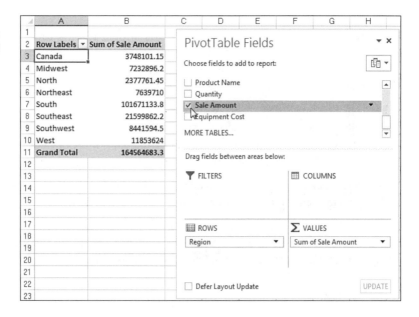

At this point, you have created your first pivot table report!

How Does Excel Know Where Your Fields Go?

As you've just experienced, the new PivotTable Field List interface enables you to add fields to your pivot table by simply placing a check next to each field name. Excel automatically adds the checked fields to the pivot table. The question is how Excel knows in which drop zone to put the fields you check. The answer is that Excel doesn't really know which drop zone to use; it makes a decision based on data type. Here's how it works: When you place a check next to a field, Excel evaluates the data type for that field. If the data type is numeric, Excel places the field into the Values drop zone; otherwise, Excel places the field into the Rows drop zone. This placement obviously underlines the importance of correctly assigning the data types for your fields.

2

> **CAUTION**
>
> Watch out for blanks in your numeric fields. If you have even one blank cell in a numeric field, Excel reads that cell as a Text field and therefore places it in the Rows drop zone!

Adding Layers to Your Pivot Table

Now you can add another layer of analysis to your report. This time you want to measure the amount of dollar sales each region earned by product category. Because your pivot table already contains the Region and Sales Amount fields, all you have to do is place a check next to the Product Category field. As you can see in Figure 2.11, your pivot table automatically added a layer for Product Category and refreshed the calculations to include subtotals for each region. Because the data is stored efficiently in the pivot cache, this change took less than a second.

Figure 2.11
Before pivot tables, adding layers to analyses would have required hours of work and complex formulas.

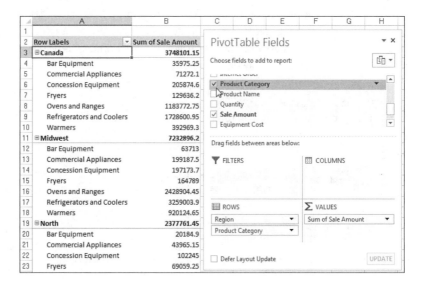

Rearranging Your Pivot Table

Suppose this view doesn't work for your manager. He wants to see Product Categories across the top of the pivot table report. To rearrange them, simply drag the Product Category field from the Rows drop zone to the Columns drop zone, as illustrated in Figure 2.12.

Figure 2.12
Rearranging a pivot table is as simple as dragging fields from one drop zone to another.

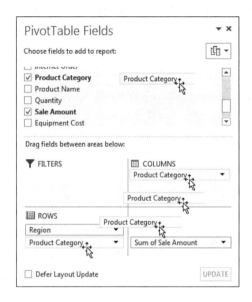

> **NOTE**
> You don't have to move your fields into a drop zone to be able to drag them around. You can actually drag fields directly from the field list into the desired drop zone. You can also move a field into a drop zone by using that field's context menu: Click the black triangle next to the field name and then select the desired drop zone.

Instantly, the report is restructured, as shown in Figure 2.13.

Figure 2.13
Your product categories are now column oriented.

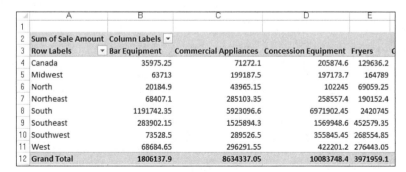

	A	B	C	D	E
1					
2	Sum of Sale Amount	Column Labels ▾			
3	Row Labels ▾	Bar Equipment	Commercial Appliances	Concession Equipment	Fryers
4	Canada	35975.25	71272.1	205874.6	129636.2
5	Midwest	63713	199187.5	197173.7	164789
6	North	20184.9	43965.15	102245	69059.25
7	Northeast	68407.1	285103.35	258557.4	190152.4
8	South	1191742.35	5923096.6	6971902.45	2420745
9	Southeast	283902.15	1525894.3	1569948.6	452579.35
10	Southwest	73528.5	289526.5	355845.45	268554.85
11	West	68684.65	296291.55	422201.2	276443.05
12	Grand Total	1806137.9	8634337.05	10083748.4	3971959.1

Longing for Drag-and-Drop Functionality?

If you're upgrading from Excel 2003, you will notice that you can no longer drag and drop fields directly onto the pivot table layout. This functionality is allowed only within the PivotTable Field List dialog (dragging into drop zones). The good news, however, is that Microsoft has provided the option of working with a classic pivot table layout, which enables the drag-and-drop functionality.

To activate the classic pivot table layout, right-click anywhere inside the pivot table and select Table Options. In the Table Options dialog, select the Display tab and place a check next to Classic PivotTable Layout, as demonstrated in Figure 2.14. Click the OK button to apply the change.

Figure 2.14
Place a check next to Classic PivotTable Layout.

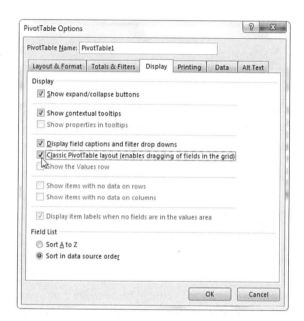

At this point, you can drag and drop fields directly onto your pivot table layout.

Unfortunately, this setting is not global. That is, you have to go through the same steps to apply the classic layout to each new pivot table you create. However, this setting persists when a pivot table is copied.

Creating a Report Filter

Often, you might be asked to produce reports for one particular region, market, or product. Instead of building separate pivot table reports for every possible analysis scenario, you can use the Filter field to create a report filter. For example, you can create a region-filtered report by simply dragging the Region field to the Filters drop zone and the Product Category field to the Rows drop zone. This way, you can analyze one particular region at a time. Figure 2.15 shows the totals for just the North region.

Figure 2.15
With this setup, you not only can see revenues by product clearly, but you also can click the Region drop-down to focus on one region.

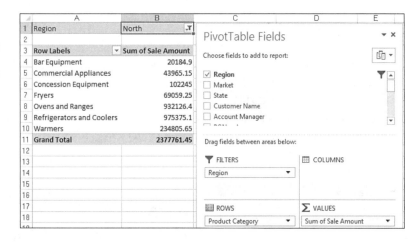

Understanding the Recommended PivotTables Feature

With Excel 2013, Microsoft introduces a new feature called Recommended PivotTables. You can find this feature next to the PivotTable icon on the Insert tab (see Figure 2.16).

Figure 2.16
The new Recommended PivotTables icon helps you start a pivot table faster.

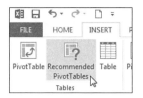

This feature is Microsoft's way of getting you up and running with pivot tables by simply creating one for you. The idea is simple. Place your cursor in a tabular range of data and then click the Recommended PivotTables icon. Excel shows you a menu of pivot tables it thinks it can create for you based on the data in your range (see Figure 2.17). When you find one that looks good to you, click it, and click OK to have Excel create it.

Another way to get to a recommended pivot table is to right-click anywhere in your data range and choose the Quick Analysis option. The context menu shown in Figure 2.18 activates, and you can select a recommended pivot table under the Tables section.

The reviews on this new feature are mixed. On one hand, it does provide a quick-and-easy way to start a pivot table, especially for those of us who are not that experienced. On the other hand, Excel's recommendations are rudimentary at best. You will often find that you need to rearrange, add, or manipulate fields in the created pivot table to suit your needs. Although Excel might get it right the first time, it's unlikely you will be able to leave the pivot table as is.

Figure 2.17
Choose from the menu of recommended pivot tables to have Excel automatically create a pivot table for you.

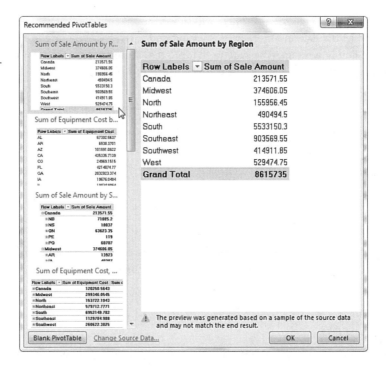

Figure 2.18
You can also choose a recommended pivot table from the Quick Analysis context menu.

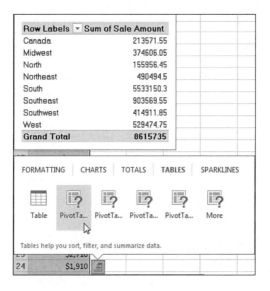

There is also a chance that Excel will simply not like the data range you pointed to. For example, the data in Figure 2.19 is a valid range, but Excel doesn't like the repeating dates. So it simply pops up a message to indicate that there are too many duplicates to recommend a pivot table; however, it will gladly create a blank one.

Figure 2.19
When Excel can't recommend a pivot table based on your data, it throws an error and gives you the option of starting with a blank pivot.

Document Number	In Balance Date	Credit Amount
D29210	01/03/12	(34.54)
D15775	01/03/12	(313.64)
D46035	01/03/12	(389.04)
D45826	01/03/12	(111.56)
D69172	01/03/12	(1,630.25)
D25388	01/03/12	(3,146.22)
D49302	01/03/12	(1,217.37)
D91669	01/03/12	(197.44)
D14289	01/03/12	(33.75)

Recommended PivotTables

We can't recommend any PivotTables for the selected data because there are too many blank cells or duplicate values, or not enough numerical columns.

Click OK to get a blank PivotTable.

Change Source Data...   OK   Cancel

All in all, the Recommended PivotTables feature can be a nice shortcut to getting a rudimentary pivot table started, but it's not a replacement for knowing how to create and manipulate pivot tables on your own.

Using Slicers

With Excel 2010, Microsoft introduced a feature called *slicers*. Slicers enable you to filter your pivot table similar to the way Filter fields filter a pivot table. The difference is that slicers offer a user-friendly interface that enables you to easily see the current filter state.

Creating a Standard Slicer

To understand the concept behind slicers, place your cursor anywhere inside your pivot table, and then select the Insert tab on the ribbon. Click the Slicer icon (see Figure 2.20).

Figure 2.20
Inserting a slicer.

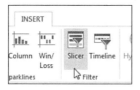

The Insert Slicers dialog shown in Figure 2.21 opens. The idea is to select the dimensions you want to filter. In this example, the Region and Market slicers are selected.

After the slicers are created, you can simply click the filter values to filter your pivot table. As you can see in Figure 2.22, clicking Midwest in the Region slicer not only filters your pivot table, but the Market slicer responds by highlighting the markets that belong to the Midwest region.

Figure 2.21
Select the dimensions for which you want to create slicers.

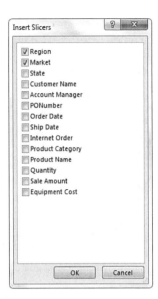

Figure 2.22
Select the dimensions you want to filter using slicers.

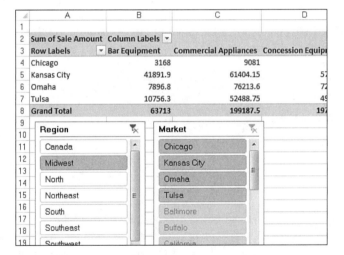

You can also select multiple values by holding down the Ctrl key on your keyboard while selecting the needed filters. In Figure 2.23, the Ctrl key was held down while Baltimore, California, Charlotte, and Chicago were selected. This not only highlights the selected markets in the Market slicer, but it also highlights their associated regions in the Region slicer.

Another advantage you gain with slicers is that you can tie each slicer to more than one pivot table. In other words, any filter you apply to your slicer can be applied to multiple pivot tables.

Figure 2.23
The fact that you can visually see the current filter state gives slicers a unique advantage over the Filter field.

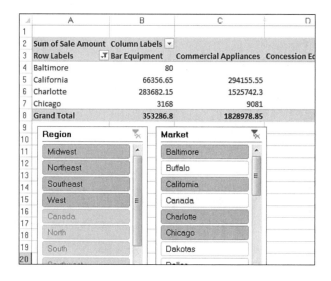

To connect your slicer to more than one pivot table, simply right-click the slicer and select Report Connections. The Report Connections dialog shown in Figure 2.24 opens. Place a check next to any pivot table that you want to filter using the current slicer.

Figure 2.24
Choose the pivot tables you want to filter by this slicer.

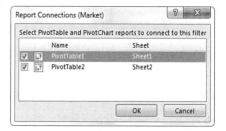

At this point, any filter applied via the slicer is applied to all the connected pivot tables. Again, slicers have a unique advantage over Filter fields in that they can control the filter state of multiple pivot tables. Filter fields can only control the pivot table in which they live.

NOTE   It's important to note that slicers are not part of the pivot table object. They are separate objects that you can use in a variety of ways. For a more detailed look at slicers, their functionality, and how to format them, pick up Que Publishing's *Special Edition Using Microsoft Excel 2013*, by Bill Jelen.

Notice that in Figure 2.24, the list of pivot tables is a bit ambiguous (PivotTable1, PivotTable2). Excel automatically gives your pivot tables these generic names; which it uses to identify them. You can imagine how difficult it would be to know which pivot table is which when working with more than a handful of pivots. In that light, you might want to consider giving your pivot tables user-friendly names so you can recognize them in dialog boxes such as the one you see in Figure 2.24.

You can easily change the name of a pivot table by placing your cursor anywhere inside the pivot table, selecting the Analyze tab, and entering a friendly name in the PivotTable Name input box found on the far left.

Creating a Timeline Slicer

The Timeline slicer is new in Excel 2013. The Timeline slicer works in the same way as a standard slicer in that it lets you filter a pivot table using a visual selection mechanism instead of the old Filter fields. The difference is the Timeline slicer is designed to work exclusively with date fields, providing an excellent visual method to filter and group the dates in your pivot table.

For you to create a Timeline slicer, your pivot table must contain a field where *all* the data is formatted as a date. It's not enough to have a column of data that contains a few dates. All the values in your date field must be formatted as a valid date. If even only one value in your date column is blank or not a valid date, Excel does not create the Timeline slicer.

To create a Timeline slicer, place your cursor anywhere inside your pivot table, select the Insert tab on the ribbon, and then click the Timeline icon (see Figure 2.25).

Figure 2.25
Inserting a Timeline slicer.

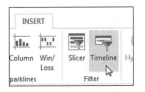

The Insert Timelines dialog seen in Figure 2.26 opens, showing you all the available date fields in the chosen pivot table. Here, you select the date fields for which you want to create slicers.

After your Timeline slicer is created, you can filter the data in your pivot table by using this dynamic data-selection mechanism. As you can see in Figure 2.27, clicking the April slicer filters the data in the pivot table to show only April data.

Figure 2.26
Select the date fields for which you want slicers created.

Figure 2.27
Click a date selection to filter your pivot table.

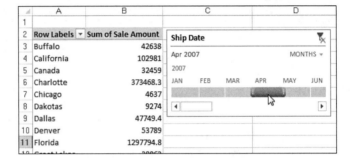

Figure 2.28 demonstrates how you can expand the slicer range with the mouse to include a wider range of dates in your filtered numbers.

Figure 2.28
You can expand the range on the Timeline slicer to include more data in the filtered numbers.

Want to quickly filter your pivot table by quarters? Well, you can easily do it with a Timeline slicer. Click the time period drop-down and select Quarters. As you can see in Figure 2.29, you also have the option of switching to Years or Days if needed.

Figure 2.29
Quickly switch between
Years, Quarters, Months,
and Days.

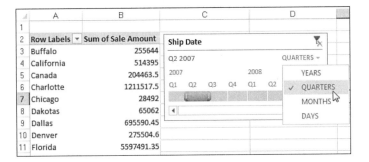

CASE STUDY: ANALYZING ACTIVITY BY MARKET

Your organization has 18 markets that sell seven types of products. You have been asked to build a report that breaks out each market and highlights the dollar sales by each product. You are starting with an intimidating transaction table that contains more than 91,000 rows of data. To start your report, do the following:

1. Place your cursor inside your data set, select the Insert tab, and click PivotTable.

2. When the Create PivotTable dialog activates, click the OK button. At this point, you should see an empty pivot table with the field list.

3. Find the Market field in the PivotTable Field List and check the box next to it.

4. Find the Sale Amount field in the PivotTable Field List and check the box next to it.

5. To get the product breakouts, find the Product Category field in the PivotTable Field List and drag it into the Columns drop zone.

In five easy steps, you have calculated and designed a report that satisfies the requirements. After a little formatting, your pivot table report should look similar to the one shown in Figure 2.30.

Figure 2.30
This summary can be created in less than a minute.

Sum of Sale Amount	Column Labels			
Row Labels	Bar Equipment	Commercial Appliances	Concession Equipment	Frye
Baltimore	80			
Buffalo	37397.9	237297.85	187711	127
California	66356.65	294155.55	416379.2	2610
CANADA	35975.25	71272.1	205874.6	129
Charlotte	283682.15	1525742.3	1569948.6	4509
Chicago	3168	9081	18218	9
Dakotas	3386.5	7287.05	30619.2	180
Dallas	59580.3	255146	306037	151
Denver	34558.85	70068.8	75712.8	1200
Florida	1132162.05	5667950.6	6665865.45	2269
Great Lakes	16798.4	36678.1	71625.8	51
Kansas City	41891.9	61404.15	57300.7	50
Knoxville	220	152		

Lest you lose sight of the analytical power you just displayed, keep in mind that your data source has more than 91,000 rows and 14 columns, which is a hefty set of data by Excel standards. Despite the amount of data, you produced a relatively robust analysis in a matter of minutes.

Keeping Up with Changes in Your Data Source

Let's go back to the family portrait analogy. As years go by, your family will change in appearance and might even grow to include some new members. The family portrait that was taken years ago remains static and no longer represents the family today. So another portrait needs to be taken.

As time goes by, your data might change and grow with newly added rows and columns. However, the pivot cache that feeds your pivot table report is disconnected from your data source, so it cannot represent any of the changes you make to your date source until you take another snapshot.

The action of updating your pivot cache by taking another snapshot of your data source is called *refreshing* your data. There are two reasons you might have to refresh your pivot table report:

■ Changes have been made to your existing data source.

■ Your data source's range has been expanded with the addition of rows or columns.

You handle these two scenarios in different ways.

Changes Have Been Made to Your Existing Data Source

If a few cells in your pivot table's source data have changed due to edits or updates, you can refresh your pivot table report with a few clicks. Simply right-click inside your pivot table report and select Refresh. This selection takes another snapshot of your data set, overwriting your previous pivot cache with the latest data.

2

> NOTE
>
> You can also refresh the data in your pivot table by selecting Analyze from the PivotTable Tools tab in the ribbon and then choosing Refresh.

> TIP
>
> Clicking anywhere inside your pivot table activates the PivotTable Tools tab just above the main ribbon.

Your Data Source's Range Has Been Expanded with the Addition of Rows or Columns

When changes have been made to your data source that affect its range (for example, you've added rows or columns), you have to update the range being captured by the pivot cache.

To do this, click anywhere inside your pivot table and then select Analyze from the PivotTable Tools tab in the ribbon. From here, select Change Data Source. This selection triggers the dialog shown in Figure 2.31.

Figure 2.31

The Change PivotTable Data Source dialog enables you to redefine the source data for your pivot table.

All you have to do here is update the range to include new rows and columns. After you have specified the appropriate range, click the OK button.

Sharing the Pivot Cache

Many times, you need to analyze the same data set in multiple ways. In most cases, this process requires you to create separate pivot tables from the same data source. Keep in mind that every time you create a pivot table, you are storing a snapshot of your entire data set in a pivot cache. Every pivot cache that is created increases your memory usage and file size. For this reason, you should consider sharing your pivot cache. In other words, in those situations when you need to create multiple pivot tables from the same data source, you can use the same pivot cache to feed multiple pivot tables. By using the same pivot cache for multiple pivot tables, you gain a certain level of efficiency when it comes to memory usage and files size.

In legacy versions of Excel, when you created a pivot table using a data set that was already being used in another pivot table, Excel actually gave you the option to use the same pivot cache. However, Excel 2013 does not give you such an option.

Instead, each time you create a new pivot table in Excel 2013, Excel automatically shares the pivot cache. Most of the time, this is beneficial; you can link as many pivot tables as you want to the same pivot cache with a negligible increase in memory and file size. On the flip side, when you group one pivot table by month and year, all of the pivot tables are grouped in a similar fashion. If you want one pivot table by month and another pivot table by week, you have to force a separate pivot cache.

You can force Excel to create a separate pivot cache by taking the following steps.

1. Press Alt+D+P on your keyboard to launch the old Pivot Table Wizard.
2. Click the Next button to get past the first screen of the wizard.
3. On the second screen, select the range for your pivot table and click the Next button.
4. Excel displays a wordy message saying that you can use less memory if you click Yes. Instead, click No.
5. On the next screen, click the Finish button.

At this point, you have a blank pivot table that pulls from its own pivot cache.

> **TIP**
> If you already have an existing pivot table, you can use this alternative method for creating a separate pivot cache. Copy and paste the existing table to a new workbook, and then copy and paste the pivot table back to a new sheet in the original workbook.

Side Effects of Sharing a Pivot Cache

It's important to note that there are a few side effects to sharing a pivot cache. For example, suppose you have two pivot tables using the same pivot cache. Certain actions affect both pivot tables:

- **Refreshing your data**—You cannot refresh one pivot table and not the other. Refreshing affects both tables.

- **Adding a calculated field**—If you create a calculated field in one pivot table, your newly created calculated field shows up in the other pivot table's field list.

- **Adding a calculated item**—If you create a calculated item in one pivot table, it shows in the other as well.

- **Grouping or ungrouping fields**—Any grouping or ungrouping you perform affects both pivot tables. For instance, suppose you group a date field in one pivot table to show months. The same date field in the other pivot table is also grouped to show months.

Although none of these side effects are critical flaws in the concept of sharing a pivot cache, it is important to keep them in mind when determining whether using a pivot table as your data source is the best option for your situation.

Saving Time with New Pivot Table Tools

Microsoft has invested a lot of time and effort in the overall pivot table experience. The results of these efforts are tools that make pivot table functionality more accessible and easier to use. The following sections look at a few of the tools that help you save time when managing your pivot tables.

Deferring Layout Updates

The frustrating part of building a pivot table from a large data source is that each time you add a field to a pivot area, you are left waiting while Excel crunches through all that data. This can become a maddeningly time-consuming process if you have to add several fields to your pivot table.

Excel 2013 offers some relief for this problem by providing a way to defer layout changes until you are ready to apply them. You can activate this option by clicking the relatively inconspicuous Defer Layout Update check box in the PivotTable Field List dialog, as shown in Figure 2.32.

Figure 2.32
Click the Defer Layout Update check box to prevent your pivot table from updating while you add fields.

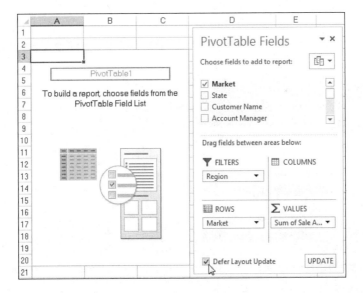

Here's how this feature works: When you place a check in the Defer Layout Update check box, you prevent your pivot table from making real-time updates as you move your fields around without your pivot table. In Figure 2.32, notice that fields in the drop zones are not in the pivot table yet. The reason is that the Defer Layout Update check box is active. When you are ready to apply your changes, click the Update button on the lower-right corner of the PivotTable Field List dialog.

> **NOTE**
>
> Remember to remove the check from the Defer Layout Update check box when you are done building your pivot table. Leaving it checked results in your pivot table remaining in a state of manual updates, preventing you from using the other features of the pivot table (that is, sorting, filtering, and grouping).

> **TIP**
>
> Incidentally, the Defer Layout Update option is available through VBA. It can help improve the performance of any macro that automates the creation of pivot tables. Using VBA to create pivot tables is covered in Chapter 13, "Using VBA to Create Pivot Tables."

Starting Over with One Click

Often you might want to start from scratch when working with your pivot table layouts. Excel 2013 provides a simple way to essentially start over without deleting your pivot cache. Select Analyze under the PivotTable Tools tab and select the Clear drop-down.

As you can see in Figure 2.33, this command enables you to either clear your entire pivot table layout or remove any existing filters you might have applied in your pivot table.

Figure 2.33
The Clear command enables you to clear your pivot table fields or remove the applied filters in your pivot table.

Relocating Your Pivot Table

You might find that, after you have created your pivot table, you need to move it to another location. It might be in the way of other analyses on the worksheet, or you might simply need to move it to another worksheet. Although there are several ways to move your pivot table, Excel 2013 provides a no-frills way to easily change the location of your pivot table.

Select Analyze under the PivotTable Tools tab and select Move PivotTable. This icon activates the Move PivotTable dialog illustrated in Figure 2.34. All you have to do here is specify where you want your pivot table moved.

Figure 2.34
The Move PivotTable dialog enables you to quickly move your pivot table to another location.

Next Steps

In the next chapter, you learn how to enhance your pivot table reports by customizing your fields, changing field names, changing summary calculations, applying formats to data fields, adding and removing subtotals, and using the Show As setting.

Customizing a Pivot Table

3

Although pivot tables provide an extremely fast way to summarize data, sometimes the pivot table defaults are not exactly what you need. In this case, you can use many powerful settings to tweak the information in your pivot table. These tweaks range from making cosmetic changes to changing the underlying calculation used in the pivot table.

In Excel 2013, you find controls to customize the pivot table in myriad places: the Analyze tab, Design tab, Field Settings dialog, Data Field Settings dialog, PivotTable Options dialog, and context menus. Rather than cover each set of controls sequentially, this chapter seeks to cover the following functional areas in making pivot table customization:

- **Minor cosmetic changes**—Change blanks to zeros, adjust the number format, and rename a field. The fact that you must correct these defaults in every pivot table that you create is annoying.
- **Layout changes**—Compare three possible layouts, show/hide subtotals and totals, and repeat row labels.
- **Major cosmetic changes**—Use table styles to format your table quickly.
- **Summary calculations**—Change from Sum to Count, Min, Max, and more. If you have a table that defaults to Count of Revenue instead of Sum of Revenue, you need to visit the section on this topic.
- **Advanced calculations**—Use settings to show data as a running total, percent of total, rank, percent of parent item, and more.
- **Other options**—Review more obscure options found throughout the Excel interface.

Making Common Cosmetic Changes

You need to make a few changes to almost every pivot table to make it easier to understand and interpret. Figure 3.1 shows a typical pivot table. To create this pivot table, open the Chapter 3 data file. Select Insert, Pivot Table, OK. Check the Sector and Revenue fields, and drag the Region field to the COLUMNS area.

Figure 3.1
A typical pivot table before customization.

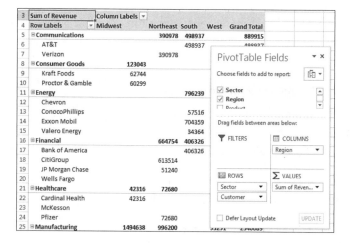

This default pivot table contains several annoying items that you might want to change quickly:

- The default table style uses no gridlines, which makes it difficult to follow the rows and columns across.

- Numbers in the VALUES area are in a general number format. There are no commas, currency symbols, and so on.

- For sparse data sets, many blanks appear in the VALUES area. The blank cell in B5 indicates that there were no Communications sales in the Midwest. Most people prefer to see zeros instead of blanks.

- Excel renames fields in the VALUES area with the unimaginative name Sum of Revenue. You can change this name.

You can correct each of these annoyances with just a few mouse clicks. The following sections address each issue.

Applying a Table Style to Restore Gridlines

The default pivot table layout contains no gridlines and is rather plain. Fortunately, you can apply a table style. Any table style that you choose is better than the default.

Follow these steps to apply a table style:

1. Make sure that the active cell is in the pivot table.

2. From the ribbon, select the Design tab.

3. Three arrows appear at the right side of the PivotTable Style gallery. Click the bottom arrow to open the complete gallery, which is shown in Figure 3.2.

Figure 3.2
The gallery contains 85 styles to choose from.

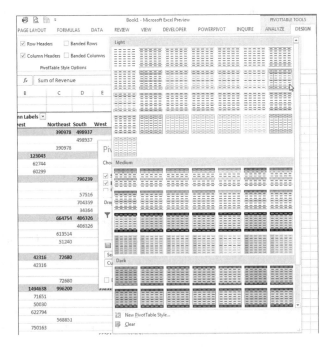

4. Choose any style other than the first style from the drop-down. Styles toward the bottom of the gallery tend to have more formatting.

5. Select the check box for Banded Rows to the left of the PivotTable Styles gallery. This draws gridlines in light styles and adds row stripes in dark styles.

It does not matter which style you choose from the gallery; any of the 84 other styles are better than the default style.

→ For more details about customizing styles, **see** "Customizing the Pivot Table Appearance with Styles and Themes," **p. 59**.

Changing the Number Format to Add Thousands Separators

If you have gone to the trouble of formatting your underlying data, you might expect that the pivot table would capture some of this formatting. Unfortunately, it does not. Even if your underlying data fields were formatted with a certain numeric format, the default pivot table presents values formatted with a general format. As a sign of some progress, when you create pivot tables from PowerPivot, you can specify the number format for a field before creating the pivot table. This functionality has not come to regular pivot tables, yet. For more about PowerPivot, read Chapter 10, "Mashing Up Data with PowerPivot."

For example, in the figures in this chapter, the numbers are in the thousands or tens of thousands. At this level of sales, you would normally have a thousands separator and probably no decimal places. Although the original data had a numeric format applied, the pivot table routinely formats your numbers in an ugly general style.

You will be tempted to format the numbers using the right-click menu and choosing Number Format. This is not the best way to go. You will be tempted to format the cells using the tools on the Home tab. This is not the way to go. Either of these methods temporarily fixes the problem, but you lose the formatting as soon as you move a field in the pivot table. The right way to solve the problem is to use the Number Format button in the Value Field Settings dialog.

You have three ways to get to this dialog:

- Right-click a number in the VALUES area of the pivot table and select Value Field Settings.

- Click the drop-down on the Sum of Revenue field in the drop zones of the PivotTable Field List and then select Value Field Settings from the context menu.

- Select any cell in the VALUES area of the pivot table. From the Analyze tab, select Field Settings from the Active Field group.

As shown in Figure 3.3, the Value Field Settings dialog is displayed. To change the numeric format, click the Number Format button in the lower-left corner.

Figure 3.3
Display the Value Field Settings dialog and then click Number Format.

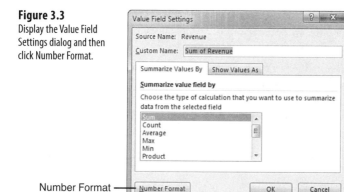

Number Format

In the Format Cells dialog, you can choose any built-in number format or choose a custom format. For example, choose Currency, as shown in Figure 3.4.

Figure 3.4

Choose an easier-to-read number format from the Format Cells dialog.

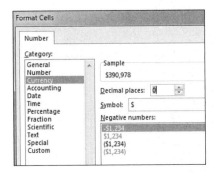

Replacing Blanks with Zeros

One of the elements of good spreadsheet design is that you should never leave blank cells in a numeric section of the worksheet. Even Microsoft believes in this rule; if your source data for a pivot table contains one million numeric cells and one blank cell, Excel 2013 treats the entire column as if it is text and chooses to Count the column instead of Sum. This is why it is incredibly annoying that the default setting for a pivot table leaves many blanks in the VALUES area of some pivot tables.

The blank tells you that there were no sales for that particular combination of labels. In the default view, an actual zero is used to indicate that there was activity, but the total sales were zero. This value might mean that a customer bought something and then returned it, resulting in net sales of zero. Although there are limited applications in which you need to differentiate between having no sales and having net zero sales, this seems rare. In 99% of the cases, you should fill in the blank cells with zeros.

Follow these steps to change this setting for the current pivot table:

1. Right-click any cell in the pivot table and choose PivotTable Options.

2. On the Layout & Format tab in the Format section, type **0** next to the field labeled For Empty Cells Show (see Figure 3.5).

3. Click OK to accept the change.

The result is that the pivot table is filled with zeros instead of blanks, as shown in Figure 3.6.

Figure 3.5
Enter a zero in the For
Empty Cells Show box to
replace the blank cells
with zero.

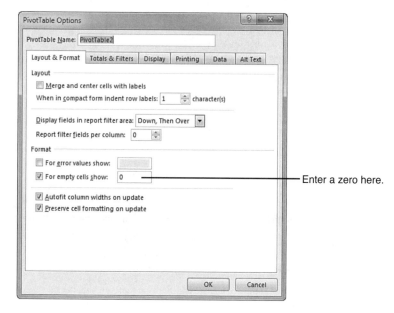

Enter a zero here.

Figure 3.6
Your report is now a solid
contiguous block of non-
blank cells.

	A	B	C	D	E	F
1						
2						
3	Sum of Revenue	Column Labels ▼				
4	Row Labels ▼	Midwest	Northeast	South	West	Grand Total
5	⊟Communications	$0	$390,978	$498,937	$0	$889,915
6	AT&T	$0	$0	$498,937	$0	$498,937
7	Verizon	$0	$390,978	$0	$0	$390,978
8	⊟Consumer Goods	$123,043	$0	$0	$0	$123,043
9	Kraft Foods	$62,744	$0	$0	$0	$62,744
10	Proctor & Gamble	$60,299	$0	$0	$0	$60,299
11	⊟Energy	$0	$0	$796,239	$54,048	$850,287
12	Chevron	$0	$0	$0	$54,048	$54,048
13	ConocoPhillips	$0	$0	$57,516	$0	$57,516
14	Exxon Mobil	$0	$0	$704,359	$0	$704,359
15	Valero Energy	$0	$0	$34,364	$0	$34,364
16	⊟Financial	$0	$664,754	$406,326	$59,881	$1,130,961

Changing a Field Name

Every field in the final pivot table has a name. Fields in the row, column, and filter areas
inherit their names from the heading in the source data. Fields in the data section are given
names such as Sum of Revenue. In some instances, you might prefer to print a different
name in the pivot table. You might prefer Total Revenue instead of the default name. In
these situations, the capability to change your field names comes in quite handy.

Although many of the names are inherited from headings in the original data set, when
your data is from an external data source, you might not have control over field names. In
these cases, you might want to change the names of the fields as well.

To change a field name in the VALUES area, follow these steps:

1. Select a cell in the pivot table that contains the appropriate type of value. You might have a pivot table with both Sum of Quantity and Sum of Revenue in the VALUES area. Choose a cell that contains a Sum of Revenue value.

2. Go to the Analyze tab in the ribbon. A Pivot Field Name text box appears below the heading of Active Field. The box currently contains Sum of Revenue.

3. Type a new name in the box, as shown in Figure 3.7. Click a cell in your pivot table to complete the entry and have the heading in A3 change. The name of the field title in the VALUES drop zone also changes to reflect the new name.

> **NOTE** One common frustration occurs when you would like to rename Sum of Revenue to Revenue. The problem is that this name is not allowed because it is not unique; you already have a Revenue field in the source data. To work around this limitation, you can name the field and add a space to the end of the name. Excel considers "Revenue " (with a space) to be different from "Revenue" (with no space). Because this change is cosmetic, the readers of your spreadsheet do not notice the space after the name.

Figure 3.7
The name typed in the Custom Name box appears in the pivot table. Although names should be unique, you can trick Excel into accepting a similar name by adding a space to the end of it.

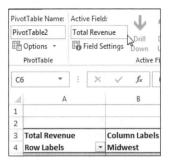

Making Report Layout Changes

Excel 2013 offers three report layout styles. The Excel team continues to offer the newer Compact Layout as the default report layout, even though I continually hound them about the fact that people who work in the real world would rather use the Tabular Report Layout, or at least would like to have a choice about which one to use as a default.

If you consider three report layouts, and the ability to show subtotals at the top or bottom, plus choices for blank rows and Repeat All Item Labels, you have 16 different layout possibilities available.

Layout changes are controlled in the Layout group of the Design tab, as shown in Figure 3.8. This group offers four icons:

- **Subtotals**—Moves subtotals to the top or bottom of each group or turns them off.
- **Grand Totals**—Turns the grand totals on or off for rows and columns.

- **Report Layout**—Uses the Compact, Outline, or Tabular forms. Offers an option to repeat item labels.

- **Blank Rows**—Inserts or removes blank lines after each group.

> **NOTE**
>
> For the statisticians in the audience, you would think that three layouts × two repeat options × two subtotal location options × two blank row options would be 24 layouts. However, choosing Repeat All Item Labels does not work with the Compact Form, thus eliminating four combinations. In addition, Subtotals at the Top of Each Group does not work with the Tabular layout, eliminating another four combinations.

Figure 3.8
The Layout group on the Design tab offers different layouts and options for totals.

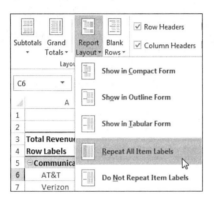

Using the New Compact Layout

By default, all new pivot tables use the Compact layout shown in Figure 3.6. In this layout, multiple fields in the row area are stacked in column A. Note in the figure that the Communications sector and the AT&T customer are both in column A.

The Compact form is suited for using the Expand and Collapse icons. Select one of the Sector value cells such as Communications in A5. Click the Collapse Field icon on the Analyze tab. Excel hides all the customer details and shows only the sectors, as shown in Figure 3.9.

After a field is collapsed, you can show detail for individual items by using the plus icons in column A, or you can click Expand Field on the Analyze tab to see the detail again.

> **TIP**
>
> If you select a cell in the innermost row field and click Expand Field on the Options tab, Excel displays the Show Detail dialog, as shown in Figure 3.10, to enable you to add a new innermost row field.

Figure 3.9
Click the Collapse Field icon to hide levels of detail.

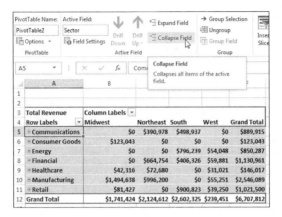

Figure 3.10
When you attempt to expand the innermost field, Excel offers to add a new innermost field.

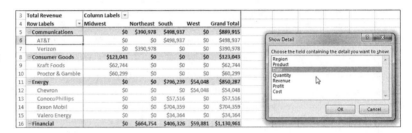

Using the Outline Form Layout

When you select Design, Layout, Report Layout, Show in Outline Form, Excel puts each row field in a separate column. The pivot table shown in Figure 3.11 is one column wider, with revenue values starting in C instead of B. This is a small price to pay for allowing each field to occupy its own column. Soon, you will find out how to convert a pivot table to values so you can further sort or filter. When you do this, you will want each field in its own column.

The Excel team added the Repeat All Item Labels option to the Report Layout tab starting in Excel 2010. This alleviated a lot of busy work because it becomes two clicks to fill in all the blank cells along the outer row fields. Choosing to repeat the item labels causes values to appear in cells A6:A7, A9:A10, and A12:A15 of Figure 3.11.

Figure 3.11 shows the pivot table in Outline form with labels repeated.

This layout is better suited if you plan to copy the values from the pivot table to a new location for further analysis. Although the Compact layout offers a clever approach by squeezing multiple fields in one column, it is not ideal for reusing the data later.

Figure 3.11
The Outline layout puts each row field in a separate column.

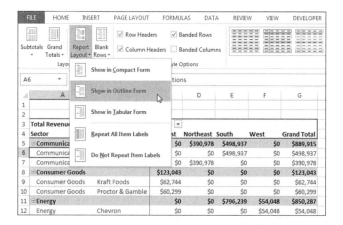

By default, both the Compact and Outline layouts put the subtotals at the top of each group. You can use the Subtotals drop-down on the Design tab to move the totals to the bottom of each group, as shown in Figure 3.12. In Outline view, this causes a not-really-useful heading row to appear at the top of each group. Cell A5 contains "Communications" without any additional data in the columns to the right. Consequently, the pivot table occupies 44 rows instead of 37 rows because each of the seven sector categories has an extra header.

Figure 3.12
With subtotals at the bottom of each group, the pivot table occupies several more rows.

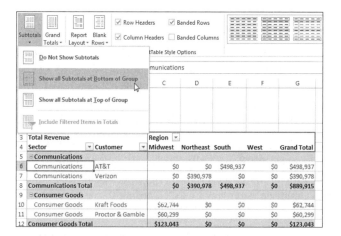

Using the Traditional Tabular Layout

Pivot table veterans will recognize the Tabular layout shown in Figure 3.13. This layout is similar to the one that has been used in pivot tables since their invention through Excel 2003. In this layout, the subtotals can never appear at the top of the group. The new Repeat All Item Labels works with this layout, as shown in Figure 3.13.

Jublia

Figure 3.13
The Tabular layout is
similar to pivot tables in
legacy versions of Excel.

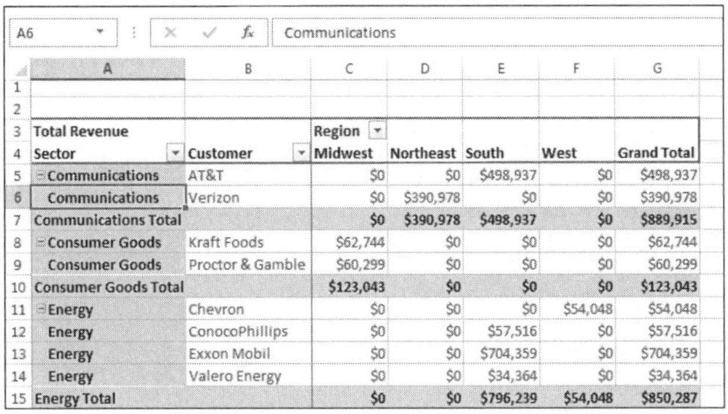

	A	B	C	D	E	F	G
1							
2							
3	Total Revenue		Region				
4	Sector	Customer	Midwest	Northeast	South	West	Grand Total
5	Communications	AT&T	$0	$0	$498,937	$0	$498,937
6	Communications	Verizon	$0	$390,978	$0	$0	$390,978
7	Communications Total		$0	$390,978	$498,937	$0	$889,915
8	Consumer Goods	Kraft Foods	$62,744	$0	$0	$0	$62,744
9	Consumer Goods	Proctor & Gamble	$60,299	$0	$0	$0	$60,299
10	Consumer Goods Total		$123,043	$0	$0	$0	$123,043
11	Energy	Chevron	$0	$0	$0	$54,048	$54,048
12	Energy	ConocoPhillips	$0	$0	$57,516	$0	$57,516
13	Energy	Exxon Mobil	$0	$0	$704,359	$0	$704,359
14	Energy	Valero Energy	$0	$0	$34,364	$0	$34,364
15	Energy Total		$0	$0	$796,239	$54,048	$850,287

The Tabular layout is the best layout if you expect to use the resulting summary data in a subsequent analysis. If you wanted to reuse the table in Figure 3.13, you would do additional "flattening" of the pivot table by choosing Subtotals, Do Not Show Subtotals, and Grand Totals, Off for Rows and Columns.

3

CASE STUDY: CONVERTING A PIVOT TABLE TO VALUES

Say that you want to convert the pivot table shown in Figure 3.13 to be a regular data set that you can sort, filter, chart, or export to another system. You don't need the Sectors totals in rows 7, 10, 15, and so on. You don't need the Grand Total at the bottom. And, depending on your future needs, you might want to move the Region field from the Columns area to the Rows area. This would allow you to add Cost and Profit as new columns in the final report.

Finally, you want to convert from a live pivot table to static values. To make these changes, follow these steps:

1. Select any cell in the pivot table.

2. From the Design tab, select Grand Totals, Off for Rows and Columns.

3. Select Design, Subtotals, Do Not Show Subtotals.

4. Drag the Region tile from the COLUMNS area in the PivotTable Field List. Drop this field between Sector and Customer in the ROWS area.

5. Check Profit and Cost in the top of the PivotTable Field List. Because both fields are numeric, they move to the VALUES area and appear in the pivot table as new columns. The report is now a contiguous solid block of data, as shown in Figure 3.14.

6. Select one cell in the pivot table. Press Ctrl+* to select all the data in the pivot table.

7. Press Ctrl+C to copy the data from the pivot table.

8. Select a blank section of a worksheet.

9. Right-click and choose Paste Values to open the fly-out menu. Select Paste Values and Number Formatting, as shown in Figure 3.15. Excel pastes a static copy of the report to the worksheet.

10. If you no longer need the original pivot table, select the entire pivot table and press the Delete key to clear the cells from the pivot table and free up the area of memory that was holding the pivot table cache.

Figure 3.14
The pivot table now contains a solid block of data.

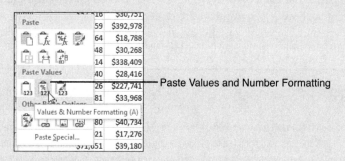

Figure 3.15
Use Paste Values to create a static version of the data.

Paste Values and Number Formatting

The result is a solid block of summary data. These 27 rows are a summary of the 500+ rows in the original data set, but they also are suitable for exporting to other systems.

Controlling Blank Lines, Grand Totals, and Other Settings

Additional settings on the Design tab enable you to toggle various elements.

The Blank Rows drop-down offers a choice for Insert Blank Row After Each Item. This setting only applies to pivot tables with two or more row fields. Blank rows are not added after each item in the inner row field. You see a blank row after each group of items in the outer row fields. As shown in Figure 3.16, the blank row after each Region makes the report easier to read. However, if you remove Sector from the report, you would have only Region in the row fields and no blank rows would appear (see Figure 3.17).

Figure 3.16
The Blank Rows setting makes the report easier to read.

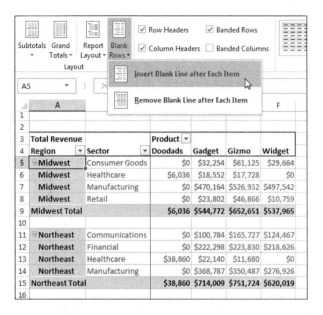

Figure 3.17
However, blank rows will not appear when there is only one item in the row field.

	A	B	C	D	E	F
1						
2						
3	Total Revenue	Product				
4	Region	Doodads	Gadget	Gizmo	Widget	Grand Total
5	Midwest	$6,036	$544,772	$652,651	$537,965	$1,741,424
6	Northeast	$38,860	$714,009	$751,724	$620,019	$2,124,612
7	South	$0	$839,551	$918,588	$844,186	$2,602,325
8	West	$28,663	$65,382	$70,057	$75,349	$239,451
9	Grand Total	$73,559	$2,163,714	$2,393,020	$2,077,519	$6,707,812

NOTE

For those of you following along with the sample files, there was quite a leap from the pivot table in Figure 3.14 to Figure 3.16, but it is still the same pivot table. Here is how to make the changes:

1. Uncheck Sector, Customer, Profit and Cost in the Pivot Table Fields task pane.
2. Drag the Product field to the Columns area.
3. Recheck the Sector field to move it to the second Row field.
4. Make sure the active cell is in column A.
5. On the Design tab of the ribbon, open Subtotals and choose Show All Subtotals at the Bottom of the Group.
6. Finally, as shown in Figure 3.16, open the Blank Rows drop-down and choose to add blank rows. To get to Figure 3.17, uncheck the Sector field.

Grand totals can appear at the bottom of each column and/or at the end of each row, or they can be turned off altogether. Settings for grand totals appear in the Grand Totals drop-down of the Layout group on the Design tab. The wording in this drop-down is a bit confusing, so Figure 3.18 shows what each option provides. The default is to show grand totals for rows and columns, as in Figure 3.17.

If you want a grand total column but no grand total at the bottom, choose On for Rows Only, as shown at the top of Figure 3.18. To me, this seems backward. To keep the grand total column, you have to choose to turn on grand totals for rows only. I guess the rationale is that each cell in F5:F8 is a grand total of the row to the left of the cell. Hence, you are showing the grand totals for each row, but not for the columns. Perhaps someday Microsoft will ship a version of Excel in English-Midwest where this setting would be called "Keep the Grand Total Column." But for now, it remains confusing.

Figure 3.18
The wording is confusing, but you can toggle off the grand total column, row, or both.

	A	B	C	D	E	F	G
1	Grand Totals On For Rows Only						
2	*Keeps the Grand Total column at the end of each row, deleted the Grand Total row.*						
3	Total Revenue	Product ▾					
4	Region ▾	Doodads	Gadget	Gizmo	Widget	Grand Total	
5	Midwest	$6,036	$544,772	$652,651	$537,965	$1,741,424	
6	Northeast	$38,860	$714,009	$751,724	$620,019	$2,124,612	
7	South	$0	$839,551	$918,588	$844,186	$2,602,325	
8	West	$28,663	$65,382	$70,057	$75,349	$239,451	
9							
10	Grand Totals On For Columns Only						
11	*Keeps the Grand Total row, deletes the Grand Total column.*						
12	Total Revenue	Product ▾					
13	Region ▾	Doodads	Gadget	Gizmo	Widget		
14	Midwest	$6,036	$544,772	$652,651	$537,965		
15	Northeast	$38,860	$714,009	$751,724	$620,019		
16	South	$0	$839,551	$918,588	$844,186		
17	West	$28,663	$65,382	$70,057	$75,349		
18	Grand Total	$73,559	$2,163,714	$2,393,020	$2,077,519		
19							
20	Off for Rows and Columns						
21	Total Revenue	Product ▾					
22	Region ▾	Doodads	Gadget	Gizmo	Widget		
23	Midwest	$6,036	$544,772	$652,651	$537,965		
24	Northeast	$38,860	$714,009	$751,724	$620,019		
25	South	$0	$839,551	$918,588	$844,186		
26	West	$28,663	$65,382	$70,057	$75,349		

In a similar fashion, to show a grand total row but no grand total column, you open the Grand Totals menu and choose On for Columns Only. Again, in some twisted version of the English language, cell B18 is totaling the cells in the column above it.

The final choice, Off for Rows and Columns, is simple enough. Excel shows neither a grand total column nor a grand total row.

Back in Excel 2003, pivot tables were shown in Tabular layout and logical headings such as "Region" and "Product" would appear in the pivot table, as shown in the top pivot table in Figure 3.19. When the Excel team switched to Compact form, they replaced those headings with "Row Labels" and "Column Labels." These add nothing to the report. To toggle off those headings, look on the far right side of the Analyze tab for an icon called Field

Headers and click it to remove "Row Labels" and "Column Labels" from your pivot tables in Compact form.

Figure 3.19
The Compact form introduced in Excel 2007 replaced useful headings with "Row Labels." You can turn these off.

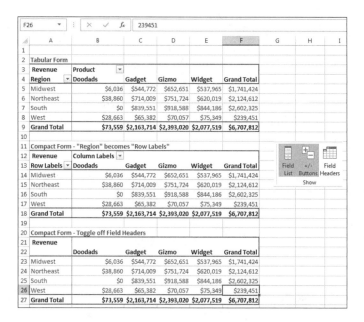

When you arrange several pivot tables vertically, as in Figure 3.19, you'll notice that changes in one pivot table change the column widths for the entire column, often causing #### to appear in the other pivot tables. By default, Excel changes the column width to AutoFit the pivot table but ignores anything else in the column. To turn off this default behavior, right-click each pivot table and choose PivotTable Options. In the first tab of the Options dialog, the second-to-last check box is AutoFit Column Widths On Update. Uncheck this box.

Customizing the Pivot Table Appearance with Styles and Themes

You can quickly apply color and formatting to a pivot table report using the 85 built-in styles in the PivotTable Styles gallery on the Design tab. These 85 styles are further modified by the four checkboxes to the left of the gallery. Combined with the 48 themes on the Page Layout tab, you have 65,280 easy ways to format a pivot table. If none of those provide what you need, you can define a new style.

Start with the four check boxes in the PivotTable Style Options group of the Design tab of the ribbon. You can choose to apply special formatting to the row headers, column headers, banded rows, or banded columns. My favorite choice here is banded rows, because it makes it easier for the reader's eye to follow a row across a wide report. You should choose from these settings first because the choices here will modify the thumbnails shown in the Styles gallery.

The PivotTable Styles gallery on the Design tab offers 85 built-in styles. Grouped into 28 styles each of Light, Medium, and Dark, the gallery offers variations on the accent colors used in the current theme. In Figure 3.20, you can see which styles in the gallery truly support banded rows and which just offer a bottom border between rows.

Note that you can modify the thumbnails for the 85 styles shown in the gallery by using the four check boxes in the PivotTable Style Options group.

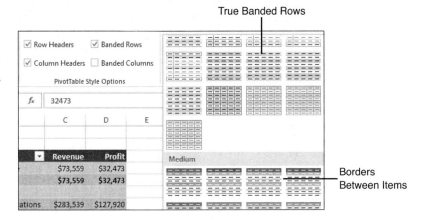

Figure 3.20
The styles are shown here with accents for row headers, column headers, and alternating colors in the columns.

The Live Preview feature in Excel 2013 works in the Styles gallery. As you hover your mouse cursor over style thumbnails, the worksheet shows a preview of the style.

Customizing a Style

You can create your own pivot table styles. The new styles are added to the gallery for the current workbook only. To use the custom style in another workbook, copy and temporarily paste the formatted pivot table to the other workbook. After the pivot table has been pasted, apply the custom style to an existing pivot table in your workbook and then delete the temporary pivot table.

Say that you want to create a pivot table style in which the banded colors are three rows high. Follow these steps to create the new style:

1. Find an existing style in the PivotTable Styles gallery that supports banded rows. Right-click the style in the gallery and select Duplicate. Excel displays the Modify PivotTable Quick Style dialog.

2. Choose a new name for the style. Excel initially appends a "2" to the existing style name, which means you have a name such as PivotStyleDark3 2. Type a better name, such as **Greenbar**.

3. In the Table Element list, click First Row Stripe. A new section called Stripe Size appears in the dialog.

4. Select 3 from the Stripe Size drop-down, as shown in Figure 3.21.

Figure 3.21
Customize the style in the Modify PivotTable Style dialog.

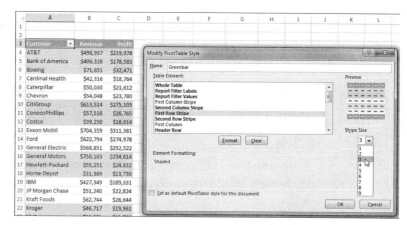

5. To change the stripe color, click the Format button. The Format Cells dialog appears. Click the Fill tab and then choose a fill color. If you want to be truly authentic, choose More Colors, Custom, and use Red=200, Green=225, Blue=204 to simulate 1980s-era greenbar paper. Click OK to accept the color and return to the Modify PivotTable Quick Style dialog.

6. In the Table Element List, click Second Row Stripe. Change the Stripe Size drop-down to be 3. Modify the format to use a lighter color such as white.

7. If you plan on creating more pivot tables in this workbook, choose the Set As Default PivotTable Style for This Document check box in the lower left.

8. Optionally edit the colors for Header Row and Grand Total Row.

9. Click OK to finish building the style. It is strange that the Excel team doesn't automatically apply this new style to the pivot table. After a few minutes of work to tweak the style, the pivot table does not change.

10. Your new style should be the first thumbnail visible in the styles gallery. Click that style to apply it to the pivot table. (Provided you have not added more than seven custom

styles, the thumbnail should be visible in the closed gallery—you can choose it without reopening the gallery.)

Modifying Styles with Document Themes

The formatting options for pivot tables in Excel 2013 are impressive. The 84 styles, combined with 16 combinations of the Style options, make for hundreds of possible format combinations.

In case you become tired of these combinations, you can visit the Themes drop-down on the Page Layout tab, where 48 built-in themes are available. Each theme has a new combination of accent colors, fonts, and shape effects.

To change a document theme, open the Themes drop-down on the Page Layout tab. Choose a new theme, and the colors used in the pivot table change to match the theme.

3

┌ C A U T I O N ─────────────────────────────────

Changing the theme affects the entire workbook. It changes the colors and fonts, and affects all charts, shapes, tables, and pivot tables on all worksheets of the active workbook.

┌───

T I P   Some of the themes use unusual fonts. You can apply the colors from a theme without changing the fonts in your document by using the Colors drop-down next to the Themes menu, as shown in Figure 3.22.

Figure 3.22
Choose new colors from the Colors menu.

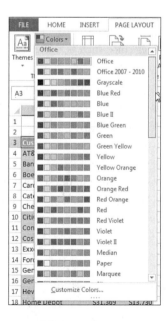

Changing Summary Calculations

When creating your pivot table report, by default Excel summarizes your data by either counting or summing the items. Instead of Sum or Count, you might want to choose functions such as Min, Max, and Count Numeric. In all, 11 options are available. However, the common reason to change a summary calculation is that Excel incorrectly chose to count instead of sum your data.

Understanding Why One Blank Cell Causes a Count

If all the cells in a column contain numeric data, Excel chooses to sum. If just one cell is either blank or contains text, Excel chooses to count.

In Figure 3.23, the worksheet contains mostly numeric entries but has a single blank cell in G2. The one blank cell is enough to cause Excel to count the data instead of summing.

Figure 3.23
The single blank cell in G2 causes problems in the default pivot table.

In Excel 2013, the first clue that you have a problem appears when you select the check box for Revenue in the Fields section of the PivotTable Field List. If Excel moves the Revenue field to the Rows drop zone, you know that Excel considers the field to be text instead of numeric.

Be vigilant while dragging fields into the Values drop zone. If a calculation appears to be dramatically low, check to see if the field name reads Count of Revenue instead of Sum of Revenue. When you create the pivot table in Figure 3.24, you should notice that your company has only $562 in revenue instead of millions. This should be a hint that the heading in B3 reads Count of Revenue instead of Sum of Revenue. In fact, 562 is one less than the number of records in the data set—Excel doesn't include the blank cell in the Count function.

Figure 3.24
Your revenue numbers look anemic. Notice in cell B3 that Excel chose to count instead of sum the revenue. This often happens if you inadvertently have one blank cell in your Revenue column.

	A	B
1		
2		
3	Row Labels ▾	Count of Revenue
4	Doodads	7
5	Gadget	178
6	Gizmo	177
7	Widget	200
8	Grand Total	562

To override the incorrect Count calculation, right-click any pivot table cell in the Revenue column. Choose Summarize Values By and then choose Sum (see Figure 3.25).

Figure 3.25
Change the function from Count to Sum in the Summarize Values By drop-down.

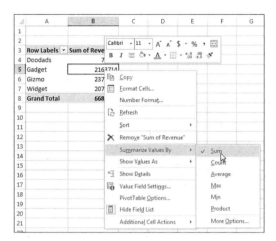

Using Functions Other Than Count or Sum

The settings for Summarize Values By and Show Values As were temporarily promoted to drop-downs in the Excel 2010 ribbon, but they are no longer in the ribbon in Excel 2013. All of the pivot table calculations icons for the Quick Access Toolbar were removed from Excel 2013. They were apparently removed to make space for Insert Timeline, Drill Down, Drill Up, and Recommended Pivot Tables. If you were a fan of Summarize Values By and Show Values As, you can continue to use them from the right-click menu or by selecting a cell and pressing Shift+F10.

The options have always been available in the Value Field Settings dialog.

Excel offers six functions through the Summarize Values By command, plus five more options when you select More Options. The options available are as follows:

- **Sum**—Provides a total of all numeric data.
- **Count**—Counts all cells, including numeric, text, and error cells. This is equivalent to the Excel function =COUNTA().
- **Average**—Provides an average.
- **Max**—Shows the largest value.
- **Min**—Shows the smallest value.
- **Product**—Multiplies all the cells together. For example, if your data set has cells with values of 3, 4, and 5, the product would be 60.
- **Count Nums**—Counts only the numeric cells. This is equivalent to the Excel function =COUNT().

- **StdDev and StdDevP**—Calculate the standard deviation. Use StdDevP if your data set contains the complete population. Use StdDev if your data set contains a sample of the population.

- **Var and VarP**—Calculate the statistical variance. Use VarP if your data contains a complete population. If your data contains only a sampling of the complete population, use Var to estimate the variance.

> **NOTE**
> Standard deviations explain how tightly results are grouped around the mean.

Adding and Removing Subtotals

Subtotals are an essential feature of pivot table reporting. Sometimes you might want to suppress the display of subtotals, and other times you might want to show more than one subtotal per field.

Suppress Subtotals When You Have Many Row Fields

When you have many row fields in your report, subtotals can mire your view. For example, in Figure 3.26, there is no need to show subtotals for each market because there is only one sales rep for each market.

Figure 3.26
Sometimes you do not need subtotals at every level.

3	Region	Market	Rep	Sum of Revenue
4	⊟Midwest	⊟Chicago	Mike	184425
5		Chicago Total		**184425**
6		⊟Cincinnati	Rose	107016
7		Cincinnati Total		**107016**
8		⊟Detroit	Henry	1372957
9		Detroit Total		**1372957**
10		⊟Louisville	Krys	42316
11		Louisville Total		**42316**
12		⊟Minneapolis	Heidi	34710
13		Minneapolis Total		**34710**
14	Midwest Total			**1741424**
15	⊟Northeast	⊟New York	Rudi	2124612
16		New York Total		**2124612**
17	Northeast Total			**2124612**

If you used the Subtotals drop-down on the Design tab, you would turn off all subtotals, including the Region subtotals and the Market subtotals. The Region subtotals are still providing good information, so you want to use the Subtotals setting in the Field Settings dialog. Choose one cell in the Market column. On the Analyze tab, choose Field Settings. Change the Subtotals setting from Automatic to None (see Figure 3.27).

Figure 3.27
Use the Subtotals setting in the field list to turn off subtotals for one field.

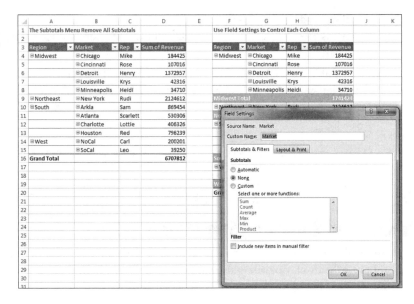

To remove subtotals for the Market field, click the Market field in the drop zone section of the PivotTable Field List. Select Field Settings. In the Field Settings dialog, select None under Subtotals, as shown in Figure 3.27.

Adding Multiple Subtotals for One Field

You can add customized subtotals to a row or column label field. Select the Region field in the bottom of the PivotTable Field List and select Field Settings.

In the Field Settings dialog for the Region field, select Custom and then select the types of subtotals you would like to see. The dialog in Figure 3.28 shows five custom subtotals selected for the Region field. It is rare to see pivot tables use this setting. It is not perfect. Note that the Count of 211 records automatically gets a currency format like the rest of the column, even though this is not a dollar figure. Also, the Average of $12,333 for South is an average of the detail records, not an average of the individual Market totals.

T I P   If you need to calculate the average of the four regions, you can do it with the DAX formula language and PowerPivot. See Chapter 10.

Figure 3.28
By selecting the Custom option in the Subtotals section, you can specify multiple subtotals for one field.

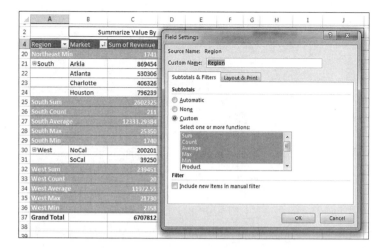

Changing the Calculation in a Value Field

The Value Field Settings dialog offers 11 options on the Summarize Values As tab and 15 main options on the Show Values As tab. Whereas the options under the first tab are the basic Sum, Average, Count, Max, and Min options that are ubiquitous throughout Excel, the 15 options under Show Values As offer interesting options such as % of Total, Running Total, and Ranks.

For Excel 2010 only, these options appeared as two drop-down menus in the ribbon. They were removed from the 2013 ribbon, but they still exist in the right-click menu. Because many of the calculations require one or two additional settings, you end up back in an extra dialog anyway. If you get in the habit of using the Value Field Settings dialog, you will have access to all the settings in one dialog.

Six of the Show Values As calculations were introduced in Excel 2010. These include % of Parent Item, Rank, and % Running Total In.

The following examples show how to use the various calculation options. To contrast the various settings, you can build a pivot table where you drag the Revenue field to the VALUES area nine separate times. Each shows up as a new column in the pivot table. Over the course of the rest of the chapter, you see the settings required for the calculations in each column.

To change the calculation for a field, select one value cell for the field and click the Field Settings button on the Analyze tab of the ribbon. The Value Field Settings dialog is similar to the Field Settings dialog, but it has two tabs. The first tab, Summarize Values By, contains Sum, Count, Average, Max, Min, Product, Count Numbers, StdDev, StdDevP, Var, and VarP. Choosing one of these 11 calculation options changes the data in the column. In Figure 3.29, columns B through D show various settings from the Summarize Values By tab.

Figure 3.29
Choose from the 11 summary calculations on this tab.

Market	Total	Average	# Orders	% of Total	% of NY	Rank	RunTotal	% RunTot	ChgFromPrev
		Summarize Value By			Show Values As				
Arkla	$869,454	$13,376	65	12.96%	40.92%	3	$869,454	12.96%	
Atlanta	$530,306	$12,052	44	7.91%	24.96%	5	$1,399,760	20.87%	-39.0%
Charlotte	$406,326	$14,512	28	6.06%	19.12%	6	$1,806,086	26.93%	-23.4%
Chicago	$184,425	$15,369	12	2.75%	8.68%	8	$1,990,511	29.67%	-54.6%
Cincinnati	$107,016	$13,377	8	1.60%	5.04%	9	$2,097,527	31.27%	-42.0%
Detroit	$1,372,957	$11,836	116	20.47%	64.62%	2	$3,470,484	51.74%	1182.9%
Houston	$796,239	$10,760	74	11.87%	37.48%	4	$4,266,723	63.61%	-42.0%
Louisville	$42,316	$10,579	4	0.63%	1.99%	10	$4,309,039	64.24%	-94.7%
Minneapolis	$34,710	$8,678	4	0.52%	1.63%	12	$4,343,749	64.76%	-18.0%
New York	$2,124,612	$11,301	188	31.67%	100.00%	1	$6,468,361	96.43%	6021.0%
NoCal	$200,201	$12,513	16	2.98%	9.42%	7	$6,668,562	99.41%	-90.6%
SoCal	$39,250	$9,813	4	0.59%	1.85%	11	$6,707,812	100.00%	-80.4%
Grand Total	$6,707,812	$11,914	563	100.00%					

Column B is the default Sum calculation. It shows the total of all records for a given market. Column C shows the Average order for each item by Market. Column D shows a count of the records. You can change the heading to say "# of Orders" or "# of Records" or whatever is appropriate. Note that the count is the actual count of records, not the count of distinct items. Counting distinct items has been difficult in pivot tables, but now is possible using PowerPivot. See Chapter 10 for more details.

Far more interesting options appear on the Show Values As tab of the Value Field Settings dialog, as shown in Figure 3.30. Fifteen options appear in the drop-down. Depending on the option you choose, you might need to specify either a Base Field or a Base Field and a Base Item. Columns E through J in Figure 3.29 show some of the calculations possible using Show Values As.

Rename the field as appropriate.

Figure 3.30
Fifteen different ways to show data are available on this tab.

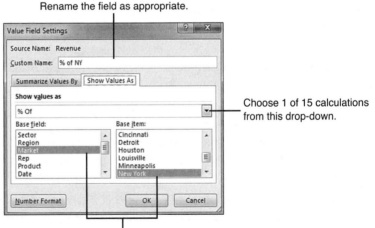

Choose 1 of 15 calculations from this drop-down.

Base Field and Base Item are selectively enabled.

Table 3.1 summarizes the Show Values As options.

Table 3.1   Calculations in Show Value As

Show Value As	Additional Required Information	Description
No Calculation	None	
% of Grand Total	None	Shows percentages so all the detail cells in the pivot table total 100%.
% of Column Total	None	Shows percentages that total up and down the pivot table to 100%.
% of Row Total	None	Shows percentages that total across the pivot table to 100%.
% of Parent Row Total	None	With multiple row fields, shows a row's percentage of the parent item's total row.
% of Parent Column Total	None	With multiple column fields, shows a column's percentage of the parent column's total.
Index	None	Calculates the relative importance of items.
% of Parent Total	Base Field only	With multiple row and/or column fields, calculates a cell's percent of the parent item's total.
Running Total In	Base Field only	Calculates a running total.
% Running Total In	Base Field only	Calculates a running total as a percentage of the total.
Rank Smallest to Largest	Base Field only	Provides a numeric rank, with 1 as the smallest item.
Rank Largest to Smallest	Base Field only	Provides a numeric rank, with 1 as the largest item.
% of	Base Field and Base Item	Expresses the values for one item as a percentage of another item.
Difference From	Base Field and Base Item	Shows the difference of one item compared to another item or to the previous item.
% Difference From	Base Field and Base Item	Shows the percent difference of one item compared to another item or to the previous item.

The capability to create custom calculations is another example of the unique flexibility of pivot table reports. With the Show Data As setting, you can change the calculation for a particular data field to be based on other cells in the VALUES area.

The following sections illustrate a number of Show Values As options.

Showing Percentage of Total

Column E of Figure 3.29 shows the % of Total. New York with $2.1 million in revenue represents 31.67% of the $6.7 million total revenue. Column E uses % of Column Total on the Show Values As tab. Two other similar options are % of Row Total and % of Grand Total. Choose one of these based on whether your text fields are going down the report, across the report, or both down and across.

Using % Of to Compare One Line to Another Line

The % Of option enables you to compare one item to another item. For example, the current data set shows that New York is the largest market. Perhaps this company started in New York and has the largest concentration of customers in New York. Perhaps the home office is in New York. The people in New York might have a New York–centric view of the world and want to show how all of the other markets are doing as a percentage of New York. Cell E6 of Figure 3.31 shows that Atlanta is about 25% the size of New York in sales.

To set up this calculation, choose Show Values As, % Of. For the Base Field, choose Market because this is the only field in the ROWS area. For the Base Item, choose New York. The result is shown in Figure 3.31.

Figure 3.31
This report is created using the % Of option with New York as the Base Item.

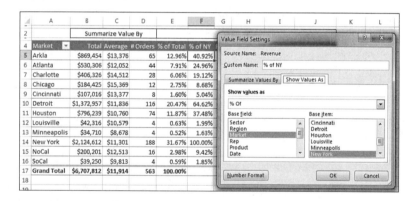

Showing Rank

Two ranking options were added in Excel 2010. Column G of Figure 3.32 shows Rank Largest to Smallest. New York is ranked #1, Minneapolis is #12. A similar option is Rank Smallest to Largest, which would be good for the pro golf tour.

To set up a rank, choose Value Field Settings, Show Values As, Rank Largest to Smallest. You are required to choose a Base Field. In this example, because Market is the only row field, it is the Base Field.

Figure 3.32
The Rank options were
added in Excel 2010.

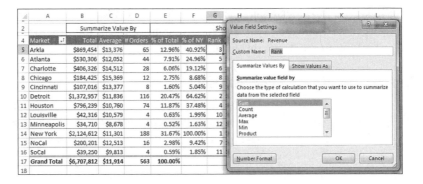

These rank options in Excel 2013 show that pivot tables have a strange way of dealing with ties. I say *strange* because they do not match any of the methods already established by the Excel functions =RANK(), =RANK.AVG(), and =RANK.EQ(). For example, if the top two markets have a tie, they are both assigned a rank of 1, and the third market is assigned a rank of 2.

Tracking Running Total and Percent of Running Total

Running total calculations is common in reports where you have months running down the column or when you want to show that the top *N* customers make up *N*% of the revenue. The Running Total In calculation has been in Excel for many versions. The % Running Total In setting was added in Excel 2010.

In Figure 3.33, cell I8 shows that the top four markets account for 76.97% of the total sales.

Figure 3.33
Show running totals or
a running percentage
of total.

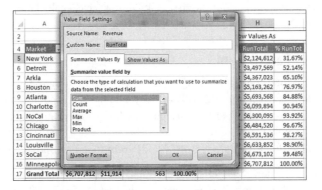

> **NOTE**
> To produce this figure, you have to use the Sort feature, which is discussed in depth in Chapter 4, "Grouping, Sorting, and Filtering Pivot Data." To create a similar analysis with the sample file, go to the drop-down in A4 and choose More Sort Options, Descending, by Total. Also note that the % Change From calculation in column J is not compatible with sorting.

To specify Running Total In (as shown in Column H) or % Running Total In (Column J), select Field Settings, Show Values As, Running Total In. You have to specify a Base Field, which in this case is the row field: Market.

Display Change from a Previous Field

Figure 3.34 shows the % Difference From setting. This calculation requires a base field and base item. You could show how each market compares to New York by specifying New York as the base item. This would be similar to Figure 3.31, except each market would be shown as a percentage of New York.

Figure 3.34
The % Difference From options enable you to compare each row to the previous or next row.

When you have date fields, it would make sense to use % Difference From and choose (previous) as the base item. Note the first cell will not have a calculation because there is no previous data in the pivot table.

Tracking Percent of Parent Item

The legacy % of Total settings always divide the current item by the grand total. In Figure 3.35, cell E4 says that Chicago is 2.75% of the total data set. A common question at the MrExcel.com message board is how to calculate Chicago's revenue as a percentage of the Midwest region total. This was possible but difficult before Excel 2010. Starting in Excel 2010, Excel added the % of Parent Row, % of Parent Column, and % of Parent Total.

To set up this calculation in Excel 2013, use Field Settings, Show Values As, % of Parent Row Total. Cell D4 in Figure 3.35 shows that Chicago's $184K is 10.59% of the Midwest Total of $1,741K.

Although it makes sense, the calculation on the subtotal rows might seem confusing. D4:D8 shows the percentage of each market as compared to the Midwest total. The values in D9, D11, D16, and D19 are comparing the region total to the grand total. For example, the 31.67% in D11 is saying that the Northeast region's $2.1 million is a little less than a third of the $6.7 million grand total.

Figure 3.35
An option in Excel 2013 enables you to calculate a percentage of the parent row.

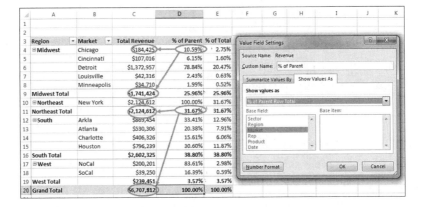

Track Relative Importance with the Index Option

The final option, Index, creates a somewhat obscure calculation. Microsoft claims that this calculation describes the relative importance of a cell within a column. In Figure 3.36, Georgia peaches have an index of 2.55 and California peaches have an index of 0.50. If the peach crop is wiped out next year, it will be more devastating to Georgia fruit production than to California fruit production.

Figure 3.36
Using the Index function, Excel shows that peach sales are more important in Georgia than in California.

	A	B	C	D	E	F	G	H	I
1	Sum of Sales	State						GA Peach	180
2	Crop	California	Georgia	Ohio	Grand Total			/ GA Total	210
3	Apple	100	10	30	140			A = Worth of Peaches to GA	0.86
4	Banana	200	10	1	211				
5	Kiwi	200	10	1	211			Peach Total	285
6	Peach	100	180	5	285			/ Total	847
7	Grand Total	600	210	37	847			B = Worth of Peaches	0.34
8									
9								Index is A/B	2.55
10	Index	State							
11	Crop	California	Georgia	Ohio	Grand Total			$= \dfrac{GeorgiaPeach \div GeorgiaTotal}{PeachTotal \div Total}$	
12	Apple	1.01	0.29	4.91	1.00				
13	Banana	1.34	0.19	0.11	1.00				
14	Kiwi	1.34	0.19	0.11	1.00				
15	Peach	0.50	2.55	0.40	1.00				
16	Grand Total	1.00	1.00	1.00	1.00				

Here is the exact calculation: First, divide Georgia peaches by Georgia total. This is 180/210, or 0.86. Next, divide total peach production (285) by total fruit production (847). This shows that peaches have an importance ratio of 0.34. Now, divide the first ratio by the second ratio: 0.86 / 0.34.

In Ohio, apples have an index of 4.91, so an apple blight would be bad for the Ohio fruit industry.

However, even after writing about this calculation for 10 years, there are parts that I don't quite comprehend. What if a state like Hawaii relied on productions of lychees but lychees were nearly immaterial to U.S. fruit production? If lychees were half of Hawaii fruit production, but 0.001 of U.S. fruit production, the Index calculation would skyrocket to 500.

Next Steps

Note that the following pivot table customizations are covered in subsequent chapters:

- Sorting a pivot table is covered in Chapter 4.
- Filtering records in a pivot table is covered in Chapter 4.
- Grouping daily dates up to months or years is covered in Chapter 4.
- Adding new calculated fields is covered in Chapter 5, "Performing Calculations Within Your Pivot Tables."
- Using data visualizations and conditional formatting in a pivot table is covered in Chapter 4.

Using these tools is a great way to focus your pivot table on the largest drivers of success for your business.

Grouping, Sorting, and Filtering Pivot Data

4

Some of the excellent new features that Microsoft added to pivot tables filtering in recent versions include the following:

- Slicers provide a visual way to filter data sets. Slicers are far superior to the old Page Filter technology. Yes, they can take up a lot more real estate, but they also vastly improve the multifiltering technology introduced in Excel 2007.

- Timelines are like a visual filter but for dealing with dates. You can filter by day, month, quarter, or year using a Timeline.

- Excel 2010 added the capability to filter a pivot table row or text field using text search. For example, this enables you to find all customers with "oil" in the name and then add all customers with "Petrol" in the name.

- Sets will someday make an impressive grouping feature in pivot tables. Unfortunately, in Excel 2013, they are limited to OLAP and PowerPivot data sets.

> **NOTE**
> Are sets good enough in Excel 2013 that you should convert your Excel data to a PowerPivot data set? Read Chapter 10, "Mashing Up Data with PowerPivot," to find out.

- Whenever the authors of this book entertain audiences at a seminar, they can be sure to "wow" the attendees with obscure features such as the Top 10 AutoShow feature, which was buried four menus deep in legacy versions of Excel. In Excel 2007, Microsoft exposed the AutoSort and AutoShow options so they are now just two clicks away from any pivot table.

- Grouping features went from being buried three levels deep in legacy versions of Excel to being a button on the ribbon in Excel 2007.

- Excel 2007 added filtering options for row and column fields that include context-sensitive filters for dates, text, and values.

This chapter covers grouping, sorting, filtering, data visualizations, and pivot table options.

Grouping Pivot Fields

Although most of your summarization and calculation needs can be accomplished with standard pivot table settings, you might want to summarize reports even further in special situations.

For example, transactional data is typically stored with a transaction date. You commonly want to report this data by month, quarter, or year. The Group option provides a straightforward way for you to consolidate transactional dates into a larger group such as month or quarter. Then you can summarize the data in those groups just as you would with any other field in your pivot table.

In the next section, you learn that grouping is not limited to date fields. In fact, you can also group non-date fields to consolidate specific pivot items into a single item.

Grouping Date Fields

Figure 4.1 shows a pivot report by date. With two years of transactional data, the report spans more than 500 columns. The columns are a summary of the original 50,563 rows, but managers often want detail by month instead of detail by day.

Figure 4.1
When reported by day, the summary report spans more than 500 columns. It would be more meaningful to report by month, quarter, and/or year instead.

	A	B	C	D	E
1					
2					
3	Sum of Revenue	Date			
4	Region	1/1/2014	1/2/2014	1/4/2014	1/7/2014
5	Midwest	$22,810	$0	$18,552	$8,456
6	Northeast	$0	$2,257	$0	$0
7	South	$0	$0	$9,152	$0
8	West	$0	$0	$0	$21,730
9	Grand Total	$22,810	$2,257	$27,704	$30,186

Excel provides a straightforward way to group date fields. Select any date heading, such as cell B4 in Figure 4.1. On the Analyze tab, click Group Field in the Group option.

When your field contains date information, the Grouping dialog appears. By default, the Months option is selected. You have choices to group by Seconds, Minutes, Hours, Days, Months, Quarters, and Years. It is possible, and usually advisable, to select more than one field in the Grouping dialog. In this case, select Months and Years, as shown in Figure 4.2.

Figure 4.2
Business users of Excel
usually group by months
(or quarters) and years.

There are several interesting points to note about the resulting pivot table. First, notice that
the Years field has been added to your Field List. Don't let this fool you. Your source data
is not changed to include the new field. Instead, this field is now part of your pivot cache in
memory. Another interesting point is that, by default, the Years field is automatically added
to the same area as the original date field in the pivot table layout, as shown in Figure 4.3.
Although this happens automatically, you are free to pivot months and years onto the opposite axis of the report. This is a quick way to create a year-over-year sales report.

Figure 4.3
By default, Excel adds the
new grouped date field to
your pivot table layout.

	A	B	C	D	E
1					
2					
3	Sum of Revenue	Years ▾	Date ▾		
4		⊟ 2014			
5	Region ▾	Jan	Feb	Mar	Apr
6	Midwest	$117,168	$78,664	$61,012	$70,455
7	Northeast	$87,483	$74,442	$87,436	$75,448
8	South	$46,841	$127,904	$109,229	$116,915
9	West	$21,730	$20,610	$8,116	$4,948
10	Grand Total	$273,222	$301,620	$265,793	$267,766
11					

Including Years When Grouping by Months

Although this point is not immediately obvious, it is important to understand that if you
group a date field by month, you also need to include the year in the grouping.

Examine the pivot table shown in Figure 4.4. This table has a date field that has been grouped by month and year. The months in column A use the generic abbreviations Jan, Feb, and so on. The sales for January 2014 are $273,222.

Figure 4.4
This table has a date field that is grouped by both month and year.

3	Sum of Revenue	Years		
4	Date	2014	2015	Grand Total
5	Jan	$273,222	$257,524	$530,746
6	Feb	$301,620	$253,977	$555,597
7	Mar	$265,793	$210,702	$476,495
8	Apr	$267,766	$271,534	$539,300
9	May	$341,412	$313,771	$655,183
10	Jun	$179,555	$239,829	$419,384
11	Jul	$385,767	$297,905	$683,672
12	Aug	$291,661	$270,747	$562,408
13	Sep	$276,524	$233,220	$509,744
14	Oct	$301,903	$308,986	$610,889
15	Nov	$230,273	$278,993	$509,266
16	Dec	$292,057	$363,071	$655,128
17	Grand Total	$3,407,553	$3,300,259	$6,707,812

However, if you choose to group the date field only by month, Excel continues to report the date field using the generic Jan abbreviation. The problem is that dates from January 2014 and January 2015 are both rolled up and reported together as Jan.

Having a report that totals Jan 2014 and Jan 2015 might be useful only if you are performing a seasonality analysis. Under any other circumstance, the report of $530,746 in January sales is too ambiguous and is likely to be interpreted wrong. To avoid ambiguous reports like the one shown in Figure 4.5, always include a year in the Group dialog when you are grouping by month. Unless, of course, you know that all the dates fall within one year.

Figure 4.5
If you fail to include the Year field in the grouping, the report mixes sales from Jan 2014 and Jan 2015 in the same number.

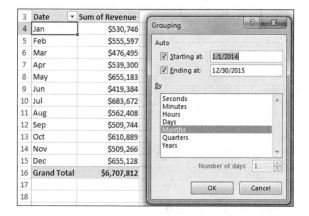

Grouping Date Fields by Week

The Grouping dialog offers choices to group by second, minute, hour, day, month, quarter, and year. It is also possible to group on a weekly or biweekly basis.

The first step is to find either a paper calendar or an electronic calendar, such as the Calendar feature in Outlook, for the year in question. If your data starts on January 4, 2013, it is helpful to know that January 4 was a Monday that year. You need to decide if weeks should start on Sunday or Monday or any other day. For example, you can check the paper or electronic calendar to learn that the nearest starting Sunday is January 3, 2013.

Select any date heading in your pivot table. Then select Group Field from the Analyze tab. In the Grouping dialog, clear all the By options and select only the Days field. This enables the spin button for Number of Days. To produce a report by week, increase the number of days from 1 to 7.

Next, you need to set up the Starting At date. If you were to accept the default of starting at January 1, 2014, all your weekly periods would run from Wednesday through Tuesday. By checking a calendar before you begin, you know that you want the first group to start on December 30, 2013 to have weeks that run Monday through Sunday. Figure 4.6 shows the settings in the Grouping dialog and the resulting report.

Figure 4.6
Group dates up to weekly periods.

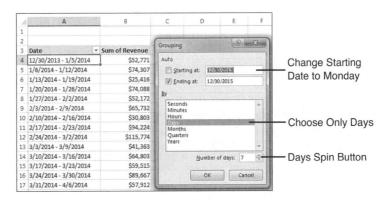

C A U T I O N

If you choose to group by week, none of the other grouping options can be selected. You cannot group this or any field by month, quarter, or year. You cannot add calculated items to the pivot table.

Ungrouping

After you have established groups, you can undo the groups by using the Ungroup icon on the Analyze tab. To undo a group, select one of the grouped cells and then click the Ungroup icon on the Analyze tab.

Grouping Numeric Fields

The Grouping dialog for numeric fields enables you to group items into equal ranges. This can be useful for creating frequency distributions. The pivot table in Figure 4.7 is quite the opposite of anything you've seen so far in this book. The numeric field—Revenue—is in the Rows area. A text field—Customer—is in the Values area. When you put a text field in the Values area, you get a count of how many records match the criteria. In its present state, this pivot table is not that fascinating; it is telling you that exactly one record in the database has a total revenue for $23,690.

Figure 4.7
Nothing interesting here—lots of order totals that appear exactly one time in the database.

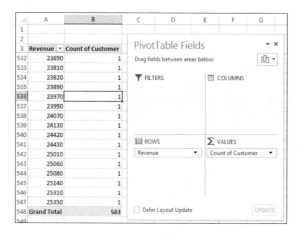

Select one number in column A of the pivot table. Select Group Field from the Analyze tab of the ribbon. Because this field is not a date field, the Grouping dialog offers fields for Starting At, Ending At, and By. As shown in Figure 4.8, you can choose to show amounts from 0 to 30,000 in groups of 5,000.

Figure 4.8
Create a frequency distribution by grouping the order size into $5,000 buckets.

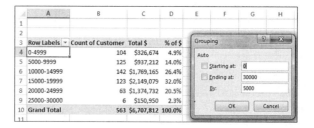

After grouping the order size into buckets, you might want to add additional fields, such as Revenue and Revenue shown as a percentage of the total.

CASE STUDY: GROUPING TEXT FIELDS FOR REDISTRICTING

You get a call from the VP of Sales. Secretly, the Sales department is considering a massive reorganization of the sales regions. The VP would like to see a report showing revenue after redistricting. You have been around long enough to know that the proposed regions will change several times before the reorganization happens, so you are not willing to change the Region field in your source data quite yet.

First, build a report showing revenue by market. The VP of Sales is proposing eliminating two regional managers and redistricting the country into two super regions. Using the Ctrl key, highlight the five regions that will make up the new West region. Figure 4.9 shows the pivot table before the first group is created.

Figure 4.9
Use the Ctrl key to select the noncontiguous cells that make up the new region.

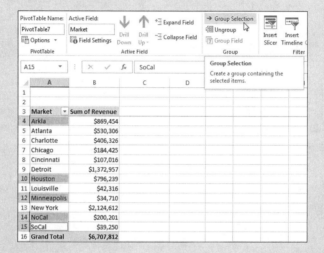

From the Analyze tab, click Group Selection. Excel adds a new field called Market2. The five selected regions are arbitrarily rolled up to a new territory called Group1. Using the Ctrl key, select the markets (now in column B) for the next region (see Figure 4.10).

Figure 4.10
The first super-region is arbitrarily called Group1.

3	Market2 ▼	Market ▼	Sum of Revenue
4	⊟ Group1	Arkla	$869,454
5		Houston	$796,239
6		Minneapolis	$34,710
7		NoCal	$200,201
8		SoCal	$39,250
9	⊟ Atlanta	Atlanta	$530,306
10	⊟ Charlotte	Charlotte	$406,326
11	⊟ Chicago	Chicago	$184,425
12	⊟ Cincinnati	Cincinnati	$107,016
13	⊟ Detroit	Detroit	$1,372,957
14	⊟ Louisville	Louisville	$42,316
15	⊟ New York	New York	$2,124,612
16	Grand Total		$6,707,812

Click Group Selection to group the markets in the proposed East region. As shown in Figure 4.11, you have grouped the markets into new regions, but there are four things that need further adjustment: the name of Group1, Group2, Market2, and the lack of subtotals for column A.

Figure 4.11
The markets are grouped, but you have to do some cleanup.

3	Market2 ▼	Market ▼	Sum of Revenue
4	⊟ Group1	Arkla	$869,454
5		Houston	$796,239
6		Minneapolis	$34,710
7		NoCal	$200,201
8		SoCal	$39,250
9	⊟ Group2	Atlanta	$530,306
10		Charlotte	$406,326
11		Chicago	$184,425
12		Cincinnati	$107,016
13		Detroit	$1,372,957
14		Louisville	$42,316
15		New York	$2,124,612
16	Grand Total		$6,707,812

Cleaning up the report will take a few moments.

1. Select cell A9. Type East to replace the arbitrary name of Group2.

2. Select cell A4. Type West to replace the arbitrary name of Group1.

3. Select the Market2 heading in A3. Type a new field name of Region New. Note that although you can reuse item values such as East and West, the name in A3 has to be unique. The pivot cache already has a field called Region, so you need to use a name such as Proposed Region, or Region2, or Region2015.

   It is strange that Excel chooses to use no subtotals for this new grouped field.

4. While you still have A3 selected, click the Field Settings dialog in the ribbon and choose Automatic for Subtotals.

The result is the pivot table in Figure 4.12.

Figure 4.12
It is now easy to see that these regions are heavily unbalanced.

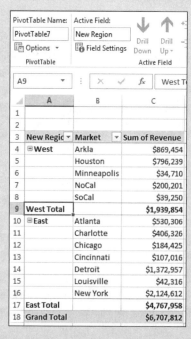

PivotTable Name:	Active Field:		
PivotTable7	New Region		
🗐 Options ▾	🗐 Field Settings	Drill Down	Drill Up ▾
PivotTable		Active Field	

A9	▼	fx	West T

⊿	A	B	C
1			
2			
3	New Regio ▼	Market ▼	Sum of Revenue
4	⊟ West	Arkla	$869,454
5		Houston	$796,239
6		Minneapolis	$34,710
7		NoCal	$200,201
8		SoCal	$39,250
9	West Total		$1,939,854
10	⊟ East	Atlanta	$530,306
11		Charlotte	$406,326
12		Chicago	$184,425
13		Cincinnati	$107,016
14		Detroit	$1,372,957
15		Louisville	$42,316
16		New York	$2,124,612
17	East Total		$4,767,958
18	Grand Total		$6,707,812

Figure 4.12 shows the report that is ready for the VP of Sales. You can probably predict that the Sales department needs to shuffle markets to balance the regions. To go back to the original regions, select East and West in column A and choose Ungroup. You can then start over grouping regions in a new combination.

Using the PivotTable Fields List

The entry points for sorting and filtering are spread throughout the Excel interface. It is worth taking a closer look at the row header drop-downs and the PivotTable Fields list before diving in to sorting and filtering.

As you've seen in these pages, I never use the Compact Form for a pivot table. My first step with any pivot table is to ditch the Compact Form and to return to Tabular Form. Although there are many good reasons for this, one is illustrated in Figures 4.13 and 4.14.

Figure 4.13
The drop-down in B3 for Customer is separate from the drop-down for Region.

In Figure 4.13, a Region drop-down appears in A3. A Customer drop-down appears in B3. Each of these separate drop-downs offers great settings for sorting and filtering.

Figure 4.14
In Compact Form, one single drop-down tries to control sorting and filtering for all the row fields.

When you leave the pivot table in the Compact Form, there are not separate headings for Region and Customer. Both fields are crammed into column A, with the silly heading of Row Labels. This means the drop-down always offers sorting and filtering options for Region. Every time you go back to the A3 drop-down with hopes of filtering or sorting the Customer field, you have to reselect Customer from a drop-down at the top of the menu. This is an extra click. If you are making five changes to the Customer field, you are reselecting Customer over and over and over and over and over. This should be enough to convince you to abandon the Compact Form.

If you decide to keep the Compact Form and get frustrated with the consolidated Row Labels drop-down, you can directly access the invisible drop-down for the correct field using the PivotTable Fields list, which contains a visible drop-down for every field in the areas at the bottom. Those visible drop-downs do not contain the sorting and filtering options.

The good drop-downs are actually in the top of the fields list, but you have to hover over the field to see the drop-down appear. After you hover as shown in Figure 4.15, you can directly access the same customer drop-down shown in Figure 4.13.

Figure 4.15
Hover over the field in the top of the fields list to directly access the sorting and filtering settings for that field.

Docking and Undocking the PivotTable Fields List

The PivotTable Fields List starts out docked on the right side of the Excel window. Hover over the green PivotTable Fields heading in the pane, and the mouse pointer changes to a four-headed arrow. Drag to the left to enable the pane to float anywhere in your Excel window.

After you have undocked the PivotTable Fields List, you might find that it is difficult to redock it on either side of the screen. To redock the fields list, you must grab the title bar and drag until at least 85% of the fields list is off the edge of the window. Pretend that you are trying to remove the floating fields list completely from the screen. Eventually, Excel gets the hint and redocks it. Note that you can dock the PivotTable Fields List on either the right or left side of the screen.

Rearranging the PivotTable Fields List

As shown in Figure 4.16, a small drop-down appears near the top right of the PivotTable Fields List. Select this drop-down to see its five possible arrangements. Although the default is to have the Fields section at the top of the list and the Areas section at the bottom of the list, four other arrangements are possible. New in Excel 2013, options let you control whether the fields in the list appear alphabetically or in the same sequence that they appeared in the original data set.

Figure 4.16
Use this drop-down to rearrange the PivotTable Fields List.

The final three arrangements offered in the drop-down are rather confusing. If someone changes the PivotTable Fields List to show only the Areas section, you cannot see new fields to add to the pivot table.

If you ever encounter a version of the PivotTable Fields List with only the Areas sections (see Figure 4.16) or only the fields, remember that you can return to a less confusing view of the data by using the arrangement drop-down.

Using the Areas Section Drop-Downs

As shown in Figure 4.17, every field in the Areas section has a visible drop-down arrow. When you select this drop-down arrow, you see four categories of choices:

- The first four choices enable you to rearrange the field within the list of fields in that area of the pivot table. You can accomplish this by dragging the field up or down in the area.

- The next four choices enable you to move the field to a new area. You could also accomplish this by dragging the field to a new area.

- The next choice enables you to remove the field from the pivot table. You can also accomplish this by dragging the field outside of the fields list.

- The final choice displays the Field Settings dialog for the field.

Figure 4.17
Use this drop-down to
rearrange the PivotTable
Fields List.

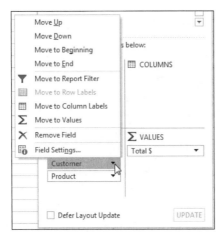

Sorting in a Pivot Table

Items in the row area and column area of a pivot table are sorted in ascending order by any custom list first. This allows weekday and month names to sort into Monday, Tuesday, Wednesday... instead of the alphabetical order of Friday, Monday, Saturday, ..., Wednesday.

If the items do not appear in a custom list, they will be sorted in ascending order. This is fine, but in many situations, you want the customer with the largest revenue to appear at the top of the list. When you sort in ascending order using a pivot table, you are setting up a rule that controls how that field is sorted, even after new fields are added to the pivot table.

> **TIP** Excel 2013 includes four custom lists by default, but you can add your own custom list to control the sort order of future pivot tables. See the "Using a Custom List for Sorting" section, later in this chapter.

Sorting Customers into High-to-Low Sequence Based on Revenue

Three pivot tables appear in Figure 4.18. The first pivot table shows the default sort for a pivot table: Customers are arranged alphabetically, starting with AT&T, Bank of America, Boeing, and so on.

In the second pivot table, the report is sorted in descending sequence by Total Revenue. This pivot table was sorted by selecting cell E3 and choosing the ZA icon in the Data tab of the ribbon. Although that sounds like a regular sort, it is better. When you sort inside a pivot table, Excel sets up a rule that will be used after you make additional changes to the pivot table.

Figure 4.18
When you override the default sort, Excel remembers the sort as additional fields are added.

	A	B	C	D	E	F	G	H	I
1	Sort AZ is the default			More Sort Options -			After adding fields, the sort rule remains		
2				Descending by Total Revenue					
3	Customer	Total $		Customer	Total $		Sector	Customer	Total $
4	AT&T	$498,937		Wal-Mart	$869,454		Manufacturing	General Motors	$750,163
5	Bank of America	$406,326		General Motors	$750,163			Ford	$622,794
6	Boeing	$71,651		Exxon Mobil	$704,359			General Electric	$568,851
7	Cardinal Health	$42,316		Ford	$622,794			IBM	$427,349
8	Caterpillar	$50,030		CitiGroup	$613,514			Boeing	$71,651
9	Chevron	$54,048		General Electric	$568,851			Hewlett-Packard	$55,251
10	CitiGroup	$613,514		AT&T	$498,937			Caterpillar	$50,030
11	ConocoPhillips	$57,516		IBM	$427,349		Manufacturing Total		$2,546,089
12	Costco	$39,250		Bank of America	$406,326		Financial	CitiGroup	$613,514
13	Exxon Mobil	$704,359		Verizon	$390,978			Bank of America	$406,326
14	Ford	$622,794		Pfizer	$72,680			Wells Fargo	$59,881
15	General Electric	$568,851		Boeing	$71,651			JP Morgan Chase	$51,240
16	General Motors	$750,163		Kraft Foods	$62,744		Financial Total		$1,130,961
17	Hewlett-Packard	$55,251		Proctor & Gamble	$60,299		Retail	Wal-Mart	$869,454

The pivot table in columns G:I shows what happens after you add Sector as a new outer row field. Within each sector, the pivot table continues to sort the data in descending order by revenue. Within Manufacturing, General Motors appears first with $750K, followed by Ford with $622K.

Furthermore, you could remove Customer from the pivot table, do more adjustments, and then add Customer back to the column area, and Excel will remember that the customers should be presented from high to low.

If you could see the entire pivot table in G3:I38 of Figure 4.18, you would notice that the sectors are sorted in descending order by revenue as well. This did not happen automatically. When you add sectors, they originally show in alphabetical sequence, with Communications first, followed by Consumer Goods, Energy, Financial, and so on.

The following tricks can be used for sorting an outer row field by revenue:

■ You can select cell G4 and then use Collapse Field on the Analyze tab to hide the customer detail. After you have only the sectors showing, select I3 and click ZA to sort descending. Excel understands that you want to set up a sort rule for the Sector field.

■ You can temporarily remove Customer from the pivot table, sort descending by revenue, and then add Customer back.

■ You can use the More Sort Options, as described in the following paragraphs.

To sort the Sector field, you should open the drop-down menu shown in Figure 4.19. If your pivot table is shown in Tabular Form or Outline Form, you can simply open the drop-down arrow in cell G3, as shown in Figure 4.19. If your pivot table is in Compact Form, you can hover over the Sector field in the top of the PivotTable Fields List to reveal a drop-down menu. Alternatively, you can open the Row Fields drop-down and choose Sector at the top of the menu.

Inside the drop-down menu, choose More Sort Options to open the Sort (Sector) dialog. In this dialog, you can choose to sort the Sector field in Descending order by Total $ (see Figure 4.20).

Figure 4.19
For explicit control over sort order, open this drop-down menu.

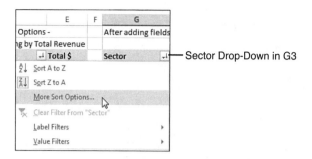

Sector Drop-Down in G3

Figure 4.20
Choose to sort Sector based on the Total $ field.

The Sort (Sector) dialog shown in Figure 4.20 includes a More Options button in the lower left. If you choose this button, you arrive at the More Sort Options dialog. Here, you can specify a custom list to be used for the first key sort order. You can also specify that the sorting should be based on a column other than Grand Total.

In Figure 4.21, the pivot table includes Product in the column area. If you wanted to sort the customers based on total gadget revenue instead of total revenue, for example, you could do so with the More Sort Options dialog. Here are the steps:

1. Open the Customer heading drop-down in B4.

2. Choose More Sort Options.

3. In the Sort (Customer) dialog, choose More Options.

4. In the More Sort Options (Customer) dialog, choose the Sort By Values in Selected Column option (see Figure 4.21).

5. Click in the reference box, and then click cell D5. Note that you cannot click the Gadget heading in D4; you have to choose one of the Gadget value cells.

6. Click OK twice to return to the pivot table.

Figure 4.21
Using More Sort Options, you can sort by a specific pivot field item.

In previous versions of Excel, there were separate sort buttons on the Analyze tab and the Data tab. The Excel team is working to simplify Excel: Rather than have different rules for sort buttons on the Data tab and Analyze tab, they now offer a single set of buttons. When you want to sort with the buttons on the Data tab, Excel attempts to figure out what you mean and then applies the rules in the dialogs shown in Figures 4.19 through 4.21.

You might wonder whether you can set up the "Sort by Doodads" rule by doing a simple sort using the Data tab. As noted in step 5, it seems like an anomaly that you have to specify a numeric cell as the Sort By reference instead of the heading. This logic continues through to the sorting IntelliSense.

In Figure 4.22, if you click in E4, D4, C4, B4, or F4 and then click the ZA button, the result always sorts descending by the Grand Total column. However, if you click in cell C5, which is a value cell, and click the ZA button to sort descending, you successfully alter the setting in More Sort Options (Customer) to sort the Customer column descending by sales of doodads.

Figure 4.22
Sort by cell E5 instead of cell E4 to set up a rule like the one shown in Figure 4.21.

	A	B	C	D	E	F
1	**Sum of Revenue**	**Product**				
2	**Customer**	**Doodads**	**Gadget**	**Gizmo**	**Widget**	**Grand Total**
3	Pfizer	$38,860	$22,140	$11,680	$0	$72,680
4	McKesson	$28,663	$2,358	$0	$0	$31,021
5	Cardinal Health	$6,036	$18,552	$17,728	$0	$42,316

Sort by Grand Total

Sort by Doodads

Using a Manual Sort Sequence

The Sort dialog offers something called a *manual sort*. Rather than using the dialog, you can invoke a manual sort in a surprising way.

Note that the products in Figure 4.23 are in the following order: Doodads, Gadget, Gizmo, and Widget. It appears that the Doodads product line is a minor product line and probably would not fall first in the product list.

Figure 4.23
Initially, the products across the top of the report are sorted alphabetically.

	A	B	C	D	E	F
1	Sum of Revenue	Product ▾				
2	Date ▾	Doodads	Gadget	Gizmo	Widget	Grand Total
3	2014	$65,216	$1,144,099	$1,152,075	$1,046,163	$3,407,553
4	2015	$8,343	$1,196,997	$1,240,945	$853,974	$3,300,259
5	Grand Total	$73,559	$2,341,096	$2,393,020	$1,900,137	$6,707,812

Place the cell pointer in cell E2 and type the word **Doodads**. When you press Enter, Excel figures out that you want to move the Doodads column to be last. All the values for this product line move from column B to column E. The values for the remaining products shift to the left.

This behavior is completely unintuitive. You should never try this behavior with a regular (non–pivot table) data set in Excel. You would never expect Excel to change the data sequence just by moving the labels. Figure 4.24 shows the pivot table after a new column heading has been typed in cell E2.

Figure 4.24
Simply type a heading in E2 to rearrange the columns.

	A	B	C	D	E	F
1	Sum of Revenue	Product ▾				
2	Date ▾	Gadget	Gizmo	Widget	Doodads	Grand Total
3	2014	$1,144,099	$1,152,075	$1,046,163	$65,216	$3,407,553
4	2015	$1,196,997	$1,240,945	$853,974	$8,343	$3,300,259
5	Grand Total	$2,341,096	$2,393,020	$1,900,137	$73,559	$6,707,812

If you prefer to use the mouse, you can drag and drop the column heading to a new location. Select a column heading. Hover over the edge of the cell selection rectangle until the mouse changes to a four-headed arrow. Drag the cell to a new location, as shown in Figure 4.25. When you release the mouse, all of the value settings move to the new column.

Figure 4.25
Use drag and drop to move a column to a new position.

	A	B	C	D	E	F
1	Sum of Revenue	Product ▾				
2	Date ▾	Gadget	Gizmo	Widget	Doodads	Grand Total
3	2014	$1,144,099	$1,152,075	C2:C5 163	$65,216	$3,407,553
4	2015	$1,196,997	$1,240,945	$853,974	$8,343	$3,300,259
5	Grand Total	$2,341,096	$2,393,020	$1,900,137	$73,559	$6,707,812

4

CAUTION

After you use a manual sort, any new products you add to the data source are automatically added to the end of the list rather than appearing alphabetically.

Using a Custom List for Sorting

Another way to permanently change the order of items along a dimension is to set up a custom list. All future pivot tables created on your computer will automatically respect the order of the items in a custom list.

The pivot table at the top of Figure 4.26 includes weekday names. The weekday names were added to the original data set using =TEXT(F2,"DDD") and copying down. Excel automatically puts Sunday first and Saturday last, even though this is not the alphabetical sequence of these words. This happens because Excel ships with four custom lists to control the days of the week, months of the year, and the three-letter abbreviations for both.

Figure 4.26

The weekday names in B2:H2 follow the order specified in the Custom Lists dialog.

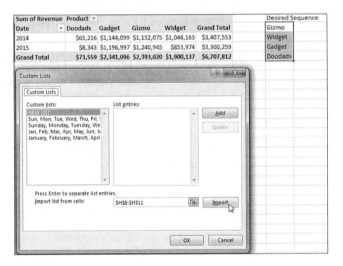

You can define your own custom list to control the sort order of pivot tables. Follow these steps to set up a custom list:

1. In an out-of-the-way section of the worksheet, type the products in their proper sequence. Type one product per cell, going down a column.

2. Select the cells containing the list of regions in the proper sequence.

3. Click the File tab and select Options.

4. Select the Advanced category in the left navigation. Scroll down to the General group. Click the Edit Custom Lists button.

5. In the Custom Lists dialog, your selection address is entered in the Import text box, as shown in Figure 4.26. Click Import to bring the products in as a new list.

6. Click OK to close the Custom Lists dialog and then click OK to close the Excel Options dialog.

The custom list is now stored on your computer and is available for all future Excel sessions. All future pivot tables will automatically show the product field in the order specified in the custom list. Figure 4.27 shows a new pivot table created after the custom list was set up.

Figure 4.27

After you define a custom list, all future pivot tables will follow the order in the list.

⊿	A	B	C	D	E	F
7	Sum of Revenue	Product ▾				
8	Date ▾	Gizmo	Widget	Gadget	Doodads	Grand Total
9	2014	$1,152,075	$1,046,163	$1,144,099	$65,216	$3,407,553
10	2015	$1,240,945	$853,974	$1,196,997	$8,343	$3,300,259
11	Grand Total	$2,393,020	$1,900,137	$2,341,096	$73,559	$6,707,812

To sort an existing pivot table by the newly defined custom list, follow these steps:

1. Open the Product header drop-down and choose More Sort Options.

2. In the Sort (Product) dialog, choose More Options.

3. In the More Sort Options (Product) dialog, clear the AutoSort check box.

4. As shown in Figure 4.28, in the More Sort Options (Product) dialog, open the First Key Sort Order drop-down and select the custom list with your product names.

Figure 4.28

Choose to sort by the custom list.

5. Click OK twice.

Filtering the Pivot Table: An Overview

Excel 2013 provides dozens of ways to filter a pivot table. Microsoft is continually investing in pivot tables, and the filter area has been expanded in 2007, 2010, and 2013.

Figure 4.29 points out some of the filters available. Each of these methods, and the best way to use each method, is discussed in the following sections.

Figure 4.29
This figure shows a fraction of the available filtering choices.

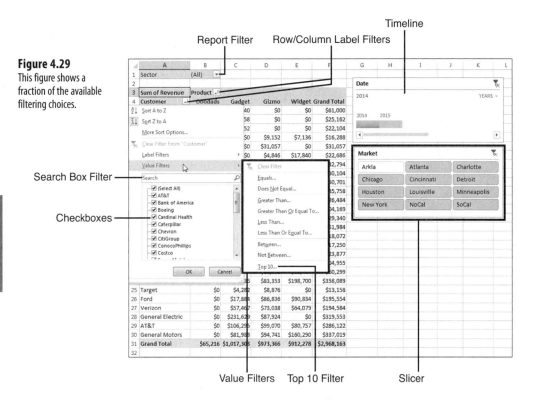

There are four ways to filter a pivot table, as shown in Figure 4.29:

- The Date timeline filter in G2:K9 is new in Excel 2013.
- The Market filter in G10:K17 is an example of the slicer introduced in Excel 2010.
- Drop-downs in B1 and B2 offer what were known as Page Filters in Excel 2003, Report Filters in Excel 2010, and now simply Filters.
- Cell G4 offers the top-secret AutoFilter location.

Drop-downs in A4 and B3 lead to even more filters:

- The traditional check box filters for each pivot item.
- A Search box filter introduced in Excel 2010.

- A fly-out menu with Label Filters.

- Depending on the field type, you might see a Value Filters fly-out menu, including the powerful Top 10 filter, which can do Top 10, Bottom 5, Bottom 3%, Top $8 Million, and more.

- Depending on the field type, you might see a Date Filters fly-out menu, with 37 virtual filters such as Next Month, Last Year, and Year to Date.

Using Filters for Row and Column Fields

If you have a field (or fields) in the row or column area of a pivot table, a drop-down with filtering choices appears on the header cell for that field. In Figure 4.29, a Customer drop-down appears in A4, and a Product drop-down appears in B3. The pivot table in that figure is using Tabular Form. If your pivot tables use Compact Form, you see a drop-down on the cell with Row Labels or Column Labels.

If you have multiple row fields, it is just as easy to sort using the invisible drop-downs that appear when you hover over a field in the top of the PivotTable Fields List.

> **NOTE** In the following figures, I use the drop-down menu in the fields list so you can see both the Filter choices and the result of those filters in the figure. When you open the filter in cell B3, it covers most of the pivot table.

Filtering Using the Check Boxes

You might have a few annoying products that appear in your pivot table. In the present example, the Doodads product line is a specialty product with very little sales. It might be an old legacy product that is out of line, but it still gets an occasional order from the scrap bin. Every company seems to have these orphan sales that no one really wants to see.

The check box filter provides an easy way to hide these items. Open the Product drop-down and uncheck Doodads. The product is hidden from view (see Figure 4.30).

What if you need to uncheck hundreds of items in order to leave only a few items selected? Toggle all items off or on using the Select All check box at the top of the list. You can then select the few items that you want to show in the pivot table.

In Figure 4.31, Select All turned off all customers and then two clicks re-selected Ford and General Motors.

The check boxes work great in this tiny data set with 26 customers. In real life, with 500 customers in the list, it will not be this easy to filter your data set using the check boxes.

Figure 4.30
Open the Product filter and uncheck Doodads.

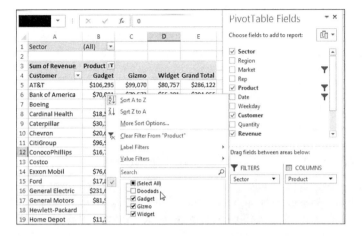

Figure 4.31
Use Select All to toggle all items off or on.

Filtering Using the Search Box

When you have hundreds of customers, the search box can be a great timesaver. In Figure 4.32, the database includes banks, credit unions, and insurance companies. If you want to narrow the list to banks and credit unions, you could follow these steps:

1. Open the Customer drop-down.
2. Type **Bank** in the search box (see Figure 4.32).
3. By default, Select All Search Results is selected. Click OK.
4. Open the Customer drop-down again.

Figure 4.32
Select the results of the
first search.

5. Type **Credit Union** in the search box.

6. Choose Add Current Selection to Filter, as shown in Figure 4.33. Click OK.

Figure 4.33
For the second search,
add these results to the
existing filter.

You now have all customers with either Bank or Credit Union in the name.

The search box isn't perfect. What if you want to find all the Insurance companies and turn those off? There is no choice for "Select Everything Except These Results." Nor is there a choice for "Toggle All Filter Choices." However, the Label Filters enable you to handle queries such as "select all customers that do not contain 'Insurance.'"

Filtering Using the Label Filters

Text fields offer a fly-out menu called Label Filters. To filter out all of the Insurance customers, you can apply a Does Not Contain filter (see Figure 4.34). In the next dialog, you can specify that you want customers that do not contain Insurance, Ins, or Ins* (see Figure 4.35).

Figure 4.34
Choose a Label Filter of Does Not Contain.

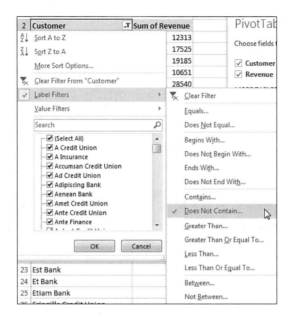

Figure 4.35
Specify to exclude customers with Insurance.

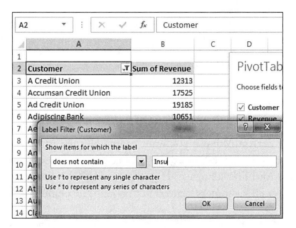

Note that Label Filters are not additive. You can only apply one Label Filter at a time. If you take the data in Figure 4.34 and apply a new Label Filter of between A and Czz, some insurance customers that were filtered out in Figure 4.35 come back in Figure 4.36.

Figure 4.36
However, a second Label Filter does not get added to the previous filter. Insurance is back in.

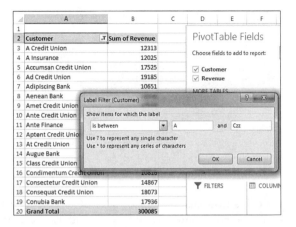

Filtering a Label Column Using Information in a Values Column

The Value Filters fly-out menu enables you to filter the customers based on information in the Values columns. Perhaps you want to see customers who had between $20,000 and $30,000 of revenue. You can use the Customer heading drop-down to control this. Here's how:

1. Open the Customer drop-down.

2. Choose Value Filters.

3. Choose Between (see Figure 4.37).

Figure 4.37
Value Filters for the Customer column will look at value in the Revenue field.

4. Type the values **20000** and **30000**, as shown in Figure 4.38.

Figure 4.38
Choose customers
between $20,000 and
$30,000, inclusive.

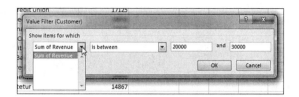

5. Click OK.

The results are inclusive; if a customer had exactly $20,000 or exactly $30,000, they are returned along with the customers between $20,000 and $30,000. Note that choosing a Value Filter clears out any previous Label Filters.

Creating a Top-Five Report Using the Top 10 Filter

One of the more interesting Value Filters is the Top 10 filter. If you are sending a report to the VP of Sales, she is not going to want to see hundreds of pages of customers. One short summary with the top customers is more than her attention span can handle. Here's how to create it:

1. Go to the Customer drop-down. Choose Value Filters, Top 10.
2. The Top 10 Filter dialog enables you to choose Top or Bottom. Leave the setting at the default of Top.
3. You can ask for any number of customers: 10, 5, 7, 12. Fill the number in the second field.
4. The third drop-down on the dialog offers Items, Percent, and Sum. You could ask for the top ten items. You could ask for the top 80% of revenue (which the theory says should be 20% of the customers). Or, you can ask for enough customers to reach a sum of $5 million (see Figure 4.39).

> **CAUTION**
>
> The $3,560,284 total shown in cell B9 of Figure 4.39 is the revenue of only the visible customers. It does not include the revenue for the remaining customers. You might want to show the grand total of all customers at the bottom of the list. You have a few options:
>
> - A setting on the Design tab, under the Subtotals drop-down, enables you to include values from filtered items in the totals. This option is only available for OLAP data sets. However, you can make a regular data set into an OLAP data set by running it through PowerPivot. See Chapter 10.

■ You can remove the grand total from the pivot table in Figure 4.39 and build another one-row pivot table just below this data set. Hide the heading row from the second pivot table, and you will appear to have the true grand total at the bottom of the pivot table.

■ If you select the blank cell to the right of the last heading (C3 in Figure 4.39), you can turn on the filter on the Data tab. This filter is not designed for pivot tables and is usually grayed out. After you've added the regular filters, open the drop-down in B3. Choose Top 10 Filter and ask for the top six items, as shown in Figure 4.40. This returns the top five customers and the grand total from the data set. Be aware that this method is taking advantage of a bug in Excel. If the underlying data changes, the Excel team will not update the filter for you.

Figure 4.39
Create a report of the top five customers.

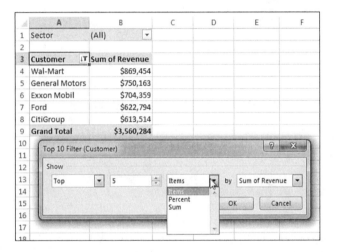

Figure 4.40
You are taking advantage of a hole in the fabric of Excel to apply a regular AutoFilter to a pivot table.

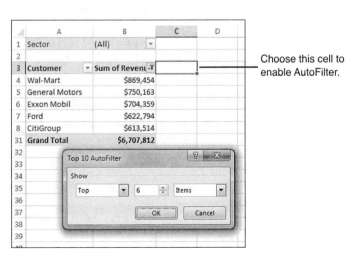

Choose this cell to enable AutoFilter.

Filtering Using the Date Filters in the Label Drop-Down

If your label field contains all dates, Excel replaces the Label Filter fly-out with a Date Filters fly-out. These filters offer many virtual filters, such as Next Week, This Month, Last Quarter, and so on (see Figure 4.41).

Figure 4.41
The Date Filters offer various virtual date periods.

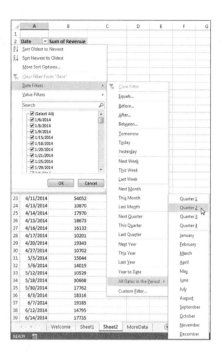

If you choose Equals, Before, After, or Between, you can specify a date or a range of dates.

Options for the current, past, or next day, week, month, quarter, or year occupy 15 options. Combined with Year to Date, these options change day after day. You can pivot a list of projects by due date and always see the projects that are due in the next week using this option. When you open the workbook on another day, the report recalculates.

> **TIP**
> A week runs from Sunday through Saturday. If you select Next Week, the report always shows a period from the next Sunday through the following Saturday.

When you select All Dates in the Period, a new fly-out menu offers options such as Each Month and Each Quarter.

┌─ CAUTION ──┐

If your date field contains dates and times, the Date Filters might not work as expected. You might ask for dates equal to 4/15/2015 and Excel will say that no records are found. The problem is that 6:00 p.m. on 4/15/2015 is stored internally as 42109.75, with the ".75" representing the 18 hours elapsed in the day between midnight and 6:00 p.m. If you want to return all records that happened at any point on April 15, check the Whole Days box in the Date Filter dialog.

└──┘

Filtering Using the Filters Area

Pivot table veterans remember the old page area section of a pivot table. This area has been renamed the Filters area and still operates basically the same as in legacy versions of Excel. Microsoft did add the capability to select multiple items from the Filters area. Although the Filters area is not as showy as the new slicer feature, it is still useful when you need to replicate your pivot table for every customer.

Adding Fields to the Filters Area

The pivot table in Figure 4.42 is a perfect ad hoc reporting tool to give to a high-level executive. He can use the drop-downs in B1:B4 and E1:E4 to find revenue quickly for any combination of sector, region, market, rep, customer, product, date, or weekday. This is a typical use of Report Filters.

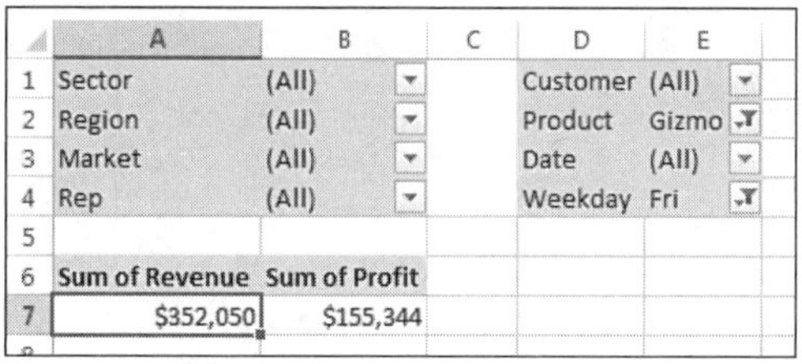

Figure 4.42
With multiple fields in the Filters area, this pivot table can answer many ad hoc queries.

To set up the report, drag Revenue and Cost to the Values drop zone and then drag as many fields as desired to the Filters drop zone.

If you add many fields to the Filters area, you might want to use one of the obscure pivot table options settings. Click Options on the Analyze tab. On the Layout & Format tab of the PivotTable Options dialog, change the Report Filter Fields Per Column from 0 to a positive number. Excel rearranges the filter fields into multiple columns. Figure 4.42 shows the report filters with four fields per column. You can also change Down, Then Over to Over, Then Down to rearrange the sequence of the filter fields.

Choosing One Item from a Filter

To filter the pivot table, click any drop-down in the Filters area of the pivot table. The drop-down always starts with (All), but then lists the complete unique set of items available in that field.

Choosing Multiple Items from a Report Filter

At the bottom of the Filters drop-down is a check box labeled Select Multiple Items. If you select this box, Excel adds a check box next to each item in the drop-down. This enables you to check multiple items from the list.

In Figure 4.43, the pivot table is filtered to show revenue from three zones.

Figure 4.43
You can select multiple items, but after the filter drop-down closes, you cannot tell which items were selected.

Replicating a Pivot Table Report for Each Item in a Filter

Although slicers are the new darlings of the pivot table report, the good-old fashioned Report Filter can still do one trick that slicers cannot do. Say you have created a report that you would like to share with the industry managers. You have a report showing customers with revenue and profit. You would like each industry manager to see only the customers in their area of responsibility.

CAUTION

Selecting multiple items from the Report Filter leads to a situation where the person reading the report will not know which items are included. Slicers solve this problem.

Follow these steps to quickly replicate the pivot table:

1. Make sure the formatting in the pivot table looks good before you start. You are about to make several copies of the pivot table, and you don't want to format each worksheet in the workbook, so double-check the number formatting and headings now.

2. Add the Sector field to the Filters area. Leave the Sector filter set to (All).

3. Select one cell in the pivot table so that you can see the Analyze tab in the ribbon.

4. Find the Options button in the left side of the Analyze tab. Next to the options tab is a drop-down. Don't click the big Options button. Instead, open the drop-down (see Figure 4.44).

Figure 4.44
Open the tiny drop-down next to the Options button.

5. Choose Show Report Filter Pages.

6. In the Show Report Filter Pages dialog, you see a list of all the fields in the report area. Because this pivot table only has the Sector field, this is the only choice (see Figure 4.45).

Figure 4.45
Select the field by which to replicate the report.

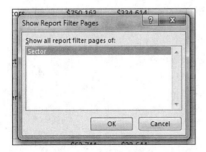

7. Click OK and stand back.

Excel inserts a new worksheet for every item in the Sector field. On the first new worksheet, Excel chooses the first sector as the filter value for that sheet. Excel renames the worksheet to match the sector. Figure 4.46 shows the new Energy worksheet, with neighboring tabs that contain Communications, Consumer Goods, Financial, and so on.

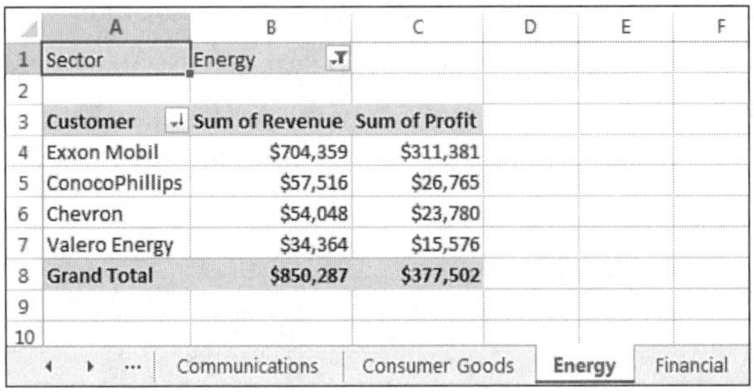

Figure 4.46
Excel quickly adds one page per sector.

	A	B	C	D	E	F
1	Sector	Energy				
2						
3	Customer	Sum of Revenue	Sum of Profit			
4	Exxon Mobil	$704,359	$311,381			
5	ConocoPhillips	$57,516	$26,765			
6	Chevron	$54,048	$23,780			
7	Valero Energy	$34,364	$15,576			
8	Grand Total	$850,287	$377,502			
9						
10						

◄ ► ⋯ | Communications | Consumer Goods | **Energy** | Financial

> **TIP**
> If the underlying data changes, you can refresh all of the Sector worksheets by using Refresh on one Sector pivot table. After you refresh the Communications worksheet, all of the pivot tables refresh.

Filtering Using Slicers and Timelines

Slicers are graphical versions of the Report Filter fields. Rather than hiding the items selected in the filter drop-down behind a heading such as (Multiple Items), the slicer provides a large array of buttons that show at a glance which items are included or excluded.

To add slicers, click the Insert Slicer icon on the Analyze tab. Excel displays the Insert Slicers dialog. Choose all the fields for which you want to create graphical filters, as shown in Figure 4.47.

Initially, Excel chooses one-column slicers of similar color in a tiled arrangement (see Figure 4.48). However, you can change these settings by selecting a slicer and using the Slicer Tools Options tab in the ribbon.

You can add more columns to a slicer. If you have to show 50 two-letter state abbreviations, that will look much better as five rows of ten columns instead of 50 rows of one column. Click the slicer to get access to the Slicer Tools Analyze tab. Use the Columns spin button to increase the number of columns in the slicer. Use the resize handles in the slicer to make the slicer wider or shorter. To add visual interest, choose a different color from the Slicer Styles gallery for each field.

Figure 4.47
Choose fields for slicers.

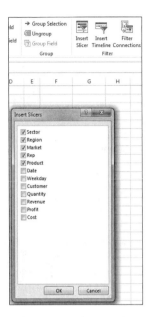

Figure 4.48
The slicers appear with
one column each.

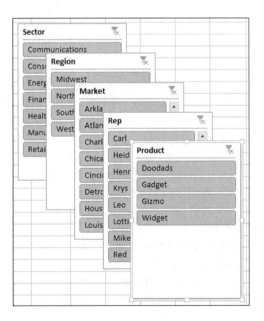

After formatting the slicers, arrange them in a blank section of the worksheet, as shown in
Figure 4.49.

Figure 4.49
After formatting, your slicers might fit on a single screen.

Rename a slicer using
the Slicer Settings dialog.

Northeast grayed out because
no customers in selected sectors.

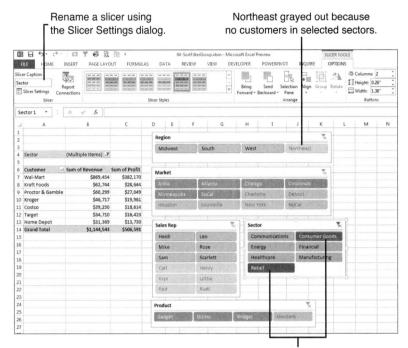

Consumer Goods and Retail Selected

Three colors might appear in a slicer. The dark color indicates items that are selected. White boxes often mean the item has no records because of other slicers. Gray boxes indicate items that are not selected.

Note that you can control the heading for the slicer and the order of items in the slicer using the Slicer Settings icon on the Slicer Tools Options tab of the ribbon. Just as you can define a new pivot table style, you can also right-click an existing slicer style and choose Duplicate. You can change the font, colors, and so on.

Using Timelines to Filter by Date

After slicers were introduced in Excel 2010, there was some feedback that slicers were not an ideal way to deal with date fields. You end up adding some fields to your original data set to show (perhaps) a decade and then use the group feature for year, quarter, and month. You would end up with a whole bunch of slicers all trying to select a time period, as shown in Figure 4.50.

For Excel 2013, Microsoft introduced a new kind of filter called a *timeline*. Select one cell in your pivot table and choose Insert Timeline from the Analyze tab. Timelines can only apply to fields that contain dates. Excel gives you a list of date fields to choose from, although in most cases, there is only one date field from which to choose.

Figure 4.50
Four different slicers
are necessary to filter
by date.

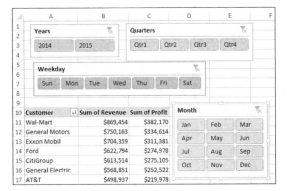

Figure 4.51 shows a timeline. Perhaps the best part of a timeline is the drop-down that lets
you repurpose the timeline for days, months, quarters, or years. This works even if you have
not grouped your daily dates up to months, quarters, or years.

Figure 4.51
A single Timeline control
can filter your pivot table
by month, quarter, year,
or day.

Driving Multiple Pivot Tables from One Set of Slicers

Chapter 12, "Enhancing Your Pivot Table Reports with Macros," includes a tiny macro that
lets you drive two pivot tables with one set of Report Filters. This has historically been difficult to do, unless you used a macro.

Now, one set of slicers or timelines can be used to drive multiple pivot tables or pivot
charts. In Figure 4.52, the Market slicer is driving three elements. It drives the pivot table
in the top left with year-over-year sales by quarter. It drives a pivot table behind the top-
right chart with sales by product line. It drives the bottom-right chart with sales by sector.

You find out how to create pivot charts in Chapter 6, "Using Pivot Charts and Other
Visualizations," so the following instructions show you how to create three pivot tables that
are tied to a single slicer:

1. Create your first pivot table.

2. Select the entire pivot table.

3. Copy with Ctrl+C or the Copy command.

4. Select a new blank area of the worksheet.

5. Paste. This creates a second pivot table. This pivot table shares the pivot cache with the
   first pivot table. In order for one slicer to run multiple pivot tables, they must share the
   same pivot cache.

Figure 4.52
Three pivot elements controlled by the same slicer.

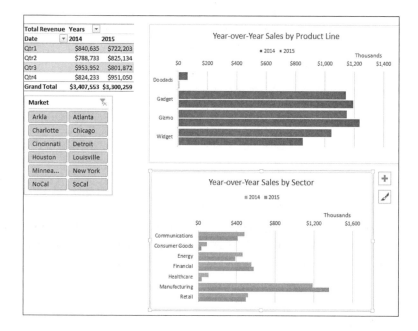

6. Change the fields in the second pivot table to show some other interesting analysis.

7. Repeat steps 2–6 to create a third copy of the pivot table.

8. Select a cell in the first pivot table. Choose Insert Slicer. Choose one or more fields to be used as a slicer. Alternatively, insert a timeline for a date field.

9. Format the slicer with columns and colors. At this point, the slicer is only driving the first pivot table.

10. Click the slicer to select it. When the slicer is selected, the Slicer Tools Design tab of the ribbon appears.

11. Select the Slicer Tools Design tab and choose Report Connections. Excel displays the Report Connections (Market) dialog. Initially, only the first pivot table is selected.

12. As shown in Figure 4.53, choose the other pivot tables in the dialog and click OK.

Figure 4.53
Choose to hook this slicer up to the other pivot tables.

13. If you created multiple slicers and/or timelines in step 8, repeat steps 11 and 12 for the other slicers.

The result is a dashboard in which all of the pivot tables and pivot charts update in response to selections made in the slicer (see Figure 4.54).

Figure 4.54

All of the pivot charts and pivot tables update when you choose from the slicer.

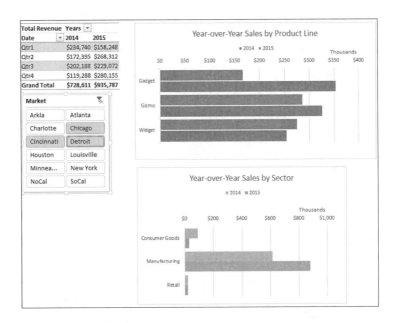

TIP | The worksheet in Figure 4.54 would be a perfect worksheet to publish to SharePoint or to your SkyDrive. You can share the workbook with co-workers and have them interact with the slicers. They won't need to worry about the underlying data or enter any numbers; they just click on the slicer to see the reports update.

Next Steps

In Chapter 5, "Performing Calculations Within Your Pivot Tables," you learn how to use pivot table formulas to add new virtual fields to your pivot table.

Performing Calculations Within Your Pivot Tables

5

Introducing Calculated Fields and Calculated Items

When analyzing data with pivot tables, you will often find the need to expand your analysis to include data based on calculations that are not in your original data set. Excel provides a way to perform calculations within your pivot table through calculated fields and calculated items.

A *calculated field* is a data field you create by executing a calculation against existing fields in the pivot table. Think of a calculated field as adding a virtual column to your data set. This column takes up no space in your source data, contains the data you define with a formula, and interacts with your pivot data as a field—just like all the other fields in your pivot table.

A *calculated item* is a data item you create by executing a calculation against existing items within a data field. Think of a calculated item as adding a virtual row of data to your data set. This virtual row takes up no space in your source data and contains summarized values based on calculations performed on other rows in the same field. Calculated items interact with your pivot data as a data item—just like all the other items in your pivot table.

With calculated fields and calculated items, you can insert a formula into your pivot table to create your own custom field or data item. Your newly created data becomes a part of your pivot table, interacting with other pivot data, recalculating when you refresh and supplying you with a calculated metric that does not exist in your source data.

The example in Figure 5.1 demonstrates how a basic calculated field can add another perspective on your data. Your pivot table shows total sales amount and contracted hours for each market. A calculated field that shows you average dollar per hour enhances this analysis and adds another dimension to your data.

Figure 5.1

Avg Dollar per Hour is a calculated field that adds another perspective to your data analysis.

	A	B	C	D
1				
2	Row Labels ▾	Sales_Amount	Contracted Hours	Avg Dollar Per Hour
3	BUFFALO	$450,478	6,864	$65.63
4	CALIFORNIA	$2,254,735	33,014	$68.30
5	CANADA	$776,245	12,103	$64.14
6	CHARLOTTE	$890,522	14,525	$61.31
7	DALLAS	$467,089	6,393	$73.06
8	DENVER	$645,583	8,641	$74.71
9	FLORIDA	$1,450,392	22,640	$64.06
10	KANSASCITY	$574,899	8,547	$67.26
11	MICHIGAN	$678,705	10,744	$63.17
12	NEWORLEANS	$333,454	5,057	$65.94
13	NEWYORK	$873,581	14,213	$61.46
14	PHOENIX	$570,255	10,167	$56.09
15	SEATTLE	$179,827	2,889	$62.25
16	TULSA	$628,405	9,583	$65.57
17	Grand Total	$10,774,172	165,380	$65.15

Now, you might look at Figure 5.1 and ask yourself, "Why go through all the trouble of creating calculated fields or calculated items? Why not just use formulas in surrounding cells or even add the calculation directly into the source table to get the information needed?"

To answer these questions, look at the different methods you could use to create the calculated field in Figure 5.1.

Method 1: Manually Add the Calculated Field to Your Data Source

You can manually add a calculated field to your data source, allowing the pivot table to pick up the field as a regular data field (see Figure 5.2). On the surface, this option looks simple, but this method of precalculating metrics and incorporating them into your data source is impractical on several levels.

Figure 5.2

Precalculating calculated fields in your data source is both cumbersome and impractical.

	N	O	P	Q	R
1	Sales_Amount	Contracted Hours	Sales_Period	Sales_Rep	Avg Dollar Per Hour
2	$197.95		2 P08	5060	$98.98
3	$197.95		2 P08	5060	$98.98
4	$191.28		3 P08	5060	$63.76
5	$240.07		4 P11	44651	$60.02
6	$147.22		2 P08	160410	$73.61
7	$163.51		2 P02	243	$81.76
8	$134.01		3 P02	243	$44.67
9	$134.01		3 P02	243	$44.67
10	$134.01		3 P02	243	$44.67
11	$239.00		3 P01	4244	$79.67
12	$215.87		4 P02	5030	$53.97
13	$180.57		4 P02	64610	$45.14
14	$240.07		4 P02	213	$60.02

If the definitions of your calculated fields change, you have to go back to the data source, recalculate the metric for each row, and refresh your pivot table. If you have to add a metric, you have go back to the data source, add a new calculated field, and then change the range of your pivot table to capture the new field.

Method 2: Use a Formula Outside Your Pivot Table to Create the Calculated Field

You can add a calculated field by performing the calculation in an external cell with a formula. In the example shown in Figure 5.3, the Average Dollar Per Hour column was created with formulas referencing the pivot table.

Figure 5.3
Typing a formula next to your pivot table essentially gives you a calculated field that refreshes when your pivot table is refreshed.

D3		f_x	=B3/C3	
	A	B	C	D
1				
2	Row Labels	Sales_Amount	Contracted Hours	Avg Dollar Per Hour
3	BUFFALO	$450,478	6,864	$65.63
4	CALIFORNIA	$2,254,735	33,014	$68.30
5	CANADA	$776,245	12,103	$64.14
6	CHARLOTTE	$890,522	14,525	$61.31
7	DALLAS	$467,089	6,393	$73.06
8	DENVER	$645,583	8,641	$74.71
9	FLORIDA	$1,450,392	22,640	$64.06
10	KANSASCITY	$574,899	8,547	$67.26
11	MICHIGAN	$678,705	10,744	$63.17
12	NEWORLEANS	$333,454	5,057	$65.94
13	NEWYORK	$873,581	14,213	$61.46
14	PHOENIX	$570,255	10,167	$56.09
15	SEATTLE	$179,827	2,889	$62.25
16	TULSA	$628,405	9,583	$65.57
17	Grand Total	$10,774,172	165,380	$65.15

Although this method gives you a calculated field that updates when your pivot table is refreshed, any changes in the structure of your pivot table have the potential of rendering your formula useless.

As you can see in Figure 5.4, moving the Market field to the Filters area changes the structure of your pivot table, exposing the weakness of makeshift calculated fields that use external formulas.

Figure 5.4
External formulas run the risk of errors when the pivot table structure is changed.

	A	B	C	D
1	Market	(All)		
2				Avg Dollar Per Hour
3	Sales_Amount	Contracted Hours		#VALUE!
4	$10,774,172	165,380		#DIV/0!
5				#DIV/0!
6				#DIV/0!
7				#DIV/0!
8				#DIV/0!
9				#DIV/0!
10				#DIV/0!
11				#DIV/0!
12				#DIV/0!
13				#DIV/0!
14				#DIV/0!
15				#DIV/0!
16				#DIV/0!
17				#DIV/0!

5

Method 3: Insert a Calculated Field Directly into Your Pivot Table

Inserting the calculated field directly into your pivot table is the best option. It eliminates the need to manage formulas, provides for scalability when your data source grows or changes, and allows for flexibility in the event that your metric definitions change.

Another huge advantage of this method is that you can alter your pivot table's structure and even measure different data fields against your calculated field without worrying about errors in your formulas or losing cell references.

The pivot table report shown in Figure 5.5 is the same one you see in Figure 5.1, except it has been restructured so that you get the average dollar per hour by market and product.

Figure 5.5

Your calculated field remains viable even when your pivot table's structure changes to accommodate new dimensions.

⬚	A	B	C	D	E
1					
2	**Market** ▾	**Product_Description** ▾	**Sales_Amount**	**Contracted Hours**	**Avg Dollar Per Hour**
3	⊟BUFFALO	Cleaning & Housekeeping Services	$66,845	982	$68.07
4		Facility Maintenance and Repair	$69,570	821	$84.74
5		Fleet Maintenance	$86,460	1,439	$60.08
6		Green Plants and Foliage Care	$34,831	490	$71.08
7		Landscaping/Grounds Care	$65,465	1,172	$55.86
8		Predictive Maintenance/Preventative Maintenance	$127,307	1,960	$64.95
9	**BUFFALO Total**		**$450,478**	**6,864**	**$65.63**
10	⊟CALIFORNIA	Cleaning & Housekeeping Services	$37,401	531	$70.44
11		Facility Maintenance and Repair	$281,198	3,103	$90.62
12		Fleet Maintenance	$337,225	5,737	$58.78
13		Green Plants and Foliage Care	$830,413	11,900	$69.78
14		Landscaping/Grounds Care	$248,343	3,421	$72.59
15		Predictive Maintenance/Preventative Maintenance	$520,156	8,322	$62.50
16	**CALIFORNIA Total**		**$2,254,735**	**33,014**	**$68.30**

The bottom line is that there are significant benefits to integrating your custom calculations into your pivot table, including the following:

- The elimination of potential formula and cell reference errors
- The ability to add and remove data from your pivot table without affecting your calculations
- The ability to auto-recalculate when your pivot table is changed or refreshed
- The flexibility to change calculations easily when your metric definitions change
- The ability to manage and maintain your calculations effectively

→   If you move your data to PowerPivot, you can use the DAX formula language to create more powerful calculations. **See** "Two Kinds of DAX Calculations" **p. 237**.

Creating Your First Calculated Field

Before you create a calculated field, you must first have a pivot table. Build the pivot table you see in Figure 5.6.

Now that you have a pivot table, it's time to create your first calculated field. To do this, you must activate the Insert Calculated Field dialog. Select Analyze under the PivotTable Tools tab and then select Fields, Items, & Sets from the Calculations group. Selecting this option activates a drop-down menu from which you can select Calculated Field, as demonstrated in Figure 5.7.

Figure 5.6
Create the pivot table
shown here.

	A	B	C
1			
2	**Market**	**Sales_Amount**	**Contracted Hours**
3	BUFFALO	$450,478	6,864
4	CALIFORNIA	$2,254,735	33,014
5	CANADA	$776,245	12,103
6	CHARLOTTE	$890,522	14,525
7	DALLAS	$467,089	6,393
8	DENVER	$645,583	8,641
9	FLORIDA	$1,450,392	22,640
10	KANSASCITY	$574,899	8,547
11	MICHIGAN	$678,705	10,744
12	NEWORLEANS	$333,454	5,057
13	NEWYORK	$873,581	14,213
14	PHOENIX	$570,255	10,167
15	SEATTLE	$179,827	2,889
16	TULSA	$628,405	9,583
17	**Grand Total**	**$10,774,172**	**165,380**

Figure 5.7
Start the creation of your
calculated field by selecting Calculated Field.

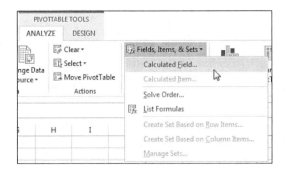

After you select Calculated Field, Excel activates the Insert Calculated Field dialog, as
shown in Figure 5.8.

Figure 5.8
The Insert Calculated
Field dialog assists you in
creating a calculated field
in your pivot table.

Notice the two input boxes, Name and Formula, at the top of the dialog box. The objective here is to give your calculated field a name and then build the formula by selecting the combination of data fields and mathematical operators that provide the metric you are looking for.

As you can see in Figure 5.9, you first give your calculated field a descriptive name—that is, a name that describes the utility of the mathematical operation. In this case, enter **Avg Dollar per Hour** in the Name input box.

Figure 5.9
Give your calculated field a descriptive name.

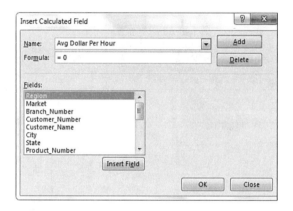

Next, you go to the Fields list and double-click the Sales_Amount field. Enter **/** to let Excel know you plan to divide the Sales_Amount field by something.

> ┌ C A U T I O N ──
> By default, the Formula input box in the Insert Calculated Field dialog box contains = 0. Ensure
> that you delete the zero before continuing with your formula.

At this point, your dialog should look similar to the one shown in Figure 5.10.

Figure 5.10
Start your formula with =
`Sales_Amount /`.

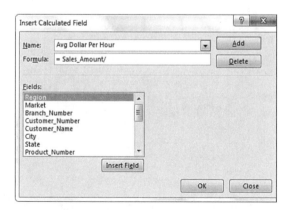

Next, double-click the Contracted Hours field to finish your formula, as illustrated in Figure 5.11.

Figure 5.11
The full formula, =
`Sales_Amount/`
`'Contracted`
`Hours'`, gives you the
calculated field you need.

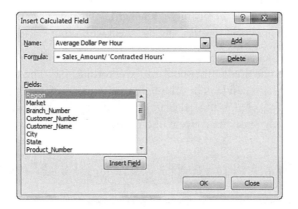

Finally, select Add and then click OK to create your new calculated field.

As you can see in Figure 5.12, not only does your pivot table create a new field called Sum of Avg Dollar Per Hour, but the PivotTable Field List includes your new calculated field as well.

Figure 5.12
You can change the
settings on your new
calculated field, just as
you would any other
field (that is, change the
field name, change the
number format, change
the color).

	A	B	C	D
1				
2	Market	Sales_Amount	Contracted Hours	Sum of Avg Dollar Per Hour
3	BUFFALO	$450,478	6,864	65.62911859
4	CALIFORNIA	$2,254,735	33,014	68.29634034
5	CANADA	$776,245	12,103	64.13660002
6	CHARLOTTE	$890,522	14,525	61.30963787
7	DALLAS	$467,089	6,393	73.06264195
8	DENVER	$645,583	8,641	74.71164101
9	FLORIDA	$1,450,392	22,640	64.06325088
10	KANSASCITY	$574,899	8,547	67.26324675
11	MICHIGAN	$678,705	10,744	63.1706022
12	NEWORLEANS	$333,454	5,057	65.93902511
13	NEWYORK	$873,581	14,213	61.46351298
14	PHOENIX	$570,255	10,167	56.08882561
15	SEATTLE	$179,827	2,889	62.24548633
16	TULSA	$628,405	9,583	65.57495878
17	Grand Total	$10,774,172	165,380	65.14797303

NOTE The resulting values from a calculated field are not formatted. You can easily apply any desired formatting using some of the techniques from Chapter 3, "Customizing a Pivot Table."

Does this mean you have just added a column to your data source? The answer is no. Calculated fields are similar to the pivot table's default subtotal and grand total calculations in that they are all mathematical functions that recalculate when the pivot table changes or is refreshed. Calculated fields merely mimic the hard fields in your data source, allowing you to drag them, change field settings, and use them with other calculated fields.

Take a moment and look at Figure 5.11 closely. Notice the formula you entered is in a format similar to the one used in the standard Excel formula bar. The obvious difference is that instead of using hard numbers or cell references, you are referencing pivot data fields to define the arguments used in this calculation. If you have worked with formulas in Excel before, you will quickly grasp the concept of creating calculated fields.

CASE STUDY: SUMMARIZING NEXT YEAR'S FORECAST

All the branch managers in your company have submitted their initial revenue forecasts for next year. Your task is to take the first-pass numbers they submitted and create a summary report showing the following:

- Total revenue forecast by market
- Total percent growth over last year
- Total contribution margin by market

Because these numbers are first-pass submissions and you know they will change over the course of the next two weeks, you decide to use a pivot table to create the requested forecast summary.

Start by building the initial pivot table, shown here in Figure 5.13, to include Revenue Last Year and Forecast Next Year for each market. After creating the pivot table, you will see that by virtue of adding the Forecast Next Year field in the data area, you have met your first requirement: to show total revenue forecast by market.

Figure 5.13
The initial pivot table is basic, but it provides the data for your first requirement: show total revenue forecast by market.

MARKET	Revenue Last Year	Forecast Next Year
BUFFALO	$450,478	$411,246
CALIFORNIA	$2,254,735	$2,423,007
CANADA	$776,245	$746,384
CHARLOTTE	$890,522	$965,361
DALLAS	$467,089	$510,635
DENVER	$645,583	$722,695
FLORIDA	$1,450,392	$1,421,507
KANSASCITY	$574,899	$607,226
MICHIGAN	$678,705	$870,447
NEWORLEANS	$333,454	$366,174
NEWYORK	$873,581	$953,010
PHOENIX	$570,255	$746,721
SEATTLE	$179,827	$214,621
TULSA	$628,405	$661,726
Grand Total	$10,774,172	$11,620,760

The next metric you need is percent growth over last year. To get this data, you need to add a calculated field that calculates the following formula:

```
(Forecast Next Year / Revenue Last Year) - 1
```

To achieve this, do the following:

1. Activate the Insert Calculated Field dialog and name your new field **Percent Growth** (see Figure 5.14).

Figure 5.14
Name your new field Percent Growth.

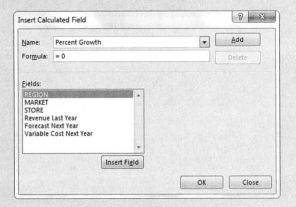

2. Delete the 0 in the Formula input box.
3. Enter **(** (an opening parenthesis).
4. Double-click the Forecast Next Year field.
5. Enter **/** (a division sign).
6. Double-click the Revenue Last Year field.
7. Enter **)** (a closing parenthesis).
8. Enter **-** (a minus sign).
9. Enter the number **1**.

> **TIP**
>
> You can use any constant in your pivot table calculations. Constants are static values that do not change. In this example, the number 1 is a constant. Though the value of Revenue Last Year or Forecast Next Year might change based on the available data, the number 1 will always have the same value.

After you have entered the full formula, your dialog should look similar to the one shown in Figure 5.15.

With your formula typed in, you can now click OK to add your new field. After changing the format of the resulting values to percent, you have a nicely formatted Percent Growth calculation in your pivot table. At this point, your pivot table should look like the one shown in Figure 5.16.

5

Figure 5.15
With just a few clicks, you have created a variance formula!

Figure 5.16
You have added a Percent Growth calculation to your pivot table.

MARKET	Revenue Last Year	Forecast Next Year	Sum of Percent Growth
BUFFALO	$450,478	$411,246	-8.7%
CALIFORNIA	$2,254,735	$2,423,007	7.5%
CANADA	$776,245	$746,384	-3.8%
CHARLOTTE	$890,522	$965,361	8.4%
DALLAS	$467,089	$510,635	9.3%
DENVER	$645,583	$722,695	11.9%
FLORIDA	$1,450,392	$1,421,507	-2.0%
KANSASCITY	$574,899	$607,226	5.6%
MICHIGAN	$678,705	$870,447	28.3%
NEWORLEANS	$333,454	$366,174	9.8%
NEWYORK	$873,581	$953,010	9.1%
PHOENIX	$570,255	$746,721	30.9%
SEATTLE	$179,827	$214,621	19.3%
TULSA	$628,405	$661,726	5.3%
Grand Total	$10,774,172	$11,620,760	7.9%

With this newly created view into your data, you can easily see that three markets need to resubmit their forecasts to reflect positive growth over last year (see Figure 5.17).

Figure 5.17
You can already discern some information from the calculated field, identifying three problem markets.

MARKET	Revenue Last Year	Forecast Next Year	Sum of Percent Growth
BUFFALO	$450,478	$411,246	-8.7%
CALIFORNIA	$2,254,735	$2,423,007	7.5%
CANADA	$776,245	$746,384	-3.8%
CHARLOTTE	$890,522	$965,361	8.4%
DALLAS	$467,089	$510,635	9.3%
DENVER	$645,583	$722,695	11.9%
FLORIDA	$1,450,392	$1,421,507	-2.0%
KANSASCITY	$574,899	$607,226	5.6%
MICHIGAN	$678,705	$870,447	28.3%
NEWORLEANS	$333,454	$366,174	9.8%
NEWYORK	$873,581	$953,010	9.1%
PHOENIX	$570,255	$746,721	30.9%
SEATTLE	$179,827	$214,621	19.3%
TULSA	$628,405	$661,726	5.3%
Grand Total	$10,774,172	$11,620,760	7.9%

5

Now it's time to focus on your last requirement, which is to find total contribution margin by market. To get this data, you need to add a calculated field that calculates the following formula:

```
Forecast Next Year + Variable Cost Next Year
```

> **NOTE**
>
> A quick look at Figure 5.17 confirms that the Variable Cost Next Year field is not displayed in the pivot table report. Can you build pivot table formulas with fields that are currently not *even in* the pivot table? The answer is yes; you can use any field that is available to you in the PivotTable Field List, regardless of the fact that the field is not shown in the pivot table itself.

To create this field, do the following:

1. Activate the Insert Calculated Field dialog box and name your new field **Contribution Margin**.
2. Delete the 0 in the Formula input box.
3. Double-click the Forecast Next Year field.
4. Enter + (a plus sign).
5. Double-click the Variable Cost Next Year field.

After you have entered the full formula, your dialog should look similar to the one shown in Figure 5.18.

Figure 5.18
With just a few clicks, you have created a formula that calculates contribution margin.

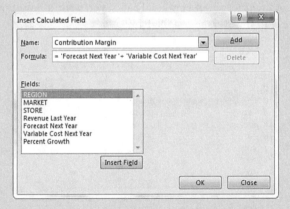

With the creation of the contribution margin, this report is ready to be delivered (see Figure 5.19).

Now that you've built your pivot table report, you can easily analyze any new forecast submissions by refreshing your report with the new updates.

Figure 5.19
Contribution margin is now a data field in your pivot table report thanks to your calculated field.

	A	B	C	D	E
1					
2					
3	MARKET	Revenue Last Year	Forecast Next Year	Sum of Percent Growth	Sum of Contribution Margin
4	BUFFALO	$450,478	$411,246	-8.7%	($169,546)
5	CALIFORNIA	$2,254,735	$2,423,007	7.5%	$1,152,641
6	CANADA	$776,245	$746,384	-3.8%	$118,415
7	CHARLOTTE	$890,522	$965,361	8.4%	$360,343
8	DALLAS	$467,089	$510,635	9.3%	($908,021)
9	DENVER	$645,583	$722,695	11.9%	($697,393)
10	FLORIDA	$1,450,392	$1,421,507	-2.0%	$865,700
11	KANSASCITY	$574,899	$607,226	5.6%	($328,773)
12	MICHIGAN	$678,705	$870,447	28.3%	($92,813)
13	NEWORLEANS	$333,454	$366,174	9.8%	($586,405)
14	NEWYORK	$873,581	$953,010	9.1%	$506,335
15	PHOENIX	$570,255	$746,721	30.9%	$318,496
16	SEATTLE	$179,827	$214,621	19.3%	($163,738)
17	TULSA	$628,405	$661,726	5.3%	($1,193,984)
18	Grand Total	$10,774,172	$11,620,760	7.9%	($818,743)

Creating Your First Calculated Item

As you learned at the beginning of this chapter, a calculated item is a virtual data item you create by executing a calculation against existing items within a data field. Calculated items come in especially handy when you need to group and aggregate a set of data items.

For example, the pivot table in Figure 5.20 gives you sales amount by sales period. Imagine that you need to compare the average performance of the most recent six sales periods to the average of the prior seven periods. That is, you want to take the average of P01–P07 and compare it to the average of P08–P13.

Figure 5.20
You want to compare the most recent six sales periods to the average of the prior seven periods.

	A	B
1		
2		
3	Row Labels	Sum of Sales_Amount
4	P01	$681,865
5	P02	$1,116,916
6	P03	$657,611
7	P04	$865,498
8	P05	$925,802
9	P06	$868,930
10	P07	$640,587
11	P08	$1,170,262
12	P09	$604,552
13	P10	$891,253
14	P11	$949,605
15	P12	$887,665
16	P13	$513,625
17	Grand Total	$10,774,172

Place your cursor on any data item in the Sales_Period field and then select Fields, Items, & Sets from the Calculations group. Next, select Calculated Item, as shown in Figure 5.21.

Figure 5.21
Start the creation of your calculated item by selecting Calculated Item.

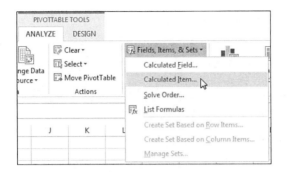

Selecting this option opens the Insert Calculated Item dialog. A quick glance at Figure 5.22 shows you that the top of the dialog identifies which field you are working with. In this case, it is the Sales_Period field. In addition, notice the Items list box is automatically filled with all the items in the Sales_Period field.

Figure 5.22
The Insert Calculated Item dialog is automatically populated to reflect the field with which you are working.

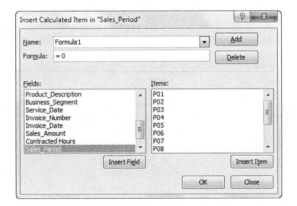

Your goal is to give your calculated item a name and then build its formula by selecting the combination of data items and operators that provide the metric you are looking for.

In this example, name your first calculated item **Avg P1-P7 Sales**, as shown in Figure 5.23.

Next, you can build your formula in the Formula input box by selecting the appropriate data items from the Items list. In this scenario, you want to create the following formula:

```
=Average(P01, P02, P03, P04, P05, P06, P07)
```

Enter the formula shown in Figure 5.24 into the Formula input box.

Click OK to activate your new calculated item. As you can see in Figure 5.25, you now have a data item called Avg P1-P7 Sales.

Figure 5.23
Give your calculated item a descriptive name.

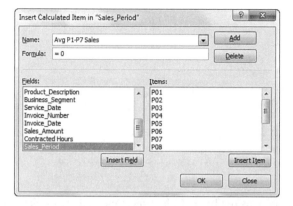

Figure 5.24
Enter a formula that gives you the average of P01–P07.

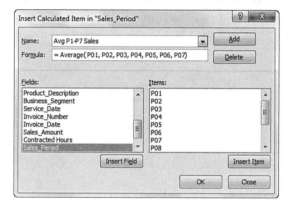

Figure 5.25
You have successfully added a calculated item to your pivot table.

	A	B
1		
2		
3	**Row Labels** ▼	**Sum of Sales_Amount**
4	P01	$681,865
5	P02	$1,116,916
6	P03	$657,611
7	P04	$865,498
8	P05	$925,802
9	P06	$868,930
10	P07	$640,587
11	P08	$1,170,262
12	P09	$604,552
13	P10	$891,253
14	P11	$949,605
15	P12	$887,665
16	P13	$513,625
17	Avg P1-P7 Sales	$822,458
18	**Grand Total**	**$11,596,630**

5

You can use any worksheet function in both a calculated field and a calculated item. The only restriction is that the function you use cannot reference external cells or named ranges. In effect, this means you can use any worksheet function that does not require cell references or defined names to work (such as COUNT, AVERAGE, IF, and OR).

Create a calculated item to represent the average sales for P08–P13, as shown in Figure 5.26.

Figure 5.26
Create a second calculated item.

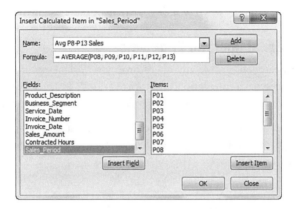

Now you can hide the individual sales periods, leaving only your two calculated items. After a little formatting, your calculated items, shown in Figure 5.27, allow you to compare the average performance of the six most recent sales periods to the average of the prior seven periods.

Figure 5.27
You can now compare the most recent six sales periods to the average of the prior seven periods.

	A	B
1		
2		
3	Row Labels	Sum of Sales_Amount
4	Avg P1-P7 Sales	$822,458
5	Avg P8-P13 Sales	$836,160
6	Grand Total	$1,658,619

CAUTION

Be aware that it is often prudent to hide the data items you used to create your calculated item. In Figure 5.27, notice that all periods have been hidden. This prevents any grand totals and subtotals from showing incorrect aggregations.

Understanding the Rules and Shortcomings of Pivot Table Calculations

Although there is no better way to integrate your calculations into a pivot table than using calculated fields and calculated items, they do come with their own set of drawbacks. It's important you understand what goes on behind the scenes when you use pivot table calculations, and even more important to be aware of the boundaries and limitations of calculated fields and calculated items to avoid potential errors in your data analysis.

The following sections highlight the rules around calculated fields and calculated items that you will most likely encounter when working with pivot table calculations.

Remembering the Order of Operator Precedence

Just as in a spreadsheet, you can use any operator in your calculation formulas, meaning any symbol that represents a calculation to perform (+, –, *, /, %, ^). Moreover, just as in a spreadsheet, calculations in a pivot table follow the order of operator precedence.

In other words, when you perform a calculation that combines several operators, as in (2+3) * 4/50%, Excel evaluates and performs the calculation in a specific order. The order of operations for Excel is as follows:

- Evaluate items in parentheses.
- Evaluate ranges (:).
- Evaluate intersections (spaces).
- Evaluate unions (,).
- Perform negation (–).
- Convert percentages (%).
- Perform exponentiation (^).
- Perform multiplication (*) and division (/), which are of equal precedence.
- Perform addition (+) and subtraction (–), which are of equal precedence.
- Evaluate text operators (&).
- Perform comparisons (=, <>, <=, >=).

> **NOTE**
> Operations that are equal in precedence are performed left to right.

Consider this basic example. The correct answer to (2+3)*4 is 20. However, if you leave off the parentheses, as in 2+3*4, Excel performs the calculation like this: 3*4 = 12 + 2 = 14. The order of operator precedence mandates that Excel perform multiplication before addition. Entering 2+3*4 gives you the wrong answer. Because Excel evaluates and performs all calculations in parentheses first, placing 2+3 inside parentheses ensures the correct answer.

Here is another widely demonstrated example. If you enter 10^2, which represents the exponent 10 to the second power as a formula, Excel returns 100 as the answer. If you enter –10^2, you would expect –100 to be the result. Instead, Excel returns 100 yet again. The reason is that Excel performs negation before exponentiation, meaning Excel is converting 10 to –10 before the exponentiation, effectively calculating –10*–10, which indeed equals 100. Using parentheses in the formula, –(10^2), ensures that Excel calculates the exponent before negating the answer, giving you –100.

Understanding the order of operations ensures that you avoid miscalculating your data.

Using Cell References and Named Ranges

When you create calculations in a pivot table, you are essentially working in a vacuum. The only data available to you is the data that exists in the pivot cache. Therefore, you cannot reach outside the confines of the pivot cache to reference cells or named ranges in your formula.

Using Worksheet Functions

When building your calculated fields or calculated items, Excel enables you to use any worksheet function that accepts numeric values as arguments and returns numeric values as the result. Of the many functions that fall into this category, some include COUNT, AVERAGE, IF, AND, NOT, and OR.

Some examples of functions you could not use are VLOOKUP, INDEX, SUMIF, COUNTIF, LEFT, and RIGHT. Again, these would all be impossible to use because they either require cell array references or return textual values as the result.

Using Constants

You can use any constant in your pivot table calculations. Constants are static values that do not change. For example, in the formula [Units Sold]*5, 5 is a constant. Though the value of Units Sold might change based on the available data, 5 always has the same value.

Referencing Totals

Your calculation formulas cannot reference a pivot table's subtotals or grand total. This means that you cannot use the result of a subtotal or grand total as a variable or argument in your calculated field.

Rules Specific to Calculated Fields

Calculated field calculations are always performed against the sum of your data. In basic terms, Excel always calculates data fields, subtotals, and grand totals before evaluating your calculated field. This means that your calculated field is always applied to the sum of the underlying data.

5

The example shown in Figure 5.28 demonstrates how this can adversely affect your data analysis.

Figure 5.28
Although the calculated field is correct for the individual data items in your pivot table, the subtotal is mathematically incorrect.

	A	B	C	D	E	F G	H
1			Data				
			Number				
2	Qtr	Product	of Units	Price	CalcField Unit*Price		
3	⊟Q1	A	10	22	$220		
4		B	5	30	$150		
5		C	5	44	$220		
6		D	11	54	$594		
7	Q1 Total		31	150	$4,650		$1,184 <--Real Q1 Subtotal

In each quarter, you need to get the total revenue for every product by multiplying the number of units sold by the price. If you look at Q1 first, you can immediately see the problem. Instead of returning the sum of 220+150+220+594, which would give you $1,184, the subtotal is calculating the sum of number of units times the sum of price, which returns the wrong answer.

As you can see in Figure 5.29, including the whole year in your analysis compounds the problem.

Figure 5.29
The grand total for the year as a whole is completely wrong.

	A	B	C	D	E	F G	H
1			Data				
			Number				
2	Qtr	Product	of Units	Price	CalcField Unit*Price		
3	⊟Q1	A	10	22	$220		
4		B	5	30	$150		
5		C	5	44	$220		
6		D	11	54	$594		
7	Q1 Total		31	150	$4,650		$1,184 <--Real Q1 Subtotal
8	⊟Q2	A	7	19	$133		
9		B	12	25	$300		
10		C	9	39	$351		
11		D	5	52	$260		
12	Q2 Total		33	135	$4,455		$1,044 <--Real Q2 Subtotal
13	⊟Q3	A	6	17	$102		
14		B	8	21	$168		
15		C	6	40	$240		
16		D	7	55	$385		
17	Q3 Total		27	133	$3,591		$895 <--Real Q3 Subtotal
18	⊟Q4	A	8	22	$176		
19		B	7	31	$217		
20		C	6	35	$210		
21		D	10	49	$490		
22	Q4 Total		31	137	$4,247		$1,093 <--Real Q4 Subtotal
23	Grand Total		122	555	$67,710		$4,216 <--Real Grand Total

Unfortunately, there is no solution to this problem, but there is a workaround. In worst-case scenarios, you can configure your settings to eliminate subtotals and grand totals and then calculate your own totals. Figure 5.30 demonstrates this workaround.

Figure 5.30
Calculating your own totals can prevent reporting incorrect data.

	A	B	C	D	E
1			Data		
2	Qtr	Product	Number of Units	Price	CalcField Unit*Price
3	Q1	A	10	22	$220
4		B	5	30	$150
5		C	5	44	$220
6		D	11	54	$594
7	Q2	A	7	19	$133
8		B	12	25	$300
9		C	9	39	$351
10		D	5	52	$260
11	Q3	A	6	17	$102
12		B	8	21	$168
13		C	6	40	$240
14		D	7	55	$385
15	Q4	A	8	22	$176
16		B	7	31	$217
17		C	6	35	$210
18		D	10	49	$490
19					
20					$4,216

Rules Specific to Calculated Items

You cannot use calculated items in a pivot table that uses averages, standard deviations, or variances. Conversely, you cannot use averages, standard deviations, or variances in a pivot table that contains a calculated item.

You cannot use a page field to create a calculated item, nor can you move any calculated item to the report filter area.

You cannot add a calculated item to a report that has a grouped field, nor can you group any field in a pivot table that contains a calculated item.

When building your calculated item formula, you cannot reference items from a field other than the one you are working with.

As you think about the section you have just read, don't be put off by these shortcomings of pivot tables. Despite the clear limitations highlighted, the capability to create custom calculations directly into your pivot table remains a powerful and practical feature that can enhance your data analysis. Now that you are aware of the inner workings of pivot table calculations and understand the limitations of calculated fields and items, you can avoid the pitfalls and use this feature with confidence.

Managing and Maintaining Your Pivot Table Calculations

In your dealings with pivot tables, you will find that sometimes you won't keep a pivot table for more than the time it takes to say, "Copy, Paste Values." Other times, however, it will be more cost effective to keep your pivot table and all its functionality intact.

When you find yourself maintaining and managing your pivot tables through changing requirements and growing data, you might find the need to maintain and manage your calculated fields and calculated items as well.

Editing and Deleting Your Pivot Table Calculations

When your calculation's parameters change or you no longer need your calculated field or calculated item, you can activate the appropriate dialog to edit or remove the calculation.

Simply activate the Insert Calculated Field or Insert Calculated Item dialog and select the Name drop-down, as demonstrated in Figure 5.31.

Figure 5.31
Opening the drop-down list under Name reveals all the calculated fields or items in the pivot table.

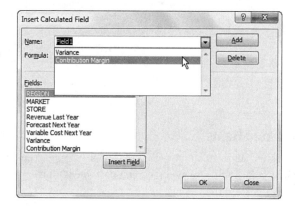

As you can see in Figure 5.32, after you select a calculated field or item, you have the option of deleting the calculation or modifying the formula.

Figure 5.32
After you select the appropriate calculated field or item, you can either delete or modify the calculation.

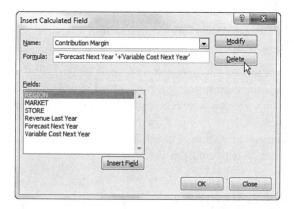

Changing the Solve Order of Your Calculated Items

If the value of a cell in your pivot table is dependent on the results of two or more calculated items, you have the option of changing the solve order of the calculated items. That is, you can specify the order in which the individual calculations are performed.

To get to the Solve Order dialog, place your cursor anywhere in the pivot table, select Fields, Items, & Sets from the Calculations group, and then select Solve Order, as shown in Figure 5.33.

Figure 5.33
Activate the Solve Order dialog.

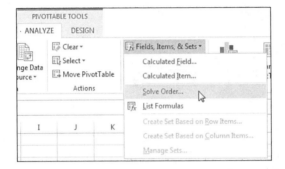

The Solve Order dialog, shown here in Figure 5.34, lists all the calculated items that currently exist in your pivot table. The idea is to select any of the calculated items you see listed to enable the Move Up, Move Down, and Delete command buttons. The order you see in the formulas in this list is the exact order the pivot table will perform each operation.

Figure 5.34
After you identify the calculated item you are working with, simply move the item up or down to change the solve order. You also have the option of deleting the item in this dialog.

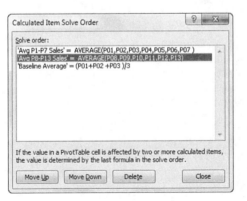

Documenting Your Formulas

Excel provides a nice little function that lists the calculated fields and calculated items used in your pivot table, along with details on the solve order and formulas. This feature comes in especially handy if you need to quickly determine what calculations are being applied in a pivot table and which fields or items those calculations affect.

To list your pivot table calculations, simply place your cursor anywhere in the pivot table and select Fields, Items, & Sets and then select List Formulas. Excel creates a new tab in your workbook listing the calculated fields and calculated items in the current pivot table. Figure 5.35 shows a sample output of the List Formulas command.

Figure 5.35

The List Formulas command enables you to document the details of your pivot table calculations quickly and easily.

Calculated Field		
Solve Order	Field	Formula
Calculated Item		
Solve Order	Item	Formula
1	'Avg P1-P7 Sales'	= AVERAGE(P01,P02,P03,P04,P05,P06,P07)
2	'Avg P8-P13 Sales'	= AVERAGE(P08,P09,P10,P11,P12,P13)
3	'Baseline Average'	=(P01+P02 +P03)/3
Note:	When a cell is updated by more than one formula,	
	the value is set by the formula with the last solve order.	
	To change formula solve orders,	
	use the Solve Order command on the Pivot Formulas drop down menu.	

What's Next

In the next chapter, you discover the fundamentals of pivot charts and the basics of representing your pivot data graphically. You also get a firm understanding of the limitations of pivot charts and alternatives to using pivot charts.

Using Pivot Charts and Other Visualizations

What Is a Pivot Chart...Really?

When sharing your analyses with others, you will quickly find that there is no getting around the fact that people want charts. Pivot tables are nice, but they leave lots of those pesky numbers that take time to absorb. Charts, on the other hand, enable users to make a split-second determination on what your data is actually revealing. Charts offer instant gratification, allowing users to immediately see relationships, point out differences, and observe trends. The bottom line is that managers today want to absorb data as fast as possible, and nothing delivers that capability faster than a chart. This is where pivot charts come into play. Whereas pivot tables offer the analytical, pivot charts offer the visual.

A common definition of a pivot chart is a graphical representation of the data in your pivot table. Although this definition is technically correct, it somehow misses the mark on what a pivot chart truly does.

When you create a standard chart from data that is not in a pivot table, you feed the chart a range made up of individual cells holding individual pieces of data. Each cell is an individual object with its own piece of data, so your chart treats each cell as an individual data point and thus charts each one separately.

However, the data in your pivot table is part of a larger object. The pieces of data you see inside your pivot table are not individual pieces of data that occupy individual cells. Rather, they are items inside a larger pivot table object that is occupying space on your worksheet.

When you create a chart from your pivot table, you are not feeding it individual pieces of data inside individual cells; you are feeding it the entire pivot table layout. Indeed, a true definition of a pivot chart is a chart that uses a PivotLayout Object to view and control the data in your pivot table.

Using the PivotLayout Object allows you to interactively add, remove, filter, and refresh data fields inside your pivot chart just like your pivot table. The result of all this action is a graphical representation of the data you see in your pivot table.

Creating Your First Pivot Chart

With all the complexity behind the make-up of a pivot chart, you might get the impression that creating one is difficult. The reality is that it's quite a simple task.

To demonstrate how simple it is to create a pivot chart, look at the pivot table in Figure 6.1. This pivot table provides for a simple view of revenue by market. The Business Segment field in the report filter area lets you parse out revenue by line of business.

Figure 6.1
This basic pivot table shows revenue by market and allows for filtering by line of business.

	A	B
1	Business_Segment (All)	▾
2		
3	Row Labels ▾	Sum of Sales_Amount
4	BUFFALO	$450,478
5	CALIFORNIA	$2,254,735
6	CANADA	$776,245
7	CHARLOTTE	$890,522
8	DALLAS	$467,089
9	DENVER	$645,583
10	FLORIDA	$1,450,392
11	KANSASCITY	$574,899
12	MICHIGAN	$678,705
13	NEWORLEANS	$333,454
14	NEWYORK	$873,581
15	PHOENIX	$570,255
16	SEATTLE	$179,827
17	TULSA	$628,405
18	Grand Total	$10,774,172

Creating a pivot chart from this data would not only allow for an instant view of the performance of each market, but would also permit you to retain the ability to filter by line of business.

To start the process, place your cursor anywhere inside the pivot table and click the Insert tab on the ribbon. On the Insert tab, you can see the Charts group displaying the various types of charts you can create. Here, you can choose the chart type you would like to use for your pivot chart. For this example, click the Column chart icon and select the first 2-D column chart, as demonstrated in Figure 6.2.

As you can see in Figure 6.3, choosing a chart type causes a chart to appear.

Figure 6.2
Select the chart type you
want to use.

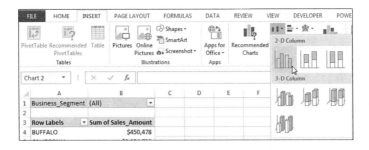

Figure 6.3
Excel creates your pivot
chart on the same sheet
as your pivot table.

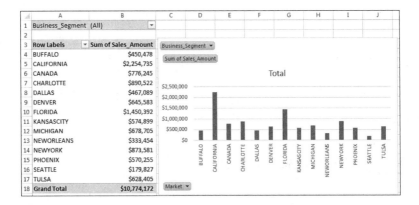

T I P

Notice that pivot charts are now, by default, placed on the same sheet as the source pivot table. If you long for the days when pivot charts were located on their own chart sheets, you are in luck. All you have to do is place your cursor inside your pivot table and then press F11 on your keyboard. This creates a pivot chart on its own sheet.

You can easily change the location of your pivot chart by right-clicking the chart itself (outside the plot area) and selecting Move Chart. This activates the Move Chart dialog, in which you can specify the new location.

6

A Word About the Pivot Field Buttons

In Figure 6.3, notice the pivot field buttons. These are gray buttons and drop-downs you see on pivot charts. Using these pivot field buttons, you can rearrange the chart and apply filters to the underlying pivot table.

Keep in mind that these pivot field buttons will be visible when you print your pivot table. If you aren't too keen on showing the pivot field buttons directly on your pivot charts, you can remove them by clicking your chart and then selecting the Analyze tab. On the Analyze tab, you can use the Field Buttons drop-down to hide some or all of the pivot field buttons.

You now have a chart that is a visual representation of your pivot table. More than that, because the pivot chart is tied to the underlying pivot table, changing the pivot table in any way changes the chart. For example, as Figure 6.4 illustrates, adding the Region field to the pivot table adds a region dimension to your chart.

Figure 6.4
Your pivot chart displays the same fields your underlying pivot table displays.

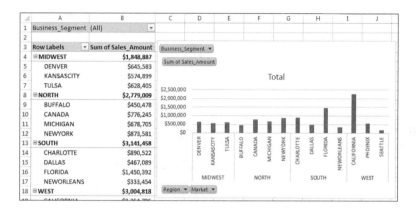

> **NOTE**
>
> The pivot chart in Figure 6.4 does not display the subtotals shown in the pivot table. When creating a pivot chart, Excel ignores subtotals and grand totals.

In addition, filtering a Business Segment not only filters the pivot table, but also the pivot chart. All this behavior comes from the fact that pivot charts use the same pivot cache and pivot layout as their corresponding pivot tables. This means that if you add or remove data from your data source and refresh your pivot table, your pivot chart updates to reflect the changes.

> **TIP**
>
> Did you know you can also use slicers with your pivot charts? Simply click your pivot chart, select the Analyze tab, and then click the Insert Slicer icon to take advantage of all the benefits of slicers with your pivot chart!
>
> Feel free to refer to the "Using Slicers" section in Chapter 2, "Creating a Basic Pivot Table," to get a quick refresher on slicers.

Take a moment to think about the possibilities. You can essentially create a fairly robust interactive reporting tool on the power of one pivot table and one pivot chart; no programming necessary.

Creating a Pivot Chart from Scratch

You don't have to build your pivot table before creating a pivot chart. You can go straight from your raw data to a pivot chart. Simply click any single cell in your data source and select the Insert tab. From there, select the PivotChart drop-down and then choose PivotChart. This activates the Create PivotChart dialog. At this point, you go through the same steps you would take if you were building a pivot table.

In Chapter 9, "Working with and Analyzing OLAP Data," you find out how to create pivot charts that are completely decoupled from any pivot table.

Keeping Pivot Chart Rules in Mind

As with other aspects of pivot table technology, pivot charts come with their own set of rules and limitations. The following sections give you a better understanding of the boundaries and restrictions of pivot charts.

Changes in the Underlying Pivot Table Affect Your Pivot Chart

The primary rule you should always be cognizant of is that your pivot chart is merely an extension of your pivot table. If you refresh, move a field, add a field, remove a field, hide a data item, show a data item, or apply a filter, your pivot chart reflects your changes.

The Placement of Data Fields in Your Pivot Table Might Not Be Best Suited for Your Pivot Chart

One common mistake people make when using pivot charts is assuming that Excel places the values in the column area of the pivot table in the x-axis of the pivot chart.

For instance, the pivot table in Figure 6.5 is in a format that is easy to read and comprehend. The structure chosen shows Sales Periods in the column area and the Region in the row area. This structure works fine in the pivot table view.

Figure 6.5
The placement of your data fields works for a pivot table view.

	A	B	C	D	E	F	G	
1	Business_Segment	(All)						
2								
3	Sum of Sales_Amount	Column Labels						
4	Row Labels	P01	P02	P03	P04	P05	P06	P0
5	MIDWEST		$109,498	$207,329	$101,861	$155,431	$159,298	$149,426	$1
6	NORTH	$180,772	$260,507	$183,151	$214,665	$235,369	$221,791	$1
7	SOUTH	$198,415	$334,189	$189,493	$255,558	$283,012	$249,258	$1
8	WEST	$193,180	$314,891	$183,106	$239,843	$248,124	$248,456	$1
9	Grand Total	$681,865	$1,116,916	$657,611	$865,498	$925,802	$868,930	$6

Suppose you decide to create a pivot chart from this pivot table. You would instinctively expect to see fiscal periods across the x-axis and lines of business along the y-axis. However, as you can see in Figure 6.6, your pivot chart comes out with Region in the x-axis and Sales Period in the y-axis.

Figure 6.6
Creating a pivot chart from your nicely structured pivot table does not yield the results you were expecting.

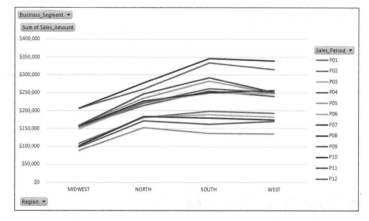

So why does the structure in your pivot table not translate to a clean pivot chart? The answer has to do with the way pivot charts handle the different areas of your pivot table.

In a pivot chart, both the x-axis and y-axis correspond to a specific area in your pivot table:

- **Y-axis**—Corresponds to the column area in your pivot table and makes up the y-axis of your pivot chart
- **X-axis**—Corresponds to the row area in your pivot table and makes up the x-axis of your pivot chart

Given this new information, look at the pivot table in Figure 6.5 again. This structure says that the Sales_Period field will be treated as the y-axis because it is in the column area. Meanwhile, the Region field will be treated as the x-axis because it is in the row area.

Now suppose you were to rearrange the pivot table to show fiscal periods in the row area and lines of business in the column area, as shown in Figure 6.7.

Figure 6.7
This format makes for slightly more difficult reading in a pivot table view but allows your pivot chart to give you the effect you are looking for.

	A	B	C	D	E	F
1	Business_Segment	(All)				
2						
3	Sum of Sales_Amount	Column Labels				
4	Row Labels	MIDWEST	NORTH	SOUTH	WEST	Grand Total
5	P01	$109,498	$180,772	$198,415	$193,180	$681,865
6	P02	$207,329	$260,507	$334,189	$314,891	$1,116,916
7	P03	$101,861	$183,151	$189,493	$183,106	$657,611
8	P04	$155,431	$214,665	$255,558	$239,843	$865,498
9	P05	$159,298	$235,369	$283,012	$248,124	$925,802
10	P06	$149,426	$221,791	$249,258	$248,456	$868,930
11	P07	$101,809	$184,350	$180,146	$174,282	$640,587
12	P08	$207,278	$277,905	$345,842	$339,236	$1,170,262
13	P09	$98,129	$172,271	$163,153	$171,000	$604,552
14	P10	$156,974	$227,469	$251,042	$255,769	$891,253
15	P11	$159,130	$246,435	$293,184	$250,855	$949,605
16	P12	$154,276	$221,242	$261,113	$251,034	$887,665
17	P13	$88,448	$153,083	$137,053	$135,041	$513,625
18	Grand Total	$1,848,887	$2,779,009	$3,141,458	$3,004,818	$10,774,172

This arrangement generates the pivot chart shown in Figure 6.8.

Figure 6.8
With the new arrangement in your pivot table, you get a pivot chart that makes sense.

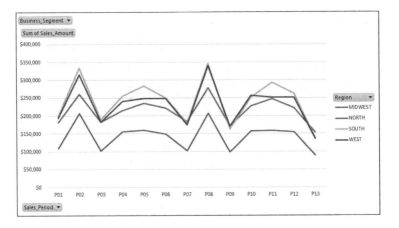

A Few Formatting Limitations Still Exist in Excel 2013

With previous versions of Excel (prior to Excel 2007), many users avoided using pivot charts because of the many formatting limitations that came with them. These limitations included the inability to resize or move key components of the pivot chart, the loss of formatting when underlying pivot tables were changed, and the inability to use certain chart types. All these limitations led to pivot charts being viewed by most users as too clunky and impractical to use.

With Excel 2007, Microsoft introduced substantial improvements to the pivot chart functionality. Users had the ability to format almost every property and component of a pivot chart. In addition, pivot charts in Excel 2007 no longer lost their formatting when the underlying pivot table changed. Pivot charts were also placed on the same worksheet as the source pivot table. Excel 2013 continues to offer the functionality introduced in Excel 2007, with a few additions (namely pivot field buttons and slicers).

Overall, the look and feel of pivot charts in Excel 2013 are very much that of standard charts, making them much more of a viable reporting option. However, a few limitations persist in this version of Excel that you should keep in mind:

- You still cannot use XY (scatter) charts, bubble charts, and stock charts when creating a pivot chart.
- Applied trend lines are often lost when you add or remove fields in the underlying pivot table.
- The chart titles in the pivot chart cannot be resized.

> **TIP**
>
> Although you cannot resize the chart titles in a pivot chart, making the font bigger or smaller indirectly resizes the chart title.

CASE STUDY: CREATING A REPORT SHOWING INVOICE FREQUENCY AND REVENUE DISTRIBUTION BY PRODUCT

You have been asked to provide both region and market managers with an interactive reporting tool that will allow them to easily see revenues across products for a variety of time periods. Your solution needs to give managers the flexibility to filter out a region or market if needed, as well as give managers the ability to dynamically filter the chart for specific periods.

Given the amount of data in your source table and the possibility that this will be a recurring exercise, you decide to use a pivot chart. Start by building the pivot table you see in Figure 6.9.

Figure 6.9
The initial pivot table meets all the data requirements.

	A	B
1		
2	Region	(All) ▾
3	Market	(All) ▾
4		
5	**Product_Description** ▾	**Sum of Sales_Amount**
6	Cleaning & Housekeeping Services	$1,138,593
7	Facility Maintenance and Repair	$2,361,158
8	Fleet Maintenance	$2,627,798
9	Green Plants and Foliage Care	$1,276,783
10	Landscaping/Grounds Care	$1,190,915
11	Predictive Maintenance/Preventative Maintenance	$2,178,925
12	**Grand Total**	**$10,774,172**

Next, place your cursor anywhere inside the pivot table and click Insert. On the Insert tab, you can see the Charts menu displaying the various types of charts you can create. Choose the Column chart icon and select the first 2-D column chart. You immediately see the chart in Figure 6.10.

Figure 6.10
Your raw pivot chart needs some formatting to meet requirements.

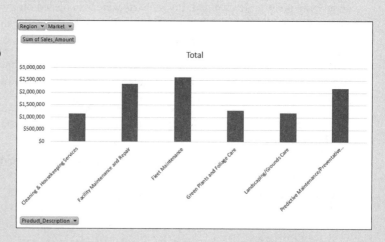

Next, click the newly created chart and select Insert Timeline from the Analyze tab under PivotChart Tools (see Figure 6.11).

Figure 6.11
Insert a Timeline slicer.

This activates the Insert Timelines dialog shown in Figure 6.12. Here, you see a list of available date fields in your pivot table. Select the Invoice_Date field.

Figure 6.12
Insert a Timeline slicer for
Invoice_Date.

At this point, you have a slicer that aggregates and filters the pivot chart by time-specific periods (see Figure 6.13).

Figure 6.13
A pivot chart and slicer
combination makes for
a powerful reporting
mechanism.

> **TIP**
> Feel free to refer to the "Using Slicers" section in Chapter 2 to get a quick refresher on Timeline slicers.

6

As a final step, remove any superfluous pivot field buttons from the chart. In this case, the only buttons you need are the Region and Market drop-downs, which give your users an interactive way to filter the pivot chart. The other gray buttons you see on the chart are not necessary.

You can remove superfluous pivot field buttons by clicking the chart and selecting the Analyze tab in the ribbon. You can then use the Field Buttons drop-down to choose the field buttons you want to be visible in the chart. In this case, you only want the Report filter field buttons visible, so only check that option (see Figure 6.14).

Figure 6.14
Use the Field Buttons drop-down to hide any unwanted pivot field buttons on the chart.

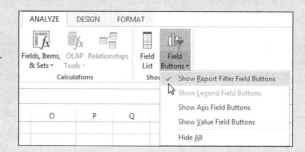

Your final pivot chart should look similar to the one in Figure 6.15.

Figure 6.15
Your final report meets all the requirements of content and interactivity.

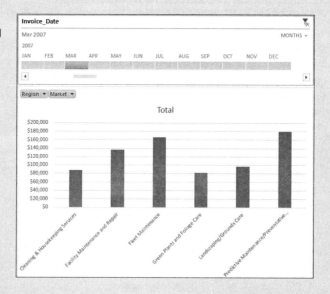

You now have a pivot chart that enables a manager to interactively review revenue by product and time period. This pivot chart also gives anyone using this report the ability to filter by region and market.

Examining Alternatives to Using Pivot Charts

There are generally two reasons why you would need an alternative to using pivot charts. First, you do not want the overhead that comes with a pivot chart. Second, you want to avoid some of the formatting limitations of pivot charts.

In fact, sometimes you might create a pivot table simply to summarize and shape your data in preparation for charting. In these situations, you don't plan on keeping your source data, and you definitely don't want a pivot cache taking up memory and file space.

In the example in Figure 6.16, you can see a pivot table that summarizes revenue by quarter for each product.

Figure 6.16

This pivot table was created to summarize and chart revenue by quarter for each product.

A	B	C	D	E	F
1					
2 Sum of Sales_Amount	Invoice_Date				
3 Product_Description	Qtr1	Qtr2	Qtr3	Qtr4	Grand Total
4 Cleaning & Housekeeping Services	$257,218	$290,074	$297,251	$294,049	$1,138,593
5 Facility Maintenance and Repair	$563,799	$621,715	$600,810	$574,834	$2,361,158
6 Fleet Maintenance	$612,496	$691,440	$674,592	$649,269	$2,627,798
7 Green Plants and Foliage Care	$293,194	$325,276	$329,787	$328,527	$1,276,783
8 Landscaping/Grounds Care	$288,797	$310,670	$303,086	$288,363	$1,190,915
9 Predictive Maintenance/Preventative Maintenance	$533,127	$567,391	$552,380	$526,027	$2,178,925
10 Grand Total	$2,548,631	$2,806,566	$2,757,906	$2,661,069	$10,774,172

The idea here is that you created this pivot table only to summarize and shape your data for charting. You don't want to keep the source data, nor do you want to keep the pivot table with all its overhead. The problem is, if you try to create a chart using the data in the pivot table, you inevitably create a pivot chart. This effectively means you have all the overhead of the pivot table looming in the background. Of course, this could be problematic if you do not want to share your source data with end users or you don't want to inundate them with unnecessarily large files.

The good news is, you can use a few simple techniques to create a chart from a pivot table but not end up with a pivot chart. Any one of the following methods does the trick.

Method 1: Turn Your Pivot Table into Hard Values

After you have created and structured your pivot table appropriately, select the entire pivot table and copy it. Then select Paste Values from the Insert tab, as demonstrated in Figure 6.17.

This action essentially deletes your pivot table, leaving you with the last values that were displayed in the pivot table. You can subsequently use these values to create a standard chart.

> **NOTE**
> This technique effectively disables the dynamic functionality of your pivot chart. That is, your pivot chart becomes a standard chart that cannot be interactively filtered or refreshed. This is also true for method 2 and method 3, which are outlined in the following sections.

Figure 6.17
The Paste Values functionality is useful when you want to create hard-coded values from pivot tables.

Method 2: Delete the Underlying Pivot Table

If you have already created your pivot chart, you can turn it into a standard chart by simply deleting the underlying pivot table. To do this, select the entire pivot table and press the Delete key on the keyboard. Keep in mind that with this method, unlike method 1, you are left with none of the values that made up the source data for the chart. In other words, if anyone asks for the data that feeds the chart, you will not have it.

> **TIP**
>
> Here is a handy tip to keep in the back of your mind: If you ever find yourself in a situation where you have a chart but the data source is not available, activate the chart's data table. The data table lets you see the data values that feed each series in the chart.

Method 3: Distribute a Picture of the Pivot Chart

Now, it might seem strange to distribute pictures of a pivot chart, but this is an entirely viable method of distributing your analysis without a lot of overhead. In addition to very small file sizes, you also get the added benefit of controlling what your clients get to see.

To use this method, simply copy the pivot chart by right-clicking the chart itself (outside the plot area) and selecting Copy. Then open a new workbook. Right-click anywhere in the new workbook, select Paste Special, and then select the picture format you prefer. A picture of your pivot chart is placed in the new workbook.

> ┌ **CAUTION** ─────────────────
>
> Be aware that if you have pivot field buttons on your chart, they will also show up in the copied picture. This will not only be unsightly, but it might leave your audience confused as to why the buttons don't work. Be sure to hide all pivot field buttons before copying a pivot chart as a picture.
>
> You can remove them by clicking on your chart and then selecting the Analyze tab. On the Analyze tab, you can use the Field Buttons drop-down to hide all of the pivot field buttons.

Method 4: Use Cells Linked Back to the Pivot Table as the Source Data for Your Chart

Many Excel users shy away from using pivot charts solely based on the formatting restrictions and issues they encounter when working with them. Often these users give up the functionality of a pivot table to avoid the limitations of pivot charts.

However, if you want to retain key functionality in your pivot table, such as report filters and top ten ranking, there is a way to link a standard chart to your pivot table without creating a pivot chart.

In the example in Figure 6.18, a pivot table shows the top ten markets by contracted hours along with their total revenue. Notice that the report filter area allows you to filter by business segment so you can see the top ten markets segment.

Figure 6.18

This pivot table allows you to filter by business segment to see the top ten markets by total contracted hours and revenue.

	A	B	C
1	Business_Segment (All)		
2			
3	**Market**	Contracted Hours	Sales_Amount
4	CALIFORNIA	33,014	$2,254,735
5	FLORIDA	22,640	$1,450,392
6	CHARLOTTE	14,525	$890,522
7	NEWYORK	14,213	$873,581
8	CANADA	12,103	$776,245
9	MICHIGAN	10,744	$678,705
10	PHOENIX	10,167	$570,255
11	TULSA	9,583	$628,405
12	DENVER	8,641	$645,583
13	KANSASCITY	8,547	$574,899
14	**Grand Total**	**144,177**	**$9,343,323**

Suppose you want to turn this view into an XY scatter chart to be able to point out the relationship between the contracted hours and revenues.

Well, a pivot chart is definitely out because you can't build pivot charts with XY scatter charts. The techniques outlined in methods 1, 2, and 3 are also out because those methods disable the interactivity you need. So what's the solution? Use the cells around the pivot table to link back to the data you need and then chart those cells. In other words, you can build a mini data set that feeds your standard chart. This data set links back to the data items in your pivot table, so when your pivot table changes, so does your data set.

Click your cursor in a cell next to your pivot table, as demonstrated in Figure 6.19, and reference the first data item that you need to create the range you will feed your standard chart.

Now copy the formula you just entered and paste that formula down and across to create your complete data set. At this point, you should have a data set that looks similar to Figure 6.20.

6

Figure 6.19
Start your linked data set by referencing the first data item you need to capture.

	A	B	C	D	E
1	Business_Segment (All)				
2					
3	**Market**	▼ Contracted Hours	Sales_Amount		
4	CALIFORNIA	33,014	$2,254,735		=B4
5	FLORIDA	22,640	$1,450,392		
6	CHARLOTTE	14,525	$890,522		
7	NEWYORK	14,213	$873,581		
8	CANADA	12,103	$776,245		
9	MICHIGAN	10,744	$678,705		
10	PHOENIX	10,167	$570,255		
11	TULSA	9,583	$628,405		
12	DENVER	8,641	$645,583		
13	KANSASCITY	8,547	$574,899		
14	**Grand Total**	**144,177**	**$9,343,323**		

Figure 6.20
Copy the formula and paste it down and across to create your complete data set.

	A	B	C	D	E	F
1	Business_Segment (All)					
2						
3	**Market**	▼ Contracted Hours	Sales_Amount		Contracted Hours	Sales_Amount
4	CALIFORNIA	33,014	$2,254,735		33,014	2,254,735
5	FLORIDA	22,640	$1,450,392		22,640	1,450,392
6	CHARLOTTE	14,525	$890,522		14,525	890,522
7	NEWYORK	14,213	$873,581		14,213	873,581
8	CANADA	12,103	$776,245		12,103	776,245
9	MICHIGAN	10,744	$678,705		10,744	678,705
10	PHOENIX	10,167	$570,255		10,167	570,255
11	TULSA	9,583	$628,405		9,583	628,405
12	DENVER	8,641	$645,583		8,641	645,583
13	KANSASCITY	8,547	$574,899		8,547	574,899
14	**Grand Total**	**144,177**	**$9,343,323**			

After your linked data set is complete, you can use it to create a standard chart. In this example, you are creating an XY scatter chart with this data. You could never do this with a pivot chart.

Figure 6.21 demonstrates how this solution offers the best of both worlds. You have kept the ability to filter out a particular business segment using the page field, and you have all the formatting freedom of a standard chart without any of the issues related to using a pivot chart.

Figure 6.21
This solution allows you to continue using the functionality of your pivot table without any of the formatting limitations you would have with a pivot chart.

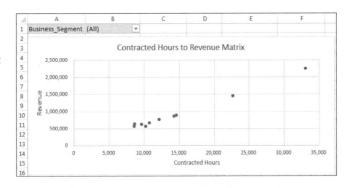

→ Another alternative to Pivot Charts is to create a Power View dashboard. See Chapter 11, "Dashboarding with Power View."

Using Conditional Formatting with Pivot Tables

In versions prior to Excel 2007, conditional formatting simply allowed you to dynamically change the color or formatting of a value or a range of cells based on a set of conditions you defined.

In Excel 2007, Microsoft introduced a more robust set of visualizations, including data bars, color scales, and icon sets. These new visualizations allow users to build dashboard-style reporting that goes far beyond the traditional red, yellow, and green designations. What's more, conditional formatting has been extended to integrate with pivot tables. This means that conditional formatting is now applied to a pivot table's structure, not just the cells it occupies.

In this section, you learn how to leverage the magic combination of pivot tables and conditional formatting to create interactive visualizations that serve as an alternative to pivot charts.

To start the first example, create the pivot table shown in Figure 6.22.

Figure 6.22
Create this pivot table.

	A	B	C
1			
2	**Market** ▾	**Sum of Sales_Amount**	**Sum of Sales_Amount2**
3	BUFFALO	$450,478	450,478
4	CALIFORNIA	$2,254,735	2,254,735
5	CANADA	$776,245	776,245
6	CHARLOTTE	$890,522	890,522
7	DALLAS	$467,089	467,089
8	DENVER	$645,583	645,583
9	FLORIDA	$1,450,392	1,450,392
10	KANSASCITY	$574,899	574,899
11	MICHIGAN	$678,705	678,705
12	NEWORLEANS	$333,454	333,454
13	NEWYORK	$873,581	873,581
14	PHOENIX	$570,255	570,255
15	SEATTLE	$179,827	179,827
16	TULSA	$628,405	628,405
17	**Grand Total**	$10,774,172	10,774,172

Suppose you want to create a report that enables your managers to see the performance of each sales period graphically. You could build a pivot chart, but you decide to use conditional formatting. In this example, let's go the easy route and quickly apply some data bars.

First, select all the Sum of Sales_Amount2 values in the values area. After you have highlighted the revenue for each Sales_Period, click the Home tab and select Conditional Formatting in the Styles group to data bars, as demonstrated in Figure 6.23.

6

Figure 6.23
Apply data bars to the
values in your pivot table.

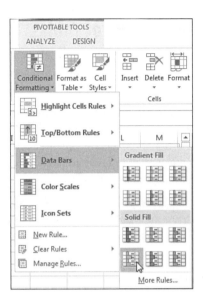

You immediately see data bars in your pivot table along with the values in the Sum of Sales_
Amount2 field. You want to show only the bar. To do this, follow these steps:

1. Click the Conditional Formatting drop-down on the Home tab and select Manage
Rules.

2. In the Rules Manager dialog, select the Data Bar rule you just created and select Edit
Rule.

3. Place a check in the option to Show Bar Only (see Figure 6.24).

Figure 6.24
Click the Show Bar Only
option to get a clean view
of just the data bars.

As you can see in Figure 6.25, you now have a set of bars that correspond to the values in your pivot table. This visualization looks like a sideways chart, doesn't it? What's more impressive is that as you filter the markets in the report filter area, the data bars dynamically update to correspond with the data for the selected market.

Figure 6.25
You have applied conditional data bars with just three easy clicks!

	A	B	C
1			
2	**Market**	**Sum of Sales_Amount**	**Sum of Sales_Amount2**
3	BUFFALO	$450,478	
4	CALIFORNIA	$2,254,735	
5	CANADA	$776,245	
6	CHARLOTTE	$890,522	
7	DALLAS	$467,089	
8	DENVER	$645,583	
9	FLORIDA	$1,450,392	
10	KANSASCITY	$574,899	
11	MICHIGAN	$678,705	
12	NEWORLEANS	$333,454	
13	NEWYORK	$873,581	
14	PHOENIX	$570,255	
15	SEATTLE	$179,827	
16	TULSA	$628,405	
17	**Grand Total**	**$10,774,172**	**10,774,172**

How can it be that you did not have to trudge through a dialog to define the condition levels?

Excel 2013 has a handful of preprogrammed scenarios that you can leverage when you want to spend less time configuring your conditional formatting and more time analyzing your data. For example, to create the data bars you've just employed, Excel uses a predefined algorithm that takes the largest and smallest values in the selected range and calculates the condition levels for each bar.

Other examples of preprogrammed scenarios include the following:

- Top *N*th Items
- Top *N*th %
- Bottom *N*th Items
- Bottom *N*th %
- Above Average
- Below Average

As you can see, Excel 2013 makes an effort to offer the conditions that are most commonly used in data analysis.

NOTE   To remove the applied conditional formatting, place your cursor inside the pivot table, click the Home tab, and select Conditional Formatting in the Styles group. From there, select Clear Rules and then select Clear Rules from This PivotTable.

6

Creating Custom Conditional Formatting Rules

It's important to note that you are by no means limited to these preprogrammed scenarios. You can still create your own custom conditions. To help illustrate this, create the pivot table shown in Figure 6.26.

Figure 6.26

This pivot shows Sales_ Amount, Contracted_ Hours, and a calculated field that calculates Dollars per Hour.

	A	B	C	D
1	Product_Description (All) ▾			
2				
3	Market ▾	Sales_Amount	Contracted Hours	Dollars Per Hour
4	BUFFALO	$450,478	6,864	$65.63
5	CALIFORNIA	$2,254,735	33,014	$68.30
6	CANADA	$776,245	12,103	$64.14
7	CHARLOTTE	$890,522	14,525	$61.31
8	DALLAS	$467,089	6,393	$73.06
9	DENVER	$645,583	8,641	$74.71
10	FLORIDA	$1,450,392	22,640	$64.06
11	KANSASCITY	$574,899	8,547	$67.26
12	MICHIGAN	$678,705	10,744	$63.17
13	NEWORLEANS	$333,454	5,057	$65.94
14	NEWYORK	$873,581	14,213	$61.46
15	PHOENIX	$570,255	10,167	$56.09
16	SEATTLE	$179,827	2,889	$62.25
17	TULSA	$628,405	9,583	$65.57
18	Grand Total	$10,774,172	165,380	$65.15

In this scenario, you want to evaluate the relationship between total revenue and dollars per hour. The idea is that some strategically applied conditional formatting helps identify opportunities for improvement.

Start by placing your cursor in the Sales_Amount column. Click the Home tab and select Conditional Formatting. Then select New Rule. This activates the New Formatting Rule dialog, shown in Figure 6.27.

The objective in this dialog is to identify the cells where the conditional formatting will be applied, specify the rule type to use, and define the details of the conditional formatting.

First, you must identify the cells where your conditional formatting will be applied. You have three choices:

- **Selected Cells**—This selection applies conditional formatting to only the selected cells.
- **All cells showing "Sales_Amount" values**—This selection applies conditional formatting to all values in the Sales_Amount column, including all subtotals and grand totals. This selection is ideal for use in analyses in which you are using averages, percentages, or other calculations where a single conditional formatting rule makes sense for all levels of analysis.

Figure 6.27
The New Formatting Rule
dialog.

All cells showing "Sales_Amount" values for "Market"—This selection applies conditional formatting to all values in the Sales_Amount column at the Market level only (excludes subtotals and grand totals). This selection is ideal for use in analyses where you are using calculations that make sense only within the context of the level being measured.

> **NOTE**
> The words *Sales_Amount* and *Market* are not permanent fixtures of the New Formatting Rule dialog. These words change to reflect the fields in your pivot table. Sales_Amount is used because your cursor is in that column. Market is used because the active data items in the pivot table are in the Market field.

In this example, the third selection (All cells showing "Sales_Amount" values for "Market") makes the most sense, so click that radio button, as demonstrated in Figure 6.28.

Next, in the Select a Rule Type section, you must specify the rule type you want to use for the conditional format. You can select one of five rule types:

■ **Format All Cells Based on Their Values**—This selection enables you to apply conditional formatting based on some comparison of the actual values of the selected range. That is, the values in the selected range are measured against each other. This selection is ideal when you want to identify general anomalies in your data set.

Figure 6.28
Click the radio button next to All cells showing "Sales_Amount" values for "Market".

■ **Format Only Cells That Contain**—This selection enables you to apply conditional formatting to those cells that meet specific criteria you define. Keep in mind that the values in your range are not measured against each other when you use this rule type. This selection is useful when you are comparing your values against a predefined benchmark.

■ **Format Only Top or Bottom Ranked Values**—This selection enables you to apply conditional formatting to those cells that are ranked in the top or bottom Nth number or percent of all the values in the range.

■ **Format Only Values That Are Above or Below the Average**—This selection enables you to apply conditional formatting to those values that are mathematically above or below the average of all values in the selected range.

■ **Use a Formula to Determine Which Cells to Format**—This selection enables you to specify your own formula and evaluate each value in the selected range against that formula. If the values evaluate as true, then the conditional formatting is applied. This selection comes in handy when you are applying conditions based on the results of an advanced formula or mathematical operation.

> **NOTE**
> You can use data bars, color scales, and icon sets only when the selected cells are formatted based on their values. This means that if you want to use data bars, color scales, and icon sets, you must select the Format All Cells Based on Their Values rule type.

In this scenario, you want to identify problem areas using icon sets; therefore, you want to format the cells based on their values.

Finally, you need to define the details of the conditional formatting in the Edit the Rule Description section. Again, you want to identify problem areas using the slick icon sets that are offered by Excel 2013. In that light, select Icon Sets from the Format Style drop-down box.

After selecting Icon Sets, select a style appropriate to your analysis. The style selected in Figure 6.29 is ideal in situations in which your pivot tables cannot always be viewed in color.

Figure 6.29
Select Icon Sets from the Format Style drop-down box.

With this configuration, Excel applies the sign icons based on the percentile bands >=67, >=33, and <33. Keep in mind that you can change the actual percentile bands based on your needs. In this scenario, the default percentile bands are sufficient.

Click the OK button to apply the conditional formatting. As you can see in Figure 6.30, you now have icons that enable you to quickly determine where each market falls in relation to other markets as it pertains to revenue.

Now apply the same conditional formatting to the Dollars Per Hour field. When you are done, your pivot table should look similar to the one shown in Figure 6.31.

Take a moment to analyze what you have here. With this view, a manager can analyze the relationship between total revenue and dollars per hour. For example, the Dallas market manager can see that he is in the bottom percentile for revenue but in the top percentile for dollars per hour. With this information, he immediately sees that his dollars per hour rates might be too high for his market. Conversely, the New York market manager can see that she is in the top percentile for revenue but in the bottom percentile for dollars per hour. This tells her that her dollars per hour rates might be too low for her market.

Figure 6.30
You have applied your first custom conditional formatting!

	A	B	C	D
1	Product_Description	(All)		
2				
3	**Market**	**Sales_Amount**	**Contracted Hours**	**Dollars Per Hour**
4	BUFFALO	◇ $450,478	6,864	$65.63
5	CALIFORNIA	◯ $2,254,735	33,014	$68.30
6	CANADA	◇ $776,245	12,103	$64.14
7	CHARLOTTE	△ $890,522	14,525	$61.31
8	DALLAS	◇ $467,089	6,393	$73.06
9	DENVER	◇ $645,583	8,641	$74.71
10	FLORIDA	△ $1,450,392	22,640	$64.06
11	KANSASCITY	◇ $574,899	8,547	$67.26
12	MICHIGAN	◇ $678,705	10,744	$63.17
13	NEWORLEANS	◇ $333,454	5,057	$65.94
14	NEWYORK	△ $873,581	14,213	$61.46
15	PHOENIX	◇ $570,255	10,167	$56.09
16	SEATTLE	◇ $179,827	2,889	$62.25
17	TULSA	◇ $628,405	9,583	$65.57
18	**Grand Total**	**$10,774,172**	**165,380**	**$65.15**

Figure 6.31
You have successfully created an interactive visualization.

	A	B	C	D
1	Product_Description	(All)		
2				
3	**Market**	**Sales_Amount**	**Contracted Hours**	**Dollars Per Hour**
4	BUFFALO	◇ $450,478	6,864 △	$65.63
5	CALIFORNIA	◯ $2,254,735	33,014 △	$68.30
6	CANADA	◇ $776,245	12,103 △	$64.14
7	CHARLOTTE	△ $890,522	14,525 ◇	$61.31
8	DALLAS	◇ $467,089	6,393 ◯	$73.06
9	DENVER	◇ $645,583	8,641 ◯	$74.71
10	FLORIDA	△ $1,450,392	22,640 △	$64.06
11	KANSASCITY	◇ $574,899	8,547 △	$67.26
12	MICHIGAN	◇ $678,705	10,744 △	$63.17
13	NEWORLEANS	◇ $333,454	5,057 △	$65.94
14	NEWYORK	△ $873,581	14,213 ◇	$61.46
15	PHOENIX	◇ $570,255	10,167 ◇	$56.09
16	SEATTLE	◇ $179,827	2,889	$62.25
17	TULSA	◇ $628,405	9,583 △	$65.57
18	**Grand Total**	**$10,774,172**	**165,380**	**$65.15**

Remember that this in an interactive report. Each manager can view the same analysis by product by simply filtering the report filter area!

What's Next

In the next chapter, you find out how to bring together disparate data sources into one pivot table. You create a pivot table from multiple data sets, and you learn the basics of creating pivot tables from other pivot tables.

Analyzing Disparate Data Sources with Pivot Tables

7

Until this point, you have been working with one local table located in the worksheet within which you are operating. Indeed, it would be wonderful if every data set you came across were neatly packed in one easy-to-use Excel table. Unfortunately, the business of data analysis does not always work out that way.

The reality is that some of the data you encounter will come from disparate data sources—meaning sets of data that are from separate systems, stored in different locations, or saved in a variety of formats. In an Excel environment, disparate data sources generally fall into one of two categories: external data or multiple ranges.

External data is exactly what it sounds like—data that is not located in the Excel workbook in which you are operating. Some examples of external data sources are text files, Access tables, SQL Server tables, and other Excel workbooks.

Multiple ranges are separate data sets located in the same workbook but separated either by blank cells or by different worksheets. For example, if your workbook has three tables on three different worksheets, each of your data sets covers a range of cells. You are therefore working with multiple ranges.

A pivot table can be an effective tool when you need to summarize data that is not neatly packed into one table. With a pivot table, you can quickly bring together either data found in an external source or data found in multiple tables within your workbook. In this chapter, you discover various techniques for working with external data sources and data sets located in multiple ranges within your workbook.

Using Multiple Consolidation Ranges

If you need to analyze data dispersed in multiple ranges, you can use the old Multiple Consolidation Ranges pivot tables. Multiple Consolidation Ranges is a concept introduced before Excel 2003 when Excel only allowed for 65,536 rows per worksheet.

In those days, if you had a very large data table exceeding the row limit, you would have to parse the table into multiple tables. This allowed for the data to be kept in a single workbook, but it was impossible to create a standard pivot table based on the data due to the fact that your data was separated into different worksheets.

However, you could create a Multiple Consolidation Ranges pivot table to bring all the data into one pivot cache. Thus, you could analyze the data more effectively.

This functionality still exists in Excel 2013, and it's worth taking a look at how it works.

Creating a Multiple Consolidation Pivot Table

Let's say you have three data ranges that you need to bring together to analyze as a group (see Figure 7.1).

Figure 7.1
Someone passed you a file that has three ranges of data. You need to bring the three ranges together so you can analyze them as a group.

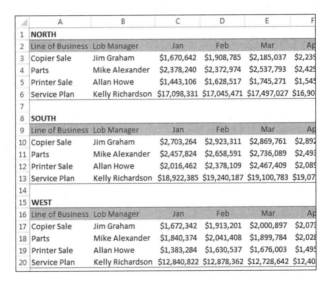

	A	B	C	D	E	F
1	NORTH					
2	Line of Business	Lob Manager	Jan	Feb	Mar	Ap
3	Copier Sale	Jim Graham	$1,670,642	$1,908,785	$2,185,037	$2,239
4	Parts	Mike Alexander	$2,378,240	$2,372,974	$2,537,793	$2,429
5	Printer Sale	Allan Howe	$1,443,106	$1,628,517	$1,745,271	$1,549
6	Service Plan	Kelly Richardson	$17,098,331	$17,045,471	$17,497,027	$16,90
7						
8	SOUTH					
9	Line of Business	Lob Manager	Jan	Feb	Mar	Ap
10	Copier Sale	Jim Graham	$2,703,264	$2,923,311	$2,869,761	$2,892
11	Parts	Mike Alexander	$2,457,824	$2,658,591	$2,736,089	$2,493
12	Printer Sale	Allan Howe	$2,016,462	$2,378,109	$2,467,409	$2,089
13	Service Plan	Kelly Richardson	$18,922,385	$19,240,187	$19,100,783	$19,07
14						
15	WEST					
16	Line of Business	Lob Manager	Jan	Feb	Mar	Ap
17	Copier Sale	Jim Graham	$1,672,342	$1,913,201	$2,000,897	$2,073
18	Parts	Mike Alexander	$1,840,374	$2,041,408	$1,899,784	$2,028
19	Printer Sale	Allan Howe	$1,383,284	$1,630,537	$1,676,003	$1,499
20	Service Plan	Kelly Richardson	$12,840,822	$12,878,362	$12,728,642	$12,40

You can create a pivot table using multiple consolidation ranges. With this pivot table option, you can quickly and easily consolidate all the data from your selected ranges into a single pivot table.

Start the process of bringing this data together with a pivot table by activating the classic PivotTable and PivotChart Wizard. You can do so by pressing Alt+D+P on your keyboard. After the PivotTable and PivotChart Wizard is activated, select the option for Multiple Consolidation Ranges, as shown in Figure 7.2.

Figure 7.2
Press Alt+D+P to activate the PivotTable and PivotChart Wizard.

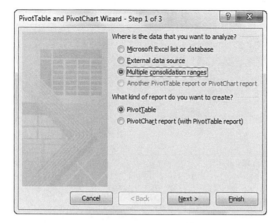

Specify whether you want Excel to create one page field for you, or whether you would like to create your own. In most cases, the page fields that Excel creates are ambiguous and of no value. Therefore, in almost all cases, you should select the option of creating your own page fields, as illustrated in Figure 7.3. Then select Next.

Figure 7.3
Specify that you want to create your own page fields and then select Next.

You need to point Excel to each of your individual data sets, one by one. Simply select the entire range of your first data set and select Add, as shown in Figure 7.4.

> **CAUTION**
>
> For your pivot table to generate properly, the first line of each range must include column labels.

Select the rest of your ranges and add them to your list of ranges. At this point, your dialog should look similar to the one in Figure 7.5.

7

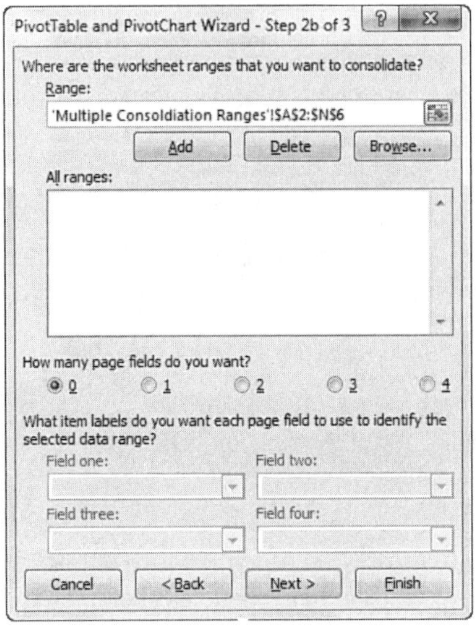

Figure 7.4
Select the entire range of your first data set and select Add.

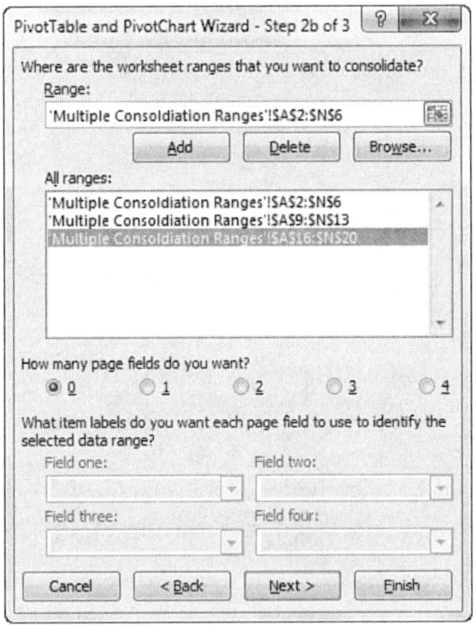

Figure 7.5
Add the other two data set ranges to your range list.

Notice that each of your data sets belongs to a region (North, South, or West). When your pivot table brings your three data sets together, you need a way to parse out each region again.

To ensure you have that capability, you need to tag each range in your list of ranges with a name identifying which data set that range came from. The result is the creation of a page field that allows you to filter each region as needed.

The first thing you have to do to create your Region page field is specify how many page fields you want to create. In your case, you want to create only one page field for your region identifier, so simply click the radio button next to the number 1, as demonstrated in Figure 7.6. This action enables the Field One input box. As you can see, you can create up to four page fields.

Figure 7.6
To be able to filter by region when your pivot table is complete, you have to create a page field. Click the radio button next to the number 1 to create one page field. This action enables the Field One input box.

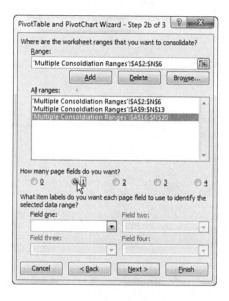

You have to tag each range, one by one, so click the first range in your range list to highlight it. Enter the region name into the Field One input box. As you can see in Figure 7.7, the first range is made up of data from the North region, so you enter **North** in the input box.

Repeat the process for the other regions, as illustrated in Figure 7.8. When you're done, select Next.

The last step is to choose the destination of your new pivot table. In this case, select the New Worksheet option, and then click Finish.

You have successfully brought three data sources together into one pivot table, as shown in Figure 7.9.

7

Figure 7.7
Select the first range that represents the data set for the North region and enter the word **North** in the input box.

Figure 7.8
Repeat the process until you have tagged all your data sets. When you're done, select Next.

Figure 7.9
You now have a pivot table that contains data from three data sources.

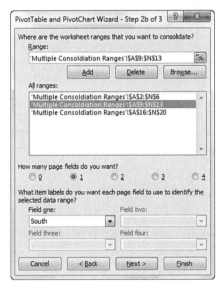

⊿	A	B	C	D	E	F	G	H	I	J	K	L	M	N	O
1	Page1	(All)													
2															
3	Count of Value	Column Labels													
4	Row Labels	Jan	Feb	Mar	Apr	May	Jun	Jul	Aug	Sep	Oct	Nov	Dec	Lob Manager	Grand Total
5	Copier Sale		3	3	3	3	3	3	3	3	3	3	3	3	3	39
6	Parts		3	3	3	3	3	3	3	3	3	3	3	3	3	39
7	Printer Sale		3	3	3	3	3	3	3	3	3	3	3	3	39
8	Service Plan		3	3	3	3	3	3	3	3	3	3	3	3	39
9	Grand Total		12	12	12	12	12	12	12	12	12	12	12	12	156

7

Analyzing the Anatomy of a Multiple Consolidation Ranges Pivot Table

Take a moment to analyze your new pivot table. You might notice a few interesting things here. First, your field list includes fields called Row, Column, Value, and Page1.

It is important to keep in mind that pivot tables using multiple consolidation ranges as their data sources can have only three base fields: Row, Column, and Value. In addition to these base fields, you can create up to four page fields.

> **TIP**
>
> Notice that the fields generated with your pivot table have fairly generic names (Row, Column, Value, Page1). You can customize the field settings for these fields to rename and format them to better suit your needs. See Chapter 3, "Customizing a Pivot Table," for a more detailed look at customizing field settings.

The Row Field

The Row field is always made up of the first column in your data source. Note that in Figure 7.1, the first column in your data source is Line of Business. Therefore, the Row field in your newly created pivot table contains Line of Business.

The Column Field

The Column field contains the remaining columns in your data source. Pivot tables that use multiple consolidation ranges combine all the fields in your original data sets (minus the first column, which is used for the Row field) into a kind of super field called the Column field. The fields in your original data sets become data items under the Column field.

Notice that your pivot table initially applies Count to your Column field. If you change the field setting of the Column field to Sum, all the data items under the Column field are affected. Figure 7.10 shows the same data as Figure 7.9, except the summarize type is set to Sum instead of the default (Count).

Figure 7.10

The data items under the Column field are treated as one entity. When you change the calculation of the Column field from Count to Sum, the change applies to all items under the Column field.

	A	B	C	D	E	F	G	N
1	Page1	(All)						
2								
3	Sum of Value	Column Labels						
4	Row Labels	Jan	Feb	Mar	Apr	May	Jun	Lob Manager
5	Copier Sale	$6,046,248	$6,745,297	$7,055,695	$7,205,183	$7,314,876	$7,307,057	$0
6	Parts	$6,676,438	$7,072,973	$7,173,666	$6,951,658	$7,034,322	$6,787,727	$0
7	Printer Sale	$4,842,852	$5,637,163	$5,888,683	$5,130,810	$5,859,476	$5,985,190	$0
8	Service Plan	$48,861,538	$49,164,020	$49,326,452	$48,381,665	$49,363,401	$47,116,246	$0
9	Grand Total	$66,427,076	$68,619,453	$69,444,496	$67,669,316	$69,572,075	$67,196,220	$0

The Value Field

The Value field contains the value for all data items under the Column field. Notice that even fields that were originally text fields in your data set are treated as numerical values. An example is Lob Manager, shown in Figure 7.10. Although this field contained manager names in the original data set, it is now treated as a number in your pivot table.

As mentioned before, pivot tables that use multiple consolidation ranges merge the fields in your original data sets (minus the first field), making them data items in the Column field. Therefore, although you might recognize fields such as Lob Manager as text fields that contain their own individual data items, they no longer hold data of their own. They have been transformed into data items themselves—data items with a value.

The net effect of this behavior is that fields originally holding text or dates show up in your pivot table as a meaningless numerical value. It's usually a good idea to simply hide these fields to avoid confusion.

> **TIP**
>
> You can learn all about hiding fields in Chapter 4, "Grouping, Sorting, and Filtering Pivot Data."

The Page Fields

Page fields are the only fields in Multiple Consolidation Ranges pivot tables that you have direct control over. You can create and define up to four page fields. The useful feature of these fields is that you can drag them to the row area or column area to add layers to your pivot table.

The Page1 field shown in the pivot table in Figure 7.10 was created to be able to filter by region. However, if you move the Page1 field to the row area of your pivot table, you can create a one-shot view of all your data by region. Figure 7.11 demonstrates this view.

Figure 7.11
Moving the Page1 field to the row area adds a layer to your pivot table report, giving you a one-shot view of all your data by region.

	A	B	C	D	E	F	G	N	O
3	Sum of Value	Column Labels							
4	Row Labels	Jan	Feb	Mar	Apr	May	Jun	Lob Manager	Grand Total
5	⊟NORTH	$22,590,319	$22,955,747	$23,965,128	$23,117,481	$23,506,822	$22,612,583	$0	$276,992,617
6	Copier Sale	$1,670,642	$1,908,785	$2,185,037	$2,239,371	$2,121,648	$2,133,291	$0	$25,893,618
7	Parts	$2,378,240	$2,372,974	$2,537,793	$2,429,561	$2,419,169	$2,271,298	$0	$29,063,171
8	Printer Sale	$1,443,106	$1,628,517	$1,745,271	$1,545,072	$1,808,141	$1,785,903	$0	$20,621,317
9	Service Plan	$17,098,331	$17,045,471	$17,497,027	$16,903,477	$17,157,864	$16,422,091	$0	$201,414,511
10	⊟SOUTH	$26,099,935	$27,200,198	$27,174,042	$26,548,945	$27,331,488	$26,646,198	$0	$319,820,310
11	Copier Sale	$2,703,264	$2,923,311	$2,869,761	$2,892,764	$3,203,760	$3,192,643	$0	$36,711,470
12	Parts	$2,457,824	$2,658,591	$2,736,089	$2,493,456	$2,583,428	$2,572,431	$0	$31,205,269
13	Printer Sale	$2,016,462	$2,378,109	$2,467,409	$2,089,987	$2,351,109	$2,480,684	$0	$28,153,264
14	Service Plan	$18,922,385	$19,240,187	$19,100,783	$19,072,738	$19,193,191	$18,400,440	$0	$223,750,307
15	⊟WEST	$17,736,822	$18,463,508	$18,305,326	$18,002,890	$18,733,765	$17,937,439	$0	$216,582,112
16	Copier Sale	$1,672,342	$1,913,201	$2,000,897	$2,073,048	$1,989,468	$1,981,123	$0	$23,976,601
17	Parts	$1,840,374	$2,041,408	$1,899,784	$2,028,641	$2,031,725	$1,943,998	$0	$23,670,053
18	Printer Sale	$1,383,284	$1,630,537	$1,676,003	$1,495,751	$1,700,226	$1,718,603	$0	$19,594,197
19	Service Plan	$12,840,822	$12,878,362	$12,728,642	$12,405,450	$13,012,346	$12,293,715	$0	$149,341,261

7

You might run into a situation in which you need to redefine your pivot table. That is, you need to add a data range, remove a data range, or redefine your page fields. To redefine your pivot table, simply activate the classic PivotTable and PivotChart Wizard and then select the Back button until you get to the dialog you need.

Using the Internal Data Model

Excel 2013 introduces a new in-memory analytics engine called the Data Model. Every workbook has one internal Data Model that enables you to work with and analyze disparate data sources like never before.

The idea behind the Data Model is simple. Let's say you have two tables: a Customers table and an Orders table. The Orders table has basic information about invoices (customer number, invoice date, and revenue). The Customers table has basic information such as customer number, customer name, and state.

If you want to analyze revenue by state, you have to join the two tables and aggregate the Revenue field in the Orders table by the State field in the Customers table.

In the past, you would have to go through a series of gyrations involving VLookups, SumIfs, or other formulas. With the new Excel 2013 Data Model, however, you can simply tell Excel how the two tables are related (they both have customer number) and then pull them into the internal Data Model. The Excel Data Model then builds an analytical cube based on that customer number relationship and exposes the data through a pivot table. With the pivot table, you can create the aggregation by state with a few clicks of the mouse.

→   The internal Data Model is secretly using the PowerPivot data engine. If you have Excel Pro Plus or higher, you can take the data model further. See Chapter 10, "Mashing Up Data with PowerPivot."

Building Out Your First Data Model

Imagine you have the Transactions table you see in Figure 7.12. On another worksheet, you have an Employees table (see Figure 7.13) that contains information about the employee.

Figure 7.12
This table shows transactions by employee number.

◢	A	B	C	D
1	Sales_Rep	Invoice_Date	Sales_Amount	Contracted Hours
2	4416	1/5/2007	111.79	2
3	4416	1/5/2007	111.79	2
4	160006	1/5/2007	112.13	2
5	6444	1/5/2007	112.13	2
6	160006	1/5/2007	145.02	3
7	52661	1/5/2007	196.58	4
8	6444	1/5/2007	204.20	4
9	51552	1/5/2007	225.24	3
10	55662	1/6/2007	86.31	2
11	1336	1/6/2007	86.31	2
12	60224	1/6/2007	86.31	2
13	54564	1/6/2007	86.31	2
14	56146	1/6/2007	89.26	2
15	5412	1/6/2007	90.24	1

7

Figure 7.13
This table provides information on employees: first name, last name, and job title.

▲	A	B	C	D
1	Employee_Number	Last_Name	First_Name	Job_Title
2	21	SIOCAT	ROBERT	SERVICE REPRESENTATIVE 3
3	42	BREWN	DONNA	SERVICE REPRESENTATIVE 3
4	45	VAN HUILE	KENNETH	SERVICE REPRESENTATIVE 2
5	104	WIBB	MAURICE	SERVICE REPRESENTATIVE 2
6	106	CESTENGIAY	LUC	SERVICE REPRESENTATIVE 2
7	113	TRIDIL	ROCH	SERVICE REPRESENTATIVE 2
8	142	CETE	GUY	SERVICE REPRESENTATIVE 3
9	145	ERSINEILT	MIKE	SERVICE REPRESENTATIVE 2
10	162	GEBLE	MICHAEL	SERVICE REPRESENTATIVE 2
11	165	CERDANAL	ALAIN	SERVICE REPRESENTATIVE 3
12	201	GEIDRIOU	DOMINIC	TEAMLEAD 1

You need to create an analysis that shows sales by job title. This would normally be difficult given the fact that sales and job title are in two separate tables. But with the new Data Model, you can follow these simple steps:

1. Click inside the Transactions data table and start a new pivot table (by using Insert, Pivot Table on the ribbon).

2. In the Create PivotTable dialog, be sure to place a check next to the Add This Data to the Data Model option (see Figure 7.14).

Figure 7.14
Create a new pivot table from the Transactions table. Make sure you select Add This Data to the Data Model.

3. Click inside the Employees data table and start a new pivot table. Again, be sure to place a check next to the Add This Data to the Data Model option, as demonstrated in Figure 7.15.

Figure 7.15
Create a new pivot table from the Employees table. Make sure to select Add This Data to the Data Model.

> **NOTE**
> Notice that in Figure 7.14 and 7.15, the Create PivotTable dialogs are referencing named ranges. That is to say, each table was given a specific name. When you're adding data to the Data Model, it's a best practice to name your data tables. This way, you can easily recognize your tables in the Data Model.
>
> If you don't name your tables, the Data Model shows them as Range1, Range2, and so on.
>
> To give your data table a name, simply highlight all the data in the table, select the Formulas tab on the ribbon, and then click the Define Name command. In the dialog, enter a name for the table. Repeat for all other tables.

4. Now that both tables have been added to the Data Model, you activate the PivotTable Fields list and choose the ALL selector, as shown in Figure 7.16. This shows both ranges in the field list.

5. Build out your pivot table as normal. In this case, Job_Title goes to the Row area and Sales_Amount goes to the Values area. As you can see in Figure 7.17, Excel immediately recognizes that you are using two tables from your Data Model and prompts you to create a relationship between them. Click the Create button.

6. Excel activates the Create Relationship dialog shown in Figure 7.18. Here, you select the tables and fields that define the relationship. In Figure 7.18, you can see that the Transaction table has a Sales_Rep field. It is related to the Employees table via the Employee_Number field.

7

Figure 7.16
Select ALL in the
PivotTable Fields list to
see both tables in your
Data Model.

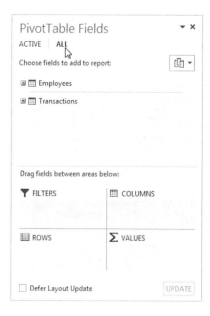

Figure 7.17
When Excel prompts
you, choose to create the
relationship between the
two tables.

Figure 7.18
Build the appropriate
relationship using the
Table and Column drop-
downs.

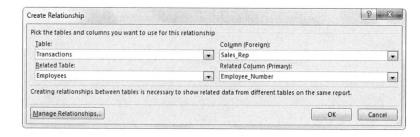

7. After you create your relationship, you have a single pivot table that effectively uses data from both tables to create the analysis you need. Figure 7.19 illustrates that using the Excel Data Model, you have achieved the goal of showing sales by job title.

Figure 7.19
You have achieved your goal of showing sales by job title.

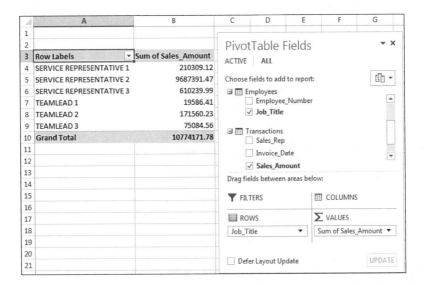

The Importance of Primary Keys

In Figure 7.18, you see that the lower-right drop-down is called Related Column (Primary). The term *Primary* means that the internal Data Model uses this field from the associated table as the primary key.

A primary key is a field that contains only unique non-null values (no duplicates or blanks). Primary key fields are necessary in the Data Model to prevent aggregation errors and duplications. Every relationship you create must have a field designated as the primary key.

So the Employees table (in the scenario in Figure 7.18) must have all unique values in the Employee_Number field; with no blanks or null values.

This is the only way Excel can ensure data integrity when joining multiple tables.

Managing Relationships in the Data Model

After you assign tables to the internal Data Model, you might need to adjust the relationships between the tables. To make changes to the relationships in a Data Model, activate the Manage Relationships dialog.

Click the Data tab in the ribbon and select the Relationships command. The dialog shown in Figure 7.20 displays.

7

Figure 7.20
The Manage
Relationships dialog
enables you to make
changes to the relation-
ships in the Data Model.

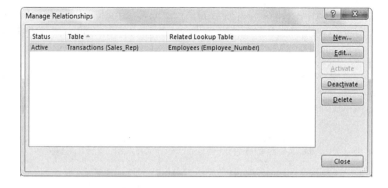

Here, you will find the following commands:

- **New**—Create a new relationship between two tables in the Data Model.
- **Edit**—Alter the selected relationship.
- **Activate**—Enforce the selected relationship, telling Excel to consider the relationship when aggregating and analyzing the data in the Data Model.
- **Deactivate**—Turn off the selected relationship, telling Excel to ignore the relationship when aggregating and analyzing the data in the Data Model.
- **Delete**—Remove the selected relationship.

Adding a New Table to the Data Model

You can add a new table to your Data Model in one of two ways.

The easiest way is to simply create a pivot table from the new table and then choose the Add This Data to the Data Model option. Excel adds your table to the Data Model and produces a pivot table. After your table has been added, you can open the Manage Relationships dialog and create the needed relationship.

The second and more flexible method is to manually define your table and add it to the Data Model. Here's how:

1. Place your cursor inside your data table and select Insert Table. The dialog in Figure 7.21 displays. Here, you specify the range for your data. Excel then turns that range into a defined table that the internal Data Model can recognize.

Figure 7.21
Convert your range into a
defined table.

2. On the Table Tools Design tab, change the Table Name field (in the Properties group) to something appropriate that's easy to remember (see Figure 7.22).

Figure 7.22
Give your newly created table a friendly name.

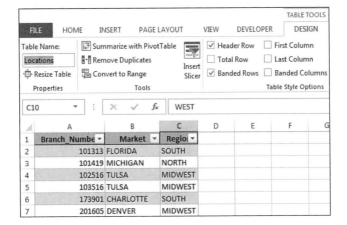

3. Go to the Data tab in the ribbon and select Connections to open the Workbook Connections dialog shown in Figure 7.23. Click the drop-down next to Add and choose the Add to the Data Model option.

Figure 7.23
Open the Workbook Connections dialog and select Add to the Data Model.

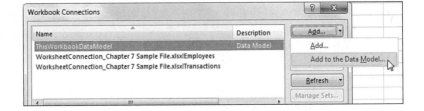

4. The Existing Connections dialog opens (see Figure 7.24). On the Tables tab, find and select your newly created table. Click the Open button to add it to the Data Model.

5. At this point, all pivot tables built on the Data Model are updated to reflect the new table. Be sure to open the Manage Relationships dialog and create the needed relationship.

CAUTION

Be aware that every table you add to the Data Model is essentially stored with the workbook, effectively increasing the size of your Excel file. Read more about the size limitations of the Excel Data Model later in the chapter.

7

Figure 7.24
Select your newly created table and click the Open button.

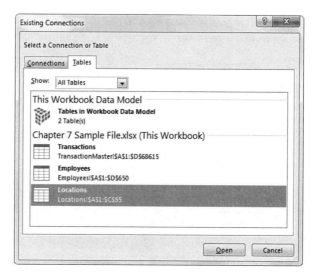

Removing a Table from the Data Model

You might find that you want to remove a table or data source altogether from the Data Model. To do so, click the Data tab in the ribbon and then click the Connections command. The Workbook Connections dialog shown in Figure 7.25 opens.

Click the table you want to remove from the Data Model (Employees, in this case) and then click the Remove button.

Figure 7.25
Use the Workbook Connections dialog to remove any table from the internal Data Model.

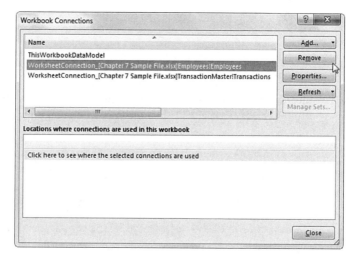

Create a New Pivot Table Using the Data Model

There might be instances when you want to create a pivot table from scratch using the existing internal Data Model as the source data. Here are the steps to do so:

1. Activate the Create PivotTable dialog by clicking Insert, PivotTable. Click the Use an External Data Source option (see Figure 7.26). Then click the Choose Connection button.

Figure 7.26
Open the Create PivotTable dialog and choose the external data source option.

2. You see the Existing Connections dialog shown in Figure 7.27. On the Tables tab, select Tables in Workbook Data Model and then click the Open button.

Figure 7.27
Use the Existing Connections dialog to select the internal Data Model as the data source for your pivot table.

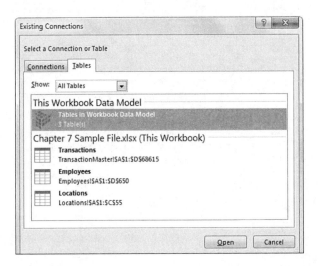

3. You go back to the Create PivotTable dialog. From here, you can click the OK button to create the pivot table.

4. If all goes well, you see a PivotTable Fields dialog with all the tables that are included in the internal Data Model (see Figure 7.28).

Figure 7.28
Your newly created pivot table shows all the tables in the internal Data Model.

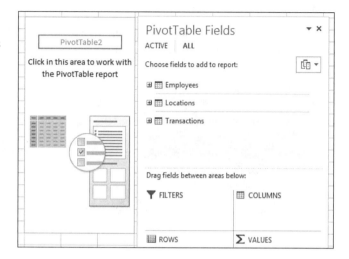

Limitations of the Internal Data Model

As with everything else in Excel, the internal Data Model does have limitations. Table 7.1 highlights the maximum and configurable limits for Excel Data Models.

Table 7.1   Data Model Limitations

Object	Specification
Data Model size	In 32-bit environments, Excel workbooks are subject to a 2GB limit. This includes the in-memory space shared by Excel, the internal Data Model, and add-ins that run in the same process.
	In 64-bit environments, there are no hard limits on file size. Workbook size is limited only by available memory and system resources.
Number of tables in the Data Model	No hard limits on the count of tables. However, all tables in the data model cannot exceed 2,147,483,647 bytes.
Number of rows in each table in the Data Model	1,999,999,997
Number of columns and calculated columns in each table in the Data Model	Cannot exceed 2,147,483,647 bytes.
Number of distinct values in a column	1,999,999,997
Characters in a column name	100 characters.
String length in each field	Limited to 536,870,912 bytes (512MB), equivalent to 268,435,456 Unicode characters (256 mega-characters).

Building a Pivot Table Using External Data Sources

There is no argument that Excel is good at processing and analyzing data. In fact, pivot tables themselves are a testament to the analytical power of Excel. However, despite all its strengths, Excel makes for a poor relational data management platform, primarily for three reasons:

■ A data set's size has a significant effect on performance, making for less efficient data crunching. The reason for this is the fundamental way Excel handles memory. When you open an Excel file, the entire file is loaded into RAM to ensure quick data processing and access. The drawback to this behavior is that Excel requires a great deal of RAM to process even the smallest change in your spreadsheet (typically giving you a "Calculating" indicator in the status bar). So although Excel 2013 offers more than 1 million rows and more than 16,000 columns, creating and managing large data sets causes Excel to slow down considerably, making data analysis a painful endeavor.

■ The lack of a relational data structure forces the use of flat tables that promote redundant data. This also increases the chance for errors.

■ There is no way to index data fields in Excel to optimize performance when you're attempting to retrieve large amounts of data.

In smart organizations, the task of data management is not performed by Excel; rather, it is primarily performed by relational database systems such as Microsoft Access and SQL Server. These databases are used to store millions of records that can be rapidly searched and retrieved.

The effect of this separation in tasks is that you have a data management layer (your database) and a presentation layer (Excel). The trick is to find the best way to get information from your data management layer to your presentation layer for use by your pivot table.

Managing your data is the general idea behind building your pivot table using an external data source. Building your pivot tables from external systems enables you to leverage environments that are better suited to data management. This means you can let Excel do what it does best: analyze and create a presentation layer for your data. The following sections walk you through several techniques for building pivot tables using external data.

Building a Pivot Table with Microsoft Access Data

Often Access is used to manage a series of tables that interact with each other, such as a Customers table, an Orders table, and an Invoices table. Managing data in Access provides the benefit of a relational database where you can ensure data integrity, prevent redundancy, and easily generate data sets via queries.

The modus operandi of most Excel users is to use an Access query to create a subset of data and then import that data into Excel. From there, the data can be analyzed with pivot tables. The problem with this method is that it forces the Excel workbook to hold two copies of the imported data sets: one on the spreadsheet and one in the pivot cache. Holding

7

two copies obviously causes the workbook to be twice as big as it needs to be, and it introduces the possibility of performance issues.

Excel 2013 offers a surprisingly easy way to use your Access data without creating two copies of it. To see how easy it is, open Excel and start a new workbook. Then click the Data tab and look for the group called Get External Data. Here, you find the From Access selection, as shown in Figure 7.29.

Figure 7.29
Click the From Access button to get data from your Access database.

Selecting the From Access button activates a dialog asking you to select the database you want to work with. Select your database.

> **T I P**
>
> The sample database used in this chapter is available for download from www.mrexcel.com/pivotbookdata2013.html.

After your database has been selected, the dialog shown in Figure 7.30 activates. This dialog lists all the tables and queries available. In this example, select the query called Sales_By_Employee and click the OK button.

Figure 7.30
Select the table or query you want to analyze.

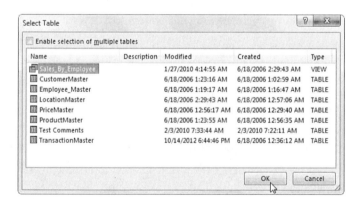

NOTE In Figure 7.30, notice that the Select Table dialog contains a column called Type. There are two types of Access objects you can work with: Views and Tables. View indicates that the data set listed is an Access query, and Table indicates that the data set is an Access table.

In this example, notice that Sales_By_Employee is actually an Access query. This means that you import the results of the query. This is true interaction at work; Access does all the back-end data management and aggregation, and Excel handles the analysis and presentation!

Next, you see the Import Data dialog, where you select the format in which you want to import the data. As you can see in Figure 7.31, you have the option of importing the data as a table, as a pivot table, or as a pivot table with an accompanying pivot chart. You also have the option to tell Excel where to place the data.

Select the radio button next to PivotTable Report and click the OK button.

Figure 7.31
Select the radio button next to PivotTable Report.

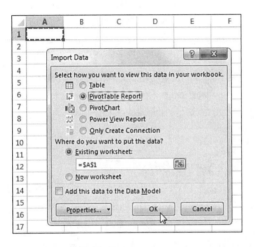

At this point, you should see the PivotTable Fields list shown in Figure 7.32. From here, you can use this pivot table just as you normally would.

The wonderful thing about this technique is that you can refresh the data simply by refreshing the pivot table. When you refresh, Excel takes a new snapshot of the data source and updates the pivot cache.

Figure 7.32
Your pivot table is ready
to use.

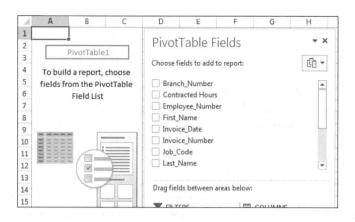

CAUTION

If you create a pivot table that uses an Access database as its source, you can refresh that pivot table only if the table or view is available. That is, deleting, moving, or renaming the database used to create the pivot table destroys the link to the external data set, thus destroying your ability to refresh the data. Deleting or renaming the source table or query has the same effect.

Following that reasoning, any clients using your linked pivot table cannot refresh the pivot table unless the source is available to them. If you need your clients to be able to refresh, you might want to make the data source available via a shared network directory.

Building a Pivot Table with SQL Server Data

In the spirit of collaboration, Excel 2013 vastly improves your ability to connect to transactional databases such as SQL Server. With the connection functionality found in Excel, creating a pivot table from SQL Server data is as easy as ever.

Start on the Data tab and select From Other Sources to see the drop-down menu shown in Figure 7.33. Then select From SQL Server.

Figure 7.33
From the drop-down
menu, select From SQL
Server.

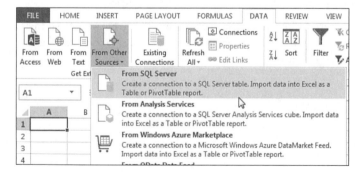

Selecting this option activates the Data Connection Wizard, as shown in Figure 7.34. The idea here is that you configure your connection settings so Excel can establish a link to the server.

> **NOTE**
> There is no sample file for this case study. The essence of this demonstration is the interaction between Excel and a SQL server data source. The actions you take to connect to your particular database are the same as demonstrated here.

The first step in this endeavor is to provide Excel with some authentication information. As you can see in Figure 7.34, you enter the name of your server as well as your username and password.

Figure 7.34
Enter your authentication information and click the Next button.

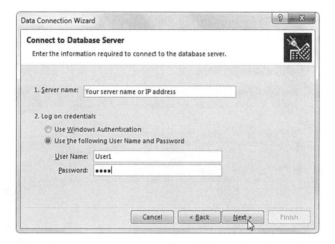

> **NOTE**
> If you are typically authenticated via Windows Authentication, you simply select the Use Windows Authentication option.

Next, you select the database with which you are working from a drop-down menu containing all available databases on the specified server. As you can see in Figure 7.35, a database called AdventureWorks2012 has been selected in the drop-down box. Selecting this database causes all the tables and views in it to be exposed in the list of objects below the drop-down menu. All there is left to do in this screen is to choose the table or view you want to analyze and then click the Next button.

7

Figure 7.35
Specify your database and then choose the table or view you want to analyze.

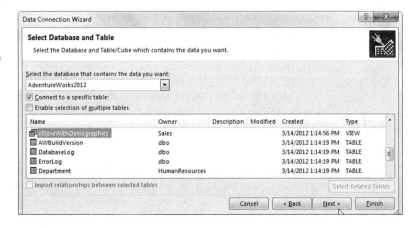

The next screen in the wizard, shown in Figure 7.36, enables you to enter some descriptive information about the connection you've just created.

Figure 7.36
Edit descriptive information for your connection.

> **NOTE**
> All the fields in the screen shown in Figure 7.36 are optional edits only. That is, if you bypass this screen without editing anything, your connection works fine.

Here are the fields you'll use most often:

- **File Name**—In the File Name input box, you can change the filename of the .odc (Office Data Connection) file generated to store the configuration information for the link you just created.

- **Save Password in File**—Under the File Name input box, you have the option of saving the password for your external data in the file itself (via the Save Password in File check box). Placing a check in this check box actually enters your password in the file. Keep in mind that this password is not encrypted, so anyone interested enough could potentially get the password for your data source simply by viewing your file with a text editor.
- **Description**—In the Description field, you can enter a plain description of what this particular data connection does.
- **Friendly Name**—The Friendly Name field enables you to specify your own name for the external source. You typically enter a name that is descriptive and easy to read.

When you are satisfied with your descriptive edits, click the Finish button to finalize your connection settings. You immediately see the Import Data dialog, shown in Figure 7.37. From here, you select a pivot table and then click the OK button to start building your pivot table.

Figure 7.37
When your connection is finalized, you can start building your pivot table.

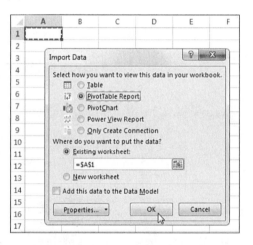

CASE STUDY: CREATING A DATA MODEL WITH MULTIPLE EXTERNAL DATA TABLES

You have an Access database that contains a normalized set of tables. You want to analyze the data in that database in Excel. You decide you want to use the new Excel Data Model to expose the data you need through a pivot table.

To accomplish your desired task, follow these steps:

1. Click the Data tab and look for the group called Get External Data. Here, you find the From Access selection, as shown in Figure 7.38.

2. Browse to your target Access database and open it. The Select Data dialog opens.

3. In the dialog, place a check next to Enable Selection of Multiple Tables (see Figure 7.39).

Figure 7.38
Click the From Access button to get data from your Access database.

Figure 7.39
Enable the selection of multiple tables.

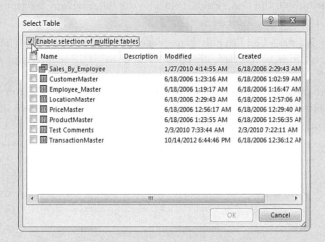

4. Place a check next to each table you want to bring into the internal Data Model. Click the OK button, as demonstrated in Figure 7.40.

Figure 7.40
Place a check next to each table you want to import to the internal Data Model, and then click OK.

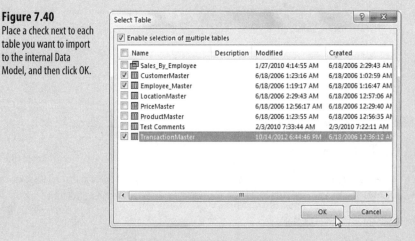

5. At this point, the Import Data dialog shown in Figure 7.41 opens. Click the drop-down arrow next to Properties and remove the check next to Import Relationships Between Tables. This ensures that Excel does not error out because of misinterpretations of how the tables are related. In other words, you want to create relationships yourself.

Figure 7.41
Remove the check next to Import Relationships Between Tables.

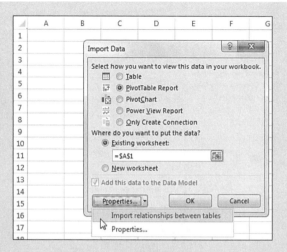

6. Still in the Import Data dialog, choose the PivotTable Report option and click OK to create the base pivot.

7. Click the Data tab in the ribbon and choose the Relationships command; this actives the Manage Relationships dialog shown in Figure 7.42. Create the needed relationships and then click the Close button.

Figure 7.42
Create the needed relationships for the tables you just imported.

8. You now have a pivot table based on external data imported into the Data Model. In just a few a few clicks, you have created a powerful platform to build and maintain pivot table analysis based on data in an Access database (see Figure 7.43).

7

Figure 7.43
You are ready to build your pivot table analysis based on multiple external data tables!

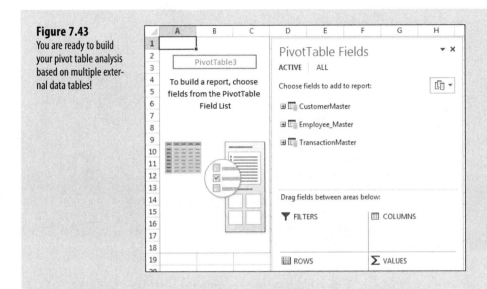

What's Next

Chapter 8, "Sharing Pivot Tables with Others," covers the ins and outs of sharing your pivot tables with the world. In that chapter, you find out how you can distribute your pivot tables through the Web.

7

Sharing Pivot Tables with Others

Say that you've built an awesome pivot table with slicers. You would like people to be able to interact with the pivot table but you don't want them to be able to rearrange the pivot table, nor do you want them to be able to access the underlying data. This is now possible via several avenues:

- The Excel Web App and SkyDrive can let you turn your Excel workbook into an interactive web app with ease. A SkyDrive account is free, and this method will accommodate files up to 10MB in size.

- If your company has a SharePoint Enterprise Server plus SQL Server BI Edition, you can publish an interactive view to SharePoint.

- You can use Office 365 and create your own SharePoint site in the cloud. Again, you still have the 10MB limit.

- If you are below the 10MB file size limit, you can publish to the SkyDrive and then embed your pivot table in a blog post or a web page.

- If your file is over the 10MB limit, or if you have a PowerPivot Data Model in the workbook, you are going to have to seek an alternative hosting company. Rob Collie at PivotStream offers cloud-based PowerPivot servers. This will get you around the 10MB limit. They are working on pricing plans aimed at Excel pros on super-tight budgets. Visit http://ppvt.pro/CloudPPV for information.

8

Designing a Workbook as an Interactive Web Page

You can use the Excel client to design a workbook for use as a web page. Imagine a set of slicers at the top, then a pivot table and a few pivot charts all on one screen of data. The person who visits your workbook in a browser can interact with the slicers and see the results. And here is the best part: You can protect your intellectual property. You can choose to publish Sheet1 in the browser and not show other worksheets. The pivot tables on Sheet1 reach back to use information on Sheet2, but no one is able to hack in and unhide Sheet2. They can't see your formulas.

Figure 8.1 shows a Top Customers report with several slicers. The source data and the source pivot table are located on back worksheets. To adapt the workbook to create a web page, you can perform these tasks:

- Isolate the visible parts of the report on a single worksheet. Cut anything that does not need to be seen from the first worksheet and paste it to the Hidden worksheet. In this example, you could cut the formula for first year interest and put it on the Hidden worksheet.

- Consider if any input cells can be changed to a slicer. Slicers are excellent for selecting values in a web page. The How Many Customers To Show slicer in Figure 8.1 is tied to a simple ten-row data set and pivot table on the Hidden worksheet. The formula in F2:F11 pulls the first value from the pivot table. When someone chooses from the slicer, the proper number of top customers are shown.

- Take a few steps to make your worksheet not look like Excel. On the View tab, uncheck Formula Bar, Gridlines, and Headings.

Figure 8.1 shows the workbook in the Excel client. This is the first worksheet. Most of the data is on the Hidden worksheet.

You need to control what is shown in the browser. Open the File menu and choose Export from the left navigation. Click Browser View Options in the center pane to cause the Browser View icon to appear. Click that icon.

In the Show tab, open the drop-down. Change Entire Workbook to Sheets. You can then uncheck the Hidden worksheet (see Figure 8.2).

Save the workbook to your SkyDrive account.

You should test the workbook before sharing it. Make sure that the parameters work and that everything looks correct. When you are signed in to the SkyDrive and open your own workbook, it might automatically open in Edit mode. Go to the View tab and choose Reading View.

Figure 8.1
Make a worksheet that
does not look like Excel.

8

Figure 8.2
Choose which worksheet
will be visible and which
will be hidden.

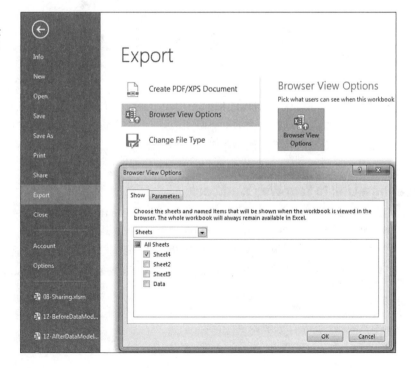

Figure 8.3 shows the workbook in the browser. If you click a slicer, the filters change and the pivot tables and pivot charts update.

Figure 8.3
This is a cool interactive web page, all created using your Excel skills.

TIP If you are reading this book, I bet that you know a lot about Microsoft Excel. You can probably knock out amazing formulas that do all sorts of calculations. Now, with just that knowledge, you can create amazing interactive web pages.

Sharing a Link to Your Web Workbook

The easiest way to share your web workbook is to use the Share with People command in the SkyDrive. This enables other people to interact with your workbook, but it also lets them download the whole workbook to their computer.

While you are viewing the workbook, use Share, Share with People, as shown in Figure 8.4.

Figure 8.4
While viewing the work-book in the SkyDrive, click Share, Share with People.

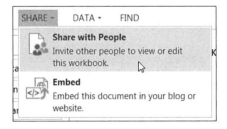

The share dialog offers three categories:

- You can send an email inviting others to use the workbook.
- You can post to Facebook, Twitter, or LinkedIn.
- You can get a link that you can distribute.

In Figure 8.5, I am posting to Facebook, Twitter, and LinkedIn. Remember the limit for Twitter is 140 characters, less the 15 characters for the link. Keep the message short and to the point.

Figure 8.5
Post to your social media accounts.

A few seconds later, the tweet appears in your Twitter feed (see Figure 8.6).

Figure 8.6
Excel shortens the URL to 14 characters and a space.

When someone sees your post and follows the link, they arrive at a read-only copy of the application shown previously in Figure 8.3. Any changes that they make to the slicer or the parameters are not saved to the workbook. The next person gets a fresh copy of the workbook.

Embedding Your Workbook in a Blog Post or Your Web Page

If you have a blog or a web page, you can embed the workbook in your web page. Go back to the Share menu in Figure 8.4 and choose the Embed option.

Excel shows a warning screen that people without your password are able to interact with the web page, as shown in Figure 8.7.

Figure 8.7
Click Generate to acknowledge the message.

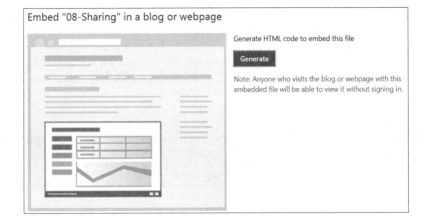

There are many things that you can customize in the next screen:

- Rather than the whole workbook, you can limit people to only see Model!A1:M20 or any other range.
- If you didn't previously hide the gridlines, you can do so.
- By default, the Include a Download Link option is checked. If you are trying to protect the data on the hidden worksheet, you should uncheck this setting.
- Choose the first item under Interaction. The first check box allows the slicers to filter the underlying pivot table. You can specify that the active cell starts in the first input cell.
- You can adjust the height and width of the embedded frame.

After you have answered all of the questions, the embed code appears at the bottom of the screen. You might have to scroll down to see the embed code. Click the Copy link to copy the embed code to your Clipboard (see Figure 8.8).

Create a new web page or blog post, and then paste the embed code at the proper place.

The result is a very safe web page that uses your formulas and data without revealing any of the tables on the back worksheets (see Figure 8.9).

Figure 8.8
Copy the embed code.

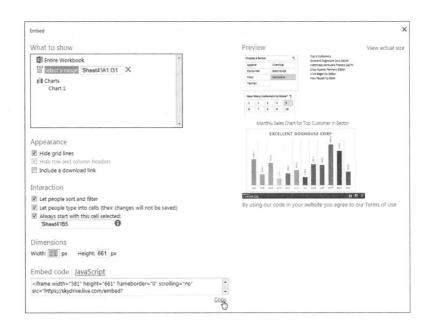

Figure 8.9
This web page was
created with Excel.

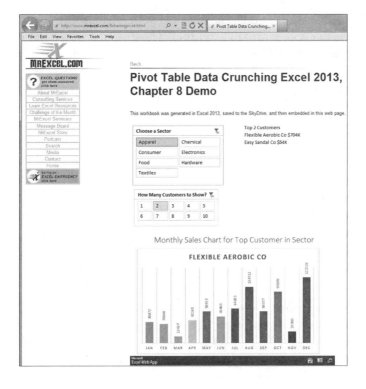

8

Sharing Pivot Tables with Other Versions of Office

The Excel team is investing heavily in pivot tables. Each new version offers new features. Unfortunately, this means a nightmare is waiting any time you try to share a pivot table with an earlier version. Here are some points to keep in mind:

- Anything created with the Data Model or PowerPivot in Excel 2013 does not open in Excel 2010, even if you have PowerPivot installed in Excel 2010.

- Timeline controls do not render in Excel 2010. An Excel shape appears where the timeline used to be.

- Percent of Parent Item, Rank, and Percent Running Total In calculations do not update in Excel 2007.

- Slicers do not appear in Excel 2007. You get the same shape as the timeline. Unfortunately, the pivot table is still filtered, even though no one can see the slicers. When they refresh the pivot table, the filters are removed and the totals change without any explanation.

- If you create a pivot table in Excel 2007 or Excel 2010 and then open it in Excel 2013, you should find no limitations. In addition, you can add Excel 2013 features to pivot tables created in earlier versions.

- If your Excel 2010 workbook contains a PowerPivot model, Excel 2013 asks if the model can be upgraded to Excel 2013. There will then be no way for the model to be opened in Excel 2010.

Working with and Analyzing OLAP Data

9

What Is OLAP?

Online Analytical Processing, or OLAP, is a category of data warehousing that enables you to mine and analyze vast amounts of data with ease and efficiency. Unlike other types of databases, OLAP databases are designed specifically for reporting and data mining. In fact, there are several key differences between your standard transactional databases, such as Access and SQL Server, and OLAP databases.

Records within a transactional database are routinely added, deleted, and updated. OLAP databases, on the other hand, contain only snapshots of data. The data in an OLAP database is typically archived data, stored solely for reporting purposes. Although new data may be appended on a regular basis, existing data is rarely edited or deleted.

Another difference between transactional databases and OLAP databases is structure. Transactional databases typically contain many tables; each table usually contains multiple relationships with other tables. Indeed, some transactional databases contain so many tables that it can be difficult to determine how each table relates to another. In an OLAP database, however, all the relationships between the various data points have been predefined and stored in *OLAP cubes*. These cubes already contain the relationships and hierarchies you need to easily navigate the data within. Consequently, you can build reports without the need to know how the data tables relate to one another.

The biggest difference between OLAP and transactional databases is the way the data is stored. The data in an OLAP cube is rarely stored in raw form. OLAP cubes typically store data in views that are already organized and aggregated. That is, grouping, sorting, and aggregations are predefined and ready to use. This makes querying and browsing for data far more efficient than in a transactional database, where you would have to group, aggregate, and sort records on the fly.

> **NOTE** An OLAP database is typically set up and maintained by the database administrator in your IT department. If your organization does not utilize OLAP databases, you might want to speak with your database administrator to discuss the possibility of some OLAP reporting solutions.

Connecting to an OLAP Cube

Before you can browse OLAP data, you must first establish a connection to an OLAP cube. Start on the Data tab and select From Other Sources to see the drop-down menu shown in Figure 9.1. Here, you select the From Analysis Services option.

Figure 9.1
Select the From Analysis Services option.

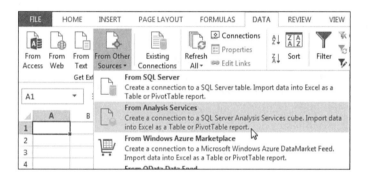

Selecting this option activates the Data Connection Wizard, shown in Figure 9.2. The idea here is that you configure your connection settings so Excel can establish a link to the server. Here are the steps to follow:

> **NOTE** The examples you see in this chapter have been created using the Analysis Services Tutorial cube that comes with SQL Server Analysis Services 2012. The actions you take to connect to and work with *your* OLAP database are the same as demonstrated here because the concepts are applicable to any OLAP cube you are using.

1. Provide Excel with some authentication information. Enter the name of your server as well as your username and password, as demonstrated in Figure 9.2. Then click Next.

Figure 9.2
Enter your authentication information and click Next.

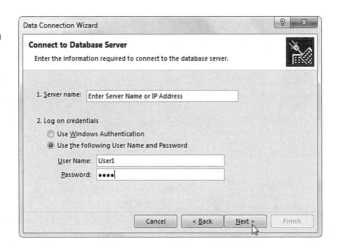

If you are typically authenticated via Windows Authentication, you simply select the Use Windows Authentication option.

2. Select the database with which you are working from the drop-down box. As Figure 9.3 illustrates, the Analysis Services Tutorial database is selected for this scenario. Selecting this database causes all the available OLAP cubes to be exposed in the list of objects below the drop-down menu. Choose the cube you want to analyze and then click Next.

Figure 9.3
Specify your database and then choose the OLAP cube you want to analyze.

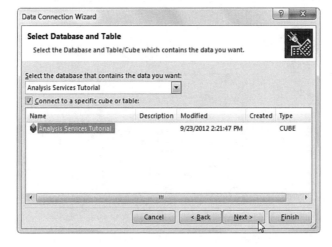

3. On the next screen, shown in Figure 9.4, enter some descriptive information about the connection you've just created.

Figure 9.4
Edit descriptive information for your connection.

> **NOTE**
> All the fields in the screen shown in Figure 9.4 are optional edits only. That is, you can bypass this screen without editing anything, and your connection will work fine.

4. Click the Finish button to finalize your connection settings. You immediately see the Import Data dialog, as shown in Figure 9.5. From here, you select PivotTable Report and then click the OK button to start building your pivot table.

Figure 9.5
When your connection is finalized, you can start building your pivot table.

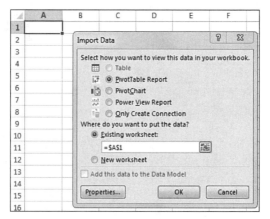

Understanding the Structure of an OLAP Cube

When your pivot table is created, you might notice that the PivotTable Fields list looks somewhat different from that of a standard pivot table. The reason is that the PivotTable Fields list for an OLAP pivot table is arranged to represent the structure of the OLAP cube you are connected to.

To effectively browse an OLAP cube, you need to understand the component parts of OLAP cubes and the way they interact with one another. Figure 9.6 illustrates the basic structure of a typical OLAP cube.

Figure 9.6
The basic structure of an OLAP cube.

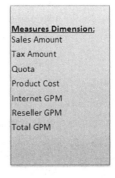

As you can see, the main components of an OLAP cube are dimensions, hierarchies, levels, members, and measures:

- **Dimensions**—Major classifications of data that contain the data items that are analyzed. Some common examples of dimensions are the Products dimension, Customer dimension, and Employee dimension. In Figure 9.6, the structure you see is that of the Products dimension.

- **Hierarchies**—Predefined aggregations of levels within a particular dimension. A hierarchy enables you to pivot and analyze multiple levels at one time without any previous knowledge of the relationships between the levels. In the example in Figure 9.6, the Products dimension has three levels that are aggregated into one hierarchy called Product Categories.

- **Levels**—Categories of data that are aggregated within a hierarchy. You can think of levels as data fields that can be queried and analyzed individually. In Figure 9.6, note that there are three levels: Category, Subcategory, and Product Name.

- **Members**—The individual data items within a dimension. Members are typically accessed via the OLAP structure of dimension, hierarchy, level, and member. In the example shown in Figure 9.6, the members you see belong to the Product Name level. The other levels have their own members and are not shown here.

- **Measures**—The actual data values within the OLAP cube. Measures are stored within their own dimension appropriately called the *Measures dimension*. The idea is that you can use any combination of dimension, hierarchy, level, and member to query the measures. This is called *slicing the measures*.

Now that you understand how the data in an OLAP cube is structured, take a look at the PivotTable Fields list again. The arrangement of the available fields starts to make sense. Figure 9.7 illustrates what the PivotTable Fields list for an OLAP pivot table might look like.

Figure 9.7
The PivotTable Fields list for an OLAP pivot table.

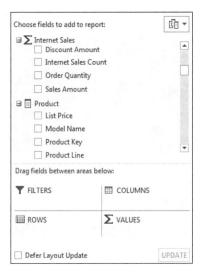

As you can see, the measures are listed first under the Sigma icon. These are the only items you can drop in the Values area of your pivot table. Next, you see dimensions represented next to the table icon. In this example, you see the Product dimension. Under the Product dimension, you see the Product Categories hierarchy that can be drilled into. Drilling into the Product Categories hierarchy enables you to see the individual levels.

The cool thing is that you are able to browse the entire cube structure by simply navigating through your PivotTable Fields list! From here, you can build your OLAP pivot table report just as you would build a standard pivot table.

Understanding the Limitations of OLAP Pivot Tables

When working with OLAP pivot tables, you must remember that the source data is maintained and controlled in the Analysis Services OLAP environment. This means that every aspect of the cube's behavior—from the dimensions and measures included in the cube, to the ability to drill into the details of a dimension—is controlled via Analysis Services. This reality translates into some limitations on the actions you can take with your OLAP pivot tables.

When your pivot table report is based on an OLAP data source...

■ You cannot place any field other than measures into the Values area of the pivot table.

■ You cannot change the function used to summarize a data field.

■ The Show Report Filter Pages command is disabled.

■ The Show Items with No Data option is disabled.

■ The Subtotal Hidden Page Items setting is disabled.

■ The Background Query option is not available.

■ Double-clicking in the Values field only returns the first 1,000 records of the pivot cache.

■ The Optimize Memory check box in the PivotTable Options dialog is disabled.

Creating Offline Cubes

With a standard pivot table, the source data is typically stored on your local drive. This way, you can work with and analyze your data while you're disconnected from the network. However, this is not the case with OLAP pivot tables. With an OLAP pivot table, the pivot cache is never brought to your local drive. This means that while you are disconnected from the network, your pivot table is out of commission. You can't even move a field while disconnected.

If you need to analyze your OLAP data while disconnected from your network, you need to create an offline cube. An *offline cube* is essentially a file that acts as a pivot cache, locally storing OLAP data so that you can browse that data while disconnected from the network.

To create an offline cube, start with an OLAP-based pivot table. Place your cursor anywhere inside the pivot table and click the OLAP Tools drop-down menu button on the PivotTable Tools Analyze tab. Here, you select Offline OLAP, as demonstrated in Figure 9.8.

Selecting this option activates the Offline OLAP Settings dialog (see Figure 9.9), where you click the Create Offline Data File button. The Create Cube File Wizard, shown in Figure 9.10, activates. Click Next to start the process.

Figure 9.8
Select the Offline OLAP option to start the creation of an offline cube.

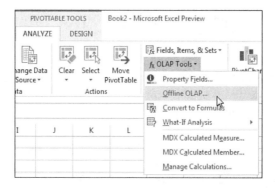

Figure 9.9
Start the Create Cube File Wizard.

As you can see in Figure 9.10, you first select the dimensions and levels you want included in your offline cube. This dialog tells Excel which data you want to import from the OLAP database. The idea is to select only the dimensions that you need available to you while disconnected from the server. The more dimensions you select, the more disk space your offline cube file takes up.

Figure 9.10
Select the dimensions and level you want included in your offline cube.

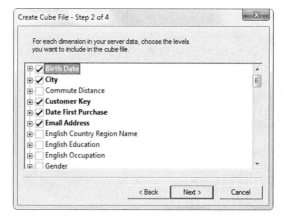

Clicking Next moves you to the next dialog, shown in Figure 9.11. Here, you are given the opportunity to filter out any members or data items you do not want included. For instance, the Extended Amount measure is not needed, so the check has been removed from its selection box. Deselecting this box ensures that this measure will not be imported and will not take up unnecessary disk space.

Figure 9.11
Deselect any members
you do not need to see
offline.

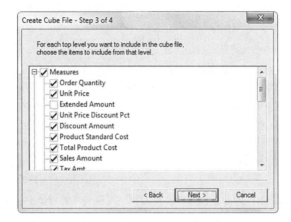

The final step is to specify a name and location for your cube file. In Figure 9.12, the cube file is named MyOfflineCube.cub, and it will be placed in a directory called Documents.

Figure 9.12
Specify a name and loca-
tion for your cube file.

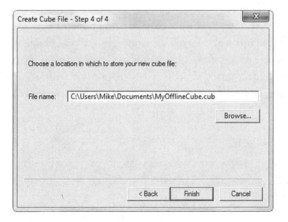

NOTE   The file extension for all offline cubes is .cub.

After a few moments of crunching, Excel outputs your offline cube file to your chosen directory. To test it, simply double-click the file to automatically generate an Excel workbook that is linked to the offline cube via a pivot table.

After your offline cube file has been created, you can distribute it to others and use it while disconnected from the network.

> **TIP**
> When you're connected to the network, you can open your offline cube file and refresh the pivot table within. This automatically refreshes the data in the cube file. The idea is that you can use the data within the cube file while you are disconnected from the network and can refresh the cube file while a data connection is available. Any attempt to refresh an offline cube while disconnected causes an error.

Breaking Out of the Pivot Table Mold with Cube Functions

Cube functions are Excel functions that can be used to access OLAP data outside a pivot table object. In pre-2010 versions of Excel, you could find cube functions only if you installed the Analysis Services add-in. In Excel 2010, cube functions were brought into the native Excel environment. To fully understand the benefit of cube functions, take a moment to walk through an example.

One of the easiest ways to start exploring cube functions is to allow Excel to convert your OLAP-based pivot table into cube formulas. Converting a pivot table to cube formulas is a delightfully easy way to create a few cube formulas without doing any of the work yourself. The idea is to tell Excel to replace all cells in the pivot table with a formula that connects back to the OLAP database. Figure 9.13 shows a pivot table connected to an OLAP database.

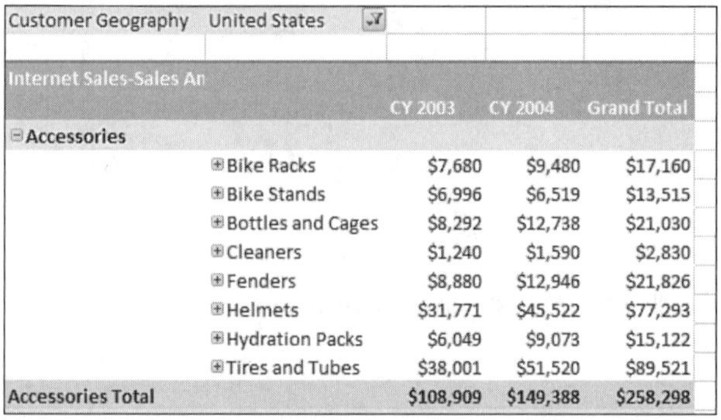

Figure 9.13
A normal OLAP pivot table.

Customer Geography	United States	☑			
Internet Sales-Sales An					
			CY 2003	CY 2004	Grand Total
⊟ Accessories					
	⊞ Bike Racks		$7,680	$9,480	$17,160
	⊞ Bike Stands		$6,996	$6,519	$13,515
	⊞ Bottles and Cages		$8,292	$12,738	$21,030
	⊞ Cleaners		$1,240	$1,590	$2,830
	⊞ Fenders		$8,880	$12,946	$21,826
	⊞ Helmets		$31,771	$45,522	$77,293
	⊞ Hydration Packs		$6,049	$9,073	$15,122
	⊞ Tires and Tubes		$38,001	$51,520	$89,521
Accessories Total			$108,909	$149,388	$258,298

With just a few clicks, you can convert any OLAP pivot table into a series of cube formulas. Place the cursor anywhere inside the pivot table and click the OLAP Tools drop-down menu button on the PivotTable Tools Options tab. Select Convert to Formulas, as demonstrated in Figure 9.14.

Figure 9.14
Select the Convert to Formulas option to convert your pivot table to cube formulas.

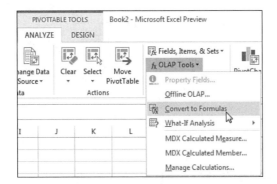

If your pivot table contains a report filter field, the dialog shown in Figure 9.15 activates. This dialog gives you the option of converting your filter drop-down selectors to cube formulas. If you select this option, the drop-down selectors are removed, leaving a static formula. If you need to have your filter drop-down selectors intact so that you may continue to interactively change the selections in the filter field, leave the Convert Report Filters option unchecked.

Figure 9.15
Excel gives you the option of converting your report filter fields.

> **NOTE** If you are working with a pivot table in compatibility mode, Excel automatically converts the filter fields to formulas.

After a second or two, the cells that used to house a pivot table are now homes for cube formulas. Note that, as in Figure 9.16, any styles you have applied are removed.

So why is this capability useful? Well, now that the values you see are no longer part of a pivot table object, you can insert rows and columns, you can add your own calculations, you can combine the data with other external data, and you can modify the report in all sorts of ways by simply moving the formulas around.

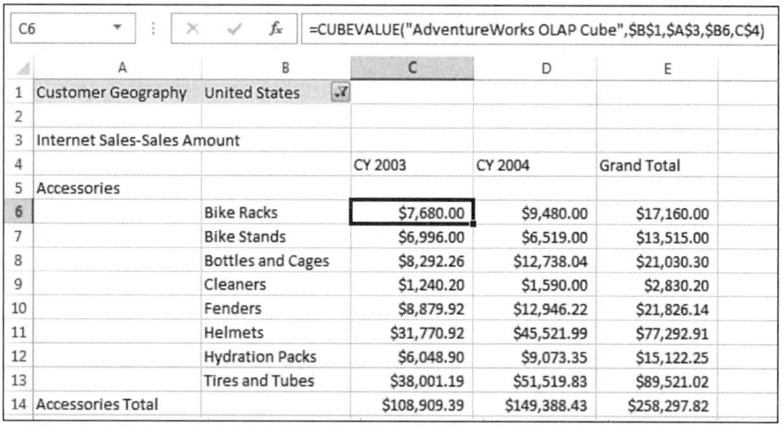

Figure 9.16
Note that in the formula bar, these cells are now a series of cube formulas!

| | C6 | ▼ | ⋮ | ✕ | ✓ | *fx* | =CUBEVALUE("AdventureWorks OLAP Cube",$B$1,$A$3,$B6,C$4) |

▲	A	B	C	D	E	
1	Customer Geography	United States	🔽			
2						
3	Internet Sales-Sales Amount					
4			CY 2003	CY 2004	Grand Total	
5	Accessories					
6		Bike Racks	$7,680.00	$9,480.00	$17,160.00	
7		Bike Stands	$6,996.00	$6,519.00	$13,515.00	
8		Bottles and Cages	$8,292.26	$12,738.04	$21,030.30	
9		Cleaners	$1,240.20	$1,590.00	$2,830.20	
10		Fenders	$8,879.92	$12,946.22	$21,826.14	
11		Helmets	$31,770.92	$45,521.99	$77,292.91	
12		Hydration Packs	$6,048.90	$9,073.35	$15,122.25	
13		Tires and Tubes	$38,001.19	$51,519.83	$89,521.02	
14	Accessories Total		$108,909.39	$149,388.43	$258,297.82	

Adding Calculations to Your OLAP Pivot Tables

In previous versions of Excel, OLAP pivot tables were limited in that you could not build your own calculations within OLAP pivot tables. This means you could not add that extra layer of analysis like you could with the Calculated Fields and Calculated Items functionality found in standard pivot tables.

> **NOTE**
> Calculated Fields and Calculated Items are covered in Chapter 5, "Performing Calculations Within Your Pivot Tables." You might find it helpful to read that chapter first in order to build the foundation for this section.

Excel 2013 changes that with the introduction of the new OLAP tools—Calculated Measures and Calculated Members. With these two new tools, you are no longer limited to just using the measures and members provided through the OLAP cube by the Database Administrator. You can add your own analysis by building your own calculations.

In this section, you explore how to build your own calculated measures and calculated members.

A Word About MDX

When you are using a pivot table with an OLAP cube, you are sending the OLAP database MDX (Multidimensional Expressions) queries. MDX is an expression language that is used to return data from multidimensional data sources (that is, OLAP cubes).

As your OLAP pivot table is refreshed or changed, subsequent MDX queries are passed to the OLAP database. The results of the query are sent back to Excel and displayed through the pivot table. This is how you are able to work with OLAP data without a local copy of a pivot cache.

When building calculated measures and calculated members, you need to utilize MDX syntax. This is the only way the pivot table can communicate your calculation to the back-end OLAP database.

The examples in this book use basic MDX constructs in order to demonstrate the new functionality found in Excel 2013. If you have the need to create complex calculated measures and calculated members, you will want to invest some time learning more about MDX.

That being said, the topic of MDX is robust and out of the scope for this book. If, after reading this section, you have a desire to learn more about MDX, consider picking up *MDX Solutions* (Wiley, ISBN: 0471748080), an excellent guide to MDX that is both easy to understand and comprehensive.

Creating Calculated Measures

A calculated measure is essentially the OLAP version of a calculated field. The idea behind a calculated measure is to create a new data field based on some mathematical operation that uses the existing OLAP fields.

In the example shown in Figure 9.17, you have an OLAP pivot table containing products along with their respective quantities and revenues. You want to add a new measure that calculates average sales price per unit.

Figure 9.17
You want to add a calculation to this OLAP pivot table showing average sales price per unit.

	A	B	C
1	Row Labels	Order Quantity	Sales Amount
2	All-Purpose Bike Stand	249	$39,591
3	Bike Wash	908	$7,219
4	Classic Vest	562	$35,687
5	Cycling Cap	2,190	$19,688
6	Fender Set - Mountain	2,121	$46,620
7	Half-Finger Gloves	1,430	$35,021
8	Hitch Rack - 4-Bike	328	$39,360
9	HL Mountain Tire	1,396	$48,860
10	HL Road Tire	858	$27,971
11	Hydration Pack	733	$40,308
12	LL Mountain Tire	862	$21,541
13	LL Road Tire	1,044	$22,436
14	Long-Sleeve Logo Jersey	1,736	$86,783
15	ML Mountain Tire	1,161	$34,818

Start by placing your cursor anywhere in the pivot table and then selecting the PivotTable Tools Analyze tab. There, you choose the MDX Calculated Measure command, as demonstrated in Figure 9.18.

This activates the New Calculated Measure dialog shown in Figure 9.19.

Figure 9.18
Choose the MDX
Calculated Measure
command.

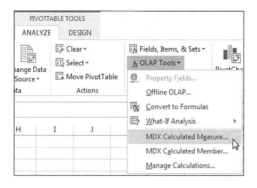

Figure 9.19
Use the New Calculated
Measure dialog to build
your calculated measure.

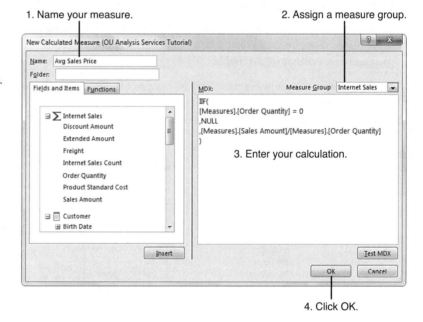

Here you take the following actions:

1. Give your calculated measure a name by entering it in the Name input box.

2. Choose a measure group to place your calculated measure. If you don't choose one, Excel automatically places your measure in the first available measure group.

3. Enter the MDX syntax for your calculation in the MDX input box. To save a little time, you can use the list on the left to choose the existing measures you need for your calculation. Simply double-click the measures needed, and Excel pops them into the MDX input box. In this example, the calculation for the average sales price is
    ```
    IIF([Measures].[Order Quantity] = 0,NULL,[Measures].[Sales Amount]/[Measures].
    [Order Quantity]).
    ```

4. Click OK.

> **NOTE**
>
> In the New Calculated Measure dialog, shown in Figure 9.19, notice a button called Test MDX. You can click this to ensure the MDX you entered is well formed. Excel lets you know via a message box if your syntax contains some error.

After you have built your calculated measure, you can go to the PivotTable Fields list and select your newly created calculation (see Figure 9.20).

Figure 9.20
Add your newly created calculation to your pivot table via the PivotTable Fields list.

As you can see in Figure 9.21, your calculated measure adds a meaningful layer of analysis to the pivot table.

Figure 9.21
Your pivot table now contains your calculated measure!

	A	B	C	D
1	Row Labels	Order Quantity	Sales Amount	Avg Sales Price
2	All-Purpose Bike Stand	249	$39,591	$159.00
3	Bike Wash	908	$7,219	$7.95
4	Classic Vest	562	$35,687	$63.50
5	Cycling Cap	2,190	$19,688	$8.99
6	Fender Set - Mountain	2,121	$46,620	$21.98
7	Half-Finger Gloves	1,430	$35,021	$24.49
8	Hitch Rack - 4-Bike	328	$39,360	$120.00
9	HL Mountain Tire	1,396	$48,860	$35.00
10	HL Road Tire	858	$27,971	$32.60
11	Hydration Pack	733	$40,308	$54.99
12	LL Mountain Tire	862	$21,541	$24.99
13	LL Road Tire	1,044	$22,436	$21.49
14	Long-Sleeve Logo Jersey	1,736	$86,783	$49.99
15	ML Mountain Tire	1,161	$34,818	$29.99

> NOTE
>
> It's important to note that when you create a calculated measure, it exists in your workbook only. In other words, you are not building your calculation directly in the OLAP cube on the server. This means no one else connected to the OLAP cube will be able to see your calculations unless you share or distribute your workbook.

Creating Calculated Members

A calculated member is essentially the OLAP version of a calculated item. The idea behind a calculated member is to create a new data item based on some mathematical operation that uses the existing OLAP members.

In the example shown in Figure 9.22, you have an OLAP pivot table containing sales information for each quarter in the year. Let's say you want to aggregate quarters 1 and 2 into a new data item called First Half of Year. You also want to aggregate quarters 3 and 4 into a new data item called Second Half of Year.

Figure 9.22
You want to add new calculated members to aggregate the four quarters into First Half of Year and Second Half of Year.

	A	B	C	D
1	Row Labels ▾	Order Quantity	Sales Amount	Avg Sales Price
2	1	15,425	$7,586,624	$491.84
3	2	17,465	$8,893,345	$509.21
4	3	13,011	$6,009,120	$461.85
5	4	14,497	$6,869,588	$473.86
6	Grand Total	60,398	$29,358,677	$486.09

Start by placing your cursor anywhere in the pivot table and then selecting the PivotTable Tools Analyze tab. There, you choose the MDX Calculated Member command, as demonstrated in Figure 9.23.

Figure 9.23
Choose the MDX Calculated Member command.

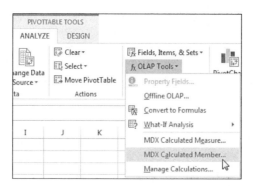

The New Calculated Member dialog opens (see Figure 9.24).

1. Name your member.   2. Choose a parent hierarchy.

Figure 9.24
Use the New Calculated
Member dialog to build
your calculated member.

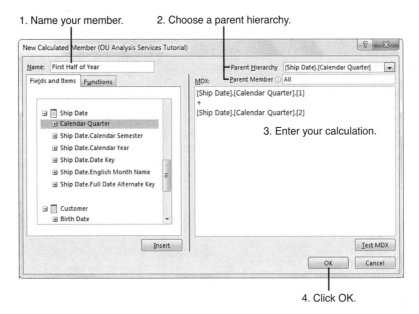

3. Enter your calculation.

9

4. Click OK.

Here you take the following actions:

1. Give your calculated member a name by entering it in the Name input box.

2. Choose the parent hierarchy for which you are creating new members. Be sure to leave the Parent Member setting on All. This ensures that Excel takes into account all members in the parent hierarchy when evaluating your calculation.

3. Enter the MDX syntax for your calculation in the MDX input box. To save a little time, you can use the list on the left to choose the existing members you need for your calculation. Simply double-click the member needed, and Excel pops them into the MDX input box. In the example in Figure 9.24, you are adding quarter 1 and quarter 2: `[Ship Date].[Calendar Quarter].[1] + [Ship Date].[Calendar Quarter].[2]`.

4. Click OK.

As soon as you click OK, Excel immediately shows your newly created calculated member in the pivot table. As you can see in Figure 9.25, your calculated member is included with the other original members of the pivot field.

Figure 9.25
Excel immediately adds
your calculated member
to your pivot field.

	A	B	C	D
1	Row Labels ▾	Order Quantity	Sales Amount	Avg Sales Price
2	1	15,425	$7,586,624	$491.84
3	2	17,465	$8,893,345	$509.21
4	3	13,011	$6,009,120	$461.85
5	4	14,497	$6,869,588	$473.86
6	First Half of Year	32,890	$16,479,969	$501.06
7	Grand Total	60,398	$29,358,677	$486.09

In Figure 9.26, you repeat the process to calculate the Second Half of Year member.

Figure 9.26
Repeat the process for any additional calculated members.

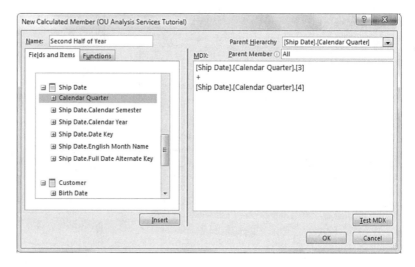

Notice in Figure 9.27 that Excel makes no attempt to remove any of the original members. In this case, you see that quarters 1 through 4 are still in the pivot table. This might be fine for your situation, but in most scenarios, you will likely hide these members to avoid confusion.

Figure 9.27
Excel shows your final calculated members along with the original members. It is a best practice to remove the original members to avoid confusion.

	A	B	C	D
1	Row Labels	Order Quantity	Sales Amount	Avg Sales Price
2	1	15,425	$7,586,624	$491.84
3	2	17,465	$8,893,345	$509.21
4	3	13,011	$6,009,120	$461.85
5	4	14,497	$6,869,588	$473.86
6	First Half of Year	32,890	$16,479,969	$501.06
7	Second Half of Year	27,508	$12,878,709	$468.18
8	**Grand Total**	**60,398**	**$29,358,677**	**$486.09**

> **NOTE**
> Remember that your calculated member exists in your workbook only. No one else connected to the OLAP cube is able to see your calculations unless you share or distribute your workbook.
>
> It is also important to note that if the parent hierarchy or parent member is changed in the OLAP cube, your calculated member ceases to function. You must re-create the calculated member.

Managing Your OLAP Calculations

Excel provides an interface to manage the calculated measures and calculated members in your OLAP pivot table.

Simply place your cursor anywhere in the pivot table and then select the PivotTable Tools Analyze tab. Choose the MDX Calculated Member command, as demonstrated in Figure 9.28.

Figure 9.28
Activate the Manage Calculations dialog.

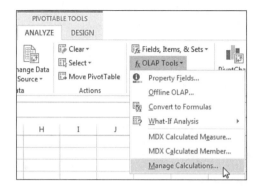

On the Manage Calculations dialog in Figure 9.29, you see the following three commands:

- **New**—Used to create a new calculated measure or calculated member
- **Edit**—Used to edit the selected calculation
- **Delete**—Used to permanently delete the selected calculation

Figure 9.29
The Manage Calculations dialog enables you to create a new calculation, edit an existing calculation, or delete an existing calculation.

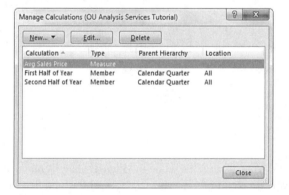

Performing What-If Analysis with OLAP Data

One final piece of functionality Excel 2013 offers is the ability to perform What-If analysis with the data in OLAP pivot tables. With this new functionality, you have the ability to actually edit the values in the pivot table and recalculate your measures and members based on your changes. You even have the ability to publish your changes back to the OLAP cube.

To make use of the What-If analysis functionality, create an OLAP pivot table and then go to the PivotTable Tools Analyze tab. Once there, select What-If Analysis, Enable What-If Analysis, as demonstrated in Figure 9.30.

Figure 9.30
Enabling What-If analysis allows you to change the values in your pivot table.

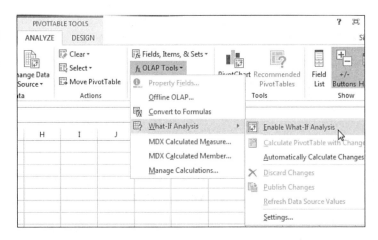

At this point, you can edit the values in your pivot table! After you have made your changes, you can right-click any of the changed values and choose Calculate PivotTable with Change (see Figure 9.31). This forces Excel to reevaluate all the calculations in the pivot table based on your edits—including your calculated members and measures.

Figure 9.31
Choose Calculate PivotTable with Change to reevaluate all your calculations.

	A	B	C	D	E
1	Row Labels	Order Quantity	Sales Amount	Avg Sales Price	
2	All-Purpose Bike Stand	249	$39,591	$159.00	
3	Bike Wash	908	$7,219	$7.95	
4	Classic Vest	562	$35,687	$63.50	
5	Cycling Cap	2,190	$19,688	$8.99	
6	Fender Set - Mountain	4,432	$46,620	$21.98	
7	Half-Finger Gloves	1,430			
8	Hitch Rack - 4-Bike	328			
9	HL Mountain Tire	1,396			
10	HL Road Tire	858			
11	Hydration Pack	733			
12	LL Mountain Tire	862			

Value has been changed
Data source value: 2,121 (click to refresh)
Calculate PivotTable with Change
Discard Change
What-If Analysis Settings

The edits you make to your pivot table while in What-If analysis mode are, by default, local edits only. If you are committed to your changes, and would like to actually make the changes on the OLAP server, you can tell Excel to publish your changes.

In the PivotTable Tools Analyze tab, select What-If Analysis, Publish Changes (see Figure 9.32). This triggers a "write-back" to the OLAP server, meaning the edited values are sent to the source OLAP cube.

> **NOTE**
> You need the adequate server permissions to publish changes to the OLAP server. Your database administrator can guide you through the process of getting write access to your OLAP database.

Figure 9.32
Excel 2013 enables you to publish your changes to the source OLAP cube!

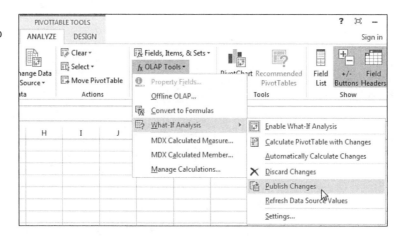

9

Next Steps

In Chapter 10, "Mashing Up Data with PowerPivot," you find out how to use PowerPivot to create powerful reporting models that are able to process and analyze millions of rows of data in a single pivot table.

Mashing Up Data with PowerPivot

PowerPivot debuted in Excel 2010 as a free add-in with six jaw-dropping features. It was an amazing product, created outside of the Excel team. For Excel 2013, the plan was to build PowerPivot functionality directly into the core Excel. The Excel team made great strides in folding the PowerPivot data model engine into Excel 2013. You've already seen the Data Model in Chapter 7, "Analyzing Disparate Data Sources with PivotTables." The Data Model is really the PowerPivot engine.

The Data Model gives you some of the features, but many more features require the PowerPivot add-in, which now ships with Office 2013 Professional Plus, or you can get it with a subscription to Office 365 Business.

If you only have Office 2013 Home and Student or Office 2013 Standard, you can still use the PowerPivot engine, but you are locked out of the PowerPivot window and some other features.

Understanding the Benefits and Drawbacks of PowerPivot and the Data Model

Let's start with the big three features and analyze what is in each version of Excel.

Merge Data from Multiple Tables Without Using VLOOKUP

This feature is available to everyone with Excel 2013. If you have the Standard edition, you won't see the PowerPivot branding (it is instead called the Data Model). You'll learn how to build a multitable analysis later in this chapter in the "Joining Multiple Tables Using the Data Model in Regular Excel 2013" section.

If you have the PowerPivot add-in, building relationships is easier using a graphic view.

Import 100 Million Rows into Your Workbook

The PowerPivot grid holds unlimited rows. I've personally seen 100 million rows. You are only limited by the 2GB maximum file size for a workbook and available memory. Plus, thanks to the VertiPaq compression algorithm, a 50MB text file frequently fits into 4MB after it is in the PowerPivot grid. For a ten-column data set, that means about 950 million rows of data is possible in one workbook. This feature is available to all versions of Excel 2013.

With Office Standard, you can import those records and produce pivot tables; however, you aren't allowed to browse the records. You need the PowerPivot add-in to browse. This is an intense psychological hurdle. I want to be able to see my data before reporting on it. It would be like putting a Maserati engine in a jalopy, but then welding the hood shut so you can't actually look at the engine. Yes, you can still drive the car really fast, but I simply have this intense need to be able to browse my data. It makes me feel better.

Create Better Calculations Using the DAX Formula Language

This feature is not available in standard editions of Excel 2013. You need the add-in to add new calculations to the PowerPivot grid and to add new calculated columns to your pivot table.

The DAX language provides a lot of flexibility. Although it's the hardest feature of PowerPivot to learn, it offers the biggest paybacks.

Other Benefits of the PowerPivot Data Model in All Editions of Excel

You get a number of other side-effect benefits of running your data through the Data Model:

- Count Distinct becomes a calculation option. This was previously hard to do. Excel tricksters would add a column to the original data that divided the COUNTIF of a field into 1. If a customer showed up five times, the calculation would evaluate to (1/5) or 0.2. They would then add up the five records with 0.2 and to get one unique customer. If you've ever gone through this painful process, you will be thrilled to know Count Distinct is two clicks away. Ditto for those of you who wanted a distinct count but could never get it to work.

- You can include filtered items in grand totals. Create a pivot table showing the top ten customers. The grand total has always been just the ten customers you see. Now, you can make that total include all of the small customers who were filtered out of the report. This feature has always been in the Subtotals drop-down on the left side of the Design tab in the ribbon, but it was perpetually grayed out. Run your data through the model, and it becomes available.

■ Named sets were introduced in Excel 2010, but only for people with OLAP data. Named sets let you create pivot tables with last year's actuals and next year's budget. By taking your data through the PowerPivot engine, you cause named sets to become available.

■ If you ever use the GETPIVOTDATA function to extract values from pivot tables, you can save a step and convert your pivot table to Cube formulas. Cut and paste these into any format desired.

Benefits of the Full PowerPivot Add-In with Excel Pro Plus

If you have Excel Pro Plus and the full PowerPivot add-in, you also have access to these features:

■ The PowerPivot grid, where you can actually browse through the 100 million rows. You can sort, filter, and add calculations in the grid.

■ A graphical design view where you can build relationships by dragging between fields.

■ The ability to change the properties of fields in the model. You can choose which fields should appear in the PivotTable Fields List and which should not.

■ You can specify that FieldA (month name) should be sorted by FieldB (month number).

■ You can define a default number format to use when the field appears in a pivot table. How many times have you wished for this in a regular pivot table?

■ You can define a field as representing a product, geography, or link to an image.

■ You get access to a weak implementation of key performance indicators. It would be simpler to use icon sets in your resultant pivot table.

■ Access to Power View dashboards and GeoFlow. Both are discussed in Chapter 11, "Dashboarding with Power View."

Understanding the Limitations of the Data Model

By using the Data Model, you've just taken your regular Excel data and built it into an OLAP model. There are annoying limitations and some benefits available to pivot tables built on OLAP models. The Excel team tried to mitigate some of the limitations for Excel 2013, but many are still present.

Here are some of the limitations:

■ **Less calculations**—Although you now have access to Distinct Count, you lose access to other calculation options such as Product.

■ **No grouping**—PowerPivot cannot use the Group feature of pivot tables. You can no longer roll daily dates up to months, quarters, and years. You can work around this by adding calculations to the original data set, but it is not as simple as using the Group feature.

10

- **Strange drilldown**—Usually, you can double-click a cell in a pivot table and see the rows that make up that cell. This now works with the Data Model, but only for the first 1,000 rows.

- **No calculated fields or calculated items**—The Data Model does not support calculated fields or calculated items. If you have PowerPivot, the DAX measures run circles around these old calculations. However, if you don't have PowerPivot, you are going to be frustrated using the Data Model.

- **Excel 2013 only**—Workbooks that use the Data Model will not work in earlier versions of Excel.

- **Bad sorting**—You've taken it for granted, but regular pivot tables know that January comes before February. That's because Excel has a custom list with the months and weekday names. Pivot tables based on the Data Model don't automatically sort using custom lists. You can fix this, but it takes eight clicks per field per pivot table.

Joining Multiple Tables Using the Data Model in Regular Excel 2013

Microsoft faced a marketing dilemma. They had built the best features of PowerPivot right into Excel 2013, yet they are trying to get customers to spend extra money for Office Pro Plus to get PowerPivot, Power View, and Inquire.

Although the name PowerPivot sounds really awesome and powerful, they had to come up with a name that describes pivot tables built in regular Excel 2013 that use the PowerPivot engine. When you see the capitalized words *Data Model* in Excel 2013, that is Microsoft's way of saying you are using PowerPivot without calling it PowerPivot. Figure 10.1 shows the Create PivotTable dialog. A new check box for Add This Data to the Data Model really means that you will be using the non-branded version of the PowerPivot engine.

Figure 10.1
When Excel 2013 refers to the Data Model, you are using the PowerPivot engine.

Preparing Data for Use in the Data Model

When you are planning on using the Data Model to join multiple tables, you should always convert your Excel ranges to tables before you begin. You theoretically do not have to convert the ranges to tables, but it will be far easier if you convert the ranges to tables and give the tables a name. If you don't convert the ranges to tables first, Excel secretly does it in the background and gives your tables meaningless names such as Range.

Figure 10.2 shows two ranges in Excel. Columns A:H contain a transactional data set. Columns J:K contain a customer lookup table to add an industry sector for each customer. You would like to create a pivot table showing revenue by sector.

Figure 10.2

You want to join these two tables together in a single pivot table.

	A	B	C	D	E	F	G	H	I	J	K
1	Region	Product	Date	Customer	Quantity	Revenue	COGS	Profit		Customer	Sector
2	East	XYZ	1/1/2015	Functiona	954	22810	10213	12597		Agile Calc	Electronics
3	Central	DEF	1/2/2015	Vivid Edge	124	2257	998	1259		Cool Bottl	Consumer
4	East	XYZ	1/4/2015	Trendy Nc	425	9152	4083	5069		Crisp Ope	Hardware
5	East	DEF	1/4/2015	Powerful	773	18552	7883	10669		Distinctivi	Electronics
6	East	ABC	1/7/2015	Improved	401	8456	3389	5067		Easy Sand	Apparel
7	East	DEF	1/7/2015	Tremendc	1035	21730	9839	11891		Excellent	Hardware
8	Central	ABC	1/9/2015	Improved	750	16416	6768	9648		Exclusive	Electronics
9	Central	XYZ	1/10/2015	Wonderfu	901	21438	9209	12229		Fine Shing	Hardware
10	Central	ABC	1/12/2015	Matchless	342	6267	2541	3726		Flexible A	Apparel
11	East	XYZ	1/14/2015	Cool Bottl	91	2401	1031	1370		Functiona	Consumer
12	East	ABC	1/15/2015	Vivid Edge	547	9345	4239	5106		Guarantee	Chemical
13	East	ABC	1/16/2015	Excellent	558	11628	5093	6535		Improved	Food
14	West	DEF	1/19/2015	Vivid Edge	100	2042	983	1059		Inventive	Hardware
15	West	ABC	1/21/2015	Powerful	250	3552	1696	1856		Magnifice	Hardware

Excel gurus are thinking, "Why don't you do a VLOOKUP to join the tables?" PowerPivot lets you avoid the VLOOKUP. In this case, the tables are small and a VLOOKUP would calculate quickly. However, imagine that you have a million records in the transactional table and ten columns in the lookup table. The VLOOKUP solution quickly becomes unwieldy. The PowerPivot engine available in the Data Model can join the tables without the overhead of VLOOKUP.

Convert the first data set to a table by following these steps:

1. Select any one cell in the first data set.

2. Press Ctrl+T or select Home, Format as Table and then select a format.

3. The Create Table dialog appears. Provided you have no blank rows, the address will be correct. Provided you have a heading above each column and three or more columns, the dialog will pre-select My Table Has Headers. Make sure to check the box if it is not already checked. Click OK to convert the range to a table. You will immediately notice the AutoFilter drop-downs in each heading and that a formatting style has been applied to the first range. This is not the important part. A new Table Tools Design tab is available in the ribbon. A Table Name field in the left part of the ribbon shows a table name such as Table1 (see Figure 10.3).

Figure 10.3
Excel uses a default table name.

Table Name

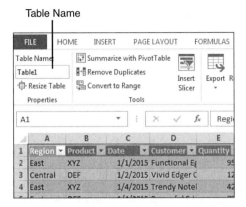

4. Click in the Table Name field and give the table a meaningful name. Database experts would call this the Fact table, but feel free to use Data, Sales, InvoiceRegister, or anything that describes the data. Sales is the table name for this example.

Now convert the second range to a table:

1. Select cell J1.

2. Press Ctrl+T. Click OK.

3. Type a table name such as **Sectors** in the Table Name field in the ribbon.

You now have two tables defined in this workbook. You are ready to begin building the pivot table.

Adding the First Table to the Data Model

Choose one cell in the first data set and select Insert, PivotTable from the ribbon. You can't use the Recommended Pivot Tables or the Analysis Lens to build a Data Model pivot table.

In the Create PivotTable dialog, the table name will appear. Choose the check box for Add This Data to the Data Model, as shown previously in Figure 10.1. Remember that "Data Model" is the nonbranded, boring name for PowerPivot. Click OK. Creating a Data Model pivot table takes several extra seconds as Excel converts and loads your data into the model.

You will get a new blank workbook with a PivotTable icon in A3:C20, just like with a regular pivot table. The PivotTable Fields task pane displays, but this is a slightly different version. Note the addition of the line with choices for Active or All (see Figure 10.4).

Expand the Sales table and choose Revenue. You see a small pivot table with the total revenue amount.

Figure 10.4
The choices for Active or
All indicate that you have
a pivot table using the
PowerPivot engine.

Adding the Second Table and Defining a Relationship

Look at the PivotTable Fields task pane. In the second line of the pane, you have a choice for Active or All. Choose All, and you see a list of all the defined tables in the workbook. At this moment, although the Fields List is showing two tables, only the Sales field is actually loaded in to the model. Click the plus sign next to the Sector table.

Drag the Sector field from the top of the PivotTable Fields List to the Columns area in the bottom of the PivotTable Fields List.

You will notice three things:

■ The bottom of the PivotTable Fields List is now showing fields from two different tables.

■ The pivot table is showing sectors, but the numbers are identical and clearly wrong in each column (see Figure 10.5).

Figure 10.5
The column labels *are*
from the second table,
but the numbers are
wrong.

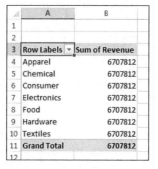

Row Labels	Sum of Revenue
Apparel	6707812
Chemical	6707812
Consumer	6707812
Electronics	6707812
Food	6707812
Hardware	6707812
Textiles	6707812
Grand Total	**6707812**

■ A yellow warning appears at the top of the PivotTable Fields List, indicating that relationships between tables may be needed and offering a Create button (see Figure 10.6).

Figure 10.6
Excel warns that you need to define a relationship between the two tables.

Click the Create button in the top of the PivotTable Fields List. Excel displays the Create Relationship dialog. Define the fields that are related in each table. Choose Sales as the first table and Customer as the column. Choose Sectors as the second table and Customer as the Related column (see Figure 10.7).

Figure 10.7
It is easy to define a relationship.

Create Relationship
Pick the tables and columns you want to use for this relationship

Table:	Column (Foreign):
Sales	Customer
Related Table:	Related Column (Primary):
Sector	Customer

Creating relationships between tables is necessary to show related data from different tables on the same report.

| Manage Relationships... | OK |

After defining the relationship, you have successfully completed the Data Model. The pivot table updates with correct numbers, as shown in Figure 10.8.

In the PivotTable Fields List, choose Active from the second line of the task pane. You will now see both tables and fields from both tables in the PivotTable Fields List. You can rearrange the fields just as in a regular pivot table.

Figure 10.8
Without doing a
VLOOKUP, you've suc-
cessfully joined data from
two tables in this report.

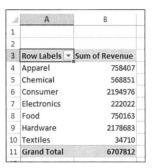

Row Labels	Sum of Revenue
Apparel	758407
Chemical	568851
Consumer	2194976
Electronics	222022
Food	750163
Hardware	2178683
Textiles	34710
Grand Total	6707812

Tell Me Again—Why Is This Better Than Doing a VLOOKUP?

If you don't have the full PowerPivot add-in, you may not be convinced that all of this hassle was worth it. You now have the ability to do some cool tricks that you could never do in a regular PivotCache pivot table. Let's look at some examples.

CASE STUDY: SHOWING TOP CUSTOMER, BUT TOTAL REVENUE

The Top 10 filter in regular pivot tables lets you show the top *N* customers, but you cannot get a true total of all records. Now that your data is in the Data Model, you can do this easily.

Starting with the pivot table that shows Sector and Revenue as in Figure 10.8, perform these steps:

1. Choose Customer from the Sales table in the PivotTable Fields List. Customer becomes the inner row field.

2. Open the Row Labels drop-down in cell A3. Open the Select Field drop-down and choose Customer.

3. Choose Value Filters and then Top 10.

4. In the Top 10 dialog, ask for the Top 1 Items by Sum of Revenue. The pivot table now shows one customer per sector. As shown in Figure 10.9, the grand total is only $3.6 million instead of the $6.7 million shown previously in Figure 10.8.

5. On the Design tab, open the Subtotals drop-down. Choose Include Filtered Items in Totals (see Figure 10.10). Each total is now marked with an asterisk and the totals include all customers, not just the customers shown.

Figure 10.9
Show Top 1 Customer per Sector. The totals are not useful.

Figure 10.10
You can see detail of the top customer, but the total revenue for all customers.

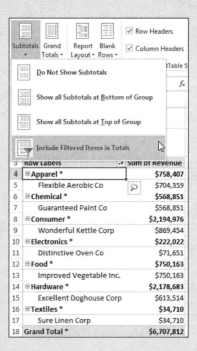

The report in Figure 10.10 is the type of report that my managers would have liked to have seen. It is not hundreds of customers, but it lets them intelligently talk about who the leading customer in each sector is. In fact, my manager just called and asked for the change shown in Figure 10.11. Add Revenue a second time to the report. Choose the second Revenue heading. Choose Field Settings. Change the calculation to Percent of Parent Row Total. You now have a report showing that Wonderful Kettle is 39.61% of the Consumer sector and that the Consumer sector is 32.72% of the total.

Figure 10.11

This will become the new favorite report of my manager for the next 3 days.

	A	B	C
	Top Customer Per Sector		
1			
2			
3	Row Labels	Sum of Revenue	% of Parent
4	⊟Apparel *	$758,407	11.31%
5	Flexible Aerobic Co	$704,359	92.87%
6	⊟Chemical *	$568,851	8.48%
7	Guaranteed Paint Co	$568,851	100.00%
8	⊟Consumer *	$2,194,976	32.72%
9	Wonderful Kettle Corp	$869,454	39.61%
10	⊟Electronics *	$222,022	3.31%
11	Distinctive Oven Co	$71,651	32.27%
12	⊟Food *	$750,163	11.18%
13	Improved Vegetable Inc.	$750,163	100.00%
14	⊟Hardware *	$2,178,683	32.48%
15	Excellent Doghouse Corp	$613,514	28.16%
16	⊟Textiles *	$34,710	0.52%
17	Sure Linen Corp	$34,710	100.00%
18	Grand Total *	$6,707,812	100.00%

Using QuickExplore

When you create your pivot table from the Data Model, you might notice a new icon that appears when you select a cell in the pivot table. This is the QuickExplore icon. It is new in Excel 2013 and only appears when the pivot table is based on a Data Model.

QuickExplore is designed to give you ideas of how to further modify the pivot table. Click the icon, and a box appears with suggestions (see Figure 10.12).

Figure 10.12

This icon only appears when the pivot table is built using the Data Model.

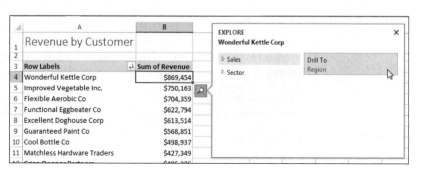

In this particular case, the QuickExplore suggestions aren't particularly useful. Figure 10.13 shows the result of drilling down by region.

Figure 10.13
This table is not that useful, but in other cases, QuickExplore might come up with something better.

	A	B
1	Customer	Wonderful Kettle Corp
2		
3	Row Labels	Sum of Revenue
4	Central	$327,958
5	East	$313,454
6	West	$228,042
7	Grand Total *	$869,454

Creating a New Pivot Table from an Existing Data Model

As you go from example to example in this book, it is easy to delete the pivot table sheet and start over with a fresh pivot table. It is slightly more complicated to start over after you already have data in the Data Model. Follow these steps:

1. In the Excel window, choose Insert, PivotTable.

2. In the Create Pivot Table dialog, choose Use an External Data Source. Even though the data is stored in the PowerPivot grid in your workbook, remember that PowerPivot started out as an external add-in. Back in Excel 2010, the PowerPivot grid was "external" to the core Excel.

3. Click the Choose Connection button. Excel displays the Existing Connections dialog.

4. Choose the second tab in the dialog for tables.

5. Choose Tables in Workbook Data Model (see Figure 10.14) and click Open.

Getting a Distinct Count

I love pivot tables. I cannot imagine life without pivot tables. But I am like a kid in a candy store with some of these new features that were previously very difficult to replicate. Before getting into how to figure out a unique count, a caution.

> **CAUTION**
>
> I usually create dozens of pivot tables a day. I start with data on one sheet and create a pivot table. When I am done or want to start over, I simply delete the pivot table worksheet and start over. You should not do this if you have a Data Model defined and you don't have the full PowerPivot add-in. The Data Model will stay, but you will not have a way to build the pivot table from it.
>
> Normally, as I go from example to example in this book, I delete the old pivot tables and create new ones. For the next example, I had to carefully undo the filtering options from the previous example.

Figure 10.14
It will take six extra clicks
to reuse an existing table.

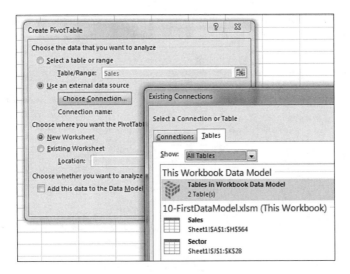

Excel pivot tables can count text values. The pivot table in Figure 10.15 is typical: Sector
in the Row area, Customer and Revenue in the Values area. You get a report showing that
there are 563 customers. This is, of course, incorrect. There were 563 records that had a
nonblank customer name, but there were not 563 different customers. This is an ugly limitation of pivot tables that we have lived with.

Figure 10.15
Count of Customer does
not mean there are 563
unique customers.

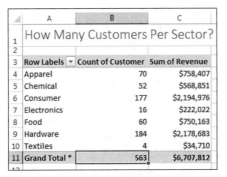

	A	B	C
1	How Many Customers Per Sector?		
2			
3	Row Labels ▼	Count of Customer	Sum of Revenue
4	Apparel	70	$758,407
5	Chemical	52	$568,851
6	Consumer	177	$2,194,976
7	Electronics	16	$222,022
8	Food	60	$750,163
9	Hardware	184	$2,178,683
10	Textiles	4	$34,710
11	Grand Total *	563	$6,707,812

If your pivot table is based on the Data Model, follow these steps:

1. Go to the Customer field in the bottom of the PivotTable Fields List. Open the drop-
down and choose Value Field Settings. This is where you could normally choose Sum,
Average, Count, and so on.

2. Scroll to the bottom of the list. Along the way, you might or might not notice that
Product and Index are missing from the list. Any sorrow over their loss will quickly be
erased when you find a new item at the bottom called Distinct Count. Choose this and
click OK.

3. The pivot table now shows that there are actually 27 unique customers in the database, 11 of which are in the hardware sector (see Figure 10.16).

Figure 10.16
Finally, an easy Distinct Count.

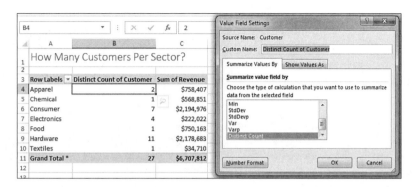

If I had a dollar for every time I needed Distinct Count in the past 10 years, I would easily have enough to afford the upgrade to Office Pro Plus. Speaking of which, the following section contrasts how to build a model if you are using the PowerPivot add-in.

Using the PowerPivot Add-In from Excel 2013 Pro Plus

If your version of Excel 2013 includes the full PowerPivot add-in, you receive several benefits:

- You have more ways to get data into PowerPivot. More data sources, plus linked tables, copy and paste, and feeds.
- You can view, sort, and filter data in the PowerPivot grid.
- You can import many millions of rows into a single worksheet in the PowerPivot grid.
- You can use DAX formula calculations, both in the grid, and as a new calculated field called a *measure*. DAX stands for Data Analysis Expressions. DAX is composed of 117 functions that let you to do two types of calculations. There are 81 typical Excel functions that you can use to add a calculated column to a table in the PowerPoint window. Then you can use 54 functions to create a new measure in the pivot table. These 54 functions add incredible power to pivot tables.
- You have more ways to create relationships, including a Diagram View to show relationships.
- You can hide or rename columns.
- You can set the numeric formatting for a column before you create a pivot table.
- You can assign categories to fields, such as Geography, Image URL, and Web URL.
- You can define key performance indicators or hierarchies.
- If you get your IT folks to install PowerPivot Server, you can publish interactive PowerPivot reports to your SharePoint site.

If you plan to deal with millions of records, you want to go with the 64-bit versions of Office and PowerPivot. You are still constrained by available memory, but because PowerPivot can compress data, you can fit ten times that amount of data in a PowerPivot file. The 64-bit version of Office can make use of memory sizes beyond the 4GB limit in 32-bit Windows.

Enabling PowerPivot

If you have Office 365, Office 2013 Pro Plus, Office 2013 Enterprise, or a stand-alone boxed version of Excel 2013, you probably have PowerPivot. To enable PowerPivot, follow these steps:

1. Open Excel 2013. Do you see a PowerPivot tab in the ribbon? If so, you can skip the remaining steps.

2. Select File, Options and choose Add-Ins from the left column. In the bottom, choose Manage: COM Add-Ins. Click Go.

3. Look for Microsoft Office PowerPivot for Excel 2013 in the list of available COM add-ins. Check the box next to this option and click OK.

> **CAUTION**
> You have to use PowerPivot for Excel 2013. The old "PowerPivot for Excel" is from Excel 2010 and will not work with Excel 2013.

4. If the PowerPivot tab does not appear in the ribbon, close Excel 2013 and restart.

After installing the add-in, you should see a PowerPivot tab on the Excel 2013 ribbon, as shown in Figure 10.17.

Figure 10.17
After successful installation, you have a PowerPivot tab in the ribbon.

The next sections walk you through your first PowerPivot data mash-up. In this example, you create a report that merges a 1.8 million–row CSV file with a store identifying data in Excel.

Import a Text File

Your main table is a 1.8 million–record CSV file called 10-BigData.txt. This file is shown in Notepad in Figure 10.18. It is important that you have column headings in row 1 of the

CSV file. The point-of-sale vendor who provides this data usually has a "Run on mm/dd/yyyy" row at the top of the file, a blank row, and then headings in row 3. You will have to convince the data provider to delete those extraneous rows before sending you the data.

Figure 10.18
This 1.8 million–row file is too big for Excel.

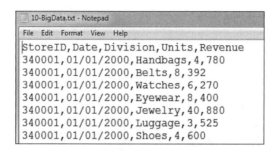

```
10-BigData.txt - Notepad
File  Edit  Format  View  Help
StoreID,Date,Division,Units,Revenue
340001,01/01/2000,Handbags,4,780
340001,01/01/2000,Belts,8,392
340001,01/01/2000,Watches,6,270
340001,01/01/2000,Eyewear,8,400
340001,01/01/2000,Jewelry,40,880
340001,01/01/2000,Luggage,3,525
340001,01/01/2000,Shoes,4,600
```

To import the 1.8 million–row file into PowerPivot, follow these steps:

1. Select the PowerPivot tab in Excel 2013.

2. Select the Manage icon. A new PowerPivot application window appears. This window eventually will contain a grid where you can browse the data in the PowerPivot model (see Figure 10.19). PowerPivot offers three ribbon tabs: Home, Design, and Advanced.

Figure 10.19
Click Manage from the PowerPivot ribbon in Excel to reach the PowerPivot Add-In window with its own ribbon.

3. You want to import your main table first. This is the large CSV file shown in Figure 10.18. From the Get External Data group, select From Other Sources. PowerPivot shows the Table Import Wizard.

4. Scroll to the bottom of the Table Import Wizard and select Text File. Click Next.

5. Optionally, type a friendly connection name.

6. Click the Browse button and locate your text file. PowerPivot detects if your data contains headers.

7. Verify that your delimiter is a comma. The drop-down offers standard delimiters, such as comma, semicolon, vertical bar, and so on.

8. If there are any columns that you don't need to import, clear the check box next to the heading for those columns. The entire file is going to be read into memory. If you have extraneous columns, particularly columns with long text values that rarely repeat, you can save memory by clearing them. Figure 10.20 shows the data preview with Units cleared.

Figure 10.20
Choose which columns to import.

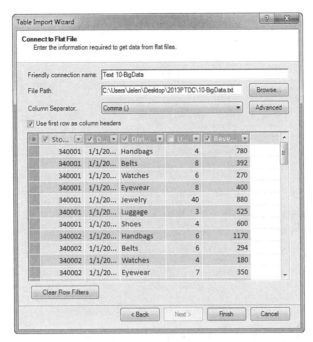

9. Note that there are filter drop-downs for each field. You can sort and filter this 1.8 million–row data set here, although it will be slower than in a few steps from now. If you open a filter field, you can choose to exclude certain values from the import.

10. Click Finish, and PowerPivot begins loading the file into memory. The wizard shows how many rows have been fetched so far (see Figure 10.21).

Figure 10.21
In less than a minute, PowerPivot is up to 1.6 million rows.

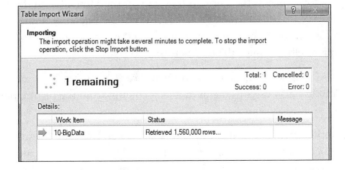

11. When the file is imported, the wizard confirms how many rows have been imported. Click Close to return to the PowerPivot window.

12. The 1.8 million–row data set is shown in the PowerPivot window (see Figure 10.22). Go ahead and grab the vertical scrollbar and scroll through the records. You can also sort, change the number format, or filter.

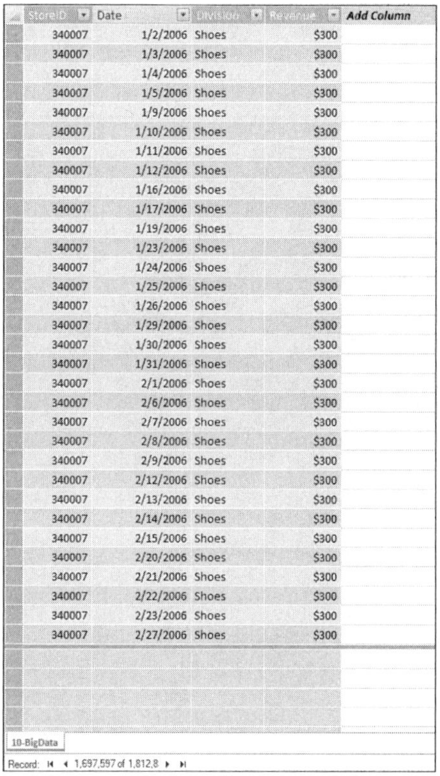

StoreID	Date	Division	Revenue	Add Column
340007	1/2/2006	Shoes	$300	
340007	1/3/2006	Shoes	$300	
340007	1/4/2006	Shoes	$300	
340007	1/5/2006	Shoes	$300	
340007	1/9/2006	Shoes	$300	
340007	1/10/2006	Shoes	$300	
340007	1/11/2006	Shoes	$300	
340007	1/12/2006	Shoes	$300	
340007	1/16/2006	Shoes	$300	
340007	1/17/2006	Shoes	$300	
340007	1/19/2006	Shoes	$300	
340007	1/23/2006	Shoes	$300	
340007	1/24/2006	Shoes	$300	
340007	1/25/2006	Shoes	$300	
340007	1/26/2006	Shoes	$300	
340007	1/29/2006	Shoes	$300	
340007	1/30/2006	Shoes	$300	
340007	1/31/2006	Shoes	$300	
340007	2/1/2006	Shoes	$300	
340007	2/6/2006	Shoes	$300	
340007	2/7/2006	Shoes	$300	
340007	2/8/2006	Shoes	$300	
340007	2/9/2006	Shoes	$300	
340007	2/12/2006	Shoes	$300	
340007	2/13/2006	Shoes	$300	
340007	2/14/2006	Shoes	$300	
340007	2/15/2006	Shoes	$300	
340007	2/20/2006	Shoes	$300	
340007	2/21/2006	Shoes	$300	
340007	2/22/2006	Shoes	$300	
340007	2/23/2006	Shoes	$300	
340007	2/27/2006	Shoes	$300	

10-BigData

Record: 1,697,597 of 1,812,8

Figure 10.22
More than a million records are in a grid that feels a lot like Excel.

Take a moment to assign a numeric format to columns. The date field starts out as date and time. If the original data did not include a time component, select the date heading and use the Format drop-down in the Formatting group of the Home tab in the PowerPivot ribbon. Choose a 3/14/2001 format. (Yes, that really is the selection in the drop-down.) Apply a currency format to the Revenue column. If you don't need to see two decimal places in your final pivot table, reduce the decimals to zero.

If you right-click a column, a menu appears where you can rename, freeze, and copy the columns. You can also use this menu to hide a column from the pivot table field list in Excel.

Note that although this feels like Excel, it is not Excel. You cannot edit an individual cell. If you add a calculation in what amounts to cell E1, that calculation is automatically copied to all rows. If you format the revenue in one cell, all the cells in that column get formatted.

You can change column widths by dragging the border between the column names just like in Excel.

The bottom line is that you have 1.8 million records you can sort, filter, and later, pivot. This is going to be cool. Note that the entire 1.8 million rows from the text file are now stored in the Excel workbook. You can copy that one .xlsx file, move it to a new computer, and all of the rows will be there. You wouldn't believe this is happening when you look at the files In Windows Explorer. The original text file is 58MB, but the Excel file is only 4MB (as a result of the vertical compression).

Add Excel Data by Copying and Pasting

The file imported previously has only StoreID as a field. It does not have the store name or location. However, you probably have a small Excel file that maps StoreID to the store name and other relevant data. You can add this data as a new tab in PowerPivot. You can use Copy and Paste, as described here, or create a linked table as described in the next section. Linked tables work better.

Follow these steps to use Copy and Paste:

1. Open a workbook containing a range that maps StoreID to Store Name in Excel.
2. Select the data with Ctrl+*.
3. Copy it with Ctrl+C.
4. Click the PowerPivot tab in Excel.
5. Click the Manage icon to open the PowerPivot window. You see your 1.8 million–row data set that you previously imported.
6. Click the Paste icon on the left side of the PowerPivot Home tab. You see a Paste Preview window.
7. Give the new table a better name than Table; try **StoreInfo**. Click OK.

You now see the store information in a new StoreInfo tab. Notice that there are now two worksheet tabs in PowerPivot.

The data that you have pasted is a static copy of the Excel data. If the original Excel data changes, you have to copy the data and do a Paste Replace in PowerPivot.

Add Excel Data by Linking

In the previous example, you added the StoreInfo table by using Copy and Paste. This creates two copies of the data. One is stored in an Excel worksheet somewhere, and the other is stored in the PowerPivot window. If the original worksheet changes, those changes will not make it through to PowerPivot. An alternative is to link the data from Excel to PowerPivot.

To link to Excel data, that data must be converted to the Table Format introduced in Excel 2007. Here are the steps to follow:

1. If you start with an Excel worksheet, make sure you have single-row headings at the top, with no blank rows or blank columns.
2. Select one cell in the worksheet and press Ctrl+T. Excel asks you to confirm the extent of your table and whether your data has headers.

10

3. Go to the Table Tools Design tab. On the left side of the ribbon, you see that this table is called Table1. Type a new name, such as **StoreInfo**.

4. On the PowerPivot tab, in the Tables group, find an icon that says Add to Data Model. When you hover over it, the tooltip says that this icon will create a linked table. Click this icon to have a copy of the table appear in the PowerPivot grid.

Define Relationships

Normally, in regular Excel you would be creating VLOOKUPs to match the two tables. This is far easier in PowerPivot. Follow these steps:

1. In the PowerPivot window, go to the Home tab and choose Diagram View. PowerPivot shows your two tables, side by side.

2. Click the StoreID field in the main table and drag to the Store field in the lookup table. Excel draws arrows indicating the relationship (see Figure 10.23).

Figure 10.23
Drag from one field to another to define a relationship.

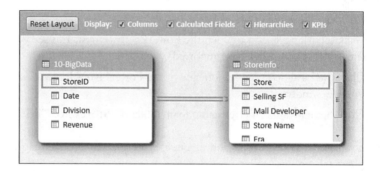

3. To return to the grid, click the Data View icon in the Home tab of the PowerPivot window.

Add Calculated Columns Using DAX

One downside to pivot tables created from PowerPivot data is that they cannot automatically group daily data up to years. Before building the pivot table, let's use the DAX formula language to add a new calculated column to the data in PowerPivot. Follow these steps to add a Year field:

1. Click the first worksheet tab at the bottom of the PowerPivot window. This is your 1.8 million–row data set.

2. The column to the right of Revenue has a heading of Add Column. Click in the first cell of this blank column.

3. Click the fx icon to the left of the formula bar. The Insert Function dialog appears with categories for All, Date & Time, Math & Trig, Statistical, Text, Logical, Filter,

Information, and Parent/Child. Select Date & Time from the drop-down. You instantly notice that this is not the same list of functions in Excel. Five of the first six functions that appear in the window are exotic and new.

4. Luckily, some familiar old functions are in the list as well. Scroll down and select the YEAR function. Click OK to insert the YEAR function in the formula bar. Click the first date in the Date column. PowerPivot proposes a formula of =year(demo[Date]. Type the closing parenthesis and press Enter. Excel fills in the column with the year associated with the date.

5. Right-click the column and select Rename Column. Type a name such as **Year**.

At this point, you might be thinking of adding many more columns, but let's move on to using the pivot table.

Build a Pivot Table

Open the PivotTable drop-down on the Home tab of the PowerPivot ribbon. As shown in Figure 10.24, you have choices for a single pivot table, a single chart, a chart and a table, two charts, Power View, and so on.

Figure 10.24
You have many options beyond a single table or chart.

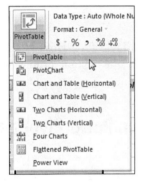

Follow these steps:

1. Select PivotTable. You now see the PowerPivot tab back in the Excel window.

2. Select to put the pivot table on a new worksheet and click OK. You are now back in Excel. The PivotTable Fields List shows both tables, although you have to use the plus symbol next to each table to see the fields in the table.

3. Expand the 10-BigData table in the PowerPivot Fields List and select Revenue. Expand the StoreInfo table and select Region. Excel builds a pivot table showing sales by region (see Figure 10.25). At this point, you have a pivot table from 1.8 million rows of data with a virtual link to a lookup table.

Figure 10.25
This pivot table summarizes 1.8 million rows and data from two tables.

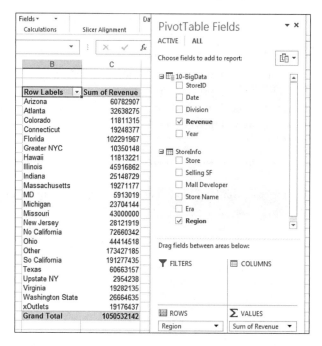

At this point, you might want to go to the PivotTable Tools tabs to further format the pivot table. You could apply a currency format and rename the Sum of Revenue field. You could also choose a format with banded rows, and so on.

Understanding Differences Between PowerPivot and Regular Pivot Tables

If you have spent your whole Excel life building pivot tables out of regular Excel data, you are going to find some annoyances with these PowerPivot pivot tables. Many of these issues are not because of PowerPivot. They are because any PowerPivot pivot table automatically is an OLAP pivot table. This means that it behaves like an OLAP pivot table.

Some items to note:

■ Days of the week do not automatically sort into the proper sequence. You have to choose More Sort Options, Ascending, More Options. Uncheck the AutoSort box. Open the First Key Sort Order drop-down and choose Sunday, Monday, Tuesday. Later in this chapter, you see how to solve this with a Calendar table.

■ There is a trick in regular Excel pivot tables that you can do instead of dragging field names to the right place. You can go to a cell that contains the word *Friday* and type **Monday** there. When you press Enter, the Monday data moves to that new column. This does not work in PowerPivot pivot tables!

- When you enter a formula in the Excel interface, you can point to a cell to include that cell in the formula. You can do this using the mouse or the arrow keys. Apparently, the PowerPivot team is made up of mouse people, because they support building a formula using the mouse in the PowerPivot grid. Old-time Lotus 1-2-3 customers who build their formulas using arrow keys will be disappointed to find that the arrow-key method doesn't work.

- The Refresh button on the Analyze tab forces Excel to update the data in the pivot table. Think before you do this in Excel 2013. In the current example, this forces Excel to go out and import the 1.8 million–row data set again.

Two Kinds of DAX Calculations

Data Analysis Expressions, or DAX, is a new formula language. You've already seen an example where you used a DAX function to add a calculated column to a table in the PowerPivot grid. The 81 DAX functions are mostly copied straight from Excel for doing these types of calculations. Most of the functions are identical to their Excel counterparts with a few exceptions listed in the next section.

You can also use DAX to create new calculated fields in the pivot table. These functions do not calculate a single cell value. They are all aggregate functions that calculate a value for the filtered rows behind any cell in the pivot table. DAX has 54 new functions to enable these calculations. The real power is in these functions.

DAX Calculations for Calculated Columns

You've already seen one example of a calculated column. The functions are remarkably similar to the same functions in Excel and mostly won't require a lot of explanation. However, there are a few oddities where Excel functions were renamed:

- The rarely documented DATEDIF function in Excel is now renamed as YEARFRAC and is rewritten to actually work.

- The TEXT function in Excel is renamed to FORMAT.

- The SUMIFS function is replaced and enhanced by CALCULATE.

- The VLOOKUP function is simplified with the RELATED function.

- DAX introduces the BLANK() function. Because some of the aggregation functions can base a calculation on either ALLNONBLANKROW or FIRSTNONBLANK, you can use the BLANK() function in an IF() function to exclude certain rows from measure calculations.

- The CHOOSE function is renamed to the SWITCH function. Whereas CHOOSE must work with values from 1 to 255, the SWITCH function can be programmed to work with other values.

Using RELATED() to Base a Column Calculation on Another Table

When you are building a calculation in the PowerPivot grid, you might need to refer to a value in another PowerPivot table. In normal Excel, you might perform a VLOOKUP. In PowerPivot, you use RELATED.

In the current example, the BigData table has StoreID and total sales for a day. One popular metric in retail reporting is sales per square foot. The StoreInfo lookup table has Store ID and Selling Square Feet, so you have all the data you need to do the calculation.

Go to the PowerPivot grid and click in a blank cell to start a new calculation. Type the equal sign and then click a cell in the Sales column. PowerPivot shows a starting formula of =[Revenue]. Type the slash to indicate division.

Now, you need to grab the Selling SF field from the StoreInfo table. Rather than do a VLOOKUP, type RELATED(. Start to type the first few letters in the table name. After typing STO, you can easily see the list of fields in the StoreInfo table (see Figure 10.26). Double-click Selling SF. Finish the formula with a closing parenthesis and Enter. Right-click the column and choose Rename. Give the field a name such as **SalesPerSquareFoot**.

Figure 10.26
Build a calculated column using DAX in the PowerPivot grid.

Using these calculated columns and relationships, you can create some interesting pivot tables. Remember that calculated columns are calculated for every row in your underlying data. The Sales Per Square Foot formula is evaluated 1.8 million times in the PowerPivot grid.

Instead, you can use DAX formulas to define a new calculated field that is only calculated once per cell in the final pivot table.

Using DAX to Create a Calculated Field in the Pivot Table

DAX calculated fields can run circles around traditional calculated fields. They are only calculated once per cell in the resultant pivot table. In Figure 10.27, the pivot table has numeric values in C5:K12. If you define a new DAX calculated field, it is only calculated for the 72 numeric cells in the pivot table. This is a lot faster than calculating 1.8 million cells and then summarizing. Before building your first calculated field, you need to understand filters.

DAX Calculated Fields Implicitly Respect the Filters

As you start to use DAX calculated fields, you have to realize that calculated fields automatically respect all filters for that cell. DAX filters first and then calculates. To understand this, consider cell D6 in Figure 10.27.

Figure 10.27
How many filters are on cell D6?

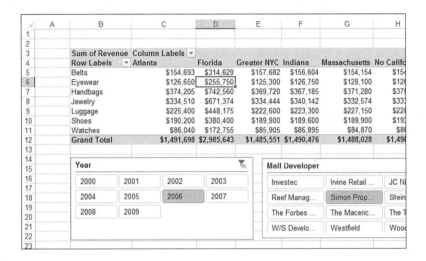

Think about how many filters are applied to cell D6. Would you say two? I think that the answer is four.

Everyone would agree that slicers are filtering the cell. Cell D6 is filtered to show only records that fall in the year 2006 based on the first slicer. Also, you are only seeing sales made at Simon Property malls based on the second slicer. That is two filters.

In addition, the Eyewear row header in B6 is really filtering everything in row 6 to only include records in the Eyewear division. That is the third filter.

Finally, the Florida heading in D4 is filtering everything in column D to only summarize records for stores that fall in the Florida region.

As you start to think about DAX calculated fields, remember that to figure out the value for a particular cell in the pivot table, the calculation engine first filters and then calculates the result using the DAX formula.

Define a DAX Calculated Field

To define a new calculated field, go to the Excel ribbon, click the PowerPivot tab, and choose Calculated Fields, New Calculated Field. Excel displays the Calculated Field dialog.

You should specify your main table as the Table Namc. Give the field a name, such as **StoreCount**. Type your formula in the formula box. Use the fx icon to insert function names. For field names, start by typing a few characters of the table name and then use the AutoComplete list to select the field.

When you are done, click the Check Formula button to check the syntax. Note that the tooltip for the function still covers up the result of check formula. Click in the Description field to hide the tooltip so you can see the result of the Check Formula button. You should see "No errors in formula" (see Figure 10.28).

Figure 10.28
Define a new calculated field.

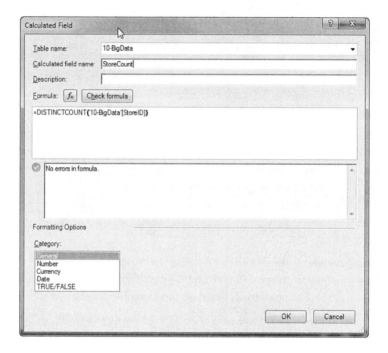

Click OK to add the new calculated field to the pivot table field list.

After you define a calculated field, you can use that field in future calculations. The SalesPerStore field in Figure 10.29 is calculated as =SUMX('10-BigData', '10-BigData'[Revenue])/[StoreCount].

You do not have to display Sum of Revenue or NumberStoresOpen in the pivot table. You could simplify the pivot table to show only SalesPerStore. PowerPivot calculates the NumberStoresOpen field for each cell in the pivot table and then displays the SalesPerStore, as shown in Figure 10.29.

Figure 10.29
SalesPerStore is calcu-
lated from a field in the
data divided by a differ-
ent DAX calculated field.

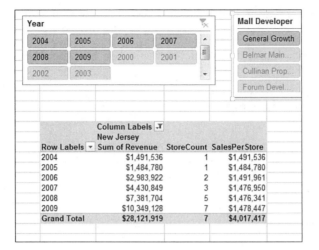

10

Is *Unfilter* Even a Word?

Here is a problem: In Figure 10.30, cell C5 is selected. That cell is filtered to total only
records where the sales rep name is Amber and where the date is 6/1/2014.

Figure 10.30
Cell C5 is implicitly
subject to a date and a
rep filter.

	A	B	C	D	E	F	G	H
1								
2								
3		Sum of Sales	Rep					
4		Date	Amber	Bill	Chris	Dale	House	Grand Total
5		6/1/2014	102	346	826	283	0	1557
6		6/2/2014	162	97	206	281	165	911
7		6/3/2014	88	57	188	123	295	751
8		6/4/2014	260	68	212	64	149	753
9		6/5/2014	117	202	38	141	274	772
10		6/6/2014	252	264	106	129	61	812
11		6/7/2014	75	54	84	120	37	370
12		6/8/2014	73	62	72	294	65	566

As you learned two sections ago, all of the filters that apply to a cell in the pivot table automatically apply to the DAX calculated field. This can be bad in some cases.

In Figure 10.30, cell G6 shows $165 in sales that were not assigned to any of the sales staff.
The policy here is that the $165 sales should be assigned to the other people who worked
that day, allocated based on their percentage of the non-house sales. Can this be solved in
the pivot table?

The huge, looming issue is that any calculations that you do for cell C5 are implicitly filtered to only show Amber's sales.

This particular DAX calculation is going to have to "unfilter" the data. It is going to have to remove the Amber filter and look at other records that are not assigned to Amber.

The DAX function CALCULATE can remove filters and apply other filters. This function is similar to SUMIFS, but more powerful.

CALCULATE **Is a Super-Enhanced Version of** SUMIFS

The CALCULATE function calculates a summary column with one or more filters. If you specify a filter for the Rep field, that filter replaces the implicit filter for Rep. By asking the filter to use Rep=House, DAX automatically ignores the implicit filter of Rep=Amber and looks at all the House records.

If you feel that using DAX is like going to the dentist, feel free to take it one step at a time. Don't try to build a function that solves the entire problem. Break the problem down into steps.

In Figure 10.31, a House calculation uses the following formula:

```
=Calculate([Sum of Sales],Sls[Rep]="House")
```

Figure 10.31

This formula forces DAX to remove the Rep filter and apply a different filter.

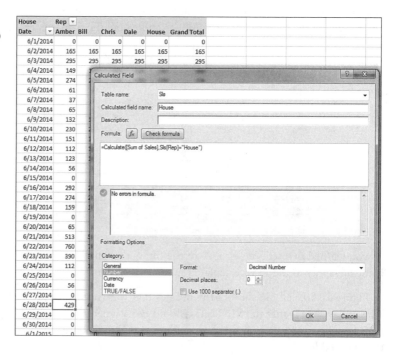

The pivot table shows that the $165 from June 2 House rep is replicated for every rep on June 2.

Define a new calculated column of NonHouse as follows:

```
=Calculate([Sum of Sales],Sls[Rep]<>"House")
```

After a calculated field is defined, you can use that field in subsequent calculated fields. Define PctNonHouse as follows:

```
=[Sum of Sales]/[NonHouse]
```

Next, define HouseAllocatedToRep as follows:

```
=[House]*[PctNonHouse]
```

Finally, define AdjSales as follows:

```
=[HouseAllocatedToRep]+[Sum of Sales]
```

In Figure 10.32, the pivot table is showing the final calculated field of AdjSales. Obviously, the PowerPivot engine has to calculate House, PctNonHouse, and NonHouse in order to calculate the result in the table.

Figure 10.32

Four calculated columns using DAX allocate the House sales to the reps who worked that day.

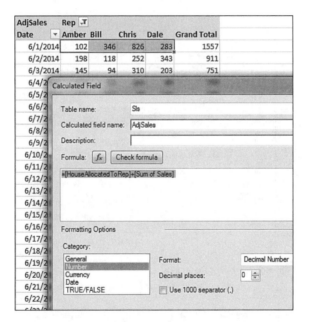

You should filter Rep to hide the House rep from the pivot table. The result is a sales amount for June 2 of $911, which matches the $911 value in H6 of Figure 10.30.

This would never be possible using calculated fields in a regular pivot table.

CASE STUDY: CALCULATE RANGE OF PRICES FOR A PRODUCT

Calculated fields in regular pivot tables always calculate on a row-by-row basis in the original data set. I had a question once on the MrExcel podcast where the person was trying to calculate the range of prices by calculating MAX(Price)−MIN(Price) in a regular pivot table. Excel would look at each row and calculate the max for that row. Because there is only one price in each row, the max of each cell is the price. Also, the min of each cell is the price. In other words, MAX−MIN is Price−Price, or 0. Thus, every product showed that the difference between the highest price and the lowest price was zero. This was clearly wrong, but it was a limitation of regular pivot tables (see Figure 10.33).

Figure 10.33
A regular pivot table has calculated columns that work at the detail level.

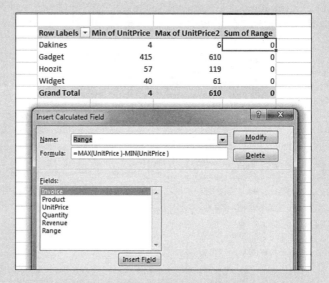

DAX offers a solution to this problem. Follow these steps:

1. Select your original data set.
2. Press Ctrl+T to define as a table.
3. On the Table Tools tab, rename the table to **Sales**.
4. Select Insert, Pivot Table. Click Add to Data Model at the bottom.
5. Add Product to the Rows area.
6. Add Unit Price to the Values area twice. (Check the field to add it the first time, drag it to add it a second time.)
7. At the bottom of the PivotTable Fields List, open the drop-down for the first UnitPrice field. Select Value Field Settings. Change the calculation to Min.
8. Repeat step 7 for the second UnitPrice field. Change the calculation to Max. Steps 7 and 8 actually define an implicit calculated field. See the following section about these fields.

9. Define a new calculated field by selecting PowerPivot, Calculated Fields, New Calculated Field. Give the field a name of **Range**. In the formula box, start to type the table name of **Sales**. From the list of fields, find `Sales[Max of Unit Price]` and press Tab. Type a minus sign. Start to type **Sales** again. Find `Sales[Min of Unit Price]` and press Tab to insert it in the formula. The Range formula is now `=[Max of UnitPrice]-[Min of UnitPrice]`.

10. Click OK to add the formula to the model. As you return to Excel, the Sales table in the PivotTable Fields List automatically contracts. Click the plus sign to see the fields again. Choose the newly added Range field. As shown in Figure 10.34, the range is correct.

Figure 10.34
By using DAX, you can perform calculations at the summary level.

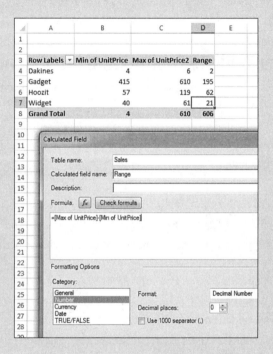

Adding Fields to the Values Area Generates DAX Calculated Fields

Behind the scenes, when you add Unit Price to the Values area and choose to show MIN, PowerPivot is secretly creating a DAX calculated field in order to show that result. This prevents you from having to enter a formula of `=MINX(Sales,Sales[Unit Price])`.

You can see these implicit calculated fields in the PowerPivot window. Choose PowerPivot, Manage. On the Advanced tab, choose Show Implicit Calculated Fields. The new fields appear in the rows along the bottom of the window.

If you hover over the field at the bottom of the window, a tooltip explains, "This calculated field was automatically generated by adding a field to the Values area of the Field List in Excel. The field is read-only and will automatically be deleted if you delete the column."

As you are building DAX, it is easier to temporarily add a field to the Values area, if only to generate the implicit field so you can make use of it in the next DAX calculation. After the new calculation is complete and in the pivot table, you can remove the implicit fields from the pivot table. They stick around in the PowerPivot window because new DAX measures reference them.

It would have been possible to generate the range calculation directly in DAX using `=Max(Sales,Sales[UnitPrice])-Minx(Sales,Sales[UnitPrice])`.

Using a Calendar Table to Enable Time Intelligence Functions

DAX offers a series of time intelligence functions. These functions require you to have a special table composed of dates.

The table should have a date column. Each date that appears in your original data set should appear on exactly one row in the date table. If you need to add additional columns to identify a date as belonging to a year, month, or weekday, add those columns to the calendar table.

There are many sources for these tables, but as Excel people, it is easiest to use pure Excel to create the table. Here are the steps to create a calendar table in Excel:

1. Go to your original data set. Select the entire column that contains the date field. Copy this column.

2. Go to a new blank worksheet. Paste the dates to column A.

3. With column A still selected, choose Data, Remove Duplicates, OK. This leaves you with exactly one occurrence of each date.

4. Add additional columns as necessary. In Figure 10.35, new columns show Year, Weekday, Weekday Name, Month, and Month Name. The formulas at the top of the figure show you how to calculate each column. If your company uses fiscal years, 4-4-5 calendars, you can add that information here as well.

Figure 10.35
Create a calendar table in Excel.

	A	B	C	D	E	F	G	H
1		B6:	=YEAR(A6)		E6:	=MONTH(A6)		
2		C6:	=WEEKDAY(A6,1)		F6:	=TEXT(A6,"mmmm")		
3		D6:	=TEXT(A6,"ddd")					
4								
5	Date	Year	Weekday	WeekdayName	Month	MonthName		
6	6/1/2014	2014	1	Sun	6	June		
7	6/2/2014	2014	2	Mon	6	June		
8	6/3/2014	2014	3	Tue	6	June		
9	6/4/2014	2014	4	Wed	6	June		
10	6/5/2014	2014	5	Thu	6	June		
11	6/6/2014	2014	6	Fri	6	June		

5. Convert the data to a table using Ctrl+T.

6. On the Table Tool Design tab, choose a table name of Calendar. It isn't necessary to use the name of Calendar, but this is a better name than Fred.

Adding the Data to PowerPivot and Formatting It

In this final example in the chapter, you go through a few extra steps designed to make the final report prettier.

First, add the Sls table and Calendar table to PowerPivot by following these steps:

1. Select a cell in the Sls table.

2. On the PowerPivot tab in Excel, choose Add to Data Model.

3. Select a cell in the Calendar table.

4. On the PowerPivot tab in Excel, choose Add to Data Model.

5. On the PowerPivot tab in Excel, choose Manage to switch to the PowerPivot window.

Next, you want to do some formatting to these two tables:

1. Select the Date column in the Sls table.

2. In the PowerPivot window, go to the Home tab. Look in the Formatting group. PowerPivot already knows this is a date, but the Date Format is wrong. Open that drop-down and choose *3/14/2001. (Yes, the menu selection really is *3/14/2001, no matter what your selected date shows.)

3. Select the Sales column in the Sls table.

4. In the Home tab, choose a format of Currency. Click Decrease Decimal two times to get rid of the decimals.

5. Select the Date column in the Sls table again.

6. On the Design tab, choose Create Relationship.

7. In the Create Relationship dialog, the first two fields already say Sls and Date. Open the drop-down for Related Lookup Table and choose Calendar. The Related Lookup Column automatically changes to Date (see Figure 10.36). Click OK to create the relationship.

8. Select the Calendar worksheet in the PowerPivot window.

9. Select the Date column.

10. Go to the Home tab and change the Date Format to *3/14/2001.

11. With the Date column still selected, go to the Design tab. Open the drop-down for Mark as Date Table. From the drop-down, choose Mark as Date Table. PowerPivot displays the Mark as Date Table dialog. The correct field of Date is already selected (see Figure 10.37). Click OK. This step is important for enabling the date filters in the PivotTable Fields List. You see the result of this step later in Figure 10.39.

Figure 10.36
Relate the Sls table to the
Calendar table.

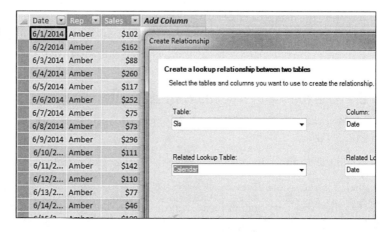

Figure 10.37
Mark the Calendar table
as a Date table.

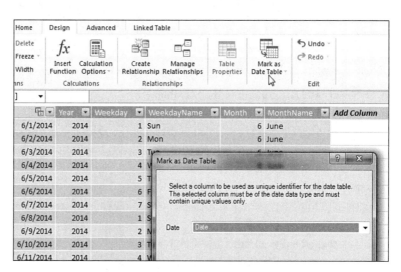

PowerPivot Doesn't Automatically Sort by Custom Lists

I am a big fan of PowerPivot, and I've been writing about it since 2009. In my first
PowerPivot book, I ruthlessly beat up on the PowerPivot team for not automatically sorting my month names into January, February, March sequence. I would show a pivot table
with months sorted into the April-August-December-February alphabetical sequence and
point out that it was clear no one on the team had ever actually had to present a report in a
boardroom.

Regular PivotCache pivot tables automatically sort all fields based on custom lists if any list
includes the items in that field. I always took this for granted until PowerPivot started *not*
sorting correctly. I found a horrible, eight-step workaround, but I was incredibly annoyed

every time I had to do those eight steps. "Why, PowerPivot Team, why do I have to repeatedly do these eight steps? The Excel team clearly has the code to sort the pivot table by the custom list. Why can't you just borrow the code from them?" This became my mantra.

Version 2 of PowerPivot has produced a solution, although it is not the solution that I envisioned. However, it is a fine solution. You do a couple of steps once and then the pivot table and slicers sort into the proper sequence.

Here is how to solve the sorting problem:

1. In PowerPivot, select the Calendar table.
2. Select one cell in the WeekdayName column.
3. On the PowerPivot Home tab, in the Sort and Filter group, is a new icon called Sort By Column. Click this icon.
4. In the Sort By Column dialog, indicate that WeekdayName should be sorted by Weekday (see Figure 10.38). Click OK.

Figure 10.38
Dear PowerPivot Team:
Thank you for providing a
solution.

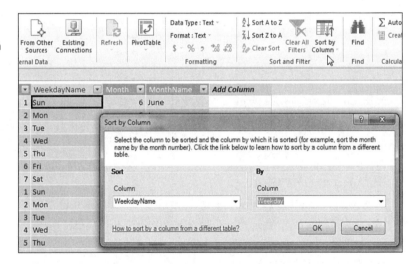

5. Select a cell in the MonthName column. Repeat steps 3 and 4 but specify that MonthName should be sorted by Month.

Create a PivotTable and Marvel at the Results

In PowerPivot, select the Sls table. In the Home tab, open the PivotTable drop-down and choose a single pivot table.

In the PowerPivot Fields List, expand the Calendar table. Hover over the Date field and open the drop-down that appears. In the fly-out menu, choose Date Filters, and you can get all the date filters that apply to a regular pivot table (see Figure 10.39). This menu is why you declared the table as a date table.

Figure 10.39
Because you declared the Calendar table as a Date table, you have access to all of the filters.

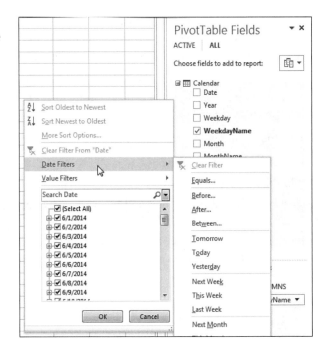

Next, add fields to your pivot table by following these steps:

1. Drag the WeekdayName field from the Calendar table to the Columns area.
2. Drag Sales from the Sls table to the Values area.
3. For good measure, go to the Analyze tab in the Excel ribbon and choose Insert Slicer. Add a slicer for Weekday.
4. In the Slicer Tools Options tab, change the Columns setting to 7.
5. Optionally, click Mon in the slicer and drag to Fri to select only the days during the week.

Figure 10.40 shows the result. Because you chose to sort WeekdayName by Weekday, the slicer has the weekdays in the right sequence. The pivot tables have the slicer in the right sequence.

If you are seeing PowerPivot for the first time, you are probably not impressed. However, if you previously beat your head against the desk seeing the alphabetical sequence of Friday, Monday, Saturday, you will appreciate the improvement.

Figure 10.40

Having weekday names in sequence in the slicer is an improvement.

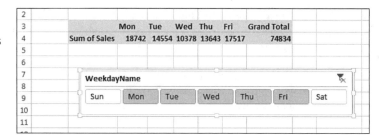

This Is a Discussion About Time Intelligence

A few pages ago, you started reading about time intelligence. All of the pre-work between then and now is designed to make the time intelligence functions actually work. If you don't go through the preceding steps, the DAX formulas will be worse than going to the dentist.

To start, rearrange the pivot table like this:

1. Open the Calendar table and drag Date to the Row Label area.
2. Open the Sls table and drag Sales to the Values area.
3. Add a slicer for Year.
4. Select 2015 from the Year slicer.

You will have the pivot table shown in Figure 10.41. Sales from June 2, 2015 were $937.

Figure 10.41

Start with a simple sales report.

	A	B	C	D	E
1					
2		Year			
3					
4		2014	2015		
5					
6					
7			Sum of Sales		
8		6/1/2015	1590		
9		6/2/2015	937		
10		6/3/2015	814		
11		6/4/2015	759		
12		6/5/2015	836		
13		6/6/2015	927		
14		6/7/2015	371		

The goal is to build calculated fields in DAX to compare sales from this day to the identical day one year ago.

As you read earlier in this chapter, that is tough to do, because cell C9 is filtered to only show records from 6/2/2015. You are going to have to unfilter the date field and reapply a filter of one year ago.

The solution involves the CALCULATE function to allow you to unfilter the date field. But how do you specify one year ago? DAX provides 30 time intelligence functions, and one of those functions is DATEADD.

DATEADD(Calendar[Date],-1,year) points to the exact same day one year ago. The third argument can be day, month, or year. Note that these are an *enumeration*, so you don't have to type quotes around the word.

> **NOTE**
>
> An enumeration is a fancy word saying that someone who programmed Excel defined a global variable with the name of year, month, or day that actually converts to some numeric code for you.

DATEADD is pretty cool. To see sales for the day before the date in column A, you use =DATEADD(Calendar[Date],-1,day). To see sales for the day 3 months ahead of today, use =DATEADD(Calendar[Date],3,month).

Remember that DATEADD is one of just 34 time intelligence functions. You could ask for DATESMTD(Calendar[Date]) to return all the dates up to the current day in this month.

> **CAUTION**
>
> Your model contains a date column in the Sls table and a date column in the Calendar table. These time intelligence functions work all the time when you refer to the Calendar[Date] field. They work 10% of the time when you refer to the Sls[Date] field. If you want to have a morning roughly akin to getting a root canal, just try to build a DAX formula that uses time intelligence functions that refer to Sls[Date]. The formula error checker says the formula is fine, but the results will not be correct in the pivot table. I can't explain why it doesn't work, but it doesn't. After you realize that you have to use the Calendar[Date] field, everything falls into place. Thanks to Rob Collie and his *DAX Formulas for PowerPivot* book for this tip.

You now have the DATEADD function, which identifies the date from one year before the date in this row of the pivot table. To actually return the sales from that date, you have to use the CALCULATE function. Remember that CALCULATE is used to override an existing implicit filter. Row 9 in the pivot table is implicitly filtered to June 2 2015. To override that filter, use CALCULATE. Here's the formula:

```
=CALCULATE([Sum of Sales],DATEADD(Calendar[Date],-1,year))
```

Follow these steps:

1. In Excel, go to the PowerPivot tab and choose Calculated Fields, Add Calculated Field.
2. Give the field a name of **SalesLastYear**.
3. Your formula is =CALCULATE([Sum of Sales],DATEADD(Calendar[Date],-1,year)).

4. In the Formatting Options, choose Currency. Specify 0 decimal places.

5. Click Check Formula to make sure the formula is typed correctly. When you can't see the results of the Check Formula because of the tooltip, click in the Description field.

6. Click OK to finish the calculated field.

7. The PivotTable Fields List redraws, which causes the Sls table to collapse back to a single line. Click the plus sign next to Sls to open the list of fields in the table.

8. Choose the SalesLastYear field to add this new calculated field to the Values area.

To finish the analysis, add a second calculated field to calculate the percentage change. Follow these steps:

1. In Excel, go to the PowerPivot tab and choose Calculated Fields, Add Calculated Field.

2. Give the field a name of **PctChange**.

3. Your formula is =[Sum of Sales]/[SalesLastYear]-1.

4. In the Formatting Options, choose Number. Open the Format drop-down and choose Percentage. Specify 1 decimal place.

5. Repeat steps 5 through 7 from the previous process.

6. Choose the PctChange field to add this new calculated field to the Values area.

Figure 10.42 shows the resulting pivot table.

Figure 10.42
Percentage change from same day last year requires a DAX calculated field.

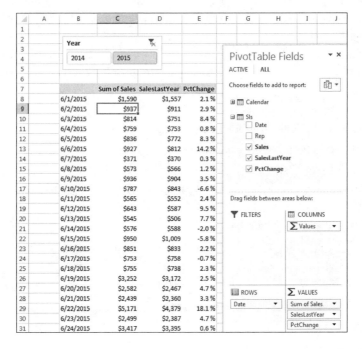

At this point, it would be possible to remove Sales and SalesLastYear from the pivot table, leaving you only with PctChange. In Figure 10.43, the Sales Rep field appears across the top of the pivot table. Each cell in the pivot table calculates the percentage change from the previous year.

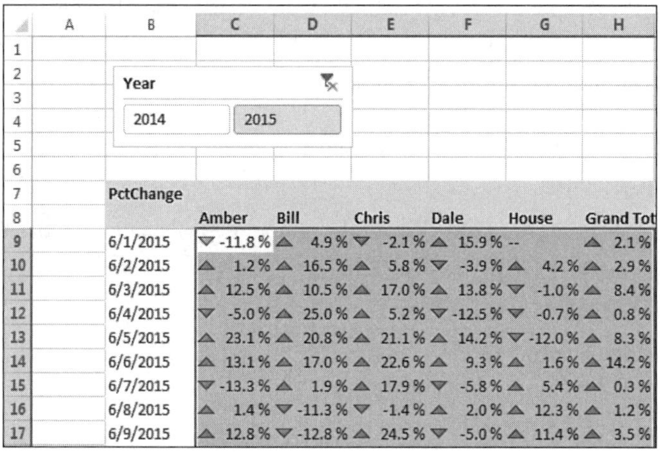

PctChange	Amber	Bill	Chris	Dale	House	Grand Tot
6/1/2015	-11.8 %	4.9 %	-2.1 %	15.9 %	--	2.1 %
6/2/2015	1.2 %	16.5 %	5.8 %	-3.9 %	4.2 %	2.9 %
6/3/2015	12.5 %	10.5 %	17.0 %	13.8 %	-1.0 %	8.4 %
6/4/2015	-5.0 %	25.0 %	5.2 %	-12.5 %	-0.7 %	0.8 %
6/5/2015	23.1 %	20.8 %	21.1 %	14.2 %	-12.0 %	8.3 %
6/6/2015	13.1 %	17.0 %	22.6 %	9.3 %	1.6 %	14.2 %
6/7/2015	-13.3 %	1.9 %	17.9 %	-5.8 %	5.4 %	0.3 %
6/8/2015	1.4 %	-11.3 %	-1.4 %	2.0 %	12.3 %	1.2 %
6/9/2015	12.8 %	-12.8 %	24.5 %	-5.0 %	11.4 %	3.5 %

Figure 10.43
Even after you pivot the report, the PctChange calculated field continues to work correctly.

Figure 10.43 includes some other steps:

1. Cell G9 showed up as an error because there were no sales in the previous year. Go to PivotTable Tools, Analyze, Options. Check the box For Error Cells Show and type -- in the box.
2. Select the numbers in the pivot table. Select Home, Conditional Formatting, Icon Sets, and choose the set called 3 Triangles, even though it is really two triangles and a dash.
3. Select Home, Conditional Formatting, Manage Rules. Select the one rule. Choose Edit Rule.
4. Open both Type drop-downs and change to Number.
5. Type **0** in both Number boxes.
6. Change the first operator drop-down from >= to just =.
7. In the top of the Edit Formatting Rule dialog, choose All Cells Showing "PctChange" Values (see Figure 10.44).
8. Click OK to finish editing the rule.
9. Click OK to close the Conditional Formatting Rules Manager dialog.

To learn more about DAX, visit Rob Collie's PowerPivotPro.com blog, or read Rob's book on DAX formulas (ISBN 978-1-61547-015-0).

Figure 10.44
Adjust the conditional formatting rules so that the yellow dash only appears for a value of zero.

Using Key Performance Indicators

Key performance indicators (KPIs) debut in this version of PowerPivot. As I write this, they are very buggy. Perhaps as you read this, they have improved.

To use a KPI, you must have one DAX calculated field defined that will be used for the KPI Base Field. Optionally, you might want a second DAX calculated field to be used as the Target Value. For example, perhaps you would have Sales as the Base Field and Quota as the Target Value.

Setting up a KPI Compared to an Absolute Value

Follow these steps to define and display a KPI:

1. In the PowerPivot tab, choose KPIs, New KPI. Excel displays the Key Performance Indicator dialog.
2. Open the Base Field drop-down and choose one of the DAX calculated measures.
3. For a target value, choose Absolute Value and type the target. There are four kinds of status thresholds:
   - Red for low, yellow for mid, green for high
   - Green for low, yellow for mid, red for high
   - Green in the center, moving to yellow, then red in each direction
   - Red in the center, moving to yellow, then green in each direction

4. Choose one of the four thresholds by clicking one of the four rectangles above the icons.

5. You *cannot* drag the text boxes that look like they should be draggable because they are not. You type new values in the text boxes above the threshold. When you type a new value and then press Tab, the text box moves to the right place.

6. Choose an icon set from the bottom of the dialog (see Figure 10.45).

Figure 10.45
Adjust the KPI settings.

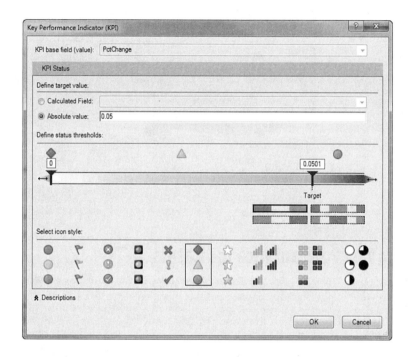

7. Click on Descriptions at the bottom of the dialog to change the field names that will appear in step 10.

8. Click OK.

9. Open the Sls table in the PivotTable Fields List. You now see a traffic light icon next to the base field.

10. Click the plus sign next to the traffic light to reveal three fields: the base field, the target field, and a field called Status. Drag Status to the Values area. The icon will appear in the pivot table. Currently, no matter what icon you choose in the dialog, you get the three circles icon with red, yellow, and green (see Figure 10.46).

Setting Up a KPI Compared to a Calculated Target Value

If you have two DAX calculated fields, such as Sales and Quota, you can set up a KPI to compare Sales for that cell to Quota for that cell. Figure 10.47 shows the dialog.

Figure 10.46
The KPI appears in the pivot table.

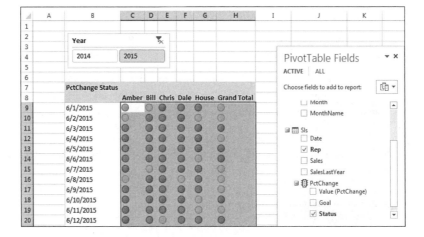

Figure 10.47
Compare Sales to the prior year's sales.

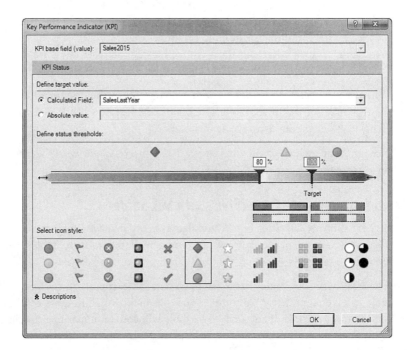

Other Notes About PowerPivot

The topic of PowerPivot deserves a whole book. (In fact, you can find my book on the subject: *PowerPivot for the Excel Data Analyst*, published by Que, ISBN 978-0-7897-4315-2.) This section covers a few miscellaneous topics that didn't make it elsewhere in this chapter.

Combination Layouts

The PivotTable drop-down in the PowerPivot Window offers eight choices. The first choice is a single pivot table and has been used throughout this chapter.

The last choice is a flattened pivot table, which is a pivot table that starts in Outline layout instead of Compact layout. The Repeat All Row Labels feature is turned on. If you plan to convert the pivot table to values to reuse it, choosing a flattened pivot table can save you a few clicks along the way.

The other six layouts include one, two, or four pivot charts. I don't get this. Pivot charts look great in Microsoft demos, but no one actually uses them. I can see why Microsoft had to put them here, because it gives them something to demo, but I cannot figure out why Microsoft gives you six different versions. If one pivot chart is bad, why would anyone ever want four of them?

However, assume you are actually trying to create a dashboard with multiple pivot charts and you found this section in the index. When you choose a combination of multiple elements, you have multiple pivot table rectangles on the worksheet. To add fields to a specific pivot table or pivot chart, put the active cell inside the rectangle for that pivot table and then add fields using the PivotTable Fields List.

When you are ready to work on another pivot table in the dashboard, choose a cell inside the rectangle for that pivot table. The Fields List resets to blank, and you can design that element. All elements share the same slicers.

Note that for each chart on your layout, Excel inserts a new worksheet to hold the actual pivot table for the chart.

Getting Your Data into PowerPivot with SQL Server

If your company has SQL Server, the data is being managed by a database administrator. That person has likely already split the company data into many tables with relationships among the tables.

There is always one table that is the main data table. If you are tracking sales, the main table will contain one record for every invoice line item. This table will have fewer fields but the most records of any table. The table will contain quantity, price, and then many fields that link out to other tables. Instead of putting the product name, this main table will have a ProductKey field. The main table will be linked to a lookup table that maps the ProductKey to a product description, list price, category, and more. Typically, the main table is linked to a dozen other lookup tables.

Database administrators call this main table the Fact table.

After specifying the connect string to your SQL Server database, you should locate the main Fact table. Select that table, and then click the button for Select Related Tables. PowerPivot reads the database schema and brings in all the tables with relationships predefined. It is, of course, then possible to add in additional Excel or text data to mash up with the SQL Server data.

Other Issues

Can multiple relationships exist between two tables? No. If you need two relationships, import the lookup table twice and link to each copy separately.

Will PowerPivot ever be available for Excel 2007? No. Will models created in Excel 2013 ever be compatible with Excel 2010? No. In both Excel 2010 and Excel 2013, significant changes happened inside of Excel.

Next Steps

While PowerPivot lets you build pivot tables from complex models, the new Power View add-in for Excel 2013 Pro Plus customers lets you combine multiple PowerPivot charts in an animated, interactive dashboard within Excel. Chapter 11 introduces Power View.

10

Dashboarding with Power View

11

Chapter 10, "Mashing Up Data with PowerPivot," introduced the PowerPivot Data Model and the Vertipaq engine. If you have the Pro Plus edition of Excel 2013, you have a new Power View add-in that creates interactive dashboard elements from your PowerPivot data.

Imagine being able to combine pivot charts, maps, and pivot tables on an interactive canvas. You can make any small tile full size with a mouse click. Select a category in one chart and the other charts highlight that data point with a bright color.

Power View, like PowerPivot, is free if you have Office 2013 Pro Plus or higher.

Preparing Your Data for Power View

When you are adding data to the Data Model for PowerPivot, you simply need to add the data tables and create the relationships. Power View has a few extra features that rely on you properly categorizing certain data fields.

The data set for this chapter is 10 years of fictitious book sales data. The main Fact table reports quarterly sales data by city and title. There are more than 400,000 records in the Fact table. Three smaller lookup tables provide category information:

- The Geography table provides City, State, and Region.
- The Products table maps the ProdID to Title, List Price, Category, Version of Excel, Level, and other category information. Power View is particularly good at letting you visualize how one category relates to another category, hence the desire to add many categories.

- You need to create a date table that converts daily dates to years and quarters. Yes, you could add 411,000 formulas in the PowerPivot grid with the =YEAR() function, but it is faster to have a date lookup table. To create the date table, copy the column of 411,000 dates in Excel to a new worksheet. Use Data, Remove Duplicates to get a unique list of daily dates. A new Year column comes from the =YEAR() function. The new Quarter column requires a VLOOKUP from MONTH() to convert to a quarter number. After you have the date columns, convert formulas to values and add this table to your model.

Consider adding a path to an image file for each product. If you store a link to a product image, you can add that image to your dashboard. This is a cool feature. If your company sells online, there is probably already a folder with a collection of image files. If you are lucky, there is a consistent naming convention where product 123 has an image called http://www.yourco.com/images/p123.jpg. In my sample data set, I learned we aren't very consistent at MrExcel.com. There were 28 products with 28 different naming conventions for the images. Note that the image files can be stored locally or on the Web. C:\Artwork\image.jpg works fine as an image URL. So does http://www.mrexcel.com/image.jpg.

You can also add a column for URL to the product page on your website. This is not as cool as showing images, however. Power View doesn't use a URL shortener, so the entire URL ends up showing in your report.

After adding your tables to PowerPivot and defining relationships, you should perform these extra steps to make your Power View experience better:

1. Format your numeric columns in PowerPivot. This matters in Power View. With a regular pivot table, if you format the underlying data and add it to the pivot table, you have to reformat it in the pivot table. The Power View people make it hard to change the numeric format in the dashboard, but they make up for it by respecting the numeric format that you define in PowerPivot. For the columns that you will be using in the report (such as Revenue and Profit), select the entire column. In the PowerPivot window, choose the Home tab and then Format as Currency. Use Decrease Decimal twice to get rid of the decimal places. Repeat for the numeric fields that you will likely include in the dashboard. For a Quantity field, use the Comma icon in the Formatting group to add commas. Even if all of your detail rows are in the 1–100 range, they will eventually total up to more than a thousand, so add the thousands separator now.

2. Select the DateTable tab in PowerPivot. On the Design tab, open the Mark as Date Table drop-down and then choose the redundant Mark as Date Table command. You have to specify which column contains a date field and contains only unique dates.

3. Go to the Advanced tab in the PowerPivot window. There is a Data Category drop-down field. Mark as many columns as you can with a Data Category. In Figure 11.1, select the entire ImagePath column and choose a data category of Image URL.

4. Mark the web page column with a category of Web URL.

5. Mark the City column with a category of City.

Figure 11.1
Assign a data category to fields that contain a link to an image.

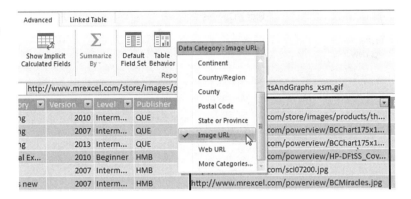

6. The data has both State and State Abbreviation columns. Mark both of these columns with a category of State or Province.

7. Mark the Product Name category with a category of Product. Note that Product is not in the drop-down. You have to choose More Categories, All, and then choose Product.

After you are done defining the relationships and the categories, close the PowerPivot window to return to Excel.

Creating a Power View Dashboard

A Power View dashboard is just another worksheet in your workbook. Go to the Insert tab in the ribbon and choose Power View. A new worksheet is inserted to the left of the current worksheet. The worksheet is given a name such as Power View1, Power View2, and so on. You can right-click the sheet tab to delete it just like a worksheet. You can drag to move it to a new location. It is just like a worksheet.

The Power View window contains a Power View Fields List, sort of like the PivotTable Fields list on the right side. A large blank canvas appears on the left. A collapsible Filters panel appears to the right of the canvas (see Figure 11.2).

The Power View Fields List is far more flexible than the PivotTable Fields List. The top is similar; you have an expandable list of tables and can limit to just active tables or all tables. The drop zones at the bottom of the Fields List change dramatically as you change a dashboard element from a table to a chart to a map to a scatter chart. Expect drop zones to come and go.

11

Blank Canvas   Filters Pane   Fields List

Figure 11.2
A new Power View
window.

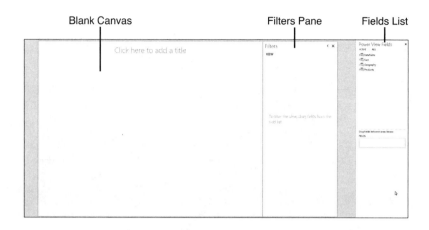

Also be careful to watch for new contextual ribbon tabs that appear to the right of the Power View tab. Inexplicably, Microsoft did not group the related contextual tabs under a Power View Tools grouping, so you might not notice that tabs labeled Formatting, Text, Analyze come and go as you select various items. When I first started working with Power View, I was hoping that Formatting would appear on the Power View tab, but the command I needed was usually on a tab just to the right of the Power View tab in the ribbon. After working with PowerPivot in Excel 2010, the usual action was to click the PowerPivot icon in the Excel ribbon to get to the PowerPivot window and more tabs. This does not work in Power View. Clicking the Power View icon inserts a new blank worksheet.

Every New Dashboard Element Starts as a Table

Expand one of the data tables in the Fields List and choose any field. That field flies over to a new element on the canvas. Every new element starts as a table. This is just a starting point. After the table is on the canvas, you can use the Switch Visualization group on the Design tab to change to one of three kinds of tables, one of three kinds of bar charts, columns charts, a pie chart, a line chart, a scatter chart, or a map.

You might build a dashboard with eight dashboard elements, but there will only be one Fields List and one Filter pane no matter what. The active element has four gray corner icons. Any changes that you make to the Fields List are applied to the active element. Right now, with your first table, this is a great feature. Check the Revenue box, and your one active element becomes a table showing revenue by region (see Figure 11.3).

After you have eight elements on the dashboard, not paying attention to which element is the active element leads to the frequent use of Undo. I keep thinking, "I am staring right at the element that I want to add the field to, but somehow, Power View can't read my mind."

Corners Indicate Active Element

Figure 11.3
A table element on a
Power View dashboard.

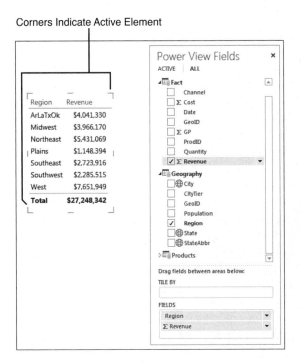

Subtlety Should Be Power View's Middle Name

I am frequently accused of being a control freak. When I look at the table in Figure 11.3, three things come screaming in to my head: Where is the sort icon? Where is the Filter icon? How can I right-justify the Revenue heading? Here are some answers:

- First, there is no sort icon. To sort by Revenue, click the Revenue heading. The first click sorts smallest to largest. Click again to sort largest to smallest. A little blue triangle appears next to the Revenue heading to let you know that the report is sorted by that column.

- Second, the filter and pop-out icons are invisible until the mouse pointer is above the table. After you hover over the table, the icons appear above the table (see Figure 11.4).

- Finally, as I am writing this, you can't right-align a heading. It might be fixed by the time you are reading this, though. The icons on the Home tab do not function in Power View. There is a Power View tab with an icon where you can change the font, the text size, and the background.

Convert the Table to a Chart

With the first table selected, you see a Design tab in the ribbon. The left group in this tab is called Switch Visualization. You have 13 choices in four drop-downs and the Map icon. The column chart drop-down offers Stacked, 100% Stacked, and Clustered Column charts. The Other Chart offers Line, Scatter, and Pie charts (see Figure 11.5).

Figure 11.4
Click a heading to sort, or hover over it for more icons.

Figure 11.5
Convert the default table to a chart or a map.

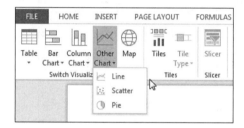

For now, choose a stacked bar chart. The element stays the exact same size, and Power View tries to fit a chart in that small area. It doesn't fit, as you can see in Figure 11.6.

Figure 11.6
The converted chart doesn't fit in the previous space.

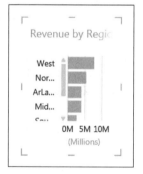

Click one of the eight resize handles and stretch the element frame until the chart looks good. As shown in Figure 11.7, you now have additional controls at the top left to control the sort order. The pop-out icon makes the element full screen temporarily. Say that you have ten small elements on the dashboard. You can click the pop-out icon to make one of the small elements full screen. After the element is full screen, a pop-out icon returns the element to the original size.

Figure 11.7
Convert the table to a
bar chart.

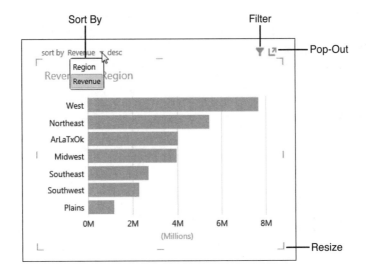

In the Fields List, drag the Channel field to the Legend area. The chart becomes a stacked
bar chart showing book sales by Online, eBook, and Brick and Mortar stores (see Figure 11.8).

Figure 11.8
Add a field to the Legend
area in the Fields List to
create a stacked chart.

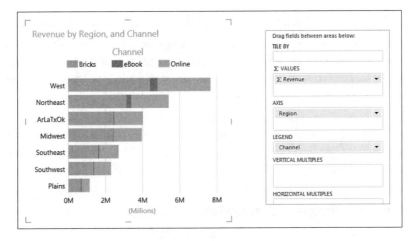

While a chart is selected, a Layout tab displays in the ribbon. Using the Layout tab, you can
move the legend to the top, add data labels, or change the type of horizontal axis.

Add Drill-Down to a Chart

The current chart has Region as an Axis field. Drag the State field and drop it as a second
Axis field. Optionally, add City as a third Axis field. After making this change, nothing
appears different in the chart. However, you've now created a hierarchy that you can drill

into. Double-click the bar for the Southwest region. The chart is replaced with a chart showing Arizona, Colorado, Utah, and New Mexico. Double-click the bar for Arizona to reveal a list of Arizona cities (see Figure 11.9). After you use drill-down, an arrow appears at the top right for drill-up.

Figure 11.9
Add field to the Axis area in the Fields List to allow drill-down.

To Begin a New Element, Drag a Field to a Blank Spot on the Canvas

To add a new element to the dashboard, you drag a field from the Fields List and drop it in a blank portion of the canvas. Just as with the first element, this element starts as a small table. You can switch it to a chart and resize and add more fields. Keep adding new elements as necessary.

You can also create a new element by copying and pasting an existing element. If you have designed one chart, right-click that chart and choose Copy. Click in a blank area of the canvas and paste. You can now change the fields in the Fields List to change the chart.

The next bit is magic.

Every Chart Point Is a Filter for Every Other Element

In Figure 11.10, two charts appear on the canvas. The right chart shows revenue by year. The left chart shows revenue by channel by region.

If you click on any part of any chart, all of the other charts will be filtered to the same element. Click the 2013 column in the right chart and the left chart is faded, except for the 2013 revenue.

To return to the unfiltered report, click the 2013 column a second time.

Figure 11.10
All elements are connected. Click a column in one chart to filter the other chart.

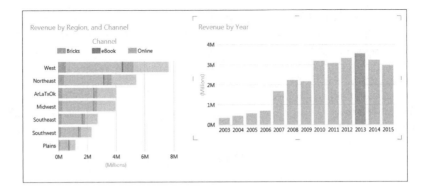

Adding a Real Slicer

The slicers in Power View look different from regular slicers, but they act the same way. To create a slicer, drag a field to a blank area of the canvas. That field starts out as a new table. Go to the Design tab of the ribbon and choose Slicer. The table is converted to a Power View slicer (see Figure 11.11).

Figure 11.11
A slicer on the canvas controls all elements on the canvas.

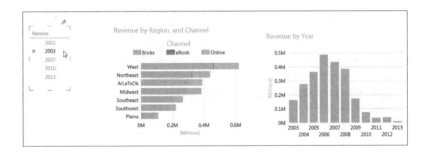

Notice these differences from a regular slicer:

- A colored square next to an item means the item is selected.
- Click an item to select that one item.
- To select multiple items, you have to Ctrl+click the other items.
- The slicer is always one column. You cannot rearrange the slicers in Power View as you can in a regular pivot table.
- An eraser icon appears in the top right of the slicer. This is the Clear Filter icon. It is equivalent to the Funnel with X icon in a regular slicer.

The Filter Pane Can Be Confusing

The last two sections showed you how to filter the canvas. There is also a filter pane. The filter pane always includes a category for View. If a table or chart is selected, there will be a category for Chart or Table.

Although these filters are on the same Filters pane, they act very differently. Consider Figure 11.12. The Version slicer in the top-left corner is affecting all three elements in the dashboard.

Figure 11.12
A Table filter applies only to the active table and is applied to the aggregate values in the table.

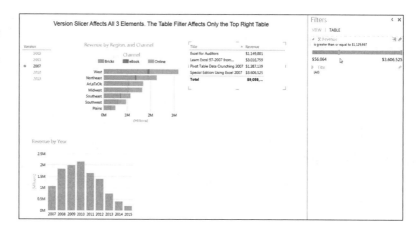

Select the top-right table and click the Filter icon to open the Table category in the Filters panel. The Table category lists all the fields currently in the active table. When you filter to ask for items over $1 million, the filter is applied at the aggregate level. After the 2007 version Slicer filter was applied, but before the Table filter was applied, the top-right table contained ten titles for a total of $11.3 million. The Table filter looks at those ten summary items and gives you only the four titles with more than a million dollars in sales (see Figure 11.12).

> **CAUTION**
> The range slider in the Filters pane is very easy to use, but it is nearly impossible to get it to stop exactly on $1,000,000. If you hold the mouse button down on the blue slider and use the left/right arrow keys, you can nudge the slider. It still will not stop exactly at $1,000,000. You can click the blue arrow to the right of the Revenue filter to open a form where you can type in the exact value of 1,000,000.

Here are the differences between the Table filter and the View filter:

■ The View filter affects all elements on the canvas.

■ The View filter starts out blank. You have to drag a field from the Field List on to the Filters pane.

■ The View filter is applied to the individual detail records in the data set. By filtering for revenue greater than approximately $2,500, Power View goes back to the original 411,000 rows of data and looks for records where the revenue on the individual line item is greater than $2,500. It is tough to sell 100 computer books in one city in one quarter. The results here are likely tied to seminar or conference purchases (see Figure 11.13).

Figure 11.13
A View filter is applied to the underlying records and affects all elements on the canvas.

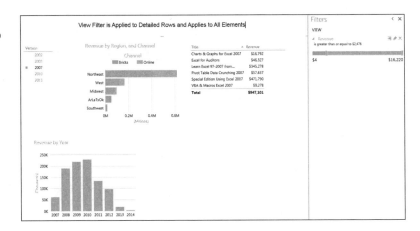

This last distinction of the filter applying at the detail level is not obvious.

Use Tile Boxes to Filter One or a Group of Charts

The Power View Fields List offers a field called Tile By. This is another way to filter an element on the dashboard.

First, select one chart or table element that you want to filter. Find the filter field in the Fields List. You can drag the field to the Tile By drop zone at the bottom of the Field List. Alternatively, you can hover over the field, open the drop-down, and choose Add as Tile By.

If you choose a regular field, the tiles appear as words. In Figure 11.14, the Image field has been added as a file.

The filter appears as tiles across the top of the chart. Notice the thick blue lines above and below the chart. These lines tell you that only the one chart between the lines is affected by the tiles (see Figure 11.14).

Tiles are cool. They provide a way to filter one chart and not the other charts. But I can already hear what you're thinking: You want to have two charts controlled by Tile 1 and another chart controlled by Tile 2. Fortunately, this can be done.

In Figure 11.14, right-click an element that is outside of the boundary and choose Cut. Click anywhere inside the Tile Boundary lines, right-click, and paste. The result will inevitably be messy, with two charts right on top of each other.

Drag the tile box up and drag the bottom boundary line to add some room. Then individually move the two charts so they fit. It is tricky to find the correct boundary box to drag. The result is shown in Figure 11.15. Both of these charts are within the boundary lines, so they are both controlled by the tiles at the top. The table outside the boundary lines is not affected by the tiles.

Figure 11.14
Only the elements between the tile boundary lines are filtered by the Tile Category Filters.

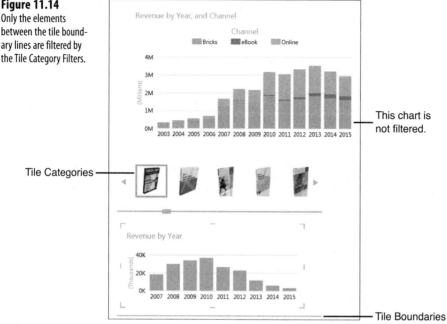

This chart is not filtered.

Tile Categories

Revenue by Year

Tile Boundaries

Both Charts in Boundary

Figure 11.15
Both elements are within the boundary lines, and they are filtered together.

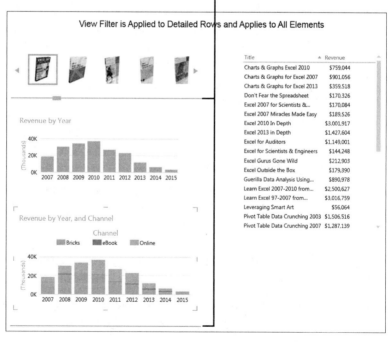

11

Replicating Charts Using Multiples

Say that you have a chart element that shows revenue by year. You could add a new field to the Legend area in order to create a stacked or clustered column chart. Alternatively, you could drag the new field to the Vertical Multiples or Horizontal Multiples field to cause Power View to replicate the chart for each value in that field. In Figure 11.16, the revenue chart appears as three charts based on the Channel field dropped in the Horizontal Multiples field.

Figure 11.16
Add a field to Horizontal
Multiples to replicate the
chart.

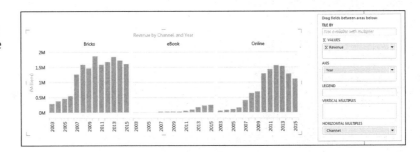

> **NOTE** When you have only a few categories, there is no difference between dropping a field in Vertical Multiples and Horizontal Multiples. If you chose a field with nine values and a Vertical Multiple, Power View uses three rows of three columns. In this example, both the Horizontal and Vertical Multiple appear as one row by three columns. The Multiples group on the Layout tab offers Grid Height and Grid Width settings where you can control the number of rows and columns used.

Showing Data on a Map

As you probably know, Microsoft owns Bing. Bing maps are pretty cool. Because Microsoft owns Bing, Microsoft seems to have free rein to use the Bing API as much as they want to, and it is evident with this feature.

In a blank section of the Power View canvas, build a table showing revenue by state. With the table active, go to the Design tab in the ribbon and choose Map from the Switch Visualization category.

A warning appears that Excel has to send a list of states to Bing. I am trying to think of a case where you would care. If you were working for a secret government agency and you were mapping the location of where the Atomic Energy Commission stores the remains of alien UFO crashes, and you think that some random person at Bing Maps is a UFO Conspiracy Theorist, then maybe you would care. However, I have to believe that Bing Maps is getting a million requests a day, and the odds of anyone figuring out that your list is of UFO storage sites instead of the location of Starbucks stores is slim.

11

After a few seconds of geocoding, a map displays. By default, the Revenue field becomes the size of the bubble in each state. When you click the map, icons let you zoom in or zoom out. Click the map and drag with the hand icon to center the map to a new position.

In Figure 11.17, the Channel field has been moved to the Color area. This creates a pie chart in each state showing the relative percentage of sales by channel. Apparently, eBooks are doing better in California than in Arizona and New Mexico.

Figure 11.17
Add Channel to the Color area.

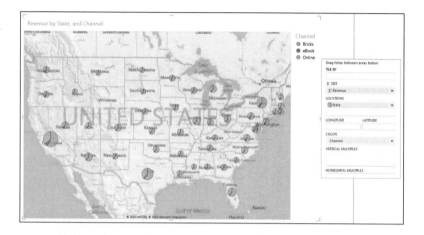

Using Table or Card View with Images

It keeps getting better. Remember that all new elements start as tables, and there are three kinds of tables: Table, Matrix, and Card.

A Matrix is similar to a regular pivot table. A Table presents the fields in a boring old table. Click any heading to sort the table by that heading. But wait! Add the Image URL field to your table. After a quick warning that Excel is getting the pictures from external sources, the images show up in the table.

Pictures also work in Card View. To switch a table to Card View, go to Design, Switch Visualizations, Table, Card View. This view presents the field title for each field in every card. Figure 11.18 shows a Card View with a Tile by Category.

Changing the Calculation

Multiple calculations are available for fields you add to an element. You can change numeric fields from Sum to Average, Min, Max, or Count. The cool addition is the ability to use Count Distinct and Count Non Blank for text fields.

In Figure 11.19, the table shows the states and then the number of distinct cities with sales in those states. Build a table with State, City, and Revenue. At the bottom of the Power View Fields List, open the drop-down for City and choose Count (Distinct).

Figure 11.18
Card View adds heading names to every record.

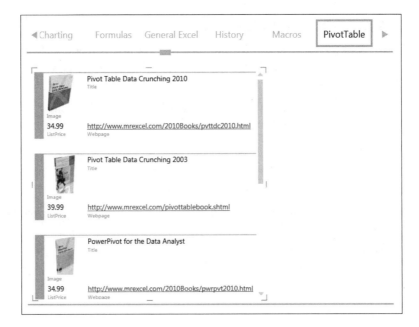

Figure 11.19
New calculations include Count Distinct.

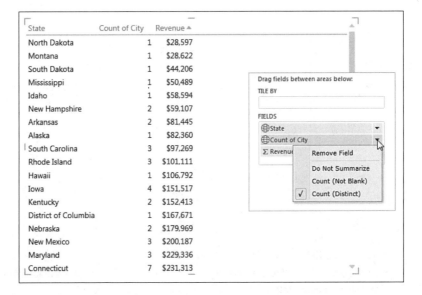

Another useful calculation option occurs when Power View summarizes a field that should not be summarized. For example, the product table has a ProductTier field with numeric values from 1 to 5. If you add this to a report, Power View might try to sum the Tier field when you wanted it to categorize by that field. Hover over the field at the bottom of the field list. Choose Do Not Summarize as the calculation.

Animating a Scatter Chart Over Time

To create a great scatter chart, you need three or four numeric fields that are related. Drag the first field to a blank section of the canvas. Choose Design, Switch Visualizations, Other Charts, Scatter.

Figure 11.20 shows the detail of the choices available in the Fields List when you are creating a scatter chart:

- Any numeric field for the x-axis.
- Any numeric field for the y-axis.
- Optionally, a field to control the size of the data point.
- A Details field. For every unique value in the Details field, you get one point in the scatter chart.
- Optionally, a color field. Each point is colored according to values in this field.
- A time field for the Play axis.

Figure 11.20
The scatter chart offers the most choices for drop zones.

If you add a field to the Play axis, a scrubber control appears along the bottom of the chart (see Figure 11.21). You can drag the marker left or right to see the chart at various points in time, or you can click the Play button to watch the chart animate.

The Play dimension is the key to having the chart animate. Unfortunately, at this time, only the scatter chart offers a Play field. You cannot animate column charts, bar charts, pie charts, or tables. Read the last section in this chapter for an advance look at GeoFlow to animate data on maps.

Figure 11.21
Use the scrubber at the bottom to see the points change over time.

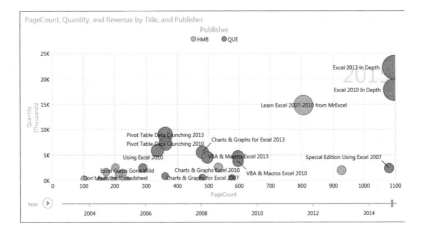

Some Closing Tips on Power View

As you experiment with Power View, keep these tips in mind:

- Be careful when clicking on charts. Click in the white space to select a chart. If you inadvertently click one of the chart columns, you've just filtered everything else on the canvas.

- The Fields List has headings for Active and All. If you just created a little chart with two fields, it is likely that the Fields List is now in Active mode, which means you only see the tables used in that chart. This is alarming, because all of your other tables and fields are missing. Don't be alarmed. Click All at the top of the field list, and they all come back.

- Don't be afraid to try new charts or tables. Create something. If it doesn't look good, right-click and select Cut. No harm. After using Power View, I am surprised how snappy and efficient it is. I have been dealing with 411,000 records in five charts and animating over time and have not had one crash.

Animating Pivot Table Data on a Map

The GeoFlow add-in for Excel 2013 will be released in early 2013 after a public beta in November 2012. The add-in will be free for anyone with Office 2013 Pro Plus. Like Power View, it offers another way to make use of data stored in the PowerPivot model.

After downloading the add-in, go to Tools, Options, Add-Ins. At the bottom of the screen, choose Manage Com Add-Ins and then choose Enable GeoFlow for Excel 2013.

After the product is installed, a 3-D Map drop-down displays on the right side of the Data tab in Excel (see Figure 11.22).

11

Figure 11.22
Explore your data set in a
3-D map.

The process of locating points on a map is called *geocoding*. When you first launch GeoFlow,
you have to choose the geography fields. Check City and State in the task pane on the right
side. Make sure that the correct geography level appears for each field. If your data contains
street addresses and GeoFlow detects these as Latitude, you will not have a good map.

After you've chosen the geography fields, click Map It in the lower-right corner (see Figure 11.23).

Figure 11.23
Choose Geography and
click Map It.

It takes a short while for GeoFlow to complete the geocoding process. You can start to
move fields around the PivotTable Fields List on the right side. Put a numeric field as the
Height field. If you want to differentiate revenue, add a field to the Category field. To animate the chart over time, put a date field in the Time drop zone.

You most likely will want to choose Temporal Accumulation. Say that you are tracking ticket sales for an event. In week 1, you sell 100 tickets. In week 2, you sell another 50 tickets. The total number of tickets sold is 150. By choosing Temporal Accumulation, GeoFlow shows 150 tickets sold as of week 2. If you don't choose Temporal Accumulation, then the 100 tickets from week 1 disappear when the time slider gets to week 2. Figure 11.24 shows the initial map. Using the scroll wheel on your mouse, you can fly around the map.

Figure 11.24
The initial map.

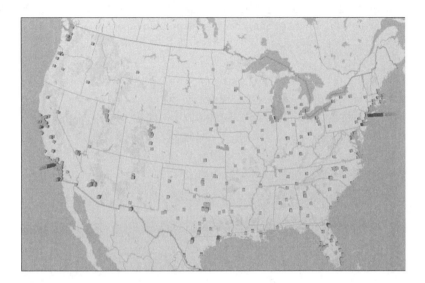

Figure 11.25 shows big sales in Manhattan and, to a lesser extent, Philadelphia.

Figure 11.25
Zoom in, all the way down to the street view, if your data is that granular.

11

Plans for GeoFlow include enabling you to build a fly-over tour by adding scenes to a Tour Manager pane. A typical tour might start with the U.S. overview for 10 seconds and then include fly-overs for each major pocket of customers.

Next Steps

Chapter 12, "Enhancing Your Pivot Table Reports with Macros," introduces you to simple macros you can use to enhance your pivot table reports.

11

Enhancing Your Pivot Table Reports with Macros

12

Why Use Macros with Your Pivot Table Reports?

Imagine that you could be in multiple locations at one time, with multiple clients at one time, helping them with their pivot table reports. Suppose you could help multiple clients refresh their data, extract top 20 records, group by months, or sort by revenue—all at the same time. The fact is you can do just that by using Excel macros.

A *macro* is a series of keystrokes that have been recorded and saved. Once saved, the macro can be played back on command. In other words, you can record your actions in a macro, save the macro, and then allow your clients to play back your actions with the touch of a button. It would be as though you were right there with them! This functionality is especially useful when you're distributing pivot table reports.

For example, suppose that you want to give your clients the option of grouping their pivot table report by month, by quarter, or by year. Although the process of grouping can be performed by anyone, some of your clients might not have a clue how to do it. In this case, you could record a macro to group by month, a macro to group by quarter, and a macro to group by year. Then you could create three buttons, one for each macro. In the end, your clients, having little experience with pivot tables, need only to click a button to group their pivot table report.

A major benefit of using macros with your pivot table reports is the power you can give your clients to easily perform pivot table actions that they would not normally be able to perform on their own, empowering them to more effectively analyze the data you provide.

Recording Your First Macro

Look at the pivot table in Figure 12.1. You know that you can refresh this pivot table by right-clicking inside the pivot table and selecting Refresh Data. Now, if you were to record your actions with a macro while you refreshed this pivot table, you, or anyone else, could replicate your actions and refresh this pivot table by running the macro.

Figure 12.1
You can easily refresh this basic pivot table by right-clicking and selecting Refresh, but if you recorded your actions with a macro, you could also refresh this pivot table simply by running the macro.

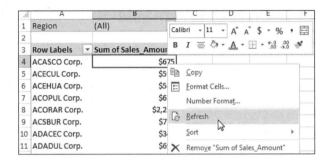

The first step in recording a macro is to initiate the Record Macro dialog. Select the Developer tab on the ribbon and then select Record Macro.

> **TIP**
> Can't find the Developer tab on the ribbon? Click the File tab on the ribbon and then choose the Options selection. The Excel Options dialog opens; click Customize Ribbon. In the list box to the far right, place a check next to Developer. Placing a check next to this option enables the Developer tab.

When the Record Macro dialog activates, you can fill in a few key pieces of information about the macro:

- **Macro Name**—Enter a name for your macro. You should generally enter a name that describes the action being performed.

- **Shortcut Key**—You can enter any letter into this input box. That letter becomes part of a set of keys on your keyboard that can be pressed to play back the macro. This is optional.

- **Store Macro In**—Specify where you want the macro to be stored. If you are distributing your pivot table report, you should select This Workbook so that the macro is available to your clients.

- **Description**—In this input box, you can enter a few words that give more detail about the macro.

Because this macro refreshes your pivot table when it is played, name your macro **RefreshData**. Also assign a shortcut key of **R**. Notice that the dialog gives you a key combination of Ctrl+Shift+R. Keep in mind that you use the key combination to play your macro after it is created. Be sure to store the macro in This Workbook. Click OK to continue. Your dialog should look like the one shown in Figure 12.2.

Figure 12.2
Fill in the Record Macro dialog as shown here, and then click OK to continue.

When you click OK in the Record Macro dialog, you initiate the recording process. At this point, any action you perform is being recorded by Excel. In this case, you want to record the process of refreshing your pivot table.

Right-click anywhere inside the pivot table and select Refresh Data. After you have refreshed your pivot table, you can stop the recording process by going up to the Developer tab and selecting the Stop Recording button.

Congratulations! You have just recorded your first macro. You can now play your macro by pressing Ctrl, Shift, and R on your keyboard at the same time.

A Word on Macro Security

You should be aware that when you record a macro yourself, your macro runs on your PC with no security restrictions. However, when you distribute workbooks that contain macros, your clients have to let Excel know that your workbook is not a security risk, thus allowing your macros to run.

Indeed, you will note that the sample file that comes with this chapter does not run unless you tell Excel to enable the macros within.

The best way to do this is to use the workbook in a *trusted location*, a directory that is deemed a safe zone where only trusted workbooks are placed. A trusted location allows you and your clients to run a macro-enabled workbook with no security restrictions, as long as the workbook is in that location.

To set up a trusted location, follow these steps:

1. Select the Macro Security button on the Developer tab. This activates the Trust Center dialog.

2. Select the Trusted Locations button.

3. Select Add New Location.

4. Click Browse to specify the directory to be considered a trusted location.

After you specify a trusted location, all workbooks opened from that location are, by default, opened with macros enabled.

12

In Excel 2013, Microsoft has enhanced the security model to remember files that you've deemed trustworthy. That is to say, when you open an Excel workbook and click the Enable button, Excel remembers that you trusted that file. Each time you open the workbook after that, Excel automatically trusts it.

For information on macro security in Excel 2013, pick up Que Publishing's *Excel 2013 In Depth* (ISBN 0-7897-4857-6) by Bill Jelen.

Creating a User Interface with Form Controls

Allowing your clients to run your macro with shortcut keys such as Ctrl+Shift+R can be a satisfactory solution if you have only one macro in your pivot table report. However, suppose you want to allow your clients to perform several macro actions. In this case, you should give your clients a clear and easy way to run each macro without having to remember a gaggle of shortcut keys. A basic user interface provides the perfect solution. You can think of a user interface as a set of controls such as buttons, scrollbars, and other devices that allow users to run macros with a simple click of the mouse.

In fact, Excel offers a set of controls designed specifically for creating user interfaces directly on a spreadsheet. These controls are called *form controls*. The general idea behind form controls is that you can place one on a spreadsheet and then assign a macro to it— meaning a macro you have already recorded. After a macro is assigned to the control, that macro is executed, or played, when the control is clicked.

You can find form controls in the Controls group on the Developer tab. To get to the form controls, simply select the Insert icon in the Controls group, as demonstrated in Figure 12.3.

12

Figure 12.3
To see the available form controls, click Insert in the Controls group on the Developer tab.

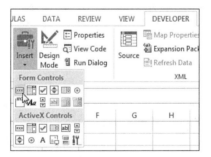

Notice that there are form controls and ActiveX controls. Although they look similar, they are quite different. Form controls, with their limited overhead and easy configuration settings, are designed specifically for use on a spreadsheet. Meanwhile, ActiveX controls are typically used on Excel user forms. As a general rule, you always want to use form controls when working on a spreadsheet.

Here, you can select the control that best suits your needs. In this example, you want your clients to be able to refresh their pivot table with the click of a button. Click the Button control to select it and then drop the control onto your spreadsheet by clicking the location you would like to place the button.

After you drop the button control onto your spreadsheet, the Assign Macro dialog, shown in Figure 12.4, opens and asks you to assign a macro to this button. Select the macro you want to assign to the button, in this case RefreshData, and then click OK.

Figure 12.4
Select the macro you want to assign to the button and then click OK. In this case, you want to select RefreshData.

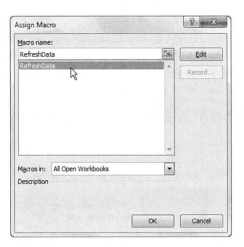

> NOTE Keep in mind that all the controls in the Forms toolbar work in the same way as the command button, in that you assign a macro to run when the control is selected.

12

As you can see in Figure 12.5, you can assign each macro in your workbook to a different form control and then name the controls to distinguish between them.

Figure 12.5
You can create a different button for each one of your macros.

Region	(All)	
Row Labels	Sum of Sales_Amount	
ACASCO Corp.	$675	
ACECUL Corp.	$593	
ACEHUA Corp.	$580	
ACOPUL Corp.	$675	
ACORAR Corp.	$2,232	
ACSBUR Corp.	$720	
ADACEC Corp.	$345	
ADADUL Corp.	$690	
ADANAS Corp.	$345	
ADCOMB Corp.	$553	

Refresh Pivot Table

See Top 20 Customers

See Bottom 20 Customers

Reset Pivot Table

Figure 12.6 demonstrates that after you have all the controls you need for your pivot table report, you can format the controls and surrounding spreadsheet to create a basic interface.

Figure 12.6
You can easily create the feeling of an interface with a handful of macros, a few form controls, and a little formatting.

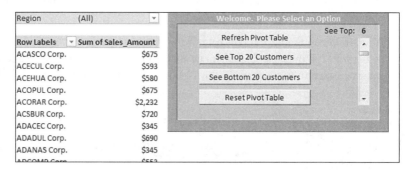

Altering a Recorded Macro to Add Functionality

When you record a macro, Excel creates a module that stores the recorded steps of your actions. These recorded steps are actually lines of VBA code that make up your macro. You can add some interesting functionality to your pivot table reports by tweaking your macro's VBA code to achieve various effects.

To get a better understanding of how this process works, start by creating a new macro that extracts the top five records by customer. Go to the Developer tab and select Record Macro. Set up the Record Macro dialog as shown in Figure 12.7. Name your new macro **TopNthCusts** and specify This Workbook as the place where you want to store the macro. Click OK to start recording.

Figure 12.7
Name your new macro and specify where you want to store it.

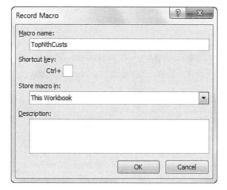

After you have started recording, right-click the Customer field and select Filter. Then select Top 10. Selecting this option opens the Filter dialog, where you specify that you want to see the top five customers by sales amount. Enter the settings shown in Figure 12.8 and then click OK.

Figure 12.8
Enter the settings you see here to get the top five customers by revenue.

After successfully recording the steps to extract the top five customers by revenue, select Stop Recording from the Developer tab.

You now have a macro that, when played, filters your pivot table to the top five customers by revenue. The plan is to tweak this macro to respond to a scrollbar. That is, you force the macro to base the number used to filter the pivot table on the number represented by a scrollbar in your user interface. In other words, a user can get the top five, top eight, or top 32 simply by moving a scrollbar up or down.

To get a scrollbar onto your spreadsheet, select the Insert icon on the Developer tab; then select the scrollbar control from the form controls. Place the scrollbar control onto your spreadsheet. You can change the dimensions of the scrollbar to an appropriate length and width by clicking and dragging the corners.

Right-click the scrollbar and select Format Control. This activates the Format Object dialog. Here, you make the following setting changes: Set Minimum Level to 1 so the scrollbar cannot go below 1, set Maximum Level to 200 so the scrollbar cannot go above 200, and set Cell Link to $M$2 so that the number represented by the scrollbar will output to cell M2. After you have completed these steps, your dialog should look like the one shown in Figure 12.9.

Figure 12.9
After you have placed a scrollbar on your spreadsheet, configure the scrollbar as shown here.

Next, assign the TopNthCusts macro you just recorded to your scrollbar, as demonstrated in Figure 12.10. Right-click the scrollbar and select Assign Macro. Select the TopNthCusts macro from the list and then click OK. Assigning this macro ensures that it plays each time the scrollbar is clicked.

Figure 12.10
Select the macro from the list.

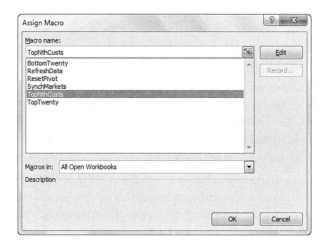

At this point, test your scrollbar by clicking it. When you click your scrollbar, two things should happen: The TopNthCusts macro should play, and the number in cell M2 should change to reflect your scrollbar's position. The number in cell M2 is important because that is the number you are going to reference in your TopNthCusts macro.

The only thing left to do is to tweak your macro to respond to the number in cell M2, effectively tying it to your scrollbar. To do this, you have to get to the VBA code that makes up the macro. You have several ways to get there, but for the purposes of this example, go to the Developer tab and select Macros. Selecting this option opens the Macro dialog, exposing several options. From here, you can run, delete, step into, or edit a selected macro. To get to the VBA code that makes up your macro, select the macro and then select Edit, as demonstrated in Figure 12.11.

The Visual Basic Editor opens with a detailed view of all the VBA code that makes up this macro (see Figure 12.12). Notice that the number 5 is hard-coded as part of your macro. The reason is that you originally recorded your macro to filter the top five customers by revenue. Your goal here is to replace the hard-coded number 5 with the value in cell M2, which is tied to your scrollbar.

You delete the number 5 and replace it with the following:

```
ActiveSheet.Range("M2").Value
```

Your macro's code should now look similar to the code shown in Figure 12.13.

Figure 12.11
To get to the VBA code that makes up the TopNthCusts macro, select the macro and then select Edit.

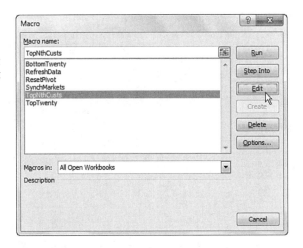

Figure 12.12
Your goal is to replace the hard-coded number 5, as specified when you originally recorded your macro, with the value in cell M2.

```
Sub TopNthCusts()
'
' TopNthCusts Macro
'

'
    Range("A4").Select
    ActiveSheet.PivotTables("PivotTable1").PivotFields("Customer_Name").ClearAllFilters

    ActiveSheet.PivotTables("PivotTable1").PivotFields("Customer_Name"). _
        PivotFilters.Add Type:=xlTopCount, DataField:=ActiveSheet.PivotTables( _
        "PivotTable1").PivotFields("Sum of Sales_Amount"), Value1:=5

End Sub
```

Figure 12.13
Simply delete the hard-coded number 5 and replace it with a reference to cell M2.

```
Sub TopNthCusts()
'
' TopNthCusts Macro
'

'
    Range("A4").Select
    ActiveSheet.PivotTables("PivotTable1").PivotFields("Customer_Name").ClearAllFilters

    ActiveSheet.PivotTables("PivotTable1").PivotFields("Customer_Name"). _
        PivotFilters.Add Type:=xlTopCount, DataField:=ActiveSheet.PivotTables( _
        "PivotTable1").PivotFields("Sum of Sales_Amount"), Value1:=ActiveSheet.Range("M2").Value

End Sub
```

Close the Visual Basic Editor to get back to your pivot table report. Test your scrollbar by setting it to 11. Your macro should play and filter out the top 11 customers by revenue, as shown in Figure 12.14.

Figure 12.14
After a little formatting, you have a clear and easy way for your clients to get the top customers by revenue.

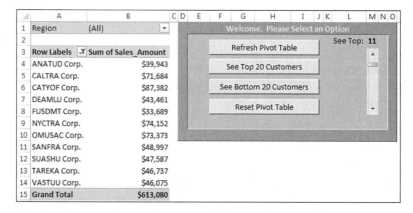

CASE STUDY: SYNCHRONIZING TWO PIVOT TABLES WITH ONE COMBO BOX

The report in Figure 12.15 contains two pivot tables. Each pivot table has a filter field for allowing you to select a market. The problem is that every time you select a market from the filter field in one pivot table, you have to select the same market from the filter field in the other pivot table to ensure you are analyzing the correct units sold versus revenue.

Not only is it a bit of a hassle to have to synchronize both pivot tables every time you want to analyze a new market's data, but there is a chance you, or your clients, might forget to do so.

Figure 12.15
This pivot table report contains two pivot tables with filter fields that filter out a market. The issue is that you have to synchronize the two pivot tables when analyzing data for a particular market.

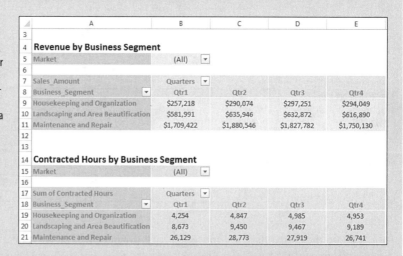

One way to synchronize these pivot tables is to use a combo box. The idea is to record a macro that selects a market from the Market field of both tables. Then you can create a combo box and fill it with the market names that exist in your two pivot tables. Finally, you can alter your macro to filter both pivot tables, using the value from your combo box. To do so, follow these steps:

1. Create a new macro and call it **SynchMarkets**. When recording starts, select the California market from the Market field in both pivot tables; then stop recording.

2. Activate the Forms toolbar and place a combo box onto your spreadsheet.

3. Create a hard-coded list of all the markets that exist in your pivot table. Note that the first entry in your list is (All). You must include this entry if you want to be able to select all markets with your combo box.

    As you can see in Figure 12.16, you place the combo box and your list of markets directly in your spreadsheet.

Figure 12.16
At this point, you should have all the tools you need: a macro that changes the Market field of both pivot tables, a combo box on your spreadsheet, and a list of all the markets that exist in your pivot table.

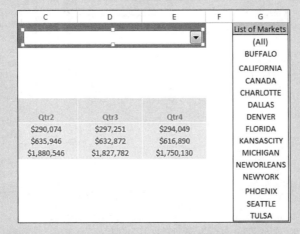

4. Right-click your combo box and select Format Control to perform the initial setup.

    First, specify an input range for the list you are using to fill your combo box. In this case, this means the market list you created in step 3. Next, specify a cell link—that is, the cell that shows the index number of the item you select (cell H1 is the cell link in this example). After you have configured your combo box, your dialog should look similar to the one shown in Figure 12.17.

12

Figure 12.17
The settings for your combo box should reference your market list as the input range and specify a cell link close to your market list. In this case, the cell link is cell H1.

At this point, you should be able to select a market from your combo box and see the associated index number in cell H1. Why an index number instead of the name of the selected market? Well, the only output of a combo box form control is an index number. This is the position number of the selected item. For instance, in Figure 12.18, the selection of Charlotte from the combo box results in the number 5 in cell H1. This means that Charlotte is the fifth item in the combo box.

Figure 12.18
Your combo box, now filled with market names, will output an index number in cell H1 when a market is selected.

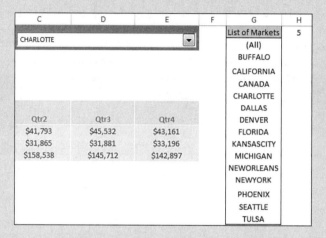

To make use of this index number, you have to pass it through the INDEX function. The INDEX function converts an index number to a value that can be recognized.

5. Enter an INDEX function (shown in Figure 12.19) that converts the index number in cell H1 to a value.

Figure 12.19
The INDEX function in cell I1 converts the index number in cell H1 to a value. You will eventually use the value in cell I1 to alter your macro.

An INDEX function requires two arguments to work properly. The first argument is the range of the list you are working with. In most cases, you use the same range that is feeding your combo box. The second argument is the index number. If the index number is in a cell (like in cell H1), you can simply reference the cell.

6. Edit the SynchMarkets macro using the value in cell I1, instead of a hard-coded value.

To get to the VBA code that makes up your macro, click the Macros button on the Developer tab. This activates the Macro dialog, shown in Figure 12.20. From here, select the SynchMarkets macro and then click Edit.

Figure 12.20
In the Macro dialog, select the SynchMarkets macro and click Edit.

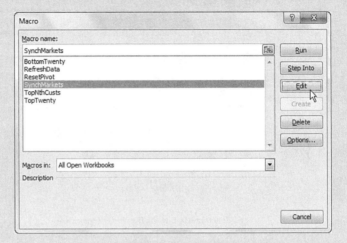

When you recorded your macro originally, you selected the California market from the Market field in both pivot tables. As you can see in Figure 12.21, California is hard-coded in your macro's VBA code.

Figure 12.21
The California market is hard-coded in your macro's VBA code.

12

Replace California with **ActiveSheet.Range("I1").Value**, as demonstrated in Figure 12.22. This code references the value in cell I1. After you have edited the macro, close the Visual Basic Editor to get back to the spreadsheet.

Figure 12.22
Replace California with ActiveSheet. Range("I1"). Value and then close the Visual Basic Editor.

7. All that is left to do is ensure that the macro will play when you select a market from the combo box. Right-click the combo box and select Assign Macro. Select the SynchMarkets macro and then click OK.

8. Clean up the formatting on your newly created report by hiding the filter fields in your pivot tables, the market list you created, and any unseemly formulas.

As you can see in Figure 12.23, this setup provides your clients with an attractive interface that allows them to make selections in multiple pivot tables using one control.

Figure 12.23
Your pivot table report is ready to use!

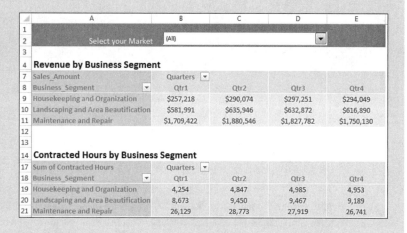

	A	B	C	D	E
1					
2	Select your Market	(All)			
3					
4	**Revenue by Business Segment**				
7	Sales_Amount	Quarters			
8	Business_Segment	Qtr1	Qtr2	Qtr3	Qtr4
9	Housekeeping and Organization	$257,218	$290,074	$297,251	$294,049
10	Landscaping and Area Beautification	$581,991	$635,946	$632,872	$616,890
11	Maintenance and Repair	$1,709,422	$1,880,546	$1,827,782	$1,750,130
12					
13					
14	**Contracted Hours by Business Segment**				
17	Sum of Contracted Hours	Quarters			
18	Business_Segment	Qtr1	Qtr2	Qtr3	Qtr4
19	Housekeeping and Organization	4,254	4,847	4,985	4,953
20	Landscaping and Area Beautification	8,673	9,450	9,467	9,189
21	Maintenance and Repair	26,129	28,773	27,919	26,741

> **TIP**
>
> When you select a new item from your combo box, the pivot tables automatically adjust the columns to fit the data. This behavior can be annoying when you have a formatted template. You can suppress this behavior by right-clicking each pivot table and selecting PivotTable Options. Selecting this option activates the PivotTable Options dialog, where you can remove the check next to the AutoFit Column Widths on Update selection.

What's Next

In the next chapter, you go beyond recording macros. Chapter 13, "Using VBA to Create Pivot Tables," shows how to utilize Visual Basic for Applications to create powerful, behind-the-scenes processes and calculations using pivot tables.

Using VBA to Create Pivot Tables

13

Version 5 of Excel introduced a powerful new macro language called Visual Basic for Applications (VBA). Every copy of Excel shipped since 1993 has had a copy of the powerful VBA language hiding behind the worksheets. VBA enables you to perform steps that you normally perform in Excel quickly and flawlessly. I have seen a VBA program change a process that would take days each month and turn it into a single button click and a minute of processing time.

Do not be intimidated by VBA. The VBA macro recorder tool gets you 90% of the way to a useful macro, and I get you the rest of the way using examples in this chapter.

Every example in this chapter is available for download from www.mrexcel.com/pivot2013data.html/.

Enabling VBA in Your Copy of Excel

By default, VBA is disabled in Office 2013. Before you can start using VBA, you need to enable macros in the Trust Center. Follow these steps:

1. Click the File menu to show the Backstage View.

2. In the left navigation, select Options. The Excel Options dialog displays.

3. In the left navigation of Excel Options, select Customize Ribbon.

4. The right list box has a list of main tabs available in Excel. By default, the Developer tab is clear. Select this tab to include it in the ribbon. Click OK to close Excel Options.

5. Click the Developer tab in the ribbon. As shown in Figure 13.1, the Code group on the left side of the ribbon includes icons for the Visual Basic Editor, Macros, Macro Recorder, and Macro Security.

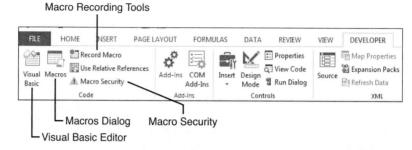

Figure 13.1
Enable the Developer tab to access the VBA tools.

Macro Recording Tools

Macros Dialog   Macro Security
Visual Basic Editor

6. Click the Macro Security icon. Excel opens the Trust Center, where you have four security choices. These choices use different words than those used in Excel 97 through Excel 2003. Step 7 explains the choices.

7. Choose one of the following options:

- **Disable All Macros with Notification**—This setting is equivalent to medium macro security in Excel 2003. When you open a workbook that contains macros, a message appears alerting you that macros are in the workbook. If you expect macros to be in the workbook, you can enable the macros. This is the safest setting because it forces you to explicitly enable macros in each workbook.

- **Enable All Macros**—This setting is not recommended because potentially dangerous code can run. However, this setting is equivalent to low macros security in Excel 2003. Because it can enable rogue macros to run in files that are sent to you by others, Microsoft recommends that you do not use this setting.

Do not choose Disable All Macros Without Notification as your macros will not be able to run. Also don't consider Disable All Macros Except Digitally Signed Macros.

Using a File Format That Enables Macros

The default Excel 2013 file format is initially the Excel Workbook (.xlsx). This workbook is defined to disallow macros. You can build a macro in an .xlsx workbook, but it won't be saved with the workbook.

You have several options for saving workbooks that enable macros:

- **Excel Macro-Enabled Workbook (.xlsm)**—This uses the XML-based method for storing workbooks and enables macros. I prefer this file type because it is compact and less prone to becoming corrupt.

- **Excel Binary Workbook (.xlsb)**—This is a binary format and always enables macros.

■ **Excel 97-2003 Workbook (.xls)**—There are billions of .xls files in existence and all of them are capable of storing macros. The downside, particularly with pivot tables, is that .xls files force Excel into compatibility mode. You lose access to slicers, new filters, rows 65537 through 1048576, columns IX through XFD, and other pivot table improvements.

When you create a new workbook, you can use File, Save As to choose the appropriate file type.

Visual Basic Editor

From Excel, press Alt+F11 or select Developer, Visual Basic to open the Visual Basic Editor, as shown in Figure 13.2. The three main sections of the VBA Editor are described here. If this is your first time using VBA, some of these items might be disabled. Follow the instructions given in the following list to make sure that each is enabled:

Figure 13.2
The Visual Basic Editor window is lurking behind every copy of Excel shipped since 1993.

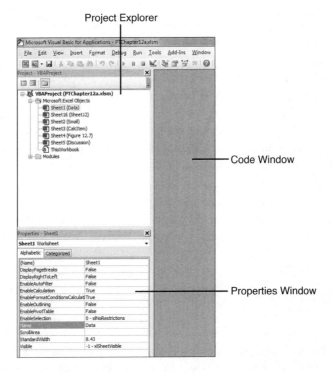

■ **Project Explorer**—This pane displays a hierarchical tree of all open workbooks. Expand the tree to see the worksheets, code modules, userforms, and class modules present in the workbook. If the Project Explorer is not visible, enable it by pressing Ctrl+R.

- **Properties window**—The Properties window is important when you begin to program user forms. It has some use when you are writing normal code, so enable it by pressing F4.

- **Code window**—This is the area where you write your code. Code is stored in one or more code modules attached to your workbook. To add a code module to a workbook, select Insert, Module from the VBA menu.

Visual Basic Tools

Visual Basic is a powerful development environment. Although this chapter cannot offer a complete course on VBA, if you are new to VBA, you should take advantage of these important tools:

- As you begin to type code, Excel might offer a drop-down with valid choices. This feature, known as AutoComplete, enables you to type code faster and eliminate typing mistakes.

- For assistance on any keyword, put the cursor in the keyword and press F1. Excel Help displays a help topic regarding the keyword.

- Excel checks each line of code as you finish it. Lines in error appear in red. Comments appear in green. You can add a comment by typing a single apostrophe. Use lots of comments so you can remember what each section of code is doing.

- Despite the aforementioned error checking, Excel might still encounter an error at runtime. If this happens, click the Debug button. The line that caused the error is highlighted in yellow. Hover your mouse cursor over any variable to see the current value of the variable.

- When you are in Debug mode, use the Debug menu to step line by line through code. If you have a wide monitor, try arranging the Excel window and the VBA window side by side. This way, you can see the effect of running a line of code on the worksheet.

- Other great debugging tools are breakpoints, the Watch window, the Object Browser, and the Immediate window. Read about these tools in the Excel VBA Help menu.

13

The Macro Recorder

Excel offers a macro recorder that is about 90% perfect. Unfortunately, the last 10% is frustrating. Code that you record to work with one data set is hard-coded to work only with that data set. This behavior might work fine if your transactional database occupies cells A1:L87601 every single day, but if you are pulling in a new invoice register every day, it is unlikely that you will have the same number of rows each day. Given that you might need to work with other data, it would be a lot better if Excel could record selecting cells using the End key. This is one of the shortcomings of the macro recorder.

In reality, Excel pros use the macro recorder to record code but then expect to have to clean up the recorded code.

Understanding Object-Oriented Code

VBA is an object-oriented language. Most lines of VBA code follow the `Noun.Verb` syntax. However, in VBA, it is called `Object.Method`. Examples of objects are workbooks, worksheets, cells, and ranges of cells. Methods can be typical Excel actions such as `.Copy`, `.Paste`, and `.PasteSpecial`.

Many methods allow adverbs—parameters you use to specify how to perform the method. If you see a construct with a colon and equal sign (`:=`), you know that the macro recorder is describing how the method should work.

You also might see the type of code in which you assign a value to the adjectives of an object. In VBA, adjectives are called *properties*. If you set `ActiveCell.Font.ColorIndex = 3`, you are setting the font color of the active cell to red. Note that when you are dealing with properties, there is only an = (equal sign), not a := (colon and equal sign).

Learning Tricks of the Trade

You need to master a few simple techniques to write efficient VBA code. These techniques help you make the jump to writing effective code.

Writing Code to Handle Any Size Data Range

The macro recorder hard-codes the fact that your data is in a range, such as A1:L87601. Although this hard-coding works for today's data set, it might not work as you get new data sets. You need to write code that can deal with different size data sets.

The macro recorder uses syntax such as `Range("H12")` to refer to a cell. However, it is more flexible to use `Cells(12, 8)` to refer to the cell in row 12, column 8. Similarly, the macro recorder refers to a rectangular range as `Range("A1:L87601")`. However, it is more flexible to use the `Cells` syntax to refer to the upper-left corner of the range and then use the `Resize()` syntax to refer to the number of rows and columns in the range. The equivalent way to describe the preceding range is `Cells(1, 1).Resize(87601,12)`. This approach is more flexible because you can replace any of the numbers with a variable.

In the Excel user interface, you can use the End key on the keyboard to jump to the end of a range of data. If you move the cell pointer to the final row on the worksheet and press the End key followed by the up-arrow key, the cell pointer jumps to the last row with data. The equivalent of doing this in VBA is to use the following code:

```
Range("A1048576").End(xlUp).Select
```

13

You do not need to select this cell; you just need to find the row number that contains the last row. The following code locates this row and saves the row number to a variable named `FinalRow`:

```
FinalRow = Range("A1048576").End(xlUp).Row
```

There is nothing magic about the variable name `FinalRow`. You could call this variable x, y, or even your dog's name. However, because VBA enables you to use meaningful variable names, you should use something such as `FinalRow` to describe the final row.

> **NOTE**
>
> Excel 2013 offers 1,048,576 rows and 16,384 columns for a regular workbook. If the workbook opens in compatibility mode, you only have 65,536 rows and 256 columns. To make your code flexible enough to handle either situation, you can use Rows.Count to learn the total number of rows in the current workbook. The preceding code can then be generalized like so:
>
> ```
> FinalRow = Cells(Rows.Count, 1).End(xlUp).Row
> ```

You also can find the final column in a data set. If you are relatively sure that the data set begins in row 1, you can use the End key in combination with the left-arrow key to jump from cell XFD1 to the last column with data. To generalize for the possibility that the code is running in legacy versions of Excel, you can use the following code:

```
FinalCol = Cells(1, Columns.Count).End(xlToLeft).Column
```

End+Down Versus End+Up

You might be tempted to find the final row by starting in cell A1 and using the End key in conjunction with the down-arrow key. Avoid this approach. Data coming from another system is imperfect. If your program imports 500,000 rows from a legacy computer system every day for the next 5 years, a day will come when someone manages to key a null value into the data set. This value will cause a blank cell or even a blank row to appear in the middle of your data set. Using Range("A1").End(xlDown) stops prematurely just above the blank cell instead of including all your data. This blank cell causes that day's report to miss thousands of rows of data, a potential disaster that calls into question the credibility of your report. Take the extra step of starting at the last row in the worksheet to greatly reduce the risk of problems.

13

Using Super-Variables: Object Variables

In typical programming languages, a variable holds a single value. You might use x = 4 to assign a value of 4 to the variable x.

Think about a single cell in Excel. Many properties describe a cell. A cell might contain a value such as 4, but the cell also has a font size, a font color, a row, a column, possibly a formula, possibly a comment, a list of precedents, and more. It is possible in VBA to create a super-variable that contains all the information about a cell or about any object. A statement to create a typical variable such as x = Range("A1") assigns the current value of A1 to the variable x.

However, you can use the Set keyword to create an object variable:

```
Set x = Range("A1")
```

You have now created a super-variable that contains all the properties of the cell. Instead of having a variable with only one value, you have a variable in which you can access the value of many properties associated with that variable. You can reference x.Formula to learn the formula in A1 or x.Font.ColorIndex to learn the color of the cell.

> **NOTE** The examples in this chapter frequently set up an object variable called PT to refer to the entire pivot table. This way, any time that the code would generally refer to ActiveSheet.PivotTables("PivotTable1"), you can specify PT to avoid typing the longer text.

Using With and End With to Shorten Code

You will frequently find that you are making several changes to the pivot table. Although the following code is explained later in this chapter, all these lines of code are for changing settings in the pivot table:

```
PT.NullString = 0
PT.RepeatAllLabels xlRepeatLabels
PT.ColumnGrand = False
PT.RowGrand = False
PT.RowAxisLayout xlTabularRow
PT.TableStyle2 = "PivotStyleMedium10"
PT.TableStyleRowStripes = True
```

For all those lines of code, the VBA engine has to figure out what you mean by PT. Your code executes faster if you only refer to PT once. Add an initial line of With PT. Then, all the remaining lines do not need to start with PT. Any line that starts with a period is assumed to be referring to the object in the With statement. Finish the code block using an End With statement:

```
With PT
    .NullString = 0
    .RepeatAllLabels xlRepeatLabels
    .ColumnGrand = False
    .RowGrand = False
    .RowAxisLayout xlTabularRow
    .TableStyle2 = "PivotStyleMedium10"
    .TableStyleRowStripes = True
End With
```

Understanding Versions

Pivot tables have been evolving. They were introduced in Excel 5 and perfected in Excel 97. In Excel 2000, pivot table creation in VBA was dramatically altered. Some new parameters

13

were added in Excel 2002. A few new properties, such as `PivotFilters` and `TableStyle2`, were added in Excel 2007. Slicers and new choices for Show Values As were added in Excel 2010. Timelines and the PowerPivot Data Model have been added in Excel 2013. Therefore, you need to be extremely careful when writing code in Excel 2013 that might be run in Excel 2007 or legacy versions of Excel.

Code for New Features Won't Work in Previous Versions

Each of the last three versions of Excel offered many new features in pivot tables. If you use code for a new feature, the code works in the current version, but it crashes in previous versions of Excel:

- Excel 2013 introduces the PowerPivot Data Model. You can add tables to the Data Model, create a relationship, and produce a pivot table. This code does not run in Excel 2010 or earlier. The function `xlDistinctCount` is new, and timelines are new.

- Excel 2010 introduced slicers, Repeat All Item Labels, named sets, and several new calculation options: `xlPercentOfParentColumn`, `xlPercentOfParentRow`, `xlPercentRunningTotal`, `xlRankAscending`, and `xlRankDescending`. These do not work in Excel 2007 or earlier.

- Excel 2007 introduced `ConvertToFormulas`, `xlCompactRow` layout, `xlAtTop` for the subtotal location, `TableStyles`, and `SortUsingCustomLists`. Macros that include this code fail in previous versions.

Building a Pivot Table in Excel VBA

This chapter does not mean to imply that you use VBA to build pivot tables to give to your clients. Instead, the purpose of this chapter is to remind you that you can use pivot tables as a means to an end. You can use a pivot table to extract a summary of data and then use that summary elsewhere.

> **NOTE** The code listings from this chapter are available for download at www.MrExcel.com/pivot2013data.html.

> **CAUTION**
> Beginning with Excel 2007, the user interface has new names for the various sections of a pivot table. Even so, VBA code continues to refer to the old names. Microsoft had to make this decision, otherwise millions of lines of code would stop working in Excel 2007 when they referred to a page field instead of a filter field. Although the four sections of a pivot table in the Excel user interface are Filters, Columns, Rows, and Values, VBA continues to use the old terms of Page fields, Column fields, Row fields, and Data fields.

In Excel 2000 and newer, you first build a pivot cache object to describe the input area of the data:

```
Dim WSD As Worksheet
Dim PTCache As PivotCache
Dim PT As PivotTable
Dim PRange As Range
Dim FinalRow As Long
Dim FinalCol As Long
Set WSD = Worksheets("Data")

' Delete any prior pivot tables
For Each PT In WSD.PivotTables
    PT.TableRange2.Clear
Next PT

' Define input area and set up a Pivot Cache
FinalRow = WSD.Cells(Rows.Count, 1).End(xlUp).Row
FinalCol = WSD.Cells(1, Columns.Count).End(xlToLeft).Column
Set PRange = WSD.Cells(1, 1).Resize(FinalRow, FinalCol)
Set PTCache = ActiveWorkbook.PivotCaches.Add(SourceType:=xlDatabase, _
    SourceData:=PRange)
```

After defining the pivot cache, use the `CreatePivotTable` method to create a blank pivot table based on the defined pivot cache:

```
Set PT = PTCache.CreatePivotTable(TableDestination:=WSD.Cells(2, FinalCol + 2), _
    TableName:="PivotTable1")
```

In the `CreatePivotTable` method, you specify the output location and optionally give the table a name. After running this line of code, you have a strange-looking blank pivot table, like the one shown in Figure 13.3. You now have to use code to drop fields onto the table.

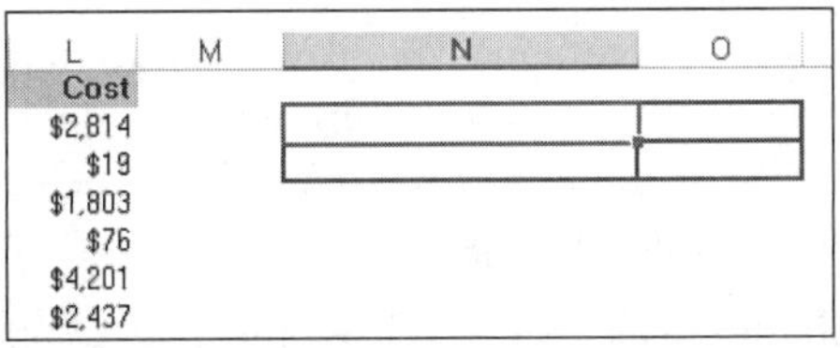

Figure 13.3
Immediately after you use the `CreatePivotTable` method, Excel gives you a four-cell blank pivot table that is not useful.

If you choose the Defer Layout Update setting in the user interface to build the pivot table, Excel does not recalculate the pivot table after you drop each field onto the table. By default in VBA, Excel calculates the pivot table as you execute each step of building the table. This could require the pivot table to be executed a half-dozen times before you get to the final result.

To speed up your code execution, you can temporarily turn off calculation of the pivot table by using the `ManualUpdate` property:

```
PT.ManualUpdate = True
```

You can now run through the steps needed to lay out the pivot table. In the `.AddFields` method, you can specify one or more fields that should be in the row, column, or filter area of the pivot table.

The `RowFields` parameter enables you to define fields that appear in the Rows layout area of the PivotTable Fields List. The `ColumnFields` parameter corresponds to the Columns layout area. The `PageFields` parameter corresponds to the Filters layout area.

The following line of code populates a pivot table with two fields in the rows area and one field in the columns area:

```
' Set up the row & column fields
PT.AddFields RowFields:=Array("Category", "Product"), _
    ColumnFields:="Region"
```

> **NOTE**
> If you are adding a single field to an area such as Region to the Columns area, you only need to specify the name of the field in quotes. If you are adding two or more fields, you have to include that list inside the array function.

Although the rows, columns, and filters fields of the pivot table can be handled with the `.AddFields` method, it is best to add fields to the data area using the code described in the next section.

Adding Fields to the Data Area

When you are adding fields to the data area of the pivot table, there are many settings that you would rather control rather than let Excel's IntelliSense decide.

Say that you are building a report with revenue. You likely want to sum the revenue. If you do not explicitly specify the calculation, Excel scans through the values in the underlying data. If 100% of the revenue cells are numeric, Excel sums. If one cell is blank or contains text, Excel decides to count the revenue. This produces confusing results.

Because of this possible variability, you should never use the `DataFields` argument in the `AddFields` method. Instead, change the property of the field to `xlDataField`. You can then specify the function to be `xlSum`.

While you are setting up the data field, you can change several other properties within the same `With...End With` block.

The `Position` property is useful when adding multiple fields to the data area. Specify 1 for the first field, 2 for the second field, and so on.

By default, Excel renames a Revenue field to something strange like Sum of Revenue. You can use the `.Name` property to change that heading back to something normal. Note that you cannot reuse the word Revenue as a name, but you can use "Revenue " (with a space).

You are not required to specify a number format, but it can make the resulting pivot table easier to understand and only takes an extra line of code:

```
' Set up the data fields
With PT.PivotFields("Revenue")
    .Orientation = xlDataField
    .Function = xlSum
    .Position = 1
    .NumberFormat = "#,##0"
    .Name = "Revenue "
End With
```

Formatting the Pivot Table

Microsoft introduced the Compact Layout for pivot tables in Excel 2007. This means that three layouts are available in Excel 2013. Excel should default to using the Tabular layout. This is good because Tabular view is the one that makes the most sense. It cannot hurt to add one line of code to ensure that you get the desired layout:

```
PT.RowAxisLayout xlTabularRow
```

In Tabular layout, each field in the row area is in a different column. Subtotals always appear at the bottom of each group. This is the layout that has been around the longest and is most conducive to reusing the pivot table report for further analysis.

The Excel user interface frequently defaults to Compact layout. In this layout, multiple columns fields are stacked up into a single column on the left side of the pivot table. To create this layout, use the following code:

```
PT.RowAxisLayout xlCompactRow
```

The one limitation of Tabular layout is that you cannot show the totals at the top of each group. If you need to do this, you'll want to switch to the Outline layout and show totals at the top of the group:

```
PT.RowAxisLayout xlOutlineRow
PT.SubtotalLocation xlAtTop
```

Your pivot table inherits the table style settings selected as the default on whatever computer happens to run the code. If you would like control over the final format, you can explicitly choose a table style. The following code applies banded rows and a medium table style:

```
' Format the pivot table
PT.ShowTableStyleRowStripes = True
PT.TableStyle2 = "PivotStyleMedium10"
```

At this point, you have given VBA all the settings required to correctly generate the pivot table. If you set ManualUpdate to False, Excel calculates and draws the pivot table. Thereafter, you can immediately set this back to True by using this code:

```
' Calc the pivot table
PT.ManualUpdate = False
PT.ManualUpdate = True
```

13

At this point, you have a complete pivot table, like the one shown in Figure 13.4.

Figure 13.4

Fewer than 50 lines of code create this pivot table in less than a second.

N	O	P	Q
Revenue		Region	
Category	Product	Midwest	North
Bar Equipment	Bar Cover	1,328	
	Cocktail Shaker 28 Oz	4,607	1,681
	Commercial Bar Blender	1,704	
	Garnish Center	455	51
	Glass Rimmers Triple Brushes	8,760	3,360
	Glass Rimmers Twin Brushes	1,278	846
	High Power Blender Easy-To-Clean Electronic Membrane	1,500	
	High Power Blender With Paddle Switches	1,125	

Listing 13.1 shows the complete code used to generate the pivot table.

Listing 13.1   Code to Generate a Pivot Table

```
Sub CreatePivot()
    '
    Dim WSD As Worksheet
    Dim PTCache As PivotCache
    Dim PT As PivotTable
    Dim PRange As Range
    Dim FinalRow As Long
    Set WSD = Worksheets("Data")

    ' Delete any prior pivot tables
    For Each PT In WSD.PivotTables
        PT.TableRange2.Clear
    Next PT
    WSD.Range("N1:AZ1").EntireColumn.Clear

    ' Define input area and set up a Pivot Cache
    FinalRow = WSD.Cells(Application.Rows.Count, 1).End(xlUp).Row
    FinalCol = WSD.Cells(1, Application.Columns.Count). _
        End(xlToLeft).Column
    Set PRange = WSD.Cells(1, 1).Resize(FinalRow, FinalCol)
    Set PTCache = ActiveWorkbook.PivotCaches.Add(SourceType:= _
        xlDatabase, SourceData:=PRange.Address)

    ' Create the Pivot Table from the Pivot Cache
    Set PT = PTCache.CreatePivotTable(TableDestination:=WSD. _
        Cells(2, FinalCol + 2), TableName:="PivotTable1")

    ' Turn off updating while building the table
    PT.ManualUpdate = True

    ' Set up the row & column fields
    PT.AddFields RowFields:=Array("Category", "Product"), _
        ColumnFields:="Region"

    ' Set up the data fields
    With PT.PivotFields("Revenue")
        .Orientation = xlDataField
        .Function = xlSum
        .Position = 1
```

13

```
      .NumberFormat = "#,##0"
   End With

   ' Format the pivot table
   PT.RowAxisLayout xlTabularRow
   PT.ShowTableStyleRowStripes = True
   PT.TableStyle2 = "PivotStyleMedium10"

   ' Calc the pivot table
   PT.ManualUpdate = False
   PT.ManualUpdate = True

   WSD.Activate
   Cells(2, FinalCol + 2).Select

End Sub
```

Dealing with Limitations of Pivot Tables

As with pivot tables in the user interface, Microsoft maintains tight control over a live pivot table. You need to be aware of these issues as your code is running on a sheet with a live pivot table.

Filling Blank Cells in the Data Area

It is always a bit annoying that Excel puts blank cells in the data area of a pivot table. In Figure 13.4, the North region had no sales of a Bar Cover, so that cell appears blank instead of with a zero.

You can override this in the Excel interface by using the For Empty Cells Show setting in the PivotTable Options dialog. The equivalent code is shown here:

```
PT.NullString = "0"
```

> **NOTE**
> Note that the Excel macro recorder always wraps that zero in quotation marks. No matter whether you specify "0" or just 0, the blank cells in the data area of the pivot table have numeric zeroes.

Filling Blank Cells in the Row Area

Excel 2010 added a much needed setting to fill in the blank cells along the left columns of a pivot table. This problem happens any time that you have two or more fields in the row area of a pivot table. Rather than repeating a label such as "Bar Equipment" in cells N5:N18, Microsoft traditionally has left those cells blank. To solve this problem in Excel 2013, use the following line of code:

```
PT.RepeatAllLabels xlRepeatLabels
```

Learning Why You Cannot Affect a Pivot Table by Inserting or Deleting Cells

You cannot use many Excel commands inside of a pivot table. Inserting rows, deleting rows, and cutting and pasting parts of a pivot table are all against the rules.

Say that you tried to delete the Grand Total column from column W in a pivot table. If you try to delete or clear column W, the macro comes to a screeching halt with a 1004 error, as shown in Figure 13.5.

Figure 13.5
You cannot delete just
part of a pivot table.

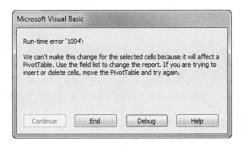

There are two strategies to get around this limitation. The first strategy is to find if there is already an equivalent command in the pivot table interface. For example, there is code to perform any of these actions:

- Remove the grand total column.
- Remove the grand total row.
- Add blank rows between each section.
- Suppress subtotals for outer row fields.

The second strategy is to convert the pivot table to values. You can then insert, cut, and clear as necessary.

Both strategies are discussed in the following sections.

Controlling Totals

The default pivot table includes a grand total row and a grand total column. You can choose to hide one or both of these elements.

To remove the grand total column from the right side of the pivot table, use

```
PT.ColumnGrand = False
```

To remove the grand total row from the bottom of the pivot table, use

```
PT.RowGrand = False
```

Turning off the subtotals rows is surprisingly complex. This issue comes up when you have multiple fields in the row area. Excel automatically turns on subtotals for the outermost row fields.

> **TIP**
>
> Did you know that you can have a pivot table show multiple subtotal rows? I have never seen anyone actually do this, but you can use the Field Settings dialog to specify that you want to see a Sum, Average, Count, Max, Min, and so on. Figure 13.6 shows this setting in the user interface.

Figure 13.6

It is rarely used, but the fact that you can specify multiple types of subtotals for a single field complicates the VBA code for suppressing subtotals.

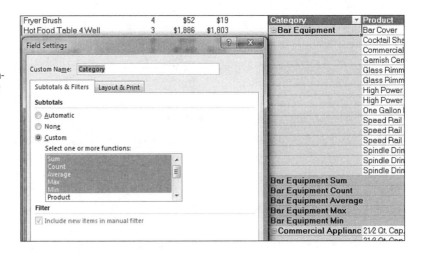

To suppress the subtotals for a field, you must set the `Subtotals` property equal to an array of 12 `False` values. The first `False` turns off automatic subtotals, the second `False` turns off the `Sum` subtotal, the third `False` turns off the `Count` subtotal, and so on. This line of code suppresses the `Category` subtotal:

```
PT.PivotFields("Category").Subtotals = Array(False, False, False, False, _
    False, False, False, False, False, False, False, False)
```

A different technique is to turn on the first subtotal. This method automatically turns off the other 11 subtotals. You can then turn off the first subtotal to make sure that all subtotals are suppressed:

```
PT.PivotFields("Category").Subtotals(1) = True
PT.PivotFields("Category").Subtotals(1) = False
```

You might be wondering about the new Distinct Count option introduced in Excel 2013. Does this force a 12th position in the array? No. The Custom subtotals option is grayed out for pivot tables that use the Data Model, so you won't ever be able to choose Sum and Distinct Count together. See the "Using the Data Model in Excel 2013" section later in this chapter for an example of using Distinct Count.

Determining the Size of a Finished Pivot Table to Convert It to Values

If you plan on converting a live pivot table to values, you need to copy the entire pivot table. This might be tough to predict. If you summarize transactional data every day, you might find that on any given day you do not have sales from one region. This can cause

13

your table to be perhaps seven columns wide on some days and only six columns wide on other days.

Excel provides two range properties that you can use to refer to a pivot table. The .TableRange2 property includes all the rows of the pivot table, including any Filter dropdowns at the top of the pivot table.

The .TableRange1 property starts just below the filter fields. It does often include the unnecessary row with Sum of Revenue at the top of the pivot table.

If your goal is to convert the pivot table to values and not move the pivot table to a new place, you can use this code:

```
PT.TableRange2.Copy
PT.TableRange2.PasteSpecial xlPasteValues
```

If you want to copy only the data section of the pivot table to a new location, you frequently use the .Offset property to start one row lower than the top of .TableRange2, like so:

```
PT.TableRange2.Offset(1,0).Copy
```

This reference copies the data area plus one row of headings.

Notice in the figure that using .OFFSET without .RESIZE causes one extra row to be copied. However, because that row is always blank, there is no need to use .RESIZE to not copy the extra blank row.

The code copies PT.TableRange2 and uses PasteSpecial on a cell six rows below the current pivot table. At that point in the code, your worksheet appears as shown in Figure 13.7. The table in cell N2 is a live pivot table, and the table in cell N57 contains the copied results.

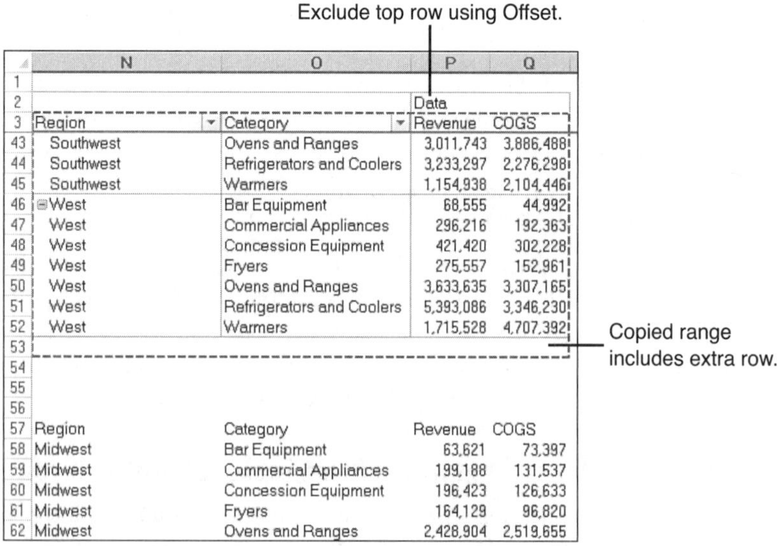

Exclude top row using Offset.

Figure 13.7
An intermediate result of the macro. The data in cell N58 has been converted to values.

	N	O	P	Q
1				
2			Data	
3	Region	Category	Revenue	COGS
43	Southwest	Ovens and Ranges	3,011,743	3,886,488
44	Southwest	Refrigerators and Coolers	3,233,297	2,276,298
45	Southwest	Warmers	1,154,938	2,104,446
46	West	Bar Equipment	68,555	44,992
47	West	Commercial Appliances	296,216	192,363
48	West	Concession Equipment	421,420	302,228
49	West	Fryers	275,557	152,961
50	West	Ovens and Ranges	3,633,635	3,307,165
51	West	Refrigerators and Coolers	5,393,086	3,346,230
52	West	Warmers	1,715,528	4,707,392
53				
54				
55				
56				
57	Region	Category	Revenue	COGS
58	Midwest	Bar Equipment	63,621	73,397
59	Midwest	Commercial Appliances	199,188	131,537
60	Midwest	Concession Equipment	196,423	126,633
61	Midwest	Fryers	164,129	96,820
62	Midwest	Ovens and Ranges	2,428,904	2,519,655

Copied range includes extra row.

You can then eliminate the pivot table by applying the `Clear` method to the entire table. If your code is then going on to do additional formatting, you should remove the pivot cache from memory by setting `PTCache` equal to `Nothing`.

The code in Listing 13.2 uses a pivot table to produce a summary from the underlying data. More than 80,000 rows are reduced to a tight 50-row summary. The resulting data is properly formatted for additional filtering, sorting, and so on. At the end of the code, the pivot table is copied to static values, and the pivot table is cleared.

Listing 13.2   Code to Produce a Static Summary from a Pivot Table

```
Sub UsePivotToCreateValues()
    '

    Dim WSD As Worksheet
    Dim PTCache As PivotCache
    Dim PT As PivotTable
    Dim PRange As Range
    Dim FinalRow As Long
    Set WSD = Worksheets("Data")

    ' Delete any prior pivot tables
    For Each PT In WSD.PivotTables
        PT.TableRange2.Clear
    Next PT
    WSD.Range("N1:AZ1").EntireColumn.Clear

    ' Define input area and set up a Pivot Cache
    FinalRow = WSD.Cells(Application.Rows.Count, 1).End(xlUp).Row
    FinalCol = WSD.Cells(1, Application.Columns.Count). _
        End(xlToLeft).Column
    Set PRange = WSD.Cells(1, 1).Resize(FinalRow, FinalCol)
    Set PTCache = ActiveWorkbook.PivotCaches.Add(SourceType:= _
        xlDatabase, SourceData:=PRange.Address)

    ' Create the Pivot Table from the Pivot Cache
    Set PT = PTCache.CreatePivotTable(TableDestination:=WSD. _
        Cells(2, FinalCol + 2), TableName:="PivotTable1")

    ' Turn off updating while building the table
    PT.ManualUpdate = True

    ' Set up the row & column fields
    PT.AddFields RowFields:=Array("Region", "Category"), _
        ColumnFields:="Data"

    ' Set up the data fields
    With PT.PivotFields("Revenue")
        .Orientation = xlDataField
        .Function = xlSum
        .Position = 1
        .NumberFormat = "#,##0"
        .Name = "Revenue "
    End With
```

13

```
With PT.PivotFields("Cost")
    .Orientation = xlDataField
    .Function = xlSum
    .Position = 2
    .NumberFormat = "#,##0"
    .Name = "COGS"
End With

' Settings to create a solid block of data
With PT
    .NullString = 0
    .RepeatAllLabels Repeat:=xlRepeatLabels
    .ColumnGrand = False
    .RowGrand = 0
    .PivotFields("Region").Subtotals(1) = True
    .PivotFields("Region").Subtotals(1) = False
End With

' Calc the pivot table
PT.ManualUpdate = False
PT.ManualUpdate = True

' Copy the pivot table as values below the pivot table
PT.TableRange2.Offset(1, 0).Copy
PT.TableRange1.Cells(1, 1).Offset(PT.TableRange1.Rows.Count + 4, 0). _
    PasteSpecial xlPasteValuesAndNumberFormats
StartRow = PT.TableRange1.Cells(1, 1).Offset(PT.TableRange1.Rows.Count _
    + 5, 0).Row

Stop  ' Figure 13.7

PT.TableRange1.Clear
Set PTCache = Nothing

WSD.Activate
Cells(StartRow, FinalCol + 2).Select

End Sub
```

The preceding code creates the pivot table. It then copies the results as values and pastes them below the original pivot table. In reality, you probably want to copy this report to another worksheet or another workbook. Examples later in this chapter introduce the code necessary for this.

So far, this chapter has walked you through building the simplest of pivot table reports. Pivot tables offer far more flexibility. Read on for more complex reporting examples.

Pivot Table 201: Creating a Report Showing Revenue by Category

A typical report might provide a list of markets by category with revenue by year. This report could be given to product line managers to show them which markets are selling well. The report in Figure 13.8 is not a pivot table, but the macro to create the report used a pivot table to summarize the data. Regular Excel commands such as Subtotal then finish off the report.

Figure 13.8
This report started as a pivot table, but finished as a regular data set.

C11			✕ ✓ *fx*	=SUBTOTAL(9,C4:C10)		

1 2 3		A	B	C	D	E	F
	1	Revenue by Category & Region					
	2						
	3	Category	Region	2014	2015	2016	Grand Total
	4	Ovens and Ranges	South	15,672K	13,796K	8,284K	37,752K
	5	Ovens and Ranges	Southeast	2,639K	2,745K	1,418K	6,802K
	6	Ovens and Ranges	West	519K	1,520K	1,594K	3,634K
	7	Ovens and Ranges	Southwest	572K	1,335K	1,104K	3,012K
	8	Ovens and Ranges	Northeast	662K	1,146K	801K	2,609K
	9	Ovens and Ranges	Midwest	290K	1,379K	760K	2,429K
	10	Ovens and Ranges	North	247K	421K	263K	931K
	11	Ovens and Ranges Total		20,602K	22,342K	14,225K	57,169K
	12	Refrigerators and Coolers	South	4,855K	4,659K	12,093K	21,606K
	13	Refrigerators and Coolers	West	1,957K	348K	3,088K	5,393K
	14	Refrigerators and Coolers	Southeast	929K	1,311K	2,062K	4,302K

In this example, you want to show the markets in descending order by revenue with years going across the columns. A sample pivot table report is shown in Figure 13.9.

Figure 13.9
A typical request is to take transactional data and produce a summary by product for product line managers.

Row Labels Repeated on Each Row

Daily Dates Rolled to Years

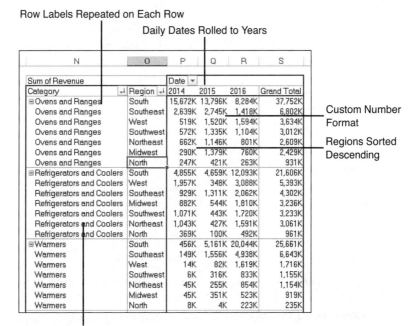

N		O	P	Q	R	S
Sum of Revenue		Date				
Category	Region	2014	2015	2016	Grand Total	
Ovens and Ranges	South	15,672K	13,796K	8,284K	37,752K	
Ovens and Ranges	Southeast	2,639K	2,745K	1,418K	6,802K	
Ovens and Ranges	West	519K	1,520K	1,594K	3,634K	
Ovens and Ranges	Southwest	572K	1,335K	1,104K	3,012K	
Ovens and Ranges	Northeast	662K	1,146K	801K	2,609K	
Ovens and Ranges	Midwest	290K	1,379K	760K	2,429K	
Ovens and Ranges	North	247K	421K	263K	931K	
Refrigerators and Coolers	South	4,855K	4,659K	12,093K	21,606K	
Refrigerators and Coolers	West	1,957K	348K	3,088K	5,393K	
Refrigerators and Coolers	Southeast	929K	1,311K	2,062K	4,302K	
Refrigerators and Coolers	Midwest	882K	544K	1,810K	3,236K	
Refrigerators and Coolers	Southwest	1,071K	443K	1,720K	3,233K	
Refrigerators and Coolers	Northeast	1,043K	427K	1,591K	3,061K	
Refrigerators and Coolers	North	369K	100K	492K	961K	
Warmers	South	456K	5,161K	20,044K	25,661K	
Warmers	Southeast	149K	1,556K	4,938K	6,643K	
Warmers	West	14K	82K	1,619K	1,716K	
Warmers	Southwest	6K	316K	833K	1,155K	
Warmers	Northeast	45K	255K	854K	1,154K	
Warmers	Midwest	45K	351K	523K	919K	
Warmers	North	8K	4K	223K	235K	

Custom Number Format

Regions Sorted Descending

No Subtotals for Categories

13

There are some tricky issues required to create this pivot table:

- You have to roll the daily dates in the original data set up to years.
- You want to control the sort order of the row fields.
- You want to fill in blanks throughout the pivot table, use a better number format, and suppress the subtotals for the Category field.

The key to producing this data quickly is to use a pivot table. The default pivot table has a number of quirky problems that you can correct in the macro. To start, use VBA to build a pivot table with Category and Region as the row fields. Add Date as a column field. Add Revenue as a data field using this code:

```
PT.AddFields RowFields:=Array("Category", _
    "Region"), ColumnFields:="Date"

' Set up the data fields
With PT.PivotFields("Revenue")
    .Orientation = xlDataField
    .Function = xlSum
    .Position = 1
    .NumberFormat = "#,##0"
End With
```

Figure 13.10 shows the default pivot table created with these settings.

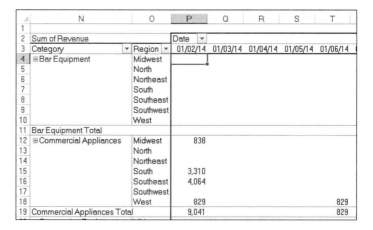

	N	O	P	Q	R	S	T
1							
2	Sum of Revenue		Date				
3	Category	Region	01/02/14	01/03/14	01/04/14	01/05/14	01/06/14
4	⊟Bar Equipment	Midwest					
5		North					
6		Northeast					
7		South					
8		Southeast					
9		Southwest					
10		West					
11	Bar Equipment Total						
12	⊟Commercial Appliances	Midwest	838				
13		North					
14		Northeast					
15		South	3,310				
16		Southeast	4,064				
17		Southwest					
18		West	829				829
19	Commercial Appliances Total		9,041				829

Here are just a few of the annoyances that most pivot tables present in their default state:

- The outline view is horrible. In Figure 13.10, the value Bar Equipment appears in the product column only once and is followed by six blank cells. Thankfully, Excel 2013 offers the RepeatAllLabels method to correct this problem. If you intend to repurpose the data, you need the row labels to be repeated on every row.

- Because the original data set contains daily dates, the default pivot table has more than 1,000 columns of daily data. No one is able to process this report. You need to roll those daily dates up to years. Pivot tables make this easy.

- The report contains blank cells instead of zeros. In Figure 13.10, the entire visible range of Bar Equipment is blank. These cells should contain zeroes instead of blanks.

- The title is boring. Most people would agree that Sum of Revenue is an annoying title.

- Some captions are extraneous. Date floating in cell P2 of Figure 13.10 does not belong in a report.

- The default alphabetical sort order is rarely useful. Product line managers are going to want the top markets at the top of the list. It would be helpful to have the report sorted in descending order by revenue.

- The borders are ugly. Excel draws in myriad borders that make the report look awful.

- Pivot tables offer no intelligent page break logic. If you want to produce one report for each product line manager, there is no fast method for indicating that each product should be on a new page.

- Because of the page break problem, you might find it is easier to do away with the pivot table's subtotal rows and have the Subtotal method add subtotal rows with page breaks. You need a way to turn off the pivot table subtotal rows offered for Category in Figure 13.10. These rows show up automatically whenever you have two or more row fields. If you had four row fields, you would want to turn off the automatic subtotals for the three outermost row fields.

Even with all these problems in default pivot tables, they are still the way to go. You can overcome each complaint either by using special settings within the pivot table or by entering a few lines of code after the pivot table is created and then copied to a regular data set.

Ensuring Table Layout Is Utilized

In legacy versions of Excel, multiple row fields appeared in multiple columns. Three layouts are now available. The Compact layout squeezes all the row fields into a single column. Compact layout is the default when a pivot table is created in the Excel interface. Currently, when you create a pivot table in VBA, the default is the Tabular layout. However, in some future version, Microsoft will correct this discrepancy, so get in the habit of explicitly changing the layout to a Tabular layout with this code:

```
PT.RowAxisLayout xlTabularRow
```

Rolling Daily Dates Up to Years

With transactional data, you often find your date-based summaries having one row per day. Although daily data might be useful to a plant manager, many people in the company want to see totals by month or quarter and year.

13

The great news is that Excel handles the summarization of dates in a pivot table with ease. For anyone who has ever had to use the arcane formula =A2+1-Day(A2) to change daily dates into monthly dates, you will appreciate the ease with which you can group transactional data into months or quarters.

Creating a date group with VBA is a bit quirky. The .Group method can be applied to only a single cell in the pivot table, and that cell must contain a date or the Date field label.

In Figure 13.10, you would have to select either the Date heading in cell P2 or one of the dates in cells P3:APM3. Selecting one of these specific cells is risky, particularly if the pivot table later starts being created in a new column. Two other options are more reliable.

If you will never use a different number of row fields, then you can assume that the Date heading is in row 1, column 3 of the area known as TableRange2. The following line of code selects this cell:

```
PT.TableRange2.Cells(1, 3).Select
```

You should probably add a comment that you need to edit the 3 in that line to another number any time that you change the number of row fields.

Another solution is to use the LabelRange property for the Date field. The following code always selects the cell containing the Date heading:

```
PT.PivotFields("Date").LabelRange.Select
```

To group the daily dates up to yearly dates, you should define a pivot table with Date in the row field. Turn off ManualUpdate to enable the pivot table to be drawn. You can then use the LabelRange property to locate the date label.

Use the .Group method on the date label cell. You specify an array of seven Boolean values for the Periods argument. The seven values correspond to seconds, minutes, hours, days, months, quarters, and years. For example, to group by years, you would use

```
PT.PivotFields("Date"),LabelRange.Group _
    Periods:=(False, False, False, False, False, False, True)
```

After you have grouped by years, the field is still called Date. This differs from the results when you group by multiple fields. To group by months, quarters, and years, you would use

```
PT.PivotFields("Date"),LabelRange.Group _
    Periods:=(False, False, False, False, True, True, True)
```

After you have grouped up to months, quarters, and years, the Date field starts referring to months. Two new virtual fields are available in the pivot table: Quarters and Years.

To group by weeks, you choose only the Day period and then use the By argument to group into seven-day periods:

```
PT.PivotFields("Date"),LabelRange.Group By:=7_
    Periods:=(False, False, False, True, False, False, False)
```

In Figure 13.10, the goal is to group the daily dates up to years, so the following code is used:

```
PT.PivotFields("Date"),LabelRange.Group _
    Periods:=(False, False, False, False, False, False, True)
```

Figure 13.11 shows the pivot table after grouping daily dates up to years.

Figure 13.11

Daily dates have been rolled up to years using the Group method.

	N	O	P	Q	R	S
1						
2	Sum of Revenue		Date			
3	Category	Region	2014	2015	2016	Grand Total
4	⊟ Bar Equipment	Midwest		22,113	41,508	63,621
5		North		5,950	14,195	20,145
6		Northeast		30,683	37,622	68,305
7		South		667,438	523,901	1,191,339
8		Southeast		165,241	118,655	283,896
9		Southwest		18,652	54,819	73,471
10		West		1,337	67,218	68,555
11	Bar Equipment Total			911,415	857,917	1,769,332
12	⊟ Commercial Appliances	Midwest	27,017	113,643	58,528	199,188
13		North	3,436	18,859	21,670	43,965
14		Northeast	15,213	114,712	155,179	285,103
15		South	271,633	2,547,905	3,103,407	5,922,945
16		Southeast	79,214	629,334	817,346	1,525,894
17		Southwest	11,678	140,920	136,928	289,527
18		West	9,182	58,739	228,295	296,216

Eliminating Blank Cells

The blank cells in a pivot table are annoying. You will want to fix two kinds of blank cells. Blank cells occur in the Values area when there were no records for a particular combination. For example, in Figure 13.11, the company did not sell bar equipment in 2014, so all of cells P4:P11 are blank. Most people would prefer to have zeroes instead of those blank cells.

Blank cells also occur in the Row Labels area when you have multiple row fields. The words Bar Equipment appear in cell N4, but then cells N5:N10 are blank.

To replace blanks in the Values area with zeroes, use

```
PT.NullString = "0"
```

> **NOTE** Although the proper code is to set this value to a text zero, Excel actually puts a real zero in the empty cells.

To fill in the blanks in the label area in Excel 2013, use

```
PT.RepeatAllLabels xlRepeatLabels
```

13

The `.RepeatAllLabels` code fails in Excel 2007 and earlier. The only solution in legacy versions of Excel is to convert the pivot table to values, and then set the blank cells to a formula that grabs the value from the row above:

```
Dim FillRange As Range
Set PT = ActiveSheet.PivotTables("PivotTable1")
' Locate outer row column
Set FillRange = PT.TableRange1.Resize(, 1)
' Convert entire table to values
PT.TableRange2.Copy
PT.TableRange2.PasteSpecial xlPasteValues
' Fill Special Cells Blanks with the value from above
FillRange.SpecialCells(xlCellTypeBlanks).FormulaR1C1 = _
    "=R[-1]C"
' Convert those formulas to values
FillRange.Value = FillRange.Value
```

Controlling the Sort Order with AutoSort

The Excel user interface offers an AutoSort option that enables you to sort a field in descending order based on revenue. The equivalent code in VBA to sort the region and category fields by descending revenue uses the `AutoSort` method:

```
PT.PivotFields("Region").AutoSort Order:=xlDescending, _
    Field:="Sum of Revenue"
PT.PivotFields("Category").AutoSort Order:=xlDescending, _
    Field:="Sum of Revenue"
```

Changing the Default Number Format

Numbers in the Values area of a pivot table need to have a suitable number format applied. You cannot count on the numeric format of the underlying field to carry over to the pivot table.

To show the Revenue values with zero decimal places and a comma, use

```
PT.PivotFields("Sum of Revenue").NumberFormat = "#,##0"
```

Some companies have customers who typically buy thousands or millions of dollars' worth of goods. You can display numbers in thousands by using a single comma after the number format. To do this, you need to include a K abbreviation to indicate that the numbers are in thousands:

```
PT.PivotFields("Sum of Revenue").NumberFormat = "#,##0,K"
```

Local custom dictates the thousands abbreviation. If you are working for a relatively young computer company where everyone uses K for the thousands separator, you are in luck because Microsoft makes it easy to use this abbreviation. However, if you work at a more than 100-year-old soap company where you use M for thousands and MM for millions, you have a few more hurdles to jump. You are required to prefix the M character with a backslash to have it work:

```
PT.PivotFields("Sum of Revenue").NumberFormat = "#,##0,\M"
```

Alternatively, you can surround the M character with double quotation marks. To put double quotation marks inside a quoted string in VBA, you must use two sequential quotation marks. To set up a format in tenths of millions that uses the `#,##0.0,,"MM"` format, you would use this line of code:

```
PT.PivotFields("Sum of Revenue").NumberFormat = "#,##0.0,,""M"""
```

Here, the format is quotation mark, pound, comma, pound, pound, zero, period, zero, comma, comma, quotation mark, quotation mark, M, quotation mark, quotation mark, quotation mark. The three quotation marks at the end are correct. You use two quotation marks to simulate typing one quotation mark in the custom number format box and a final quotation mark to close the string in VBA.

Figure 13.12 shows the pivot table blanks filled in, numbers shown in thousands, and category and region sorted descending.

Figure 13.12

After filling in blanks and sorting, you only have a few extraneous totals and labels to remove.

	N	O	P	Q	R	S
1						
2	Sum of Revenue		Date			
3	Category	Region	2014	2015	2016	Grand Total
4	⊟Ovens and Ranges	South	15,672K	13,796K	8,284K	37,752K
5	Ovens and Ranges	Southeast	2,639K	2,745K	1,418K	6,802K
6	Ovens and Ranges	West	519K	1,520K	1,594K	3,634K
7	Ovens and Ranges	Southwest	572K	1,335K	1,104K	3,012K
8	Ovens and Ranges	Northeast	662K	1,146K	801K	2,609K
9	Ovens and Ranges	Midwest	290K	1,379K	760K	2,429K
10	Ovens and Ranges	North	247K	421K	263K	931K
11	Ovens and Ranges Total		20,602K	22,342K	14,225K	57,169K
12	⊟Refrigerators and Coolers	South	4,855K	4,659K	12,093K	21,606K
13	Refrigerators and Coolers	West	1,957K	348K	3,088K	5,393K
14	Refrigerators and Coolers	Southeast	929K	1,311K	2,062K	4,302K
15	Refrigerators and Coolers	Midwest	882K	544K	1,810K	3,236K
16	Refrigerators and Coolers	Southwest	1,071K	443K	1,720K	3,233K
17	Refrigerators and Coolers	Northeast	1,043K	427K	1,591K	3,061K
18	Refrigerators and Coolers	North	369K	100K	492K	961K
19	Refrigerators and Coolers Total		11,105K	7,833K	22,856K	41,794K
20	⊟Warmers	South	456K	5,161K	20,044K	25,661K

Suppressing Subtotals for Multiple Row Fields

As soon as you have more than one row field, Excel automatically adds subtotals for all but the innermost row field. That extra row field can get in the way if you plan on reusing the results of the pivot table as a new data set for some other purpose. In the current example, you have taken 87,000 rows of data and produced a tight 50-row summary of yearly sales by category and region. That new data set would be interesting for sorting, filtering, and charting, if you could remove the total row and the category subtotals.

To remove the subtotal, you first set the Subtotals(1) property to True to turn off the other ten possible subtotals. You can then turn off the first subtotal to make sure that all subtotals are suppressed:

```
PT.PivotFields("Category").Subtotals(1) = True
PT.PivotFields("Category").Subtotals(1) = False
```

13

To remove the grand total row, use

```
PT.ColumnGrand = False
```

Figure 13.13 shows the first section of the pivot table with the subtotals removed.

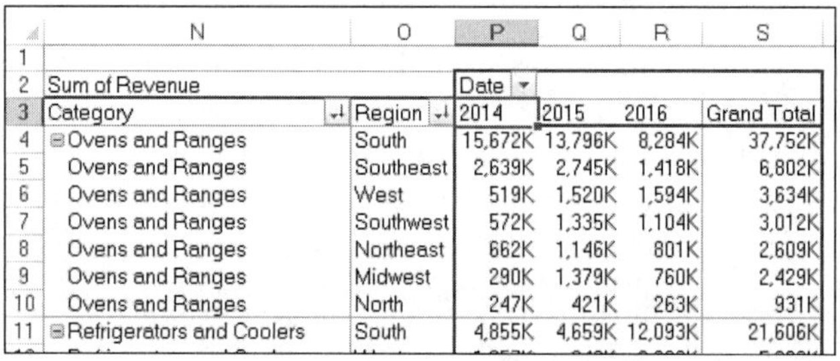

Figure 13.13
Remove the subtotal rows from column A.

	N	O	P	Q	R	S
1						
2	Sum of Revenue		Date ▼			
3	Category	Region	2014	2015	2016	Grand Total
4	⊟ Ovens and Ranges	South	15,672K	13,796K	8,284K	37,752K
5	Ovens and Ranges	Southeast	2,639K	2,745K	1,418K	6,802K
6	Ovens and Ranges	West	519K	1,520K	1,594K	3,634K
7	Ovens and Ranges	Southwest	572K	1,335K	1,104K	3,012K
8	Ovens and Ranges	Northeast	662K	1,146K	801K	2,609K
9	Ovens and Ranges	Midwest	290K	1,379K	760K	2,429K
10	Ovens and Ranges	North	247K	421K	263K	931K
11	⊟ Refrigerators and Coolers	South	4,855K	4,659K	12,093K	21,606K

Copying a Finished Pivot Table as Values to a New Workbook

If you plan on repurposing the results of the pivot table, you need to convert the table to values. This section shows you how to copy the pivot table to a brand-new workbook.

To make the code more portable, assign object variables to the original workbook, new workbook, and first worksheet in the new workbook. At the top of the procedure, add these statements:

```
Dim WSR As Worksheet
Dim WBO As Workbook
Dim WBN As Workbook
Set WBO = ActiveWorkbook
Set WSD = Worksheets("Data")
```

After the pivot table has been successfully created, build a blank Report workbook with this code:

```
' Create a New Blank Workbook with one Worksheet
Set WBN = Workbooks.Add(xlWorksheet)
Set WSR = WBN.Worksheets(1)
WSR.Name = "Report"
' Set up Title for Report
With WSR.Range("A1")
    .Value = "Revenue by Category, Region and Year"
    .Style = "Title"
End With
```

There are a few remaining annoyances in the pivot table. The borders are annoying, and there are stray labels such as Sum of Revenue and Date in the first row of the pivot table. You can solve these problems by excluding the first row(s) of PT.TableRange2 from the .Copy method and then using PasteSpecial(xlPasteValuesAndNumberFormats) to copy the data to the report sheet.

> **CAUTION**
>
> In legacy versions of Excel (2003 and earlier), `xlPasteValuesAndNumberFormats` was not available. Instead, you had to use Paste Special twice: once as `xlPasteValues` and once as `xlPasteFormats`.

In the current example, the `.TableRange2` property includes only one row to eliminate, row 2, as shown in Figure 13.13. If you had a more complex pivot table with several column fields and/or one or more page fields, you would have to eliminate more than just the first row of the report. It helps to run your macro to this point, look at the result, and figure out how many rows you need to delete. You can effectively not copy these rows to the report by using the `Offset` property. Copy the `TableRange2` property, offset by one row.

Purists will note that this code copies one extra blank row from below the pivot table, but this really does not matter because the row is blank. After copying, you can erase the original pivot table and destroy the pivot cache:

```
' Copy the Pivot Table data to row 3 of the Report sheet
' Use Offset to eliminate the title row of the pivot table
PT.TableRange2.Offset(1, 0).Copy
WSR. Range("A3").PasteSpecial Paste:=xlPasteValuesAndNumberFormats
PT.TableRange1.Clear
Set PTCache = Nothing
```

> **TIP**
>
> Note that you use the Paste Special option to paste just values and number formats. This gets rid of both borders and the pivot nature of the table. You might be tempted to use the All Except Borders option under Paste, but this keeps the data in a pivot table, and you will not be able to insert new rows in the middle of the data.

Handling Final Formatting

The last steps for the report involve some basic formatting tasks and then adding the subtotals. You can bold and right-justify the headings in row 3. Set up rows 1–3 so that the top three rows print on each page:

```
' Do some basic formatting
' Autofit columns, format the headings , right-align
Range("A3").EntireRow.Style = "Heading 4"
Range("A3").CurrentRegion.Columns.AutoFit
Range("A3").EntireRow.HorizontalAlignment = xlRight
Range("A3:B3").HorizontalAlignment = xlLeft
  ' Repeat rows 1-3 at the top of each page
WSR.PageSetup.PrintTitleRows = "$1:$3"
```

13

Adding Subtotals to Get Page Breaks

Automatic subtotals is a powerful feature found on the Data tab. Figure 13.14 shows the Subtotal dialog. Note the option Page Break Between Groups.

Figure 13.14

Use automatic subtotals because doing so enables you to add a page break after each category. Using this feature ensures that each category manager has a clean report with only her data on it.

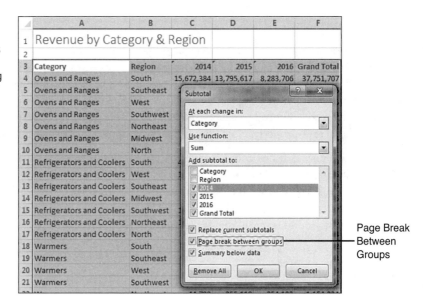

If you were sure that you would always have 3 years and a total, the code to add subtotals for each Line of Business group would be the following:

```
' Add Subtotals by Category.
' Be sure to add a page break at each change in category
Selection.Subtotal GroupBy:=1, Function:=xlSum, TotalList:=Array(3, 4, 5, 6), _
    PageBreaks:=True
```

However, this code fails if you have more or less than 3 years. The solution is to use the following convoluted code to dynamically build a list of the columns to total, based on the number of columns in the report:

```
Dim TotColumns()
Dim I as Integer
FinalCol = Cells(3, Columns.Count).End(xlToLeft).Column
ReDim Preserve TotColumns(1 To FinalCol - 2)
For i = 3 To FinalCol
    TotColumns(i - 2) = i
Next i
Selection.Subtotal GroupBy:=1, Function:=xlSum, TotalList:=TotColumns,_
    Replace:=True, PageBreaks:=True, SummaryBelowData:=True
```

Finally, with the new totals added to the report, you need to autofit the numeric columns again with this code:

```
Dim GrandRow as Long
' Make sure the columns are wide enough for totals
GrandRow = Cells(Rows.Count, 1).End(xlUp).Row
Cells(3, 3).Resize(GrandRow - 2, FinalCol - 2).Columns.AutoFit
Cells(GrandRow, 3).Resize(1, FinalCol - 2).NumberFormat = "#,##0,K"
' Add a page break before the Grand Total row, otherwise
' the  manager for the final category will have two totals
WSR.HPageBreaks.Add Before:=Cells(GrandRow, 1)
```

Putting It All Together

Listing 13.3 produces the product line manager reports in a few seconds.

Listing 13.3   Code That Produces the Category Report in Figure 13.15

```
Sub CategoryRegionReport()
    ' Category and Region as Row
    ' Years as Column
    Dim WSD As Worksheet
    Dim PTCache As PivotCache
    Dim PT As PivotTable
    Dim PRange As Range
    Dim FinalRow As Long
    Dim TotColumns()

    Set WSD = Worksheets("Data")
    Dim WSR As Worksheet
    Dim WBO As Workbook
    Dim WBN As Workbook
    Set WBO = ActiveWorkbook

    ' Delete any prior pivot tables
    For Each PT In WSD.PivotTables
        PT.TableRange2.Clear
    Next PT
    WSD.Range("N1:XFD1").EntireColumn.Clear

    ' Define input area and set up a Pivot Cache
    FinalRow = WSD.Cells(Application.Rows.Count, 1).End(xlUp).Row
    FinalCol = WSD.Cells(1, Application.Columns.Count). _
        End(xlToLeft).Column
    Set PRange = WSD.Cells(1, 1).Resize(FinalRow, FinalCol)
    Set PTCache = ActiveWorkbook.PivotCaches.Add(SourceType:= _
        xlDatabase, SourceData:=PRange.Address)

    ' Create the Pivot Table from the Pivot Cache
    Set PT = PTCache.CreatePivotTable(TableDestination:=WSD. _
        Cells(2, FinalCol + 2), TableName:="PivotTable1")

    ' Turn off updating while building the table
    PT.ManualUpdate = True

    ' Set up the row fields
```

13

```
    PT.AddFields RowFields:=Array("Category", _
        "Region"), ColumnFields:="Date"

    ' Set up the data fields
    With PT.PivotFields("Revenue")
        .Orientation = xlDataField
        .Function = xlSum
        .Position = 1
        .NumberFormat = "#,##0"
    End With

    ' Ensure tabular layout is used
    PT.RowAxisLayout xlTabularRow

    ' Calc the pivot table before grouping dates
    PT.ManualUpdate = False
    PT.ManualUpdate = True
    Stop
    PT.PivotFields("Date").LabelRange.Group _
        Periods:=Array(False, False, False, False, False, False, True)

    ' Change number format of Revenue
    PT.PivotFields("Sum of Revenue").NumberFormat = "#,##0,K"

    ' Fill in blank cells
    PT.NullString = "0"
    PT.RepeatAllLabels xlRepeatLabels

    ' Sort both label fields by descending revenue
    PT.PivotFields("Category").AutoSort Order:=xlDescending, _
        field:="Sum of Revenue"
    PT.PivotFields("Region").AutoSort Order:=xlDescending, _
        field:="Sum of Revenue"


    ' Suppress Category totals
    PT.PivotFields("Category").Subtotals(1) = True
    PT.PivotFields("Category").Subtotals(1) = False
    PT.ColumnGrand = False

    ' Calc the pivot table
    PT.ManualUpdate = False
    PT.ManualUpdate = True

    ' Create a New Blank Workbook with one Worksheet
    Set WBN = Workbooks.Add(xlWBATWorksheet)
    Set WSR = WBN.Worksheets(1)
    WSR.Name = "Report"
    ' Set up Title for Report
    With WSR.[A1]
        .Value = "Revenue by Category & Region"
        .Style = "Title"
    End With

    ' Copy the Pivot Table data to row 3 of the Report sheet
    ' Use Offset to eliminate the title row of the pivot table
```

```
PT.TableRange1.Offset(1, 0).Copy
WSR.[A3].PasteSpecial Paste:=xlPasteValuesAndNumberFormats
PT.TableRange2.Clear
Set PTCache = Nothing

' Do some basic formatting
' Autofit columns, bold the headings, right-align
Range("A3").EntireRow.Style = "Heading 4"
Range("A3").CurrentRegion.Columns.AutoFit
Range("A3").EntireRow.HorizontalAlignment = xlRight
Range("A3:B3").HorizontalAlignment = xlLeft

' Repeat rows 1-3 at the top of each page
WSR.PageSetup.PrintTitleRows = "$1:$3"

' Add subtotals
FinalCol = Cells(3, 255).End(xlToLeft).Column
ReDim Preserve TotColumns(1 To FinalCol - 2)
For i = 3 To FinalCol
    TotColumns(i - 2) = i
Next i
Range("A3").CurrentRegion.Subtotal GroupBy:=1, Function:=xlSum, _
    TotalList:=TotColumns, Replace:=True, _
    PageBreaks:=True, SummaryBelowData:=True

' Make sure the columns are wide enough for totals
GrandRow = Cells(Rows.Count, 1).End(xlUp).Row
Cells(3, 3).Resize(GrandRow - 2, FinalCol - 2).Columns.AutoFit
Cells(GrandRow, 3).Resize(1, FinalCol - 2).NumberFormat = "#,##0,K"
' Add a page break before the Grand Total row, otherwise
' the product manager for the final Line will have two totals
WSR.HPageBreaks.Add Before:=Cells(GrandRow, 1)

End Sub
```

Figure 13.15 shows the report produced by this code.

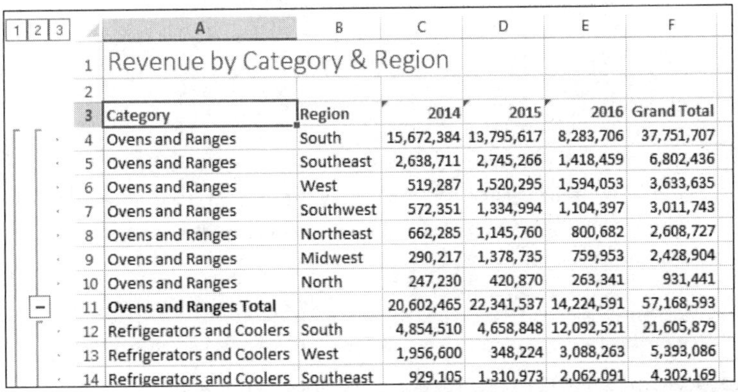

Figure 13.15

Converting 80,000 rows of transactional data to this useful report takes less than 2 seconds if you use the code that produced this example. Without pivot tables, the code would be far more complex.

	A	B	C	D	E	F
1	Revenue by Category & Region					
2						
3	Category	Region	2014	2015	2016	Grand Total
4	Ovens and Ranges	South	15,672,384	13,795,617	8,283,706	37,751,707
5	Ovens and Ranges	Southeast	2,638,711	2,745,266	1,418,459	6,802,436
6	Ovens and Ranges	West	519,287	1,520,295	1,594,053	3,633,635
7	Ovens and Ranges	Southwest	572,351	1,334,994	1,104,397	3,011,743
8	Ovens and Ranges	Northeast	662,285	1,145,760	800,682	2,608,727
9	Ovens and Ranges	Midwest	290,217	1,378,735	759,953	2,428,904
10	Ovens and Ranges	North	247,230	420,870	263,341	931,441
11	**Ovens and Ranges Total**		20,602,465	22,341,537	14,224,591	57,168,593
12	Refrigerators and Coolers	South	4,854,510	4,658,848	12,092,521	21,605,879
13	Refrigerators and Coolers	West	1,956,600	348,224	3,088,263	5,393,086
14	Refrigerators and Coolers	Southeast	929,105	1,310,973	2,062,091	4,302,169

13

You have now seen the VBA code to produce useful summary reports from transactional data. The next section deals with additional features in pivot tables.

Calculating with a Pivot Table

So far, the pivot tables have presented a single field in the Values area of the pivot table, and that field has always shown as a Sum calculation. You can add more fields to the Values area. You can change from Sum to any of 11 functions or alter the Sum to display running totals, percentage of total, and more. You can also add new calculated fields or calculated items to the pivot table.

Addressing Issues with Two or More Data Fields

It is possible to have multiple fields in the Values section of a pivot report. For example, you might have Quantity, Revenue, and Cost in the same pivot table.

When you have two or more data fields in an Excel 2013 pivot table that you built in the Excel interface, the value fields go across the columns. However, VBA builds the pivot table with the values fields going down the innermost row field. This creates the bizarre-looking table shown in Figure 13.16.

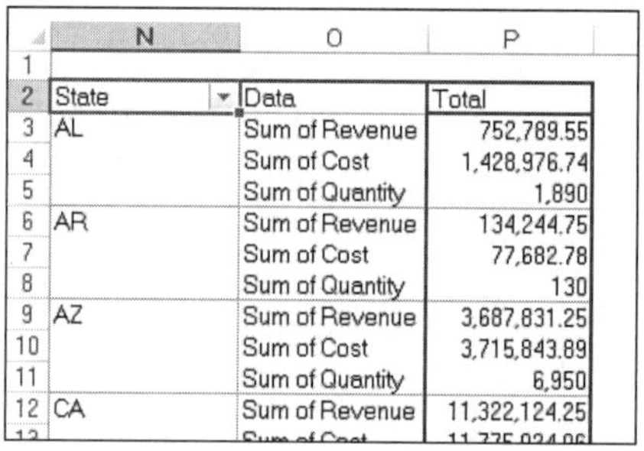

Figure 13.16
This ugly view was banished in the Excel interface after Excel 2003. VBA still produces it by default.

	N	O	P
1			
2	State	Data	Total
3	AL	Sum of Revenue	752,789.55
4		Sum of Cost	1,428,976.74
5		Sum of Quantity	1,890
6	AR	Sum of Revenue	134,244.75
7		Sum of Cost	77,682.78
8		Sum of Quantity	130
9	AZ	Sum of Revenue	3,687,831.25
10		Sum of Cost	3,715,843.89
11		Sum of Quantity	6,950
12	CA	Sum of Revenue	11,322,124.25
13		Sum of Cost	11,775,024.06

To correct this problem, you should specify that a virtual field called "Data" is one of the column fields.

> **NOTE**
> In this instance, note that "Data" is not a column in your original data; it is a special name used to indicate the orientation of the multiple values fields.

To have multiple values fields go across the report, use this code:

```
PT.AddFields RowFields:="State", ColumnFields:="Data"
```

After adding a column field called Data, you would then go on to define multiple data fields:

```
' Set up the data fields
With PT.PivotFields("Revenue")
    .Orientation = xlDataField
    .Function = xlSum
    .Position = 1
    .NumberFormat = "#,##0.00"
End With

With PT.PivotFields("Cost")
    .Orientation = xlDataField
    .Function = xlSum
    .Position = 2
    .NumberFormat = "#,##0.00"
End With

With PT.PivotFields("Quantity")
    .Orientation = xlDataField
    .Function = xlSum
    .Position = 3
    .NumberFormat = "#,##0"
End With
```

This code produces a pivot table, as shown in Figure 13.17.

Figure 13.17
When you specify the virtual field "Data" as a column field, multiple values go across the report.

	N	O	P	Q
1				
2		Data		
3	State	Sum of Revenue	Sum of Cost	Sum of Quantity
4	AL	752,789.55	1,428,976.74	1,890
5	AR	134,244.75	77,682.78	130
6	AZ	3,687,831.25	3,715,843.89	6,950
7	CA	11,322,124.25	11,775,024.06	14,585
8	CO	1,280,417.15	892,116.17	1,730
9	FL	65,272,493.30	122,148,378.05	103,763
10	GA	27,955,642.10	50,758,752.59	48,897
11	IA	816,462.00	542,146.20	950
12	ID	229,274.00	132,473.73	276

Using Calculations Other Than Sum

So far, all of the pivot tables in this chapter have used the Sum function to calculate. There are 11 functions available, including Sum. To specify a different calculation, specify one of these values as the .Function property:

- xlAverage—Average
- xlCount—Count
- xlCountNums—Count numerical values only
- xlMax—Maximum
- xlMin—Minimum
- xlProduct—Multiply

13

- xlStDev—Standard deviation, based on a sample
- xlStDevP—Standard deviation, based on the whole population
- xlSum—Sum
- xlVar—Variation, based on a sample
- xlVarP—Variation, based on the whole population

Although Count Distinct is new in Excel 2013, you cannot create Count Distinct in a regular pivot cache pivot table. See "Using the Data Model in Excel 2013" at the end of this chapter.

Note that when you add a field to the Values area of the pivot table, Excel modifies the field name with the function name and the word *of*. For example, "Revenue" becomes "Sum of Revenue." "Cost" might become "StdDev of Cost." If you later need to refer to those fields in your code, you need to do so using the new name, such as Average of Quantity.

You can improve the look of your pivot table by changing the .Name of the field. If you do not want "Sum of Revenue" appearing in the pivot table, change the .Caption to Total Revenue. This sounds less awkward than Sum of Revenue. Remember that you cannot have a name that exactly matches an existing field name in the pivot table. "Revenue" is not suitable as a name. However, " Revenue" (with a leading space) is fine to use as a name.

For text fields, the only function that makes sense is a count. You will frequently count the number of records by adding a text field to the pivot table and using the Count function.

The following code fragment calculates total revenue, a count of records by counting a text field, and average quantity:

```
With PT.PivotFields("Revenue")
    .Orientation = xlDataField
    .Function = xlSum
    .Position = 1
    .NumberFormat = "$#,##0.00"
    .Name = " Revenue"
End With

With PT.PivotFields("Customer")
    .Orientation = xlDataField
    .Function = xlCount
    .Position = 2
    .NumberFormat = "#,##0"
    .Name = "# of Records"
End With

With PT.PivotFields("Revenue")
    .Orientation = xlDataField
    .Function = xlAverage
    .Position = 3
    .NumberFormat = "#,##0.00"
    .Name = "Average Revenue"
End With
' Ensure that we get zeroes instead of blanks in the data area
```

13

```
PT.NullString = "0"
PT.TableStyle2 = "PivotStyleMedium3"
```

Figure 13.18 shows the pivot table that would result from this code.

Figure 13.18
You can change the function used to summarize columns in the Values area of the pivot table.

Rep	Data Revenue	# of Records	Average Revenue
Alda Carden	$2,225,244	799	2,785.0
Annabel Locklear	$48,013	61	787.1
Ashleigh Friedman	$5,582,120	2,910	1,918.3
Austen Cope	$282,422	159	1,776.2
Carma Gough	$848,890	466	1,821.7
Donte Drummond	$3,820	4	955.0
Dustin Gamboa	$1,308,212	1,059	1,235.3
Edward Cooley	$65,016	58	1,121.0
Jasper Witcher	$381,836	348	1,097.2
Kirstie Paulson	$36,442	48	759.2
Maleah Menard	$292,028	262	1,114.6
Marlin Stubblefield	$331,932	396	838.2
Martin Stamps	$575,548	385	1,494.9
Megan Winston	$206,988	191	1,083.7
Norman Stackhouse	$177,349	185	958.6
Pauline Mccollum	$13	1	13.0
Tory Hanlon	$3,045,306	1,192	2,554.8
Truman Dubois	$173,245	182	951.9
Grand Total	**$15,584,422**	**8,706**	**1,790.1**

Calculated Data Fields

Pivot tables offer two types of formulas. The most useful type defines a formula for a calculated field. This adds a new field to the pivot table. Calculations for calculated fields are always done at the summary level.

To set up a calculated field, use the Add method with the CalculatedFields object. You have to specify a field name and a formula, like so:

```
PT.CalculatedFields.Add Name:="GrossProfit", Formula:="=Revenue-Cost"
PT.CalculatedFields.Add "GP_Pct", "=GrossProfit/Revenue"
```

After you define the field, add it as a data field:

```
With PT.PivotFields("GrossProfit")
    .Orientation = xlDataField
    .Function = xlSum
    .Position = 3
    .NumberFormat = "$#,##0"
    .Caption = "Gross Profit"
End With
With PT.PivotFields("GP_Pct")
    .Orientation = xlDataField
    .Function = xlSum
    .Position = 4
    .NumberFormat = "0.0%"
    .Caption = "GP%"
End With
```

13

Figure 13.19 shows the Gross Profit calculated field.

Figure 13.19
A calculated field adds
Gross Profit to the pivot
table.

	Data		
Category	Sum of Revenue	Sum of Cost	Gross Profit
Bar Equipment	$1,769,332	$799,967	$969,365
Commercial Appliances	$8,562,837	$3,848,608	$4,714,229
Concession Equipment	$9,876,342	$4,436,685	$5,439,657
Fryers	$3,835,963	$1,723,930	$2,112,033
Ovens and Ranges	$57,168,593	$25,787,407	$31,381,186
Refrigerators and Coolers	$41,793,565	$18,828,219	$22,965,346
Warmers	$37,482,133	$16,876,630	$20,605,503
Grand Total	$160,488,764	$72,301,446	$88,187,318

A calculated field can be referenced in subsequent calculated fields. The following code uses the Gross Profit field to calculate Gross Profit Percent. Although the .Caption property renamed the field to "Gross Profit" (with a space), the field name in the preceding code is "GrossProfit" (without a space). Use the field name in the following calculation:

```
PT.CalculatedFields.Add "GP_Pct", "=GrossProfit/Revenue", True
With PT.PivotFields("GP_Pct")
    .Orientation = xlDataField
    .Function = xlSum
    .Position = 4
    .NumberFormat = "0.0%"
    .Caption = "GP%"
End With
```

Figure 13.20 shows a report with GP%.

Figure 13.20
GP% is based on a field in
the data set and another
calculated field.

	Data			
Category	Sum of Revenue	Sum of Cost	Gross Profit	GP%
Bar Equipment	$1,769,332	$799,967	$969,365	54.8%
Commercial Appliances	$8,562,837	$3,848,608	$4,714,229	55.1%
Concession Equipment	$9,876,342	$4,436,685	$5,439,657	55.1%
Fryers	$3,835,963	$1,723,930	$2,112,033	55.1%
Ovens and Ranges	$57,168,593	$25,787,407	$31,381,186	54.9%
Refrigerators and Coolers	$41,793,565	$18,828,219	$22,965,346	54.9%
Warmers	$37,482,133	$16,876,630	$20,605,503	55.0%
Grand Total	$160,488,764	$72,301,446	$88,187,318	54.9%

Calculated Items

Calculated items have the potential to produce incorrect results in your pivot table. Say that you have a report of sales by nine states. You want to show a subtotal of four of the states. A calculated item would add a ninth item to the state column. Although the pivot table gladly calculates this new item, it causes the grand total to appear overstated.

Figure 13.21 shows a pivot table with these nine states. The total revenue is $10 million. When a calculated item provides a subtotal of four states (see Figure 13.22), the grand total increases to $15 million. This means that the items that make up the calculated item are included in the total twice. If you like restating numbers to the Securities and Exchange Commission, feel free to use calculated items.

Figure 13.21
This pivot table adds up to $10 million

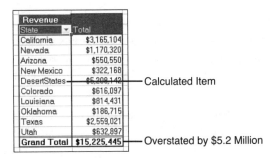

Revenue	
State	Total
Arizona	$550,550
California	$3,165,104
Colorado	$616,097
Louisiana	$814,431
Nevada	$1,170,320
New Mexico	$322,168
Oklahoma	$186,715
Texas	$2,559,021
Utah	$632,897
Grand Total	**$10,017,303**

Figure 13.22
Add a calculated item and the total is overstated.

Revenue		
State	Total	
California	$3,165,104	
Nevada	$1,170,320	
Arizona	$550,550	
New Mexico	$322,168	
DesertStates	$5,208,142	——Calculated Item
Colorado	$616,097	
Louisiana	$814,431	
Oklahoma	$186,715	
Texas	$2,559,021	
Utah	$632,897	
Grand Total	**$15,225,445**	——Overstated by $5.2 Million

The code to produce the calculated item is shown here. Calculated items are added as the final position along the field, so this code changes the `.Position` property to move the Desert States item to the proper position:

```
PT.PivotFields("State").CalculatedItems.Add _
    Name:="DesertStates", _
    Formula:="=California +Nevada +Arizona +'New Mexico'"
PT.PivotFields("State").PivotItems("California").Position = 1
PT.PivotFields("State").PivotItems("Nevada").Position = 2
PT.PivotFields("State").PivotItems("Arizona").Position = 3
PT.PivotFields("State").PivotItems("New Mexico").Position = 4
PT.PivotFields("State").PivotItems("DesertStates").Position = 5
```

If you hope to use a calculated item, you should either remove the grand total row or remove the four states that go into the calculated item. This code hides the four states. The resulting pivot table returns to the correct total, as shown in Figure 13.23.

```
PT.PivotFields("State").CalculatedItems.Add _
    Name:="DesertStates", _
    Formula:="=California +Nevada +Arizona +'New Mexico'"
' Hide the items included in the new subtotal
With PT.PivotFields("State")
    .PivotItems("California").Visible = False
    .PivotItems("Nevada").Visible = False
    .PivotItems("Arizona").Visible = False
    .PivotItems("New Mexico").Visible = False
End With
```

13

Figure 13.23
One way to use a calcu-
lated item is to remove
any elements that went
into it.

Revenue	
State ⬇	Total
DesertStates	$5,208,142
Colorado	$616,097
Louisiana	$814,431
Oklahoma	$186,715
Texas	$2,559,021
Utah	$632,897
Grand Total	**$10,017,303**

A better solution, which is discussed in the next section, is to skip calculated items and to use text grouping.

Calculating Groups

If you need to calculate subtotals for certain regions, a better solution is to use text grouping to define the groups. If you group the four states, Excel adds a new field to the row area of the pivot table. Although this process requires some special handling, it is worthwhile and creates a nice-looking report.

To group four states in the Excel interface, you select the cells that contain those four states and select Group Selection from the PivotTable Tools Options tab. This immediately does several things:

■ The items in the group are moved together in the row area.

■ A new field is added to the left of the state field. If the original field was called State, the new field is called State2.

■ Annoyingly, the subtotals property for the new State2 field is set to None instead of Automatic.

■ A subtotal for the selected items is added with the name of Group1.

■ Any items not in a group have a new subtotal added to State2 with the state name repeated.

In VBA, it is somewhat tricky to select the cells that contain the proper states. The following code uses the LabelRange property to point to the cells and then uses the UNION method to refer to the four noncontiguous cells:

```
Set R1 = PT.PivotFields("State").PivotItems("California").LabelRange
Set R2 = PT.PivotFields("State").PivotItems("Arizona").LabelRange
Set R3 = PT.PivotFields("State").PivotItems("New Mexico").LabelRange
Set R4 = PT.PivotFields("State").PivotItems("Nevada").LabelRange
Union(R1, R2, R3, R4).Group
```

After setting up the first group, rename the newly created States2 field to have a suitable name:

```
PT.PivotFields("State2").Caption = "State Group"
```

Then, change the name of this region from Group1 to the desired group name:

```
PT.PivotFields("State Group").PivotItems("Group1").Caption = "Desert States"
```

Change the subtotals property to Automatic from None:

```
PT.PivotFields("State Group").Subtotals(1) = True
```

After you have set up the first group, you can define the remaining groups with this code:

```
Set R1 = PT.PivotFields("State").PivotItems("Utah").LabelRange
Set R2 = PT.PivotFields("State").PivotItems("Colorado").LabelRange
Union(R1, R2).Group
PT.PivotFields("State Group").PivotItems("Group2").Caption = "Rockies"

Set R1 = PT.PivotFields("State").PivotItems("Texas").LabelRange
Set R2 = PT.PivotFields("State").PivotItems("Louisiana").LabelRange
Set R3 = PT.PivotFields("State").PivotItems("Oklahoma").LabelRange
Union(R1, R2, R3).Group
PT.PivotFields("State Group").PivotItems("Group3").Caption = "Oil States"
```

The result is a pivot table with new virtual groups as shown in Figure 13.24.

Figure 13.24
Grouping text fields allows for reporting by territories that are not in the original data.

Revenue		
State Group ▾	State ▾	Total
⊟ Desert State	Arizona	$550,550
	California	$3,165,104
	Nevada	$1,170,320
	New Mexico	$322,168
Desert States Total		**$5,208,142**
⊟ Rockies	Colorado	$616,097
	Utah	$632,897
Rockies Total		**$1,248,994**
⊟ Oil States	Louisiana	$814,431
	Oklahoma	$186,715
	Texas	$2,559,021
Oil States Total		**$3,560,167**
Grand Total		**$10,017,303**

Using Show Values As to Perform Other Calculations

The Show Values As tab in the Value Field Settings dialog offers 15 different calculations. These calculations enable you to change from numbers to percentage of total, running totals, ranks, and more.

Change the calculation by using the `.Calculation` option for the pivot field.

> **NOTE**
> Note that the `.Calculation` property works with the `.BaseField` and `.BaseItem` properties. Depending on the selected calculation, you might be required to specify a BaseField and BaseItem, or sometimes only a BaseField, or sometimes neither of them.

13

Some calculations such as % of Column and % of Row need no further definition; you do not have to specify a base field. Here is code to show revenue as a percentage of total revenue:

```
With PT.PivotFields("Revenue")
    .Orientation = xlDataField
    .Function = xlSum
    .Calculation = xlPercentOfTotal
    .Position = 2
    .NumberFormat = "0.0%"
    .Name = "% of Total"
End With
```

Other calculations need a base field. If you are showing revenue and ask for the descending rank, you could specify that the base field is the state field. In this case, you are asking for this state's rank based on revenue:

```
With PT.PivotFields("Revenue")
    .Orientation = xlDataField
    .Calculation = xlRankDecending
    .BaseField = "State"
    .Position = 4
    .NumberFormat = "0%"
    .Name = "RankD"
End With
```

A few calculations require both a base field and a base item. If you wanted to show every state's revenue as a percentage of California revenue, you would have to specify % Of as the calculation, State as the base field, and California as the base item:

```
With PT.PivotFields("Revenue")
    .Orientation = xlDataField
    .Calculation = xlPercentOf
    .BaseField = "State"
    .BaseItem = "California"
    .Position = 5
    .NumberFormat = "0%"
    .Name = "% of CA"
End With
```

Some of the calculation fields were new in Excel 2010. In Figure 13.25, column I uses the new % of Parent calculation and column H uses the old % of Total calculation. In both columns, Desert States is 52% of the Grand Total (cells H8 and I8). However, cell I5 shows that California is 60.8% of Desert States, whereas cell H5 shows that California is 31.6% of the grand total.

Table 13.1 shows the complete list of .Calculation options. The second column indicates whether the calculation is compatible with previous versions of Excel. The third column indicates whether you need a base field and base item.

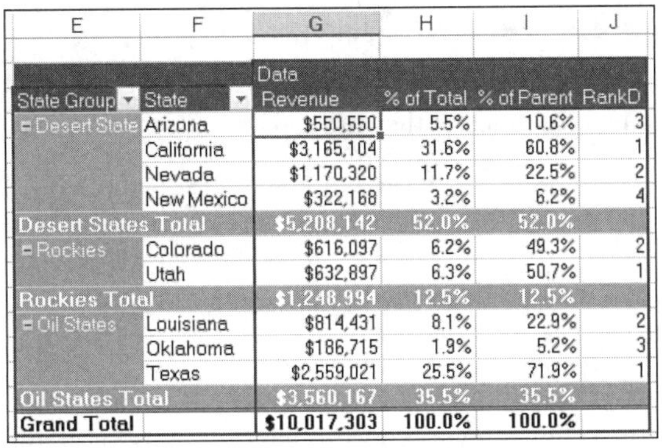

Figure 13.25
% of Parent in column I is
new in Excel 2013.

	E	F	G	H	I	J
	State Group ▼	State ▼	Data Revenue	% of Total	% of Parent	RankD
	⊟Desert State	Arizona	$550,550	5.5%	10.6%	3
		California	$3,165,104	31.6%	60.8%	1
		Nevada	$1,170,320	11.7%	22.5%	2
		New Mexico	$322,168	3.2%	6.2%	4
	Desert States Total		$5,208,142	52.0%	52.0%	
	⊟Rockies	Colorado	$616,097	6.2%	49.3%	2
		Utah	$632,897	6.3%	50.7%	1
	Rockies Total		$1,248,994	12.5%	12.5%	
	⊟Oil States	Louisiana	$814,431	8.1%	22.9%	2
		Oklahoma	$186,715	1.9%	5.2%	3
		Texas	$2,559,021	25.5%	71.9%	1
	Oil States Total		$3,560,167	35.5%	35.5%	
	Grand Total		$10,017,303	100.0%	100.0%	

Table 13.1   Calculation Options Available in Excel 2013 VBA

Calculation	Version	BaseField/BaseItem
xlDifferenceFrom	All	Both required
xlIndex	All	Neither
xlNoAdditionalCalculation	All	Neither
xlPercentDifferenceFrom	All	Both required
xlPercentOf	All	Both required
xlPercentOfColumn	All	Neither
xlPercentOfParent	2010 and later	BaseField only
xlPercentOfParentColumn	2010 and later	Both required
xlPercentOfParentRow	2010 and later	Both required
xlPercentOfRow	All	Neither
xlPercentOfTotal	All	Neither
xlPercentRunningTotal	2010 and later	BaseField only
xlRankAscending	2010 and later	BaseField only
xlRankDescending	2010 and later	BaseField only
xlRunningTotal	All	BaseField only

13

Using Advanced Pivot Table Techniques

Even if you are a pivot table pro, you might never have run into some of the really advanced techniques available with pivot tables. The following sections discuss such techniques.

Using AutoShow to Produce Executive Overviews

If you are designing an executive dashboard utility, you might want to spotlight the top five markets. This setting lets you select either the top or bottom *n* records based on any data field in the report.

The code to use AutoShow in VBA uses the .AutoShow method:

```
' Show only the top 5 Markets
PT.PivotFields("Market").AutoShow Top:=xlAutomatic, Range:=xlTop, _
    Count:=5, Field:= "Sum of Revenue"
```

When you create a report using the .AutoShow method, it is often helpful to copy the data and then go back to the original pivot report to get the totals for all markets. In the following code, this is achieved by removing the Market field from the pivot table and copying the grand total to the report. Listing 13.4 produces the report shown in Figure 13.26.

Figure 13.26

The Top 5 Markets report contains two pivot tables.

	A	B	C
1	Top 5 Markets		
2			
3	**Market**	**Bar Equipment**	**Commercial Appliances**
4	Florida	1,131,779	5,667,799
5	Charlotte	283,676	1,525,742
6	California	66,233	294,080
7	Dallas	59,560	255,146
8	Buffalo	37,366	237,298
9	Top 5 Total	1,578,614	7,980,064
10			
11	Total Company	1,769,332	8,562,837
12			

Listing 13.4   Code Used to Create the Top 5 Markets Report

```
Sub Top5Markets()
    ' Produce a report of the top 5 markets
    Dim WSD As Worksheet
    Dim WSR As Worksheet
    Dim WBN As Workbook
    Dim PTCache As PivotCache
    Dim PT As PivotTable
    Dim PRange As Range
    Dim FinalRow As Long
    Set WSD = Worksheets("Data")

    ' Delete any prior pivot tables
    For Each PT In WSD.PivotTables
        PT.TableRange2.Clear
    Next PT
    WSD.Range("M1:Z1").EntireColumn.Clear

    ' Define input area and set up a Pivot Cache
    FinalRow = WSD.Cells(Application.Rows.Count, 1).End(xlUp).Row
    FinalCol = WSD.Cells(1, Application.Columns.Count). _
        End(xlToLeft).Column
```

```vba
Set PRange = WSD.Cells(1, 1).Resize(FinalRow, FinalCol)
Set PTCache = ActiveWorkbook.PivotCaches.Add(SourceType:= _
    xlDatabase, SourceData:=PRange.Address)

' Create the Pivot Table from the Pivot Cache
Set PT = PTCache.CreatePivotTable(TableDestination:=WSD. _
    Cells(2, FinalCol + 2), TableName:="PivotTable1")

' Turn off updating while building the table
PT.ManualUpdate = True

' Set up the row fields
PT.AddFields RowFields:="Market", ColumnFields:="Category"

' Set up the data fields
With PT.PivotFields("Revenue")
    .Orientation = xlDataField
    .Function = xlSum
    .Position = 1
    .NumberFormat = "#,##0"
    .Name = "Total Revenue"
End With

' Ensure that we get zeroes instead of blanks in the data area
PT.NullString = "0"

' Sort markets descending by sum of revenue
PT.PivotFields("Market").AutoSort Order:=xlDescending, _
    field:="Total Revenue"

' Show only the top 5 markets
PT.PivotFields("Market").AutoShow Type:=xlAutomatic, Range:=xlTop, _
    Count:=5, field:="Total Revenue"

' Calc the pivot table to allow the date label to be drawn
PT.ManualUpdate = False
PT.ManualUpdate = True

' Create a new blank workbook with one worksheet
Set WBN = Workbooks.Add(xlWBATWorksheet)
Set WSR = WBN.Worksheets(1)
WSR.Name = "Report"
' Set up ritle for report
With WSR.[A1]
    .Value = "Top 5 Markets"
    .Font.Size = 14
End With

' Copy the pivot table data to row 3 of the report sheet
' Use offset to eliminate the title row of the pivot table
PT.TableRange2.Offset(1, 0).Copy
WSR.[A3].PasteSpecial Paste:=xlPasteValuesAndNumberFormats
LastRow = WSR.Cells(Rows.Count, 1).End(xlUp).Row
WSR.Cells(LastRow, 1).Value = "Top 5 Total"
```

```
' Go back to the pivot table to get totals without the AutoShow
PT.PivotFields("Market").Orientation = xlHidden
PT.ManualUpdate = False
PT.ManualUpdate = True
PT.TableRange2.Offset(2, 0).Copy
WSR.Cells(LastRow + 2, 1).PasteSpecial Paste:=xlPasteValuesAndNumberFormats
WSR.Cells(LastRow + 2, 1).Value = "Total Company"

' Clear the pivot table
PT.TableRange2.Clear
Set PTCache = Nothing

' Do some basic formatting
' Autofit columns, bold the headings, right-align
WSR.Range(WSR.Range("A3"), WSR.Cells(LastRow + 2, 9)).Columns.AutoFit
Range("A3").EntireRow.Font.Bold = True
Range("A3").EntireRow.HorizontalAlignment = xlRight
Range("A3").HorizontalAlignment = xlLeft

Range("A2").Select
MsgBox "CEO Report has been Created"

End Sub
```

The Top 5 Markets report actually contains two snapshots of a pivot table. After using the AutoShow feature to grab the top five markets with their totals, the macro went back to the pivot table, removed the AutoShow option, and grabbed the total of all markets to produce the Total Company row.

Using ShowDetail to Filter a Recordset

Take any pivot table in the Excel user interface. Double-click any number in the table. Excel inserts a new sheet in the workbook and copies all the source records that represent that number. In the Excel user interface, this is a great way to perform a drill-down query into a data set.

The equivalent VBA property is ShowDetail. By setting this property to True for any cell in the pivot table, you generate a new worksheet with all the records that make up that cell:

```
PT.TableRange1.Offset(2, 1).Resize(1, 1).ShowDetail = True
```

Listing 13.5 produces a pivot table with the total revenue for the top three stores and ShowDetail for each of those stores. This is an alternative method to using the Advanced Filter report. The results of this macro are three new sheets. Figure 13.27 shows the first sheet created.

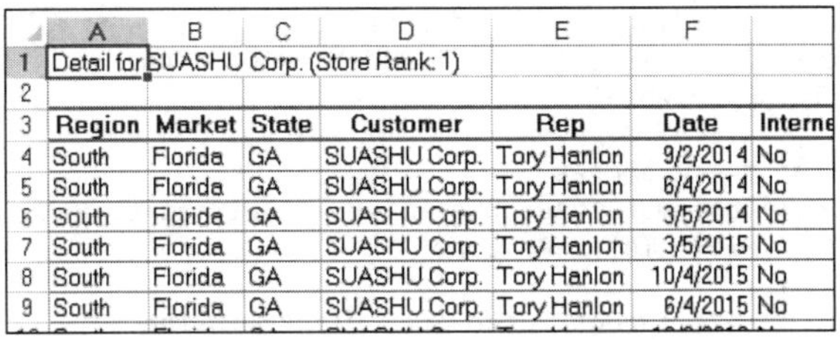

Figure 13.27

Pivot table applications are incredibly diverse. This macro created a pivot table of the top three stores and then used the `ShowDetail` property to retrieve the records for each of those stores.

⊿	A	B	C	D	E	F	
1	Detail for SUASHU Corp. (Store Rank: 1)						
2							
3	**Region**	**Market**	**State**	**Customer**	**Rep**	**Date**	**Interne**
4	South	Florida	GA	SUASHU Corp.	Tory Hanlon	9/2/2014	No
5	South	Florida	GA	SUASHU Corp.	Tory Hanlon	6/4/2014	No
6	South	Florida	GA	SUASHU Corp.	Tory Hanlon	3/5/2014	No
7	South	Florida	GA	SUASHU Corp.	Tory Hanlon	3/5/2015	No
8	South	Florida	GA	SUASHU Corp.	Tory Hanlon	10/4/2015	No
9	South	Florida	GA	SUASHU Corp.	Tory Hanlon	6/4/2015	No

Listing 13.5   Code Used to Create a Report for Each of the Top Three Customers

```
Sub RetrieveTop3CustomerDetail()
    ' Retrieve Details from Top 3 Customers
    Dim WSD As Worksheet
    Dim WSR As Worksheet
    Dim WBN As Workbook
    Dim PTCache As PivotCache
    Dim PT As PivotTable
    Dim PRange As Range
    Dim FinalRow As Long
    Set WSD = Worksheets("Data")

    ' Delete any prior pivot tables
    For Each PT In WSD.PivotTables
        PT.TableRange2.Clear
    Next PT
    WSD.Range("M1:Z1").EntireColumn.Clear

    ' Define input area and set up a Pivot Cache
    FinalRow = WSD.Cells(Application.Rows.Count, 1).End(xlUp).Row
    FinalCol = WSD.Cells(1, Application.Columns.Count). _
        End(xlToLeft).Column
    Set PRange = WSD.Cells(1, 1).Resize(FinalRow, FinalCol)
    Set PTCache = ActiveWorkbook.PivotCaches.Add(SourceType:= _
        xlDatabase, SourceData:=PRange.Address)

    ' Create the Pivot Table from the Pivot Cache
    Set PT = PTCache.CreatePivotTable(TableDestination:=WSD. _
        Cells(2, FinalCol + 2), TableName:="PivotTable1")

    ' Turn off updating while building the table
    PT.ManualUpdate = True

    ' Set up the row fields
    PT.AddFields RowFields:="Customer", ColumnFields:="Data"

    ' Set up the data fields
    With PT.PivotFields("Revenue")
        .Orientation = xlDataField
        .Function = xlSum
        .Position = 1
        .NumberFormat = "#,##0"
        .Name = "Total Revenue"
    End With
```

13

```
    ' Sort Stores descending by sum of revenue
    PT.PivotFields("Customer").AutoSort Order:=xlDescending, _
        field:="Total Revenue"

    ' Show only the top 3 stores
    PT.PivotFields("Customer").AutoShow Type:=xlAutomatic, Range:=xlTop, _
        Count:=3, field:="Total Revenue"

    ' Ensure that we get zeroes instead of blanks in the data area
    PT.NullString = "0"

    ' Calc the pivot table to allow the date label to be drawn
    PT.ManualUpdate = False
    PT.ManualUpdate = True

    ' Produce summary reports for each customer
    For i = 1 To 3
        PT.TableRange2.Offset(i + 1, 1).Resize(1, 1).ShowDetail = True
        ' The active sheet has changed to the new detail report
        ' Add a title
        Range("A1:A2").EntireRow.Insert
        Range("A1").Value = "Detail for " & _
            PT.TableRange2.Offset(i + 1, 0).Resize(1, 1).Value & _
            " (Store Rank: " & i & ")"
    Next i

    MsgBox "Detail reports for top 3 stores have been created."

End Sub
```

Creating Reports for Each Region or Model

A pivot table can have one or more Filters fields. A Filters field goes in a separate set of rows above the pivot report. It can serve to filter the report to a certain region, certain model, or certain combination of region and model. In VBA, Filters fields are called *page fields*.

You might create a pivot table with several filter fields to allow someone to do ad-hoc analyses. However, it is more likely that you will use the filter fields in order to produce reports for each region.

To set up a filter in VBA, add the PageFields parameter to the AddFields method. The following line of code creates a pivot table with Region in the Filters:

```
PT.AddFields RowFields:= "Product", ColumnFields:= "Data", PageFields:= "Region"
```

The preceding line of code sets up the Region filter with the value (All), which returns all regions. To limit the report to just the North region, use the CurrentPage property:

```
PT.PivotFields("Region").CurrentPage = "North"
```

13

One use of a filter is to build a user form in which someone can select a particular region or particular product. You then use this information to set the `CurrentPage` property and display the results of the user form.

One amazing trick is to use the Show Pages feature to replicate a pivot table for every item in one filter field drop-down. After creating and formatting a pivot table, you can run this single line of code. If you have eight regions in the data set, eight new worksheets are inserted in the workbook, one for each region. The pivot table appears on each worksheet, with the appropriate region chosen from the drop-down:

```
PT.ShowPages PageField:=Region
```

> **CAUTION**
>
> Be careful with `ShowPages`. If you use `ShowPages` on the Customer field and you have 1,000 customers, Excel attempts to insert 1,000 worksheets in the workbook, each with a pivot table. All of those pivot tables share the same pivot cache in order to minimize memory usage. However, you will eventually run out of memory and the program will end with a debug error when no additional worksheets will fit in available memory.
>
> The other problem with `ShowPages` is that it creates the individual reports as worksheets in a single workbook. In real life, you probably want separate workbooks for each region so that you can email the reports to the appropriate office. You can loop through all `PivotItems` and display them one at a time in the page field. You can quickly produce top ten reports for each region using this method.

To determine how many regions are available in the data, use `PT.PivotFields("Region").PivotItems.Count`. Either of these loops would work:

```
For i = 1 To PT.PivotFields("Region").PivotItems.Count
    PT.PivotFields("Region").CurrentPage = _
            PT.PivotFields("Region").PivotItems(i).Name
    PT.ManualUpdate = False
    PT.ManualUpdate = True
Next i

For Each PivItem In PT.PivotFields("Region").PivotItems
    PT.PivotFields("Region").CurrentPage = PivItem.Name
    PT.ManualUpdate = False
    PT.ManualUpdate = True
Next PivItem
```

Of course, in both of these loops, the three region reports fly by too quickly to see. In practice, you would want to save each report while it is displayed.

So far in this chapter, you have been using PT.TableRange2 when copying the data from the pivot table. The TableRange2 property includes all rows of the pivot table, including the page fields. There is also a .TableRange1 property, which excludes the page fields. You can use either statement to get the detail rows:

```
PT.TableRange2.Offset(3, 0)
PT.TableRange1.Offset(1, 0)
```

Which you use is your preference, but if you use TableRange2, you will not have problems when you try to delete the pivot table with PT.TableRange2.Clear. If you were to accidentally attempt to clear TableRange1 when there are page fields, you would end up with the dreaded "Cannot move or change part of a pivot table" error.

Listing 13.6 produces a new workbook for each region, as shown in Figure 13.28.

Figure 13.28
By looping through all items found in the Region page field, the macro produced one workbook for each regional manager.

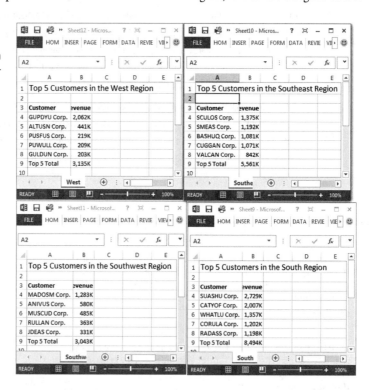

Listing 13.6   Code That Creates a New Workbook per Region

```
Sub Top5ByRegionReport()
    ' Produce a report of top 5 customers for each region
    Dim WSD As Worksheet
    Dim WSR As Worksheet
    Dim WBN As Workbook
    Dim PTCache As PivotCache
    Dim PT As PivotTable
    Dim PRange As Range
    Dim FinalRow As Long
```

```
Set WSD = Worksheets("Data")

' Delete any prior pivot tables
For Each PT In WSD.PivotTables
    PT.TableRange2.Clear
Next PT
WSD.Range("M1:Z1").EntireColumn.Clear

' Define input area and set up a Pivot Cache
FinalRow = WSD.Cells(Application.Rows.Count, 1).End(xlUp).Row
FinalCol = WSD.Cells(1, Application.Columns.Count). _
    End(xlToLeft).Column
Set PRange = WSD.Cells(1, 1).Resize(FinalRow, FinalCol)
Set PTCache = ActiveWorkbook.PivotCaches.Add(SourceType:= _
    xlDatabase, SourceData:=PRange.Address)

' Create the Pivot Table from the Pivot Cache
Set PT = PTCache.CreatePivotTable(TableDestination:=WSD. _
    Cells(2, FinalCol + 2), TableName:="PivotTable1")

' Turn off updating while building the table
PT.ManualUpdate = True

' Set up the row fields
PT.AddFields RowFields:="Customer", ColumnFields:="Data", _
    PageFields:="Region"

' Set up the data fields
With PT.PivotFields("Revenue")
    .Orientation = xlDataField
    .Function = xlSum
    .Position = 1
    .NumberFormat = "#,##0,K"
    .Name = "Total Revenue"
End With
Stop

' Sort stores descending by sum of revenue
PT.PivotFields("Customer").AutoSort Order:=xlDescending, _
    field:="Total Revenue"

' Show only the top 5 stores
PT.PivotFields("Customer").AutoShow Type:=xlAutomatic, Range:=xlTop, _
    Count:=5, field:="Total Revenue"

' Ensure that we get zeroes instead of blanks in the data area
PT.NullString = "0"

' Calc the pivot table
PT.ManualUpdate = False
PT.ManualUpdate = True
Stop
Ctr = 0

' Loop through each region
For Each PivItem In PT.PivotFields("Region").PivotItems
    Ctr = Ctr + 1
    PT.PivotFields("Region").CurrentPage = PivItem.Name
```

13

```
        PT.ManualUpdate = False
        PT.ManualUpdate = True
        Stop

        ' Create a new blank workbook with one worksheet
        Set WBN = Workbooks.Add(xlWBATWorksheet)
        Set WSR = WBN.Worksheets(1)
        WSR.Name = PivItem.Name
        ' Set up Title for Report
        With WSR.[A1]
            .Value = "Top 5 Customers in the " & PivItem.Name & " Region"
            .Font.Size = 14
        End With

        ' Copy the pivot table data to row 3 of the report sheet
        ' Use offset to eliminate the page & title rows of the pivot table
        PT.TableRange2.Offset(3, 0).Copy
        WSR.[A3].PasteSpecial Paste:=xlPasteValuesAndNumberFormats
        LastRow = WSR.Cells(65536, 1).End(xlUp).Row
        WSR.Cells(LastRow, 1).Value = "Top 5 Total"

        ' Do some basic formatting
        ' Autofit columns, bold the headings, right-align
        WSR.Range(WSR.Range("A2"), WSR.Cells(LastRow, 3)).Columns.AutoFit
        Range("A3").EntireRow.Font.Bold = True
        Range("A3").EntireRow.HorizontalAlignment = xlRight
        Range("A3").HorizontalAlignment = xlLeft
        Range("B3").Value = "Revenue"

        Range("A2").Select

    Next PivItem

    ' Clear the pivot table
    PT.TableRange2.Clear
    Set PTCache = Nothing

    MsgBox Ctr & " Region reports have been created"

End Sub
```

Manually Filtering Two or More Items in a PivotField

In addition to setting up a calculated pivot item to display the total of a couple of products that make up a dimension, you can manually filter a particular PivotField.

For example, you have one client who sells shoes. In the report showing sales of sandals, he wants to see just the stores that are in warm-weather states. The code to hide a particular store is

```
PT.PivotFields("Store").PivotItems("Minneapolis").Visible = False
```

You must be very careful never to set all items to False; otherwise, the macro ends with an error. This tends to happen more than you would expect. An application may first show products A and B and then on the next loop show products C and D. If you attempt to make A and B not visible before making C and D visible, no products will be visible along the PivotField, which causes an error. To correct this, always loop through all PivotItems, making sure to turn them back to visible before the second pass through the loop.

This process is easy in VBA. After building the table with Product in the page field, loop through to change the Visible property to show only the total of certain products:

```
' Make sure all PivotItems along line are visible
For Each PivItem In _
    PT.PivotFields("Product").PivotItems
    PivItem.Visible = True
Next PivItem

' Now - loop through and keep only certain items visible
For Each PivItem In _
    PT.PivotFields("Product").PivotItems
    Select Case PivItem.Name
        Case "Landscaping/Grounds Care", _
            "Green Plants and Foliage Care"
            PivItem.Visible = True
        Case Else
            PivItem.Visible = False
    End Select
Next PivItem
```

Using the Conceptual Filters

Beginning with Excel 2007, conceptual filters for date fields, numeric fields, and text fields are provided. In the PivotTable Fields List, hover the mouse cursor over any active field in the field list portion of the dialog. In the drop-down that appears, you can choose Label Filters, Date Filters, or Value Filters.

To apply a label filter in VBA, use the PivotFilters.Add method. The following code filters to the customers that start with 1:

```
PT.PivotFields("Customer").PivotFilters.Add _
    Type:=xlCaptionBeginsWith, Value1:="1"
```

To clear the filter from the Customer field, use the ClearAllFilters method:

```
PT.PivotFields("Customer").ClearAllFilters
```

To apply a date filter to the date field to find records from this week, use this code:

```
PT.PivotFields("Date").PivotFilters.Add Type:=xlThisWeek
```

The value filters allow you to filter one field based on the value of another field. For example, to find all the markets where the total revenue is more than $100,000, you would use this code:

```
PT.PivotFields("Market").PivotFilters.Add _
    Type:=xlValueIsGreaterThan, _
```

13

```
DataField:=PT.PivotFields("Sum of Revenue"), _
Value1:=100000
```

Other value filters might allow you to specify that you want branches where the revenue is between $50,000 and $100,000. In this case, you would specify one limit as Value1 and the second limit as Value2:

```
PT.PivotFields("Market").PivotFilters.Add _
    Type:=xlValueIsBetween, _
    DataField:=PT.PivotFields("Sum of Revenue"), _
    Value1:=50000, Value2:=100000
```

Table 13.2 lists all the possible filter types.

Table 13.2   Filter Types

Filter Type	Description
xlBefore	Filters for all dates before a specified date
xlBeforeOrEqualTo	Filters for all dates on or before a specified date
xlAfter	Filters for all dates after a specified date
xlAfterOrEqualTo	Filters for all dates on or after a specified date
xlAllDatesInPeriodJanuary	Filters for all dates in January
xlAllDatesInPeriodFebruary	Filters for all dates in February
xlAllDatesInPeriodMarch	Filters for all dates in March
xlAllDatesInPeriodApril	Filters for all dates in April
xlAllDatesInPeriodMay	Filters for all dates in May
xlAllDatesInPeriodJune	Filters for all dates in June
xlAllDatesInPeriodJuly	Filters for all dates in July
xlAllDatesInPeriodAugust	Filters for all dates in August
xlAllDatesInPeriodSeptember	Filters for all dates in September
xlAllDatesInPeriodOctober	Filters for all dates in October
xlAllDatesInPeriodNovember	Filters for all dates in November
xlAllDatesInPeriodDecember	Filters for all dates in December
xlAllDatesInPeriodQuarter1	Filters for all dates in Quarter 1
xlAllDatesInPeriodQuarter2	Filters for all dates in Quarter 2
xlAllDatesInPeriodQuarter3	Filters for all dates in Quarter 3
xlAllDatesInPeriodQuarter4	Filters for all dates in Quarter 4
xlBottomCount	Filters for the specified number of values from the bottom of a list
xlBottomPercent	Filters for the specified percentage of values from the bottom of a list

13

Filter Type	Description
xlBottomSum	Sums the values from the bottom of the list
xlCaptionBeginsWith	Filters for all captions beginning with the specified string
xlCaptionContains	Filters for all captions that contain the specified string
xlCaptionDoesNotBeginWith	Filters for all captions that do not begin with the specified string
xlCaptionDoesNotContain	Filters for all captions that do not contain the specified string
xlCaptionDoesNotEndWith	Filters for all captions that do not end with the specified string
xlCaptionDoesNotEqual	Filters for all captions that do not match the specified string
xlCaptionEndsWith	Filters for all captions that end with the specified string
xlCaptionEquals	Filters for all captions that match the specified string
xlCaptionIsBetween	Filters for all captions that are between a specified range of values
xlCaptionIsGreaterThan	Filters for all captions that are greater than the specified value
xlCaptionIsGreaterThan-OrEqualTo	Filters for all captions that are greater than or match the specified value
xlCaptionIsLessThan	Filters for all captions that are less than the specified value
xlCaptionIsLessThanOrEqualTo	Filters for all captions that are less than or match the specified value
xlCaptionIsNotBetween	Filters for all captions that are not between a specified range of values
xlDateBetween	Filters for all dates that are between a specified range of dates
xlDateLastMonth	Filters for all dates that apply to the previous month
xlDateLastQuarter	Filters for all dates that apply to the previous quarter
xlDateLastWeek	Filters for all dates that apply to the previous week
xlDateLastYear	Filters for all dates that apply to the previous year
xlDateNextMonth	Filters for all dates that apply to the next month
xlDateNextQuarter	Filters for all dates that apply to the next quarter
xlDateNextWeek	Filters for all dates that apply to the next week
xlDateNextYear	Filters for all dates that apply to the next year
xlDateThisMonth	Filters for all dates that apply to the current month
xlDateThisQuarter	Filters for all dates that apply to the current quarter
xlDateThisWeek	Filters for all dates that apply to the current week
xlDateThisYear	Filters for all dates that apply to the current year
xlDateToday	Filters for all dates that apply to the current date
xlDateTomorrow	Filters for all dates that apply to the next day
xlDateYesterday	Filters for all dates that apply to the previous day
xlNotSpecificDate	Filters for all dates that do not match a specified date

13

continues

Table 13.2   Continued

Filter Type	Description
xlSpecificDate	Filters for all dates that match a specified date
xlTopCount	Filters for the specified number of values from the top of a list
xlTopPercent	Filters for the specified percentage of values from a list
xlTopSum	Sums the values from the top of the list
xlValueDoesNotEqual	Filters for all values that do not match the specified value
xlValueEquals	Filters for all values that match the specified value
xlValueIsBetween	Filters for all values that are between a specified range of values
xlValueIsGreaterThan	Filters for all values that are greater than the specified value
xlValueIsGreaterThanOrEqualTo	Filters for all values that are greater than or match the specified value
xlValueIsLessThan	Filters for all values that are less than the specified value
xlValueIsLessThanOrEqualTo	Filters for all values that are less than or match the specified value
xlValueIsNotBetween	Filters for all values that are not between a specified range of values
xlYearToDate	Filters for all values that are within one year of a specified date

Using the Search Filter

Excel 2010 added a Search box to the filter drop-down. Although this is a slick feature in the Excel interface, there is no equivalent magic in VBA. Figure 13.29 shows the Select All Search Results check box after the search for "be". Using the macro recorder during this process creates a 5,876-line macro that goes through and turns all customers without "be" to invisible.

```
With ActiveSheet.PivotTables("PivotTable3").PivotFields("Customer")
    .PivotItems("ACASCO Corp.").Visible = False
    .PivotItems("ACECUL Corp.").Visible = False
    .PivotItems("ACEHUA Corp.").Visible = False
' snipped 5000_ similar lines
    .PivotItems("ZUQHYR Corp.").Visible = False
    .PivotItems("ZUSOEA Corp.").Visible = False
    .PivotItems("ZYLSTR Corp.").Visible = False
End With
```

There is nothing new in Excel 2013 VBA to emulate the Search box. To achieve the same results in VBA, use the xlCaptionContains filter described in Table 13.2.

Figure 13.29
The Excel 2013 interface offers a Search box. In VBA, you can emulate this using the old `xlCaptionContains` filter.

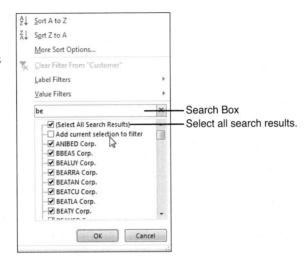

Search Box
Select all search results.

Setting up Slicers to Filter a Pivot Table

Excel 2010 introduced the concept of slicers to filter a pivot table. A slicer is a visual filter. You can resize and reposition slicers. You can control the color of the slicer and control the number of columns in a slicer. You can also select or clear items from a slicer using VBA.

Figure 13.30 shows a pivot table with two slicers. The State slicer has been modified to have five columns. The slicer with a caption "Territory" is actually based on the Region field. You can give the slicers a friendlier caption, which might be helpful when the underlying field is called IDKTxtReg or some other bizarre name invented by the IT department.

Region caption changed to Territory.

Figure 13.30
Slicers provide a visual filter for State and Region.

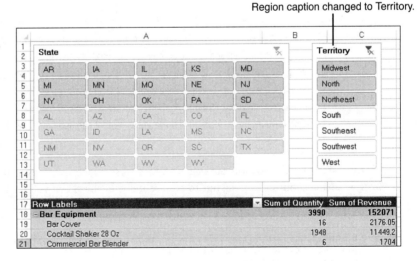

13

A slicer is composed of a `SlicerCache` and a `Slicer`. To define a slicer cache, you need to specify a pivot table as the source and a field name as the `SourceField`. The `SlicerCache` is defined at the workbook level. This enables you to have the slicer on a different worksheet than the actual pivot table.

```
Dim SCS as SlicerCache
Dim SCR as SlicerCache
Set SCS = ActiveWorkbook.SlicerCaches.Add(Source:=PT, SourceField:="State")
Set SCR = ActiveWorkbook.SlicerCaches.Add(Source:=PT, SourceField:="Region")
```

After you have defined the `SlicerCache`, you can add the `Slicer`, which is defined as an object of the slicer cache. Specify a worksheet as the destination. The `Name` argument controls the internal name for the slicer. The `Caption` argument is the heading that will be visible in the slicer. Specify the size of the slicer using height and width in points. Specify the location using top and left in points. In the following code, the values for top, left, height, and width are assigned to be equal to the location or size of certain cell ranges:

```
Dim SLS as Slicer
Set SLS = SCS.Slicers.Add(SlicerDestination:=WSD, Name:="State", _
    Caption:="State", _
    Top:=WSD.Range("O2").Top, _
    Left:=WSD.Range("O2").Left, _
    Width:=WSR.Range("O2:U2").Width, _
    Height:=WSD.Range("O2:O17").Height)
' Format the color and number of columns
```

All slicers start out as one column. You can change the style and number of columns with this code:

```
With SLS
    .Style = "SlicerStyleLight6"
    .NumberOfColumns = 5
End With
```

> **NOTE** I find that when I create slicers in the Excel interface, I spend many mouse clicks making adjustments to them. After adding two or three slicers, I position them in an overlapping tile arrangement. I always tweak the location, size, number of columns, and so on. For many years in my seminars, I bragged that I can create a pivot table in six mouse clicks. That was before slicers were introduced. Slicers are admittedly powerful, but seem to take 20 mouse clicks before they look right. Having a macro make all of these adjustments at once is a time-saver.

After the slicer is defined, you can use VBA to choose which items are activated in the slicer. It seems counterintuitive, but to choose items in the slicer, you have to change the `SlicerItem`, which is a member of the `SlicerCache`, not a member of the `Slicer`.

```
With SCR
    .SlicerItems("Midwest").Selected = True
    .SlicerItems("North").Selected = True
    .SlicerItems("Northeast").Selected = True
```

```
            .SlicerItems("South").Selected = False
            .SlicerItems("Southeast").Selected = False
            .SlicerItems("Southwest").Selected = False
            .SlicerItems("West").Selected = False
End With
```

You might need to deal with slicers that already exist. If a slicer is created for the state field, the name of the `SlicerCache` will be `"Slicer_State"`. The following code was used to format the slicers in Figure 13.30:

```
Sub MoveAndFormatSlicer()
    Dim SCS As SlicerCache
    Dim SLS As Slicer
    Dim SCR As SlicerCache
    Dim SLR As Slicer
    Dim WSD As Worksheet
    Set WSD = ActiveSheet

    Set SCS = ActiveWorkbook.SlicerCaches("Slicer_State")
    Set SLS = SCS.Slicers("State")
    With SLS
        .Style = "SlicerStyleLight6"
        .NumberOfColumns = 5
        .Top = WSD.Range("A1").Top + 5
        .Left = WSD.Range("A1").Left + 5
        .Width = WSD.Range("A1:B14").Width - 60
        .Height = WSD.Range("A1:B14").Height
    End With

    Set SCR = ActiveWorkbook.SlicerCaches("Slicer_Region")
    Set SLR = SCR.Slicers("Region")
    With SLR
        .Style = "SlicerStyleLight3"
        .NumberOfColumns = 1
        .Top = WSD.Range("C1").Top + 5
        .Left = WSD.Range("C1").Left - 20
        .Width = WSD.Range("C1").Width
        .Height = WSD.Range("C1:C14").Height
        .Caption = "Territory"
    End With

    ' Choose three regions
    With SCR
        .SlicerItems("Midwest").Selected = True
        .SlicerItems("North").Selected = True
        .SlicerItems("Northeast").Selected = True
        .SlicerItems("South").Selected = False
        .SlicerItems("Southeast").Selected = False
        .SlicerItems("Southwest").Selected = False
        .SlicerItems("West").Selected = False
    End With

End Sub
```

13

Using the Data Model in Excel 2013

Excel 2013 incorporates parts of PowerPivot into the core Excel product. Items in the Excel ribbon are incorporated into the Data Model; items in the PowerPivot ribbon are not. This means you can add two tables to the Data Model, create a relationship, and then build a pivot table from the Data Model.

To follow along with the example in this section, open the 13-BeforeDataModel.xlsm file from the sample download files. This workbook has two tables: Sales and Sector. Sector is a lookup table that is related to the Sales table via a customer field. To build the pivot table, you follow these general steps in the macro:

1. Add the main table to the model.

2. Add the lookup table to the model.

3. Link the two tables with a relationship.

4. Create a pivot cache from `ThisWorkbookDataModel`.

5. Create a pivot table from the cache.

6. Add row fields.

7. Define a measure. Add the measure to the pivot table.

Add Both Tables to the Data Model

You should already have a data set in the workbook that has been converted to a table using the Ctrl+T shortcut. On the Table Tools Design tab, change the table name to Sales. To link this table to the Data Model, use this code:

```
' Build Connection to the main Sales table
Set WBT = ActiveWorkbook
TableName = "Sales"
WBT.Connections.Add Name:="LinkedTable_" & TableName, _
    Description:="", _
    ConnectionString:="WORKSHEET;" & WBT.FullName, _
    CommandText:=WBT.Name & "!" & TableName, _
    lCmdType:=7, _
    CreateModelConnection:=True, _
    ImportRelationships:=False
```

Several variables in this code use the table name, the workbook path, and/or the workbook name. By storing the table name in a variable at the top of the code, you can build the connection name, connection string, and command text using the variables.

Adapting the preceding code to link to the lookup table then requires only changing the `TableName` variable:

```
TableName = "Sector"
WBT.Connections.Add Name:="LinkedTable_" & TableName, _
    Description:="", _
    ConnectionString:="WORKSHEET;" & WBT.FullName, _
    CommandText:=WBT.Name & "!" & TableName, _
```

```
    lCmdType:=7, _
    CreateModelConnection:=True, _
    ImportRelationships:=False
```

Create a Relationship Between the Two Tables

When you create a relationship in the Excel interface, you specify four items in the Create Relationship dialog (see Figure 13.31).

Figure 13.31
To create a relationship, specify a field in both tables.

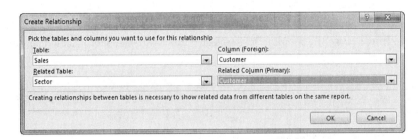

The code to create the relationship is more streamlined. There can only be one Data Model per workbook. Set an object variable named MO to refer to the model in this workbook. Use the ModelRelationships.Add method, specifying the two fields that are linked.

```
' Relate the two tables
Dim MO As Model
Set MO = ActiveWorkbook.Model
MO.ModelRelationships.Add _
    ForeignKeyColumn:=MO.ModelTables("Sales").ModelTableColumns("Customer"), _
    PrimaryKeyColumn:=MO.ModelTables("Sector").ModelTableColumns("Customer")
```

Define the Pivot Cache and Build the Pivot Table

The code to define the pivot cache specifies that the data is external. Even though the linked tables are in your workbook, and even though the Data Model is stored as a binary large object within the workbook, this is still considered an external data connection. The connection is always called ThisWorkbookDataModel.

```
' Define the PivotCache
Set PTCache = WBT.PivotCaches.Create(SourceType:=xlExternal, _
    SourceData:=WBT.Connections("ThisWorkbookDataModel"), _
    Version:=xlPivotTableVersion15)

' Create the Pivot Table from the Pivot Cache
Set PT = PTCache.CreatePivotTable( _
    TableDestination:=WSD.Cells(1, 1), TableName:="PivotTable1")
```

Add Model Fields to the Pivot Table

You will really add two types of fields to the pivot table. Text fields such as Customer, Sector, and Product are simply fields that can be added to the row or column area of the pivot table. No calculation has to happen to these fields. The code for adding text fields is

13

shown in this section. When you add a numeric field to the Values area in the Excel interface, you are actually implicitly defining a new calculated field. To do this in VBA, you have to explicitly define the field and then add it.

Let's look at the simpler example of adding a text field to the row area. The VBA code generically looks like this:

```
With PT.CubeFields("[TableName].[FieldName]")
    .Orientation = xlRowField
    .Position = 1
End With
```

In the current example, add the Sector field from the Sector table using this code:

```
With PT.CubeFields("[Sector].[Sector]")
    .Orientation = xlRowField
    .Position = 1
End With
```

Add Numeric Fields to the Values Area

In Excel 2010, PowerPivot calculated fields were called *measures*. In Excel 2013, the Excel interface calls them *calculations*. However, the underlying VBA code still calls them *measures*.

If you have a Data Model pivot table and you check the Revenue field, you see the Revenue field move to the Values area. Behind the scenes, though, Excel is implicitly defining a new measure called Sum of Revenue. (You can see the implicit measures in the PowerPivot window if you use Excel 2013 Pro Plus.) In VBA, your first step is to define a new measure for Sum of Revenue. To make it easier to refer to this measure later, assign the new measure to an object variable:

```
' Before you can add Revenue to the pivot table,
' you have to define the measure.
' This happens using the GetMeasure method.
' Assign the cube field to CFRevenue object
Dim CFRevenue As CubeField
Set CFRevenue = PT.CubeFields.GetMeasure( _
    AttributeHierarchy:="[Sales].[Revenue]", _
    Function:=xlSum, _
    Caption:="Sum of Revenue")
' Add the newly created cube field to the pivot table
PT.AddDataField Field:=CFRevenue, _
    Caption:="Total Revenue"
PT.PivotFields("Total Revenue").NumberFormat = "$#,##0,K"
```

You can use the sample code to create a new measure. The following measure uses the new Distinct Count function to count the number of unique customers in each sector:

```
' Add Distinct Count of Customer as a Cube Field
Dim CFCustCount As CubeField
Set CFCustCount = PT.CubeFields.GetMeasure( _
    AttributeHierarchy:="[Sales].[Customer]", _
    Function:=xlDistinctCount, _
    Caption:="Customer Count")
```

13

```
' Add the newly created cube field to the pivot table
PT.AddDataField Field:=CFCustCount, _
    Caption:="Customer Count"
```

> **CAUTION**
>
> Before you get too excited, the Excel team drew an interesting line in the sand with regard to
> what parts of PowerPivot are available via VBA. Any functionality that is available in Office 2013
> Standard is available in VBA. If you try to define a new calculated field that uses the DAX language,
> it does not work in VBA.

Putting It All Together

Figure 13.32 shows the Data Model pivot table created using the code in Listing 13.7.

Figure 13.32
Two tables linked with a pivot table and two measures, all via a macro.

	A	B	C
1	Row Labels ▼	Total Revenue	Customer Count
2	Apparel	$758,407	2
3	Chemical	$568,851	1
4	Consumer	$2,194,976	7
5	Electronics	$222,022	4
6	Food	$750,163	1
7	Hardware	$2,178,683	11
8	Textiles	$34,710	1
9	Grand Total	$6,707,812	27

Listing 13.7   Code to Create a Data Model Pivot Table

```
Sub BuildModelPivotTable()
    Dim WBT As Workbook
    Dim WC As WorkbookConnection
    Dim MO As Model
    Dim PTCache As PivotCache
    Dim PT As PivotTable
    Dim WSD As Worksheet
    Dim CFRevenue As CubeField
    Dim CFCustCount As CubeField

    Set WBT = ActiveWorkbook
    Set WSD = WBT.Worksheets("Report")

    ' Build Connection to the main Sales table
    TableName = "Sales"
    WBT.Connections.Add Name:="LinkedTable_" & TableName, _
        Description:="MainTable", _
        ConnectionString:="WORKSHEET;" & WBT.FullName, _
        CommandText:=WBT.Name & "!" & TableName, _
        lCmdType:=7, _
        CreateModelConnection:=True, _
        ImportRelationships:=False
```

13

```
' Build Connection to the Sector lookup table
TableName = "Sector"
WBT.Connections.Add Name:="LinkedTable_" & TableName, _
    Description:="LookupTable", _
    ConnectionString:="WORKSHEET;" & WBT.FullName, _
    CommandText:=WBT.Name & "!" & TableName, _
    lCmdType:=7, _
    CreateModelConnection:=True, _
    ImportRelationships:=False

' Relate the two tables
Set MO = ActiveWorkbook.Model
MO.ModelRelationships.Add _
    ForeignKeyColumn:=MO.ModelTables("Sales").ModelTableColumns("Customer"), _
    PrimaryKeyColumn:=MO.ModelTables("Sector").ModelTableColumns("Customer")

' Delete any prior pivot tables
For Each PT In WSD.PivotTables
    PT.TableRange2.Clear
Next PT

' Define the PivotCache
Set PTCache = WBT.PivotCaches.Create(SourceType:=xlExternal, _
    SourceData:=WBT.Connections("ThisWorkbookDataModel"), _
    Version:=xlPivotTableVersion15)

' Create the Pivot Table from the Pivot Cache
Set PT = PTCache.CreatePivotTable( _
    TableDestination:=WSD.Cells(1, 1), TableName:="PivotTable1")

' Add the Sector field from the Sector table to the Row areas
With PT.CubeFields("[Sector].[Sector]")
    .Orientation = xlRowField
    .Position = 1
End With

' Before you can add Revenue to the pivot table,
' you have to define the measure.
' This happens using the GetMeasure method
' Assign the cube field to CFRevenue object
Set CFRevenue = PT.CubeFields.GetMeasure( _
    AttributeHierarchy:="[Sales].[Revenue]", _
    Function:=xlSum, _
    Caption:="Sum of Revenue")
' Add the newly created cube field to the pivot table
PT.AddDataField Field:=CFRevenue, _
    Caption:="Total Revenue"
PT.PivotFields("Total Revenue").NumberFormat = "$#,##0,K"

' Add Distinct Count of Customer as a Cube Field
Set CFCustCount = PT.CubeFields.GetMeasure( _
    AttributeHierarchy:="[Sales].[Customer]", _
    Function:=xlDistinctCount, _
```

```
        Caption:="Customer Count")
    ' Add the newly created cube field to the pivot table
    PT.AddDataField Field:=CFCustCount, _
        Caption:="Customer Count"

End Sub
```

Next Steps

In the next chapter, you learn many techniques for handling common questions and issues with pivot tables.

Advanced Pivot Table Tips and Techniques

14

In this chapter, you discover some techniques that provide unique solutions to some of the more common pivot table problems. Take some time to glance at the topics covered here. Who knows? You might find a few unique tips that can help you tackle some of your pivot table conundrums!

Tip 1: Force Pivot Tables to Refresh Automatically

In some situations you might need to have your pivot tables refresh themselves automatically. For instance, suppose you created a pivot table report for your manager. You might not be able to trust that he will refresh the pivot table when needed.

You can force each pivot table to automatically refresh when the workbook opens by following these steps:

1. Right-click your pivot table and select PivotTable Options.
2. In the activated dialog, select the Data tab.
3. Place a check next to Refresh Data When Opening the File property.

When this property is activated, the pivot table refreshes itself each time the workbook in which it's located is opened.

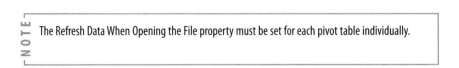

> **NOTE**   The Refresh Data When Opening the File property must be set for each pivot table individually.

Tip 2: Refresh All Pivot Tables in a Workbook at the Same Time

When you have multiple pivot tables in a workbook, refreshing all of them can be bothersome. There are several ways to avoid the hassle of manually refreshing multiple pivot tables. Here are a few options:

- **Option 1**—You can configure each pivot table in your workbook to automatically refresh when the workbook opens. To do so, right-click your pivot table and select PivotTable Options. This activates the PivotTable Options dialog. Here, select the Data tab and place a check next to Refresh Data When Opening the File property. After you have configured all pivot tables in the workbook, they will automatically refresh when the workbook is opened.

- **Option 2**—You can create a macro to refresh each pivot table in the workbook. This option is ideal when you need to refresh your pivot tables on demand, rather than only when the workbook opens. The idea is to start recording a macro. While the macro is recording, simply go to each pivot table in your workbook and refresh. After all pivot tables are refreshed, stop recording. The result is a macro that can be fired any time you need to refresh all pivot tables.

> **TIP**   Revisit Chapter 12, "Enhancing Your Pivot Table Reports with Macros," to get more detail on using macros with pivot tables.

- **Option 3**—You can use VBA to refresh all pivot tables in the workbook on demand. This option can be used when it is impractical to record and maintain macros that refresh all pivot tables. This approach entails the use of the RefreshAll method of the Workbook object. To employ this technique, start a new module and enter the following code:

```
Sub Refresh_All()
ThisWorkbook.RefreshAll
End Sub
```

You can now call this procedure any time you want to refresh all pivot tables within your workbook.

> **NOTE**   Keep in mind that the RefreshAll method refreshes all external data ranges along with pivot tables. This means that if your workbook contains data from external sources, such as databases and external files, that data is refreshed along with your pivot tables.

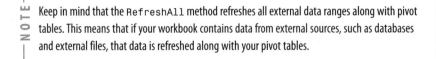

Tip 3: Sort Data Items in a Unique Order Not Ascending or Descending

Figure 14.1 shows the default sequence of regions in a pivot table report. Alphabetically, the regions are shown in sequence of Midwest, North, South, West. If your company is based in California, company traditions might dictate that the West region should be shown first, followed by Midwest, North, and South. Unfortunately, neither an ascending sort order nor a descending sort order can help you.

Figure 14.1

Company traditions dictate that the Region field should be in West-Midwest-North-South sequence.

	A	B	C	D	E	F
1						
2						
3	Sum of Sales_Amount	Column Labels				
4	Row Labels	MIDWEST	NORTH	SOUTH	WEST	Grand Total
5	Cleaning & Housekeeping Services	$174,518	$534,282	$283,170	$146,623	$1,138,593
6	Facility Maintenance and Repair	$463,077	$606,747	$846,515	$444,820	$2,361,158
7	Fleet Maintenance	$448,800	$610,791	$1,046,231	$521,976	$2,627,798
8	Green Plants and Foliage Care	$93,562	$155,021	$157,821	$870,379	$1,276,783
9	Landscaping/Grounds Care	$190,003	$299,309	$335,676	$365,928	$1,190,915
10	Predictive Maintenance/Preventative Maintenance	$478,928	$572,860	$472,045	$655,092	$2,178,925
11	Grand Total	$1,848,887	$2,779,009	$3,141,458	$3,004,818	$10,774,172

You can rearrange data items in your pivot table manually by simply typing the exact name of the data item where you would like to see its data. You can also drag the data item where you want it.

To solve the problem in this example, you simply type the **West** in cell B4 and then press Enter. The pivot table responds by resequencing the regions. The $3 million in sales for the West region automatically moves from column E to column B. The remaining regions move over to the next three columns.

Tip 4: Turn Pivot Tables into Hard Data

You created your pivot table only to summarize and shape your data. You do not want to keep the source data, nor do you want to keep the pivot table with all its overhead.

Turning your pivot table into hard data enables you to utilize the results of the pivot table without having to deal with the source data or a pivot cache. How you turn your pivot table into hard data depends on how much of your pivot table you are going to copy.

If you are copying just a portion of your pivot table, do the following:

1. Select the data you want to copy from the pivot table. Then right-click and select Copy.

2. Right-click anywhere on a spreadsheet and select Paste.

14

If you are copying your entire pivot table, follow these steps:

1. Select the entire pivot table, right-click, and select Copy. Alternatively, you can choose the Analyze tab, click Select, and then click Entire PivotTable.

2. Right-click anywhere on a spreadsheet and select Paste Special.

3. Select Values and then click OK.

> **TIP**
>
> You might want to consider removing any subtotals before turning your pivot table into hard data. Subtotals typically aren't very useful when you are creating a standalone data set.
>
> To remove the subtotals from your pivot table, first identify the field for which subtotals are being calculated. Then right-click the field's header (either in the pivot table itself or in the PivotTable Fields list) and select Field Settings. Selecting this option opens the Field Settings dialog. Here, you change the Subtotals option to None. After you click OK, your subtotals are removed.

Tip 5: Fill the Empty Cells Left by Row Fields

When you turn a pivot table into hard data, you are left not only with the values created by the pivot table, but also the pivot table's data structure. For example, the data in Figure 14.2 came from a pivot table that had a tabular layout.

Notice that the Market field kept the same row structure it had when this data was in the row area of the pivot table. It would be unwise to use this table anywhere else without filling in the empty cells left by the row field, but how do you easily fill these empty cells?

Figure 14.2
It would be impractical to use this data anywhere else without filling in the empty cells left by the row field.

	A	B	C	D
3	Region ▾	Market ▾	Product_Description ▾	Sum of Sales_Amount ▾
4	⊟MIDWEST	⊟DENVER	Cleaning & Housekeeping Services	$12,564
5			Facility Maintenance and Repair	$160,324
6			Fleet Maintenance	$170,190
7			Green Plants and Foliage Care	$42,409
8			Landscaping/Grounds Care	$73,622
9			Predictive Maintenance/Preventative Maintenance	$186,475
10		DENVER Total		$645,583
11		⊟KANSASCITY	Cleaning & Housekeeping Services	$65,439
12			Facility Maintenance and Repair	$132,120
13			Fleet Maintenance	$133,170
14			Green Plants and Foliage Care	$35,315
15			Landscaping/Grounds Care	$52,442
16			Predictive Maintenance/Preventative Maintenance	$156,412
17		KANSASCITY Total		$574,899
18		⊟TULSA	Cleaning & Housekeeping Services	$96,515
19			Facility Maintenance and Repair	$170,632
20			Fleet Maintenance	$145,440
21			Green Plants and Foliage Care	$15,838
22			Landscaping/Grounds Care	$63,939
23			Predictive Maintenance/Preventative Maintenance	$136,041
24		TULSA Total		$628,405
25	MIDWEST Total			$1,848,887

Excel 2013 actually provides you two effective ways of fixing this problem.

Option 1: Implement the Repeat All Data Items Feature

The first option is to apply the Repeat Item Labels functionality. This feature ensures that all item labels are repeated to create a solid block of contiguous cells. To implement this feature, place your cursor anywhere in your pivot table. Then go to the ribbon and select Design, Report Layout, Repeat All Item Labels (see Figure 14.3).

Figure 14.3
The Repeat All Item Labels option enables you to show your pivot data in one contiguous block of data.

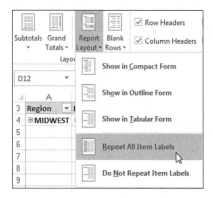

Figure 14.4 shows what a pivot table with this feature applied looks like.

Now you can turn this pivot table into hard values, ending up with a contiguous table of data without gaps.

Figure 14.4
The Repeat All Item Labels option fills all cells with data items.

	A	B	C	D
3	Region	Market	Product_Description	Sum of Sales_Amount
4	⊟MIDWEST	⊟DENVER	Cleaning & Housekeeping Services	$12,564
5	MIDWEST	DENVER	Facility Maintenance and Repair	$160,324
6	MIDWEST	DENVER	Fleet Maintenance	$170,190
7	MIDWEST	DENVER	Green Plants and Foliage Care	$42,409
8	MIDWEST	DENVER	Landscaping/Grounds Care	$73,622
9	MIDWEST	DENVER	Predictive Maintenance/Preventative Maintenance	$186,475
10	MIDWEST	DENVER Total		$645,583
11	MIDWEST	⊟KANSASCITY	Cleaning & Housekeeping Services	$65,439
12	MIDWEST	KANSASCITY	Facility Maintenance and Repair	$132,120
13	MIDWEST	KANSASCITY	Fleet Maintenance	$133,170
14	MIDWEST	KANSASCITY	Green Plants and Foliage Care	$35,315
15	MIDWEST	KANSASCITY	Landscaping/Grounds Care	$52,442
16	MIDWEST	KANSASCITY	Predictive Maintenance/Preventative Maintenance	$156,412
17	MIDWEST	KANSASCITY Total		$574,899
18	MIDWEST	⊟TULSA	Cleaning & Housekeeping Services	$96,515
19	MIDWEST	TULSA	Facility Maintenance and Repair	$170,632
20	MIDWEST	TULSA	Fleet Maintenance	$145,440
21	MIDWEST	TULSA	Green Plants and Foliage Care	$15,838
22	MIDWEST	TULSA	Landscaping/Grounds Care	$63,939
23	MIDWEST	TULSA	Predictive Maintenance/Preventative Maintenance	$136,041
24	MIDWEST	TULSA Total		$628,405
25	MIDWEST Total			$1,848,887

14

Option 2: Use Excel's Go To Special Functionality

The other solution to this problem involves using Excel's Go To Special functionality.

First convert your pivot table into hard data as demonstrated in Tip 4. Next, select the range in columns A and B that extends from the first row with blanks to the row just above the grand total. In the present example, this is A4:B100. Press the F5 key on your keyboard to activate the Go To dialog. The Go To Special dialog is a powerful feature that enables you to modify your selection based on various conditions. In the lower-left corner of the Go To dialog, choose the Special button. This activates the Go To Special dialog shown in Figure 14.5. From here, you choose the option for Blanks.

Figure 14.5
Using the Go To Special dialog enables you to select all the blank cells to be filled.

The result is that only the blank cells within your selection are selected.

Enter a formula to copy the pivot item values from the cell above to the blank cells. You can do this with four keystrokes. Type an equal sign. Press the up-arrow key. Hold down the Ctrl key while pressing Enter.

The equal sign tells Excel that you are entering a formula in the active cell. Pressing the up-arrow key points to the cell above the active cell. Pressing Ctrl+Enter tells Excel to enter a similar formula in all the selected cells instead of just the active cell. As Figure 14.6 illustrates, with these few keystrokes, you enter a formula to fill in all the blank cells at once.

You still should convert those formulas to values. However, if you attempt to copy the current selection, Excel presents an error; you cannot copy a selection that contains multiple selections. By selecting Blanks from the Go To Special dialog, you actually selected many areas of the spreadsheet.

You must reselect the original range A4:B100. You can then press Ctrl+C to copy and choose Edit, Paste Special, Values to convert the formulas to values.

This method provides a quick way to easily fill in the outline view provided by the pivot table.

Figure 14.6
Pressing Ctrl+Enter
enters the formula in all
selected cells.

	A	B	C	D
3	Region	Market	Product_Description	Sum of Sales_Amount
4	MIDWEST	DENVER	Cleaning & Housekeeping Services	$12,564
5	MIDWEST	DENVER	Facility Maintenance and Repair	$160,324
6	MIDWEST	DENVER	Fleet Maintenance	$170,190
7	MIDWEST	DENVER	Green Plants and Foliage Care	$42,409
8	MIDWEST	DENVER	Landscaping/Grounds Care	$73,622
9	MIDWEST	DENVER	Predictive Maintenance/Preventative Maintenance	$186,475
10	MIDWEST	DENVER Total		$645,583
11	MIDWEST	KANSASCITY	Cleaning & Housekeeping Services	$65,439
12	MIDWEST	KANSASCITY	Facility Maintenance and Repair	$132,120
13	MIDWEST	KANSASCITY	Fleet Maintenance	$133,170
14	MIDWEST	KANSASCITY	Green Plants and Foliage Care	$35,315
15	MIDWEST	KANSASCITY	Landscaping/Grounds Care	$52,442
16	MIDWEST	KANSASCITY	Predictive Maintenance/Preventative Maintenance	$156,412
17	MIDWEST	KANSASCITY Total		$574,899
18	MIDWEST	TULSA	Cleaning & Housekeeping Services	$96,515
19	MIDWEST	TULSA	Facility Maintenance and Repair	$170,632
20	MIDWEST	TULSA	Fleet Maintenance	$145,440
21	MIDWEST	TULSA	Green Plants and Foliage Care	$15,838
22	MIDWEST	TULSA	Landscaping/Grounds Care	$63,939
23	MIDWEST	TULSA	Predictive Maintenance/Preventative Maintenance	$136,041
24	MIDWEST	TULSA Total		$628,405

Tip 6: Add a Rank Number Field to Your Pivot Table

When you are sorting and ranking a field with a large number of data items, it can be
difficult to determine the number ranking of the current data item you are analyzing.
Furthermore, you might want to turn your pivot table into hard values for further analysis.
An integer field that contains the actual rank number of each data item could prove to be
helpful in analysis outside the pivot table.

Start with a pivot table similar to the one shown in Figure 14.7. Notice that the same data
measure is shown twice (in this case, SumOfSalesAmount).

Figure 14.7
Start with a pivot table
where the data value is
listed twice.

	A	B	C
1			
2			
3	Market	Sum of Sales_Amount	Sum of Sales_Amount2
4	BUFFALO	450478.27	450478.27
5	CALIFORNIA	2254735.38	2254735.38
6	CANADA	776245.27	776245.27
7	CHARLOTTE	890522.49	890522.49
8	DALLAS	467089.47	467089.47
9	DENVER	645583.29	645583.29
10	FLORIDA	1450392	1450392
11	KANSASCITY	574898.97	574898.97
12	MICHIGAN	678704.95	678704.95
13	NEWORLEANS	333453.65	333453.65
14	NEWYORK	873580.91	873580.91
15	PHOENIX	570255.09	570255.09
16	SEATTLE	179827.21	179827.21
17	TULSA	628404.83	628404.83
18	Grand Total	10774171.78	10774171.78

14

Right-click the second instance of data measure, select Show Values As, and then Rank Largest to Smallest (see Figure 14.8).

Figure 14.8
Adding a Rank field is simple with Excel 2013's Show Values As option.

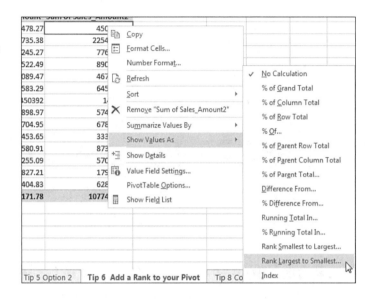

When your ranking is applied, you can adjust the labels and formatting as demonstrated in Figure 14.9. This leaves you with a clean-looking ranking report.

Figure 14.9
Your final pivot table with ranking applied.

Market	Sum of Sales_Amount	Rank
BUFFALO	$450,478	12
CALIFORNIA	$2,254,735	1
CANADA	$776,245	5
CHARLOTTE	$890,522	3
DALLAS	$467,089	11
DENVER	$645,583	7
FLORIDA	$1,450,392	2
KANSASCITY	$574,899	9
MICHIGAN	$678,705	6
NEWORLEANS	$333,454	13
NEWYORK	$873,581	4
PHOENIX	$570,255	10
SEATTLE	$179,827	14
TULSA	$628,405	8
Grand Total	$10,774,172	

Tip 7: Reduce the Size of Your Pivot Table Reports

When you initiate the creation of a pivot table report, Excel takes a snapshot of your data set and stores it in a *pivot cache*, which is nothing more than a special memory subsystem in which your data source is duplicated for quick access. That is to say, Excel literally makes a copy of your data and then stores it in a cache that is attached to your workbook.

Of course, the benefit you get from a pivot cache is optimization. Any changes you make to the pivot table report, such as rearranging fields, adding new fields, and hiding items, are made rapidly and with minimal overhead.

The downside of the pivot cache is that it basically doubles the size of your workbook. So every time you make a new pivot table from scratch, you essentially add to the file size of your workbook.

Delete Your Source Data Tab

If your workbooks have both your pivot table and your source data tab, you are wasting space. That is, you are essentially distributing two copies of the same data.

You can delete your source data and your pivot table will function just fine. After deleting the source data, saving shrinks the file.

Your clients can use the pivot table as normal, and your workbook is half as big. The only functionality you lose is the ability to refresh the pivot data because the source data is not there.

So what happens if your clients need to see the source data? Well, they can simply double-click the intersection of the row and column grand totals. This tells Excel to output the contents of the pivot table's cache into a new worksheet. So, with one double-click, your clients can re-create the source data that makes up the pivot table!

Tip 8: Create an Automatically Expanding Data Range

You will undoubtedly encounter situations in which you have pivot table reports that are updated daily (that is, records are constantly being added to the source data). When records are added to a pivot table's source data set, you must redefine the range that is captured before the new records are brought into the pivot table. Redefining the source range for a pivot table once in a while is no sweat, but when the source data is changed on a daily or weekly basis, it can start to get bothersome.

The solution is to turn your source data table into an "Excel table" before creating your pivot table. Again, Excel tables enable you to create a defined range that automatically shrinks or expands with the data. This enables any component, chart, pivot table, or formula tied to that range to keep up with changes in your data.

To implement this trick, simply highlight your source data and then click the Table icon on the Insert tab (see Figure 14.10). Confirm the range to be included in your table and then click OK.

After your source data has been converted to an Excel table, any pivot table you build on top of it automatically includes all records when your source data expands or shrinks.

14

Figure 14.10
Convert your source data into an Excel table.

> **NOTE**
> Keep in mind that although you won't have to redefine the source range anymore, you will still need to trigger a Refresh in order to have your pivot table show the current data.

Tip 9: Compare Tables Using a Pivot Table

If you've been an analyst for more than a week, you've been asked to compare two separate tables to come up with some brilliant analysis about the differences between them. This is a common scenario where leveraging a pivot table can save you some time.

In this scenario, imagine you have two tables that show customers in 2011 and in 2012. Figure 14.11 illustrates that these are two separate tables. For this example, the tables were made small for instructional purposes. Imagine you're working with something bigger here.

Figure 14.11
You need to compare these two tables.

	A	B	C	D	E	F	G
1	**2011 Customers**				**2012 Customers**		
2	Customer_Name	Fiscal Year	Revenue		Customer_Name	Fiscal Year	Revenue
3	PHALCO Corp.	2011	$456.27		PHALSM Corp.	2012	$1,902.25
4	PHALLA Corp.	2011	$3,974.07		PHALTA Corp.	2012	$2,095.01
5	PHALSE Corp.	2011	$565.34		PHALWH Corp.	2012	$1,740.27
6	PHALSM Corp.	2011	$1,902.25		PHMAN Corp.	2012	$3,228.33
7	POMTRA Corp.	2011	$2,201.90		POPPIT Corp.	2012	$604.18
8	POPAUS Corp.	2011	$1,891.73		POPUSL Corp.	2012	$870.28
9	POPCOA Corp.	2011	$1,284.61		POPUSP Corp.	2012	$2,421.01
10	PORADA Corp.	2011	$10,131.22		PORADA Corp.	2012	$10,131.22
11	PORCFA Corp.	2011	$1,187.71		PORADY Corp.	2012	$1,012.94
12					PORCFA Corp.	2012	$1,187.71

The idea is to create one table you can use to pivot. Be sure you have a way to tag which data comes from which table. As you can see in Figure 14.12, you have a column called Fiscal Year that serves this purpose.

Figure 14.12
Combine your tables into
one table.

	Customer_Name	Fiscal Year	Revenue
2	Customer_Name	Fiscal Year	Revenue
3	PHALCO Corp.	2011	$456.27
4	PHALLA Corp.	2011	$3,974.07
5	PHALSE Corp.	2011	$565.34
6	PHALSM Corp.	2011	$1,902.25
7	POMTRA Corp.	2011	$2,201.90
8	POPAUS Corp.	2011	$1,891.73
9	POPCOA Corp.	2011	$1,284.61
10	PORADA Corp.	2011	$10,131.22
11	PORCFA Corp.	2011	$1,187.71
12	PHALSM Corp.	2012	$1,902.25
13	PHALTA Corp.	2012	$2,095.01
14	PHALWH Corp.	2012	$1,740.27
15	PHMAN Corp.	2012	$3,228.33
16	POPPIT Corp.	2012	$604.18
17	POPUSL Corp.	2012	$870.28
18	POPUSP Corp.	2012	$2,421.01
19	PORADA Corp.	2012	$10,131.22
20	PORADY Corp.	2012	$1,012.94
21	PORCFA Corp.	2012	$1,187.71

After you have combined your tables, use the combined data set to create a new pivot table. Format the pivot table so that the table tag (the identifier telling you which table the data came from) is in the column area of the pivot table. In Figure 14.13, years are in the column area, and customers in the row area. The data area contains the count records for each customer name.

As you can see in Figure 14.13, you instantly get a visual indication of which customers are only in the 2011 table, which are in the 2012 table, and which are in both tables.

Figure 14.13
Create a pivot table to see
an easy-to-read visual
comparison of the two
data sets.

	A	B	C	D
1				
2	Count of Customer_Name	Fiscal Year ▾		
3	Customer_Name ▾	2011	2012	Grand Total
4	PHALCO Corp.	1		1
5	PHALLA Corp.	1		1
6	PHALSE Corp.	1		1
7	PHALSM Corp.	1	1	2
8	PHALTA Corp.		1	1
9	PHALWH Corp.		1	1
10	PHMAN Corp.		1	1
11	POMTRA Corp.	1		1
12	POPAUS Corp.	1		1
13	POPCOA Corp.	1		1
14	POPPIT Corp.		1	1
15	POPUSL Corp.		1	1
16	POPUSP Corp.		1	1
17	PORADA Corp.	1	1	2
18	PORADY Corp.		1	1
19	PORCFA Corp.	1	1	2
20	Grand Total	9	10	19

14

Tip 10: AutoFilter a Pivot Table

The conventional wisdom is that you can't apply an AutoFilter to a pivot table. Technically, that's true. But there is a way to trick Excel into making it happen.

The trick is to place your cursor directly adjacent to the last title in the pivot table, as demonstrated in Figure 14.14. Once you have it there, you can go to the application menu and select Data and then select AutoFilter.

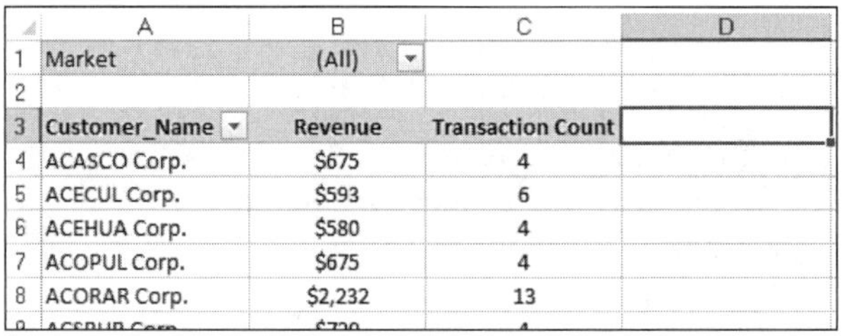

Figure 14.14
Place your cursor just outside your pivot table.

◢	A	B	C	D
1	Market	(All) ▼		
2				
3	Customer_Name ▼	Revenue	Transaction Count	
4	ACASCO Corp.	$675	4	
5	ACECUL Corp.	$593	6	
6	ACEHUA Corp.	$580	4	
7	ACOPUL Corp.	$675	4	
8	ACORAR Corp.	$2,232	13	
9	ACEBUR Corp.	$730	4	

At this point, you have AutoFilters on your pivot table! With this, you can do something cool, such as apply a custom AutoFilter to find all customers with an above-average transaction count (see Figure 14.15).

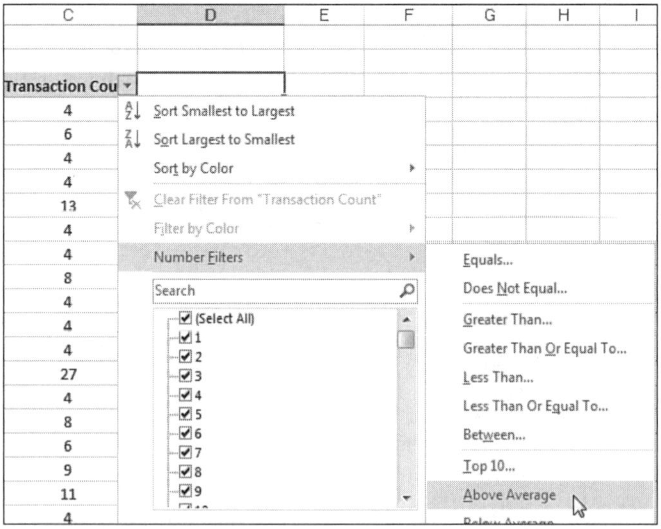

Figure 14.15
With AutoFilters implemented, you can take advantage of custom filtering not normally available to pivot tables.

C	D	E	F	G	H	I
Transaction Cou ▼						
4	Sort Smallest to Largest					
6	Sort Largest to Smallest					
4	Sort by Color ▶					
4						
13	Clear Filter From "Transaction Count"					
4	Filter by Color ▶					
4	Number Filters ▶	Equals...				
8		Does Not Equal...				
4	Search 🔍					
4	☑ (Select All)	Greater Than...				
4	☑ 1	Greater Than Or Equal To...				
27	☑ 2					
4	☑ 3	Less Than...				
8	☑ 4	Less Than Or Equal To...				
6	☑ 5					
9	☑ 6	Between...				
11	☑ 7	Top 10...				
4	☑ 8					
	☑ 9	Above Average ⌖				
		Below Average				

This is a fantastic way to add an extra layer of analytical capabilities to your pivot table reports.

14

Tip 11: Transpose a Data Set with a Pivot Table

In Chapter 2, "Creating a Basic Pivot Table," you learned that the perfect layout for the source data in a pivot table is a tabular layout. A tabular layout is a particular table structure where the following attributes exist: There are no blank rows or columns, every column has a heading, every field has a value in every row, and columns do not contain repeating groups of data.

Unfortunately, you often encounter data sets like the one shown in Figure 14.16. The problem is that the month headings are spread across the top of the table, pulling double duty as column labels and actual data values. In a pivot table, this format would force you to manage and maintain 12 fields, each representing a different month.

Figure 14.16
You need to convert this matrix-style table to a tabular data set.

⊿	A	B	C	D	E	F	G
1	Month	Product_Description	Jan	Feb	Mar	Apr	May
2	BUFFALO	Cleaning & Housekeeping Services	$6,219.66	$4,263.92	$5,386.12	$6,443.99	$4,36
3	BUFFALO	Facility Maintenance and Repair	$3,255.82	$9,490.00	$4,409.23	$4,957.62	$8,85
4	BUFFALO	Fleet Maintenance	$5,350.03	$8,924.71	$6,394.43	$6,522.46	$9,46
5	BUFFALO	Green Plants and Foliage Care	$2,415.08	$2,579.61	$2,401.91	$2,981.01	$2,70
6	BUFFALO	Landscaping/Grounds Care	$5,474.22	$4,500.52	$5,324.36	$5,705.68	$5,26
7	BUFFALO	Predictive Maintenance/Preventative Maintenance	$9,810.95	$10,180.23	$9,626.31	$11,700.73	$10,94
8	CALIFORNIA	Cleaning & Housekeeping Services	$2,840.76	$2,997.18	$2,096.78	$4,102.20	$47
9	CALIFORNIA	Facility Maintenance and Repair	$16,251.01	$35,878.99	$18,368.55	$21,843.53	$28,72
10	CALIFORNIA	Fleet Maintenance	$22,574.77	$36,894.89	$22,016.38	$27,871.10	$31,98
11	CALIFORNIA	Green Plants and Foliage Care	$48,250.90	$90,013.42	$51,130.17	$75,527.58	$69,41
12	CALIFORNIA	Landscaping/Grounds Care	$19,401.16	$21,190.57	$21,292.00	$20,918.35	$19,46
13	CALIFORNIA	Predictive Maintenance/Preventative Maintenance	$28,713.24	$46,073.56	$43,040.05	$46,000.02	$41,00

Interestingly enough, you can fix this issue by using a multiple consolidated pivot table. Follow these basic steps to convert this matrix-style data set to one that is appropriate for use with a pivot table.

Step 1: Combine All Non-Column-Oriented Fields into One Dimension Field

Due to the nature of multiple consolidation pivot tables, it's important that you have only one dimension column.

In this example, anything that isn't a month field is considered a dimension. So the Market and Product_Description fields need to be pulled into one column.

To do this you can simply type a formula that concatenates these two fields with a semicolon delimiter. Be sure you give your new column a name. You can see the exact formula to use in the formula bar shown in Figure 14.17.

After you create your concatenated column, be sure to convert the formulas into hard data. Select the newly created concatenated column, and then press Ctrl+C to copy and choose Edit, Paste Special, Values to convert the formulas to values.

Now you can remove the Market and Product_Description fields (see Figure 14.18).

14

Figure 14.17
Concatenate the Market and Product_Description fields with a semicolon delimiter.

Figure 14.18
Be sure to remove all but one dimension field.

Step 2: Create a Multiple Consolidation Ranges Pivot Table

The next step is to start the old PivotTable and PivotChart Wizard. Type Alt+D+P on your keyboard to call up the old wizard. You need this wizard because it's the only place you find the Multiple Consolidation Ranges option. Here are the steps to walk through the wizard:

1. Click the option for Multiple Consolidation Ranges and then click the Next button.

2. Select the I Will Create the Page Fields option and then click the Next button.

3. Define the range you are working with and then click Finish.

Step 3: Double-Click the Grand Total Intersection of Row and Column.

At this point, you should have a multiple consolidation pivot table that looks practically useless. Go to the intersection of the row and column Grand Totals and double-click the number (see Figure 14.19).

Figure 14.19
Double-click the intersection of row and column Grand Totals.

You get a new sheet similar to the one shown in Figure 14.20. This is essentially a transposed version of your data.

Figure 14.20

Your data set has been transposed.

	A	B	C
1	Row	Column	Value
2	BUFFALO;Cleaning & Housekeeping Services	Jan	6219.66
3	BUFFALO;Cleaning & Housekeeping Services	Feb	4263.92
4	BUFFALO;Cleaning & Housekeeping Services	Mar	5386.12
5	BUFFALO;Cleaning & Housekeeping Services	Apr	6443.99
6	BUFFALO;Cleaning & Housekeeping Services	May	4360.14
7	BUFFALO;Cleaning & Housekeeping Services	Jun	5097.46
8	BUFFALO;Cleaning & Housekeeping Services	Jul	7566.19
9	BUFFALO;Cleaning & Housekeeping Services	Aug	4263.92
10	BUFFALO;Cleaning & Housekeeping Services	Sep	7245.64
11	BUFFALO;Cleaning & Housekeeping Services	Oct	3847.15
12	BUFFALO;Cleaning & Housekeeping Services	Nov	6540.21
13	BUFFALO;Cleaning & Housekeeping Services	Dec	5610.45

Step 4: Parse Your Dimension Column into Separate Fields

Now all there is left to do is parse out the "Row" column into separate fields again. The first step in that process is to ensure there are enough columns to parse into. Because your "Row" column has one semicolon, you need one extra empty column. So, as demonstrated in Figure 14.21, add a new empty column next to the "Row" column.

Figure 14.21

Add an empty column so that there is enough room to parse the Row field into.

	A	B	C	D
1	Row	Column1	Column	Value
2	BUFFALO;Cleaning & Housekeeping Services		Jan	6219.66
3	BUFFALO;Cleaning & Housekeeping Services		Feb	4263.92
4	BUFFALO;Cleaning & Housekeeping Services		Mar	5386.12
5	BUFFALO;Cleaning & Housekeeping Services		Apr	6443.99
6	BUFFALO;Cleaning & Housekeeping Services		May	4360.14
7	BUFFALO;Cleaning & Housekeeping Services		Jun	5097.46
8	BUFFALO;Cleaning & Housekeeping Services		Jul	7566.19
9	BUFFALO;Cleaning & Housekeeping Services		Aug	4263.92
10	BUFFALO;Cleaning & Housekeeping Services		Sep	7245.64
11	BUFFALO;Cleaning & Housekeeping Services		Oct	3847.15
12	BUFFALO;Cleaning & Housekeeping Services		Nov	6540.21
13	BUFFALO;Cleaning & Housekeeping Services		Dec	5610.45

Select the "Row" (column A) and call up the Text to Columns dialog. Go to the ribbon and select Data, Text to Columns. The idea is to parse out the concatenated field using the semicolon delimiter.

In the wizard, select the Delimited option and then click Next.

On the next screen, select the Semicolon option, as demonstrated in Figure 14.22, and then click Finish.

After a few relabeling and formatting actions, your transposed data set should look similar to what's shown in Figure 14.23.

14

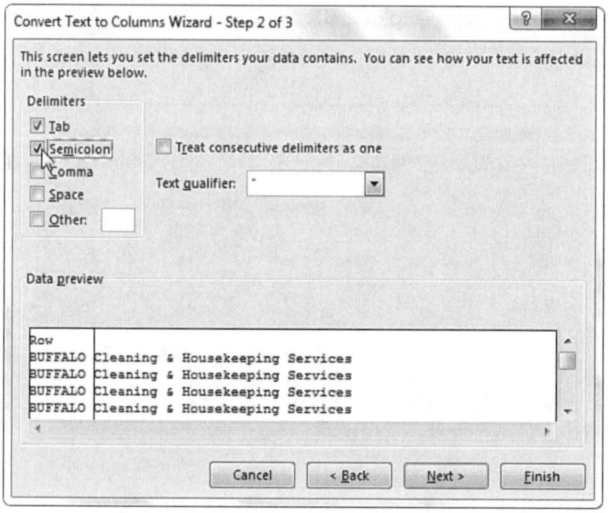

Figure 14.22
Choose the delimiter
option, and then click
Finish

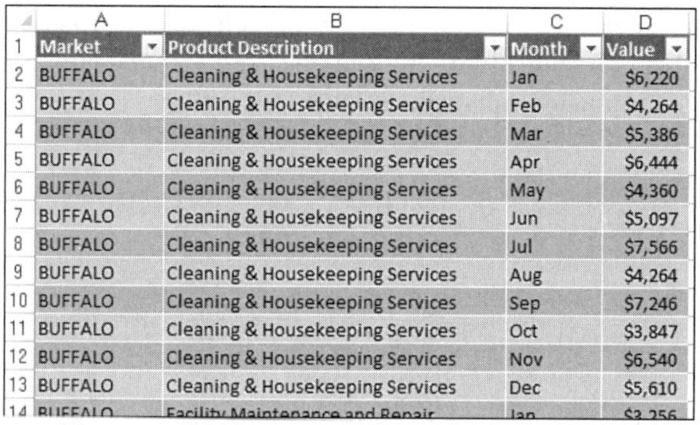

Figure 14.23
Your final transposed
data set.

Tip 12: Force Two Number Formats in a Pivot Table

Every now and then, you have to deal with a situation where a normalized data set makes it difficult to build an appropriate pivot table. For example, the data set shown in Figure 14.24 contains metrics information for each market. Notice a column that identifies the measure and a column that specifies the corresponding value.

Although this is generally a nicely formatted table, notice that some of the measures are meant to be Number format whereas others are meant to be Percentage. In the database where this data set originated, the Values field is a Double data type, so this works.

The problem is that when you create a pivot table out of this data set, you can't assign two different number formats for the Values field. After all, one field—one number format.

So as you can see in Figure 14.25, trying to set the number format for the percentage measures also changes the format for the measures that are supposed to be straight numbers.

14

Figure 14.24
This metric table has many different data types in one Value field.

	A	B	C	D	E
1	Region	Market	Product_Description	Measure	Value
2	MIDWEST	DENVER	Cleaning & Housekeeping Services	Revenue	12563.91
3	MIDWEST	DENVER	Cleaning & Housekeeping Services	Conversion Rate	0.62
4	MIDWEST	DENVER	Facility Maintenance and Repair	Revenue	160324.22
5	MIDWEST	DENVER	Facility Maintenance and Repair	Conversion Rate	0.64
6	MIDWEST	DENVER	Fleet Maintenance	Revenue	170190.26
7	MIDWEST	DENVER	Fleet Maintenance	Conversion Rate	0.20
8	MIDWEST	DENVER	Green Plants and Foliage Care	Revenue	42408.61
9	MIDWEST	DENVER	Green Plants and Foliage Care	Conversion Rate	0.88
10	MIDWEST	DENVER	Landscaping/Grounds Care	Revenue	73621.62
11	MIDWEST	DENVER	Landscaping/Grounds Care	Conversion Rate	0.92
12	MIDWEST	DENVER	Predictive Maintenance/Preventative	Revenue	186474.67
13	MIDWEST	DENVER	Predictive Maintenance/Preventative	Conversion Rate	0.93
14	MIDWEST	KANSASCITY	Cleaning & Housekeeping Services	Revenue	65439.14
15	MIDWEST	KANSASCITY	Cleaning & Housekeeping Services	Conversion Rate	0.61

Figure 14.25
You can only have one number format assigned to each data measure.

	A	B	C
1	Market	BUFFALO	
2			
3	Sum of Value	Measure	
4	Product_Description	Conversion Rate	Revenue
5	Cleaning & Housekeeping Services	27.08%	6684485.00%
6	Facility Maintenance and Repair	99.53%	6956962.00%
7	Fleet Maintenance	75.26%	8646011.00%
8	Green Plants and Foliage Care	0.36%	3483113.00%
9	Landscaping/Grounds Care	5.38%	6546546.00%
10	Predictive Maintenance/Preventative Maintenanc	31.58%	12730710.00%

The solution is to apply a custom number format that formats any value greater than 1.5 to a number. Any value less than 1.5 is formatted as a Percent. In the Format Cells dialog, click Custom and then enter the following syntax in the Type input (see Figure 14.26):

```
[>=1.5]$#,##0;[<1.5]0.0%
```

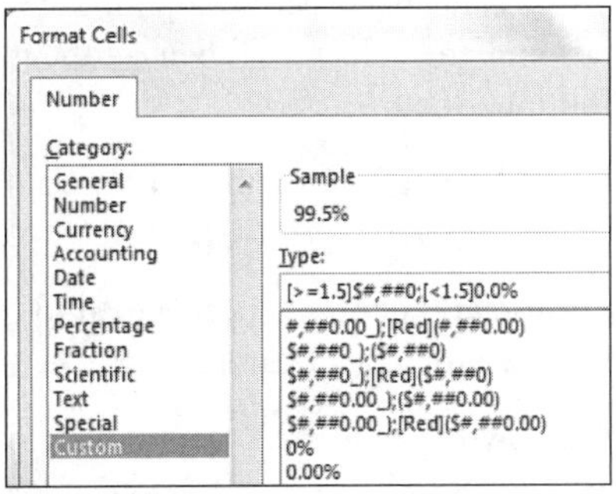

Figure 14.26
Apply a custom number format, telling Excel to format any number less than 1.5 to a percent.

The result, shown in Figure 14.27, is that each measure is now formatted appropriately. Obviously, you have to get a little lucky with the parameters of the situation you're working in. Although this technique doesn't work in all scenarios, it does open some interesting options.

Figure 14.27

Two formats in one Data field. Amazing!

▲	A	B	C
1	Market	BUFFALO .T	
2			
3	Sum of Value	Measure ▾	
4	Product_Description ▾	Conversion Rate	Revenue
5	Cleaning & Housekeeping Services	27.1%	$66,845
6	Facility Maintenance and Repair	99.5%	$69,570
7	Fleet Maintenance	75.3%	$86,460
8	Green Plants and Foliage Care	0.4%	$34,831
9	Landscaping/Grounds Care	5.4%	$65,465
10	Predictive Maintenance/Preventative Maintenance	31.6%	$127,307

Tip 13: Create a Frequency Distribution with a Pivot Table

If you've created a frequency distribution with the FREQUENCY function, you know it can quickly devolve into a confusing mess. The fact that it's an array formula doesn't help matters. Then there's that Histogram functionality you find in the Analysis ToolPak. That doesn't make life much better. Each time you have to change your bin ranges, you have to restart the entire process again.

In this tip, you learn how you can use a pivot table to quickly implement a simple frequency distribution.

First, you need to create a pivot table where the data values are plotted in the Rows area (not the Values area). Notice that in Figure 14.28, the Sales_Amount field is placed in the Rows area.

Next, right-click any value in the Rows area and select Group. In the Grouping dialog (shown in Figure 14.29), set the start and end values and then set the intervals. This essentially creates your frequency distribution.

After you click the OK button, you can leverage the result to create a distribution view of your data.

In Figure 14.30, you can see that Customer_Name has been added to get a frequency distribution of the number of customer transactions by dollar amount.

The obvious benefit to this technique is you can use the pivot table's Report Filter to interactively filter the data based on other dimensions such as Region and Market. Also, unlike with the Analysis ToolPak Histogram, you can quickly adjust your frequency intervals by simply right-clicking any number in the Rows area and selecting Group.

Figure 14.28
Place your data measure into the Rows area.

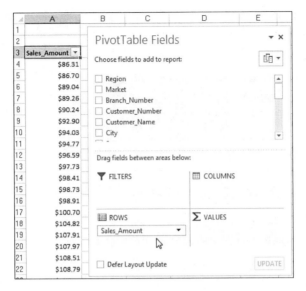

Figure 14.29
Use the Grouping functionality to create your frequency intervals.

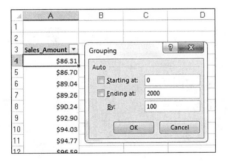

Figure 14.30
The frequency distribution of customer transactions by dollar amount.

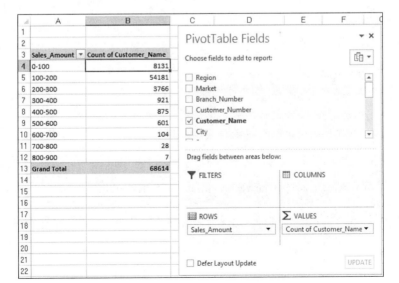

Tip 14: Use a Pivot Table to Explode a Data Set to Different Tabs

One of the most common requests an analyst gets is to create a separate pivot table report for each region, market, manager, or whatever. These types of requests usually lead to a painful manual process in which you copy a pivot table onto a new worksheet and then change the filter field to the appropriate region or manager. You then repeat this process as many times as you need to get through each selection.

Creating separate pivot table reports is one area where Excel really comes to the rescue. Excel has a function called Show Report Filter Pages that automatically creates a separate pivot table for each item in your filter fields.

To use this function, simply create a pivot table with a filter field, as shown in Figure 14.31.

Figure 14.31
Start with a pivot table that contains a filter field.

	A	B	C	D
1	Market	(All)		
2				
3	Sum of Sales_Amount	Sales_Period		
4	Product_Description	P01	P02	P03
5	Cleaning & Housekeeping Services	$80,083	$89,750	$78,182
6	Facility Maintenance and Repair	$121,304	$305,832	$115,232
7	Fleet Maintenance	$148,565	$297,315	$145,821
8	Green Plants and Foliage Care	$75,716	$135,529	$72,293
9	Landscaping/Grounds Care	$92,353	$99,173	$87,138
10	Predictive Maintenance/Preventative	$163,844	$189,317	$158,946
11	Grand Total	$681,865	$1,116,916	$657,611

Place your cursor anywhere on the pivot table and then go up to the ribbon to select the Analyze tab. On the Analyze tab, go to the PivotTable group and click the Options drop-down. Click the Show Report Filter Pages button, as demonstrated in Figure 14.32.

Figure 14.32
Click the Show Report Filter Pages button.

A dialog opens, enabling you to choose the filter field for which you would like to create separate pivot tables. Select the appropriate filter field and click OK.

Your reward is a sheet for each item in your filter field containing its own pivot table. Figure 14.33 illustrates the result. Note the newly created tabs are named to correspond with the filter item shown in the pivot table.

Figure 14.33
With just a few clicks, you can have a separate pivot table for each market!

A	B	C	D	E
1 Market	BUFFALO ⊤			
2				
3 Sum of Sales_Amount	Sales_Period ▼			
4 Product_Description ▼	P01	P02	P03	P04
5 Cleaning & Housekeeping Services	$6,220	$4,264	$4,873	$5,707
6 Facility Maintenance and Repair	$3,256	$9,490	$3,591	$3,780
7 Fleet Maintenance	$5,350	$8,925	$5,295	$6,671
8 Green Plants and Foliage Care	$2,415	$2,580	$1,961	$2,856
9 Landscaping/Grounds Care	$5,474	$4,501	$5,113	$4,691
10 Predictive Maintenance/Preventative Maintenance	$9,811	$10,180	$9,250	$10,365
11 Grand Total	$32,526	$39,939	$30,084	$34,070
12				
28				

◀ ▶ ⋯ | **BUFFALO** | CALIFORNIA | CANADA | CHARLOTTE | DALLAS | DENVER | FLORIDA

> **NOTE**
> Be aware that you can use Show Report Filter Pages on only one filter field at a time.

Tip 15: Use a Pivot Table to Explode a Data Set to Different Workbooks

Imagine you have a data set with 50,000+ rows of data. You have been asked to create a separate workbook for each market in this data set. In this tip, you discover how you can accomplish this task by using a pivot table and a little VBA.

Place the field you need to use as the group dimension (in this case, Market) into the Filter field. Place the count of Market into the data field. Your pivot table should look similar to the one shown in Figure 14.34.

Figure 14.34
Create a simple pivot table with one data field and a Report Filter.

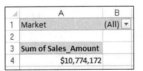

A	B
1 Market	(All) ▼
2	
3 Sum of Sales_Amount	
4	$10,774,172

As you know, you can manually select a market in the Page/Filter field and then double-click the Count of Market. This gives a new tab containing all the records that make up the number you double-clicked. You can imagine how you could do this for every market in the Market field and save the resulting tabs to their own workbook.

Using this same concept, you can implement the following VBA that goes through each item in your chosen page field and essentially calls the ShowDetail method for you, creating a raw data tab. The procedure then saves that raw data tab to a new workbook.

```
Sub ExplodeTable()
Dim PvtItem As PivotItem
Dim PvtTable As PivotTable
```

14

```
'Change variables to suit your scenario
    Const strFieldName = "Market"     '<-Change Field Name
    Const strTriggerRange = "B4"      '<-Change Trigger Range

'Set the pivot table name if needed
    Set PvtTable = ActiveSheet.PivotTables("PivotTable1") '<-Change PivotTable
    ➥Name if Needed

'Start looping through each item in the selected field
    For Each PvtItem In PvtTable.PivotFields(strFieldName).PivotItems
        PvtTable.PivotFields(strFieldName).CurrentPage = PvtItem.Name
        Range(strTriggerRange).ShowDetail = True

        'Name the temp sheet for easy cleanup later
        ActiveSheet.Name = "TempSheet"

        'copy data to new workbook and delete the temp sheet
        ActiveSheet.Cells.Copy
        Workbooks.Add
        ActiveSheet.Paste
        Cells.EntireColumn.AutoFit

        Application.DisplayAlerts = False
        ActiveWorkbook.SaveAs Filename:=ThisWorkbook.Path & "\" & PvtItem.Name &
        ➥".xls"
        ActiveWorkbook.Close
        Sheets("Tempsheet").Delete
        Application.DisplayAlerts = True

    Next PvtItem

End Sub
```

To implement this technique, enter this code into a new VBA module. Be sure to change these constants as appropriate for your scenario:.

- **Const strFieldName**—The field name is the name of the field you want to separate the data by (the field you put in the Page/Filter area of the pivot table).

- **Const strTriggerRange**—The trigger range is essentially the range that holds the one number in the pivot table's Data area. For example, if you look at Figure 14.34, you see the trigger cell in A4.

As you can see in Figure 14.35, running this procedure will output data for each market into its own separate workbook.

14

Figure 14.35
After you run this VBA, you have a separate workbook for each filtered dimension.

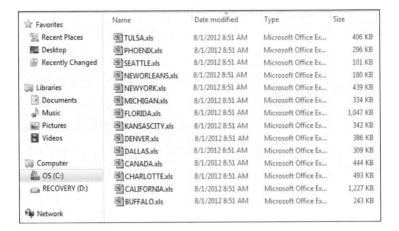

What's Next

In Chapter 15, "Dr. Jekyll and Mr. GetPivotData," you learn about one of the most hated pivot table features: the GetPivotData function. However, you also learn how to use this function to create refreshable reports month after month.

14

Dr. Jekyll and Mr. GetPivotData

15

This chapter shows you a technique that solves many annoying pivot table problems. If you have been using pivot tables for a while, you might have run into the following problems:

- Formatting tends to be destroyed when you refresh your pivot table. Numeric formats are lost. Column widths go away.

- There is no easy way to build an asymmetric pivot table. Named sets are one way, but they are only available in a pivot table model, not in a regular pivot cache pivot table.

- Excel cannot remember a template. If you frequently have to re-create a pivot table, you must redo the groupings, calculated fields, calculated items, and so on.

The technique shown in this chapter solves all these problems. It is not new. In fact, it has been around since Excel 2002. I have taught Power Excel seminars to thousands of accountants who use Excel 40–60 hours a week. Out of those thousands of people, I have only had three people say that they use this technique.

Ironically, far more than 0.3% of people know of this feature. One common question I get at seminars is, "Why did this feature show up in Excel 2002, and how the heck can you turn it off?" This same feature, which is reviled by most Excellers, is the key to creating reusable pivot table templates.

The credit for this chapter must go to Rob Collie, who spent years on the Excel project management team. He spent the Excel 2010 development cycle working on the PowerPivot product. Rob happened to relocate to Cleveland, Ohio. Because Cleveland is not a hotbed of Microsoft developers, Dave Gainer gave me a heads-up that Rob was moving to my area, and we started having lunch.

Rob and I talked about Excel and had some great conversations. During our second lunch, Rob said something that threw me for a loop. He said, "We find that our internal customers use GetPivotData all the time to build their reports, and we are not sure they will like the way PowerPivot interacts with GetPivotData."

I stopped Rob to ask if he was crazy. I told him that in my experience with about 5,000 accountants, only three of them had ever admitted to liking GetPivotData. What did he mean that he finds customers actually using GetPivotData?

Rob explained the key word in his statement: He was talking about *internal* customers, which are the people inside Microsoft who use Excel to do their jobs. Those people had become incredibly reliant on GetPivotData. He agreed that outside of Microsoft, hardly anyone ever uses GetPivotData. In fact, the only question he ever gets outside of Microsoft is how to turn off the stupid feature.

I had to know more, so I asked Rob to explain how the evil GetPivotData could ever be used for good purposes. Rob explained it to me, and I use this chapter to explain it to you. However, I know that 99% of you are reading this chapter because of the following reasons:

- You ran into the evil GetPivotData.
- You turned to the index of this book to find information on GetPivotData.
- You are expecting me to tell you how to turn off GetPivotData.

So, let's start there.

Turning Off the Evil GetPivotData Problem

GetPivotData has been the cause of many headaches since around the time of Excel 2002 when suddenly, without any fanfare, pivot table behavior changed slightly. Any time you build formulas outside a pivot table that point back inside the pivot table, you run into the evil GetPivotData problem.

For example, say you build the pivot table shown in Figure 15.1. Those years across the top are built by grouping daily dates into years. You would like to compare this year versus last year. Unfortunately, you are not allowed to add calculated items to a grouped field. So, you follow these steps:

1. Add a **% Growth** heading in cell D4.
2. Copy the formatting from C4 over to D4.
3. In cell D5, type an equal sign.
4. Click cell C5.
5. Type **/** (a slash) for division.
6. Click B5.

Figure 15.1

You want to add a formula to show the percentage of growth year after year.

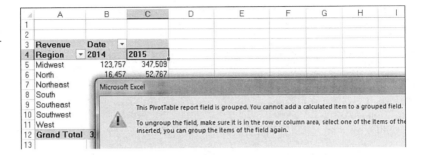

	A	B	C	D	E	F	G	H	I
1									
2									
3	Revenue	Date ▾							
4	Region ▾	2014	2015						
5	Midwest	123,757	347,509						
6	North	16,457	52,767						
7	Northeast								
8	South								
9	Southeast								
10	Southwest								
11	West								
12	Grand Total	3							
13									

Microsoft Excel

This PivotTable report field is grouped. You cannot add a calculated item to a grouped field.

⚠ To ungroup the field, make sure it is in the row or column area, select one of the items of the inserted, you can group the items of the field again.

7. Type **-1** and press Ctrl+Enter to stay in the same cell.Format the result as a percentage. You see that the Midwest region grew by 180.8%. That is impressive growth (see Figure 15.2).

Figure 15.2

Build the formula in D5 using the mouse or the arrow keys.

	A	B	C	D
1				
2				
3	Revenue	Date ▾		
4	Region ▾	2014	2015	% Growth
5	Midwest	123,757	347,509	180.8%
6	North	16,457	52,767	
7	Northeast	122,611	152,341	
8	South	2,185,357	3,196,892	
9	Southeast	359,782	801,992	
10	Southwest	141,861	191,353	
11	West	337,634	189,723	
12	Grand Total	3,287,458	4,932,576	
13				

NOTE

If you started using spreadsheets back in the days of Lotus 1-2-3, you can use this alternative method to build the formula in D5: Type = (an equal sign) and press the left arrow once. Type / (for division). Press the left arrow twice. Press Enter. As you see, the evil GetPivotData problem strikes no matter which method you use.

8. After entering your first formula, select cell D5.

9. Double-click the tiny square dot in the lower-right corner of the cell. This is the Fill handle, and it copies the formula down to the end of the report.

Immediately, you notice something is wrong because every region managed to grow by exactly 180.83% (see Figure 15.3).

There is no way that this happens in real life. The data must be fabricated. Look around: Are you working at Enron? If not, there must be another solution.

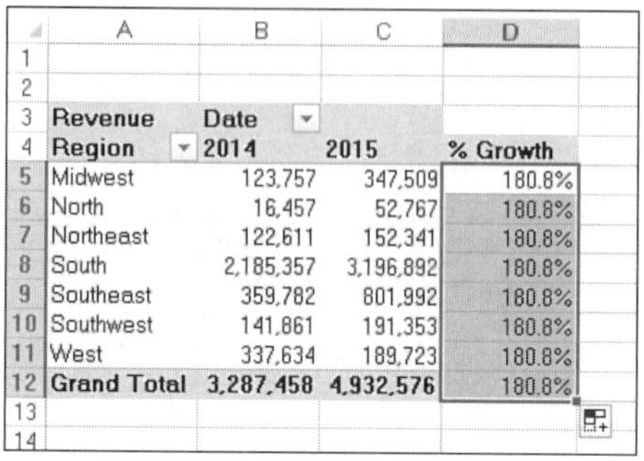

Figure 15.3
When the formula is copied down, somehow the growth is 180.83% for every region.

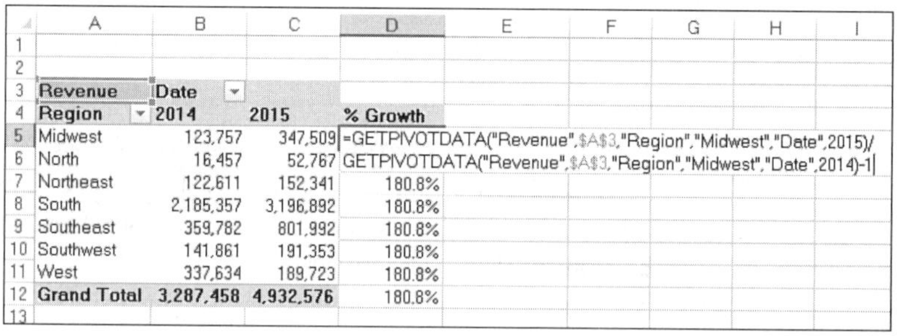

	A	B	C	D
1				
2				
3	Revenue	Date		
4	Region	2014	2015	% Growth
5	Midwest	123,757	347,509	180.8%
6	North	16,457	52,767	180.8%
7	Northeast	122,611	152,341	180.8%
8	South	2,185,357	3,196,892	180.8%
9	Southeast	359,782	801,992	180.8%
10	Southwest	141,861	191,353	180.8%
11	West	337,634	189,723	180.8%
12	Grand Total	3,287,458	4,932,576	180.8%
13				
14				

Think about the formula you built: 2015 divided by 2014 minus 1. You probably could create that formula with your eyes closed (that is, if you use arrow keys to create formulas instead of your mouse).

This is what makes you not notice something completely evil when you built the formula. When you went through the steps to build the formula, as a rational person you would expect Excel to create a formula such as =C5/B5-1. However, go back to cell D5 and press the F2 key to look at the formula (see Figure 15.4). Something evil has happened. The simple formula of =C5/B5-1 is no longer there. Instead, Excel generated some GetPivotData nonsense. Although the formula works in D5, it does not work when you copy the formula down.

Figure 15.4
Where did GetPivotData come from?

	A	B	C	D	E	F	G	H	I
1									
2									
3	Revenue	Date							
4	Region	2014	2015	% Growth					
5	Midwest	123,757	347,509	=GETPIVOTDATA("Revenue",$A$3,"Region","Midwest","Date",2015)/				
6	North	16,457	52,767	GETPIVOTDATA("Revenue",$A$3,"Region","Midwest","Date",2014)-1				
7	Northeast	122,611	152,341	180.8%					
8	South	2,185,357	3,196,892	180.8%					
9	Southeast	359,782	801,992	180.8%					
10	Southwest	141,861	191,353	180.8%					
11	West	337,634	189,723	180.8%					
12	Grand Total	3,287,458	4,932,576	180.8%					
13									

When this occurs, your reaction is something like, "What is GetPivotData, and why is it screwing up my report?" Your next reaction is, "How can I turn it off?" You might even wonder, "Why would Microsoft put this evil thing in there?"

Excel started inserting GetPivotData in Excel 2002. After being stung by GetPivotData repeatedly, I learned to hate it. I was thrown for a loop in one of the Power Analyst Boot Camps when someone asked me how it could possibly be used. I had never considered that question. In my mind, and in most people's minds, GetPivotData was evil and no good.

If you are one of those users who would just like to turn off GetPivotData, great news— there are two ways to do so, as presented in the following two sections.

Preventing GetPivotData by Typing the Formula

The simple method for avoiding GetPivotData is to create your formula without touching the mouse or the arrow keys. To do this, follow these steps:

1. Go to cell D5; type **=**.
2. Type **C5**.
3. Type **/**.
4. Type **B5**.
5. Type **-1**.
6. Press Enter.

You have now built a regular Excel formula that you can copy down to produce real results, as shown in Figure 15.5.

Figure 15.5
Type =**C5/B5-1**, and the formula works as expected.

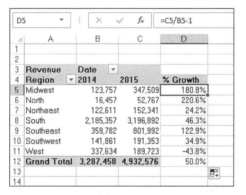

D5		:	✕	✓	f_x	=C5/B5-1

⊿	A	B	C	D
1				
2				
3	Revenue	Date ▾		
4	Region ▾	2014	2015	% Growth
5	Midwest	123,757	347,509	180.8%
6	North	16,457	52,767	220.6%
7	Northeast	122,611	152,341	24.2%
8	South	2,185,357	3,196,892	46.3%
9	Southeast	359,782	801,992	122.9%
10	Southwest	141,861	191,353	34.9%
11	West	337,634	189,723	-43.8%
12	Grand Total	3,287,458	4,932,576	50.0%
13				
14				

It is a relief to see you can still build formulas outside of pivot tables that point into a pivot table. I have run into people who simply thought this could not be done.

You might be a bit annoyed that you have to abandon your normal way of entering formulas. If so, the next section offers an alternative.

GetPivotData Is Surely Evil—Turn It Off

If you do not plan to read the second half of this chapter, you can simply turn off GetPivotData forever. Who needs it? It is evil, so just turn it off.

Back in Excel 2002 and Excel 2003, GetPivotData was hard to turn off. You had to go to Tools, Customize, Commands. Select Data from the left list box and then scroll 83% of the way through the right list box to find an icon called Generate GetPivotData. Drag that icon onto the Excel 2003 toolbar and close the dialog. Click the icon once to turn it off. Then, you could Alt+drag the icon off the toolbar because you would never need to turn on this evil feature again!

In Excel 2013, follow these steps:

1. Move the cell pointer back inside a pivot table so that the PivotTable Tools tabs appear.
2. Click the Analyze tab.
3. Notice the Options icon on the left side of the ribbon (see Figure 15.6). Do not click the icon. Next to the options icon, click the drop-down arrow.

Figure 15.6
Don't click the large Options icon. Click the tiny drop-down arrow next to the icon.

Options Drop-down

4. Inside the Options drop-down is a choice for Generate GetPivotData (see Figure 15.7). By default, this option is selected. Click that item to clear this check box.

Figure 15.7
Select Generate GetPivotData to turn the feature off.

The previous steps assume that you have a pivot table in the workbook that you can select in order to access the PivotTable tabs. If you don't have a pivot table in the current workbook, you can use File, Options. In the Formulas category, uncheck Use GetPivotData Functions for PivotTable References.

Why Did Microsoft Force GetPivotData on Us?

If GetPivotData is so evil, why did the fine people at Microsoft turn on the feature by default? Everyone simply wants to turn it off. Why would they bother to leave it on? Are they trying to make sure that there is a market for my Power Excel seminars?

I have a theory about this that I came up with during the Excel 2007 launch. I had written many books about Excel 2007, somewhere around 1,800 pages of content. When the Office 2007 launch events were happening around the country, I was given an opportunity to work at the event. I watched with interest when the presenter talked about the new features in Excel 2007.

There were at least 15 amazing features in Excel 2007. The presenter took three minutes and glossed over perhaps two and a half of the features.

I was perplexed. How could Microsoft marketing do such a horrible job of showing what was new in Excel? Then, I realized that this must always happen. Marketing asks the development team what is new. The project manager gives them a list of 15 items. The marketing guy says something like, "There is not room for 15 items in the presentation. Can you cut 80% of those items out of the list and give me just the ones with glitz and sizzle?"

Whoever worked on GetPivotData certainly knew that GetPivotData would never have enough sizzle to make it into the marketing news about Excel 2002. So, by making it the default, they hoped someone would notice GetPivotData and try to figure out how it could be used. Instead, most people, including me, just turned it off and thought it was another step in the Microsoft plot to make our lives miserable by making it harder to work in Excel.

Using GetPivotData to Solve Pivot Table Annoyances

You would not be reading this book if you hadn't realized that pivot tables are the greatest invention ever. Six clicks can create a pivot table that obsoletes the arcane process of using Advanced Filter, =DSUM, and data tables. Pivot tables enable you to produce one-page summaries of massive data sets. So what if the formatting is ugly? And so what if you usually end up converting most pivot tables to values so you can delete the columns you do not need but cannot turn off?

Figure 15.8 illustrates a typical pivot table experience. In this case, you should start with raw data. You then produce a pivot table and use all sorts of advanced pivot table tricks to get it close. You conclude by converting the pivot table to values and performing the final formatting in regular Excel.

Figure 15.8
Typical pivot table process.

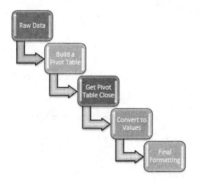

> NOTE
>
> I rarely get to refresh a pivot table because I never let pivot tables live long enough to have new data. The next time I get data, I start creating the pivot table all over again. If it is a long process, I write a macro that lets me fly through the five steps in Figure 15.8 in a couple of keystrokes.

The new method introduced by Rob Collie and described in the rest of this chapter puts a different spin on all this. In this method, you build an ugly pivot table. You do not care about the formatting of this pivot table. You then go through a one-time, relatively painful process of building a nicely formatted shell to hold your final report. Finally, you use GetPivotData to populate the shell report quickly.

From then on when you get new data, you simply put it on the data sheet, refresh the ugly pivot table, and print the shell report. Figure 15.9 illustrates this process.

Figure 15.9
How people who work at Microsoft use pivot tables.

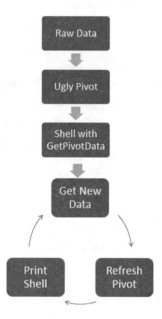

There are huge advantages to this method. For example, you do not have to worry about formatting the report after the first time. It comes much closer to an automated process.

The rest of this chapter walks you through the steps to build a dynamic report that shows actuals for months that have been completed and a forecast for future months.

Build an Ugly Pivot Table

You have transactional data showing budget and actuals for each region of a company. The budget data is at a monthly level. The actuals data is at a daily level. Budget data exists for the entire year. Actuals exist only for the months that have been completed. Figure 15.10 shows the original data set.

Because you will be updating this report every month, it makes the process easier if you have a pivot table data source that grows as you add new data to the bottom. Whereas legacy versions of Excel would achieve this through a named dynamic range using the OFFSET function, you can do this in Excel 2013 by selecting one cell in your data and pressing Ctrl+T. Click OK to confirm that your data has headers.

You now have a formatted data set, as shown in Figure 15.10.

Figure 15.10
The original data includes budget and actuals.

	A	B	C	D
1	Region	Date	Measure	Revenue
2	Midwest	1/1/2015	Budget	248000
3	North	1/1/2015	Budget	90000
4	Northeast	1/1/2015	Budget	266000
5	South	1/1/2015	Budget	360000
6	Southeast	1/1/2015	Budget	675000
7	Southwest	1/1/2015	Budget	293000
8	West	1/1/2015	Budget	563000
9	Midwest	2/1/2015	Budget	248000
10	North	2/1/2015	Budget	90000
11	Northeast	2/1/2015	Budget	266000
12	South	2/1/2015	Budget	360000
13	Southeast	2/1/2015	Budget	675000
14	Southwest	2/1/2015	Budget	293000
15	West	2/1/2015	Budget	563000

Your next step is to create a pivot table that has every possible value needed in your final report. You've learned that GetPivotData is powerful, but it can only return values that are visible in the actual pivot table. It cannot reach through to the pivot cache to calculate items that are not in the pivot table.

Create the pivot table by following these steps:

1. Select Insert, PivotTable, OK.

2. In the PivotTable Field List, select the Date field. Daily dates appear down the left side (see Figure 15.11).

Figure 15.11
Start with daily dates down the left.

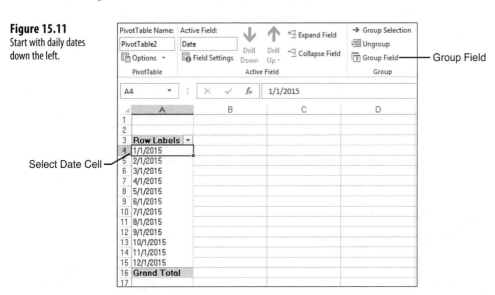

3. Select the first date cell in A4. From the PivotTable Options tab, select Group Field. Select Months and Years, as shown in Figure 15.12. Click OK. You now have actual month names down the left side, as shown in Figure 15.13.

Figure 15.12
Group the daily dates up to months and years.

Figure 15.13
You have month names instead of dates.

4. Drag the Years and Date field to the Column Labels drop zone in the Pivot Table Field List.

5. Drag Measure to the Column Labels drop zone.

6. Select Region to have it appear along the left column of the pivot table.

7. Select Revenue to have it appear in the Values area of the pivot table.

As shown in Figure 15.14, you now have one ugly pivot table. You might hate the words "Row Labels" and "Column Labels." And having a total of January Actuals plus January Budget in column D is completely pointless. This is ugly. And for once, you do not care because no one other than you will ever see this pivot table.

Figure 15.14
The world's ugliest pivot table. Summing Actuals + Budget in column D is completely meaningless.

▲	A	B	C	D	E	F
1						
2						
3	Sum of Revenue	Column Labels ▼				
4		⊟2015				
5		⊟Jan			Jan Total	⊟Feb
6	Row Labels ▼	Actuals	Budget		Actuals	Budget
7	Midwest	312387	248000	560387	266949	248000
8	North	100742	90000	190742	95197	90000
9	Northeast	277435	266000	543435	336005	266000
10	South	4182773	360000	4542773	4182773	360000
11	Southeast	926977	675000	1601977	789647	675000
12	Southwest	361686	293000	654686	329772	293000
13	West	578379	563000	1141379	596267	563000
14	**Grand Total**	**6740379**	**2495000**	**9235379**	**6596610**	**2495000**
15						

At this point, the goal is to have a pivot table with every possible data point you could ever need in your final report. It is fine if the pivot table has extra data you will never need in your report.

Build the Shell Report

Insert a blank worksheet in your workbook. Put away your pivot table hat and take out your straight Excel hat. You are going to use basic Excel formulas and formatting to create a nicely formatted report suitable for giving to your manager.

Follow these steps:

1. Put a report title in cell A1.

2. Use the Cell Styles drop-down on the Home tab to format cell A1 as a Title.

3. Put a date in cell A2 by using the formula =EOMONTH(TODAY(),0). This enters the serial number of the last day of the previous month in cell B1. If you want to see how the formula is working, you can format the cell as a Date. If you are reading this on July 14, 2015, the date that appears in cell B1 is June 30, 2015.

4. Select cell A2. Press Ctrl+1 to go to Format Cells. On the Number tab, click Custom. Type a custom number format of **"Actuals Through "mmmm, yyyy**. This causes the calculated date to appear as text.

5. There is a chance that the text in cell A2 is going to be wider than you want column A to be. Select both cells A2 and B2. Press Ctrl+1 to format the cells. On the Alignment tab, select Merge Cells. This allows the formula in cell A2 to spill over into B2 if necessary.

6. Type a Region heading in cell A5.

7. Down the rest of column A, type your region names. These names should match the names in the pivot table.

8. Where appropriate, add labels in column A for Division totals.

9. Add a line for Total Company at the bottom of the report.

10. Month names stretch from cells B4 to M4. Enter this formula in cell B4: `=DATE(YEAR($A$2),COLUMN(A1),1)`.

11. Select cell B4. Press Ctrl+1 to format the cells. On the Number tab, select Custom and type a custom number format of **MMM**.

12. Right-justify cell B4. Use the Cell Styles drop-down to select Heading 4.

13. Copy cell B4 to cells C4:M4. You now have true dates across the top that appear as month labels.

14. Enter this formula in cell B5: `=IF(MONTH(B4)<=MONTH($A$2),"Actuals","Budget")`. Right-justify cell B5. Copy across to cells C5:M5. This should provide the word *Actuals* for past months, but the word *Budget* for future months.

15. Add a Total column heading in cell N5. Add a Total Budget column in cell O5. Enter **Var %** in cell P5.

16. Fill in the regular Excel formulas necessary to provide division totals, the total company row, the grand total column, and the variance % column. For example:

   ■ Enter `=SUM(B6:B7)` in cell B8 and copy across.

   ■ Enter `=SUM(B6:M6)` in cell N6 and copy down.

   ■ Enter `=IFERROR((N6/O6)-1,0)` in cell P6 and copy down.

   ■ Enter `=SUM(B10:B12)` in cell B13 and copy across.

   ■ Enter `=SUM(B15:B16)` in cell B17 and copy across.

   ■ Enter `=SUM(B6:B18)/2` in cell B19 and copy across.

17. Apply the Heading 4 cell style to the labels in column A and the headings in rows 4:5.

18. Apply the **#,##0** number format to cells B6:O19.

19. Apply the **0.0%** number format to column P.

> **NOTE**
> If the names in the pivot table are region codes, you can hide the codes in a new hidden column A and put friendly region names in column B.

You now have a completed shell report, as shown in Figure 15.15. This report has all the necessary formatting as desired by your manager. It has totals that add up the numbers that eventually come from the pivot table.

In the next section, you use GetPivotData to complete the report.

Figure 15.15

The shell report before the GetPivotData formulas added.

	A	B	C	D	E	F	G	H	I	J	K	L	M	N	O	P
4		Jan	Feb	Mar	Apr	May	Jun	Jul	Aug	Sep	Oct	Nov	Dec		Total	
5	Region	Actuals	Actuals	Actuals	Actuals	Actuals	Actuals	Actuals	Budget	Budget	Budget	Budget	Budget	Total	Budget	Var. %
6	Northeast													0		0.0%
7	Southeast													0		0.0%
8	East Division Total	0	0	0	0	0	0	0	0	0	0	0	0	0	0	0.0%
9																
10	Midwest													0		0.0%
11	North													0		0.0%
12	South													0		0.0%
13	Central Division Total	0	0	0	0	0	0	0	0	0	0	0	0	0	0	0.0%
14																
15	West													0		0.0%
16	Southwest													0		0.0%
17	West Division Total	0	0	0	0	0	0	0	0	0	0	0	0	0	0	0.0%
18																
19	Total Company	0	0	0	0	0	0	0	0	0	0	0	0	0	0	0.0%

15

Using GetPivotData to Populate the Shell Report

At this point, you are ready to take advantage of the thing that has been driving you crazy for years—that crazy Generate GetPivotData setting. If you cleared the setting back in Figure 15.7, go in and select this again. When it is selected, you see a check mark next to Generate GetPivotData.

Go to cell B6 on the shell report (this is the cell for Northeast region, January, Actuals) and then follow these steps:

1. Type = (equal sign) to start a formula (see Figure 15.16).

Figure 15.16

Start a formula on the shell report.

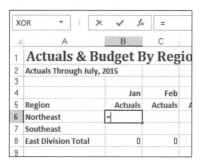

2. Move to the pivot table worksheet and click the cell for Northeast, January, Actuals. In Figure 15.17, this is cell B9.

3. Press Enter to return to the shell report and complete the formula. Excel adds a GetPivotData function in cell B6.

The formula says that the Northeast region actuals are $277,435.

> **TIP**
>
> Jot down this number because you will want to compare it to the result of the formula that you later edit.

Figure 15.17
Using the mouse, click the correct cell in the pivot table.

	A	B	C	D	E
B9	▼ : × ✓ *fx*	=GETPIVOTDATA("Revenue",UglyPivotT			
1					
2					
3	Sum of Revenue	Column Labels ▼			
4		⊟2015			
5		⊟Jan		Jan Total	⊟Feb
6	Row Labels ▼	Actuals	Budget		Actuals Bu
7	Midwest	312387	248000	560387	266949
8	North	100742	90000	190742	95197
9	Northeast	277435	266000	543435	336005
10	South	4182773	360000	4542773	4182773
11	Southeast	926977	675000	1601977	789647
12	Southwest	361686	293000	654686	329772
13	West	578379	563000	1141379	596267
14	Grand Total	6740379	2495000	9235379	6596610 24
15					

The initial formula is as follows:

```
=GETPIVOTDATA("Revenue",UglyPivotTable!$A$3,"Region","Northeast","Date",1, _
    "Measure","Actuals","Years",2015)
```

After years of ignoring the GetPivotData formula, you need to look at this monster formula closely to understand what it is doing. Figure 15.18 shows the formula in edit mode, along with the formula tooltip.

Figure 15.18
The GetPivotData formula generated by Microsoft.

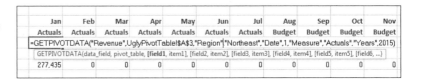

Jan	Feb	Mar	Apr	May	Jun	Jul	Aug	Sep	Oct	Nov
Actuals	Actuals	Actuals	Actuals	Actuals	Actuals	Actuals	Budget	Budget	Budget	Budget
=GETPIVOTDATA("Revenue",UglyPivotTable!$A$3,"Region"|"Northeast","Date",1,"Measure","Actuals","Years",2015)										
GETPIVOTDATA(data_field, pivot_table, [field1, item1], [field2, item2], [field3, item3], [field4, item4], [field5, item5], [field6, ...])										
277,435	0	0	0	0	0	0	0	0	0	0

Here are the arguments in the formula:

- **Data Field**—This is the field in the Value area of the pivot table. Note that you use Revenue, not Sum of Revenue.

- **Pivot Table**—This is Microsoft's way of asking, "Which pivot table do you mean?" All you have to do here is point to one single cell within the pivot table. The entry of UglyPivotTable!$A$3 is the first populated cell in the pivot table. You are free to choose any cell in the pivot table you want. However, because it does not matter which cell you choose, don't worry about getting clever here. Leave the formula pointing to $A$3, and you will be fine.

- **Field 1, Item 1**—The formula generated by Microsoft shows Region as the field name and Northeast as the item value. Aha! So this is why the GetPivotData formulas that Microsoft generates cannot be copied. They are essentially hard-coded to point to one specific value. You want your formula to change as you copy it through your report. Edit the formula to change Northeast to $A6. By using only a single dollar sign before A, you are enabling the row portion of the reference to vary as you copy the formula down.

■ **Field 2, Item 2**—The next two pairs of arguments specify that the Date field should be 1. When the original pivot table was grouped by month and year, the month field retained the original field name of Date. The value for month is 1, which means January. You probably thought I was insane to build that outrageous formula and custom number format in cell B4. That formula becomes useful now. Instead of hard-coding a 1, use MONTH(B$4). Again, the single dollar sign before row 4 indicates that the formula can get data from other months as it is copied across, but it should always reach back up to row 4 as it is copied down.

■ **Field 3, Item 3**—The field name is Measure and the item is Actuals. This happens to be correct for January, but when you get to future months, you want the measure to switch to Budget. Change the hard-coded Actuals to point to B$5.

■ **Field 4, Item 4**—This is Years and 2015. I was almost ready to leave this one alone because it would be months before we have a new year. However, why not change 2015 to YEAR($A$2)?

The new formula is shown in Figure 15.19. Rather than a formula that is hard-coded to work with only one value, you have created a formula that can be copied throughout the data set.

Figure 15.19

After being edited, the GetPivotData formula is ready for copying.

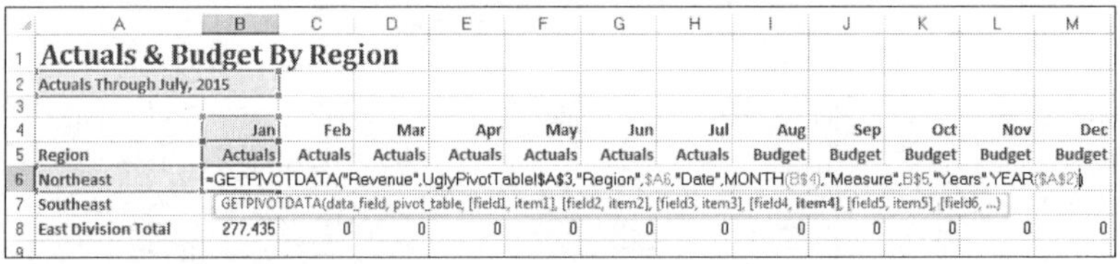

	A	B	C	D	E	F	G	H	I	J	K	L	M
1	**Actuals & Budget By Region**												
2	Actuals Through July, 2015												
3													
4		Jan	Feb	Mar	Apr	May	Jun	Jul	Aug	Sep	Oct	Nov	Dec
5	Region	Actuals	Actuals	Actuals	Actuals	Actuals	Actuals	Actuals	Budget	Budget	Budget	Budget	Budget
6	Northeast	=GETPIVOTDATA("Revenue",UglyPivotTable!$A$3,"Region",$A6,"Date",MONTH(B$4),"Measure",B$5,"Years",YEAR($A$2))											
7	Southeast	GETPIVOTDATA(data_field, pivot_table, [field1, item1], [field2, item2], [field3, item3], [field4, item4], [field5, item5], [field6, ...])											
8	East Division Total	277,435	0	0	0	0	0	0	0	0	0	0	0
9													

When you press Enter, you have the exact same answer that you had before editing the formula. Compare this with the number you jotted down earlier to make sure.

The edited formula is as follows:

```
=GETPIVOTDATA("Revenue", UglyPivotTable!$A$3,"Region",$A6,"Date", MONTH(B$4), _
   "Measure",B$5,"Years",YEAR($A$2))
```

Copy this formula to all the blank calculation cells in columns B:M. Do not copy the formula to column O yet. Now that you have real numbers in the report, you might have to adjust some column widths.

You can tweak the GetPivotData formula for the months to get the total budget. If you copy one formula to cell O6, you get a #REF! error because the word *Total* in cell O4 does not evaluate to a month. Edit the formula to the pairs of arguments for Month and Years. You still have an error.

For GetPivotData to work, the number you are looking for must be in the pivot table. Because the original pivot table had Measure as the third column field, there is no actual column for Budget total. Move the Measure field to be the first Column field, as shown in Figure 15.20.

15

Figure 15.20
Tweak the layout of the Column Labels fields so you have a Budget Total column.

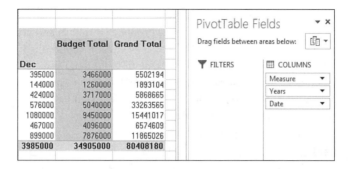

When you return to the shell report, you find that the Total Budget formula in cell O6 is now working fine. Copy that formula down to the other blank data cells in column O (see Figure 15.21). Note with amazement that all the other formulas work, even though everything in the underlying pivot table moved.

Figure 15.21
After rearranging the pivot table, you have a working formula for Total Budget.

The formula in O6 is as follows:

```
=GETPIVOTDATA("Revenue",UglyPivotTable!$A$3,"Region",$A6,"Measure",O$5)
```

You now have a nicely formatted shell report that grabs values from a live pivot table. It certainly takes more time to set up this report for the first month that you have to produce it, but it will be a breeze to update the report in future months.

Updating the Report in Future Months

In future months, you can update your report by following these steps:

1. Paste actuals for the new month just below the original data set. Because the original data set is a table, the table formatting automatically extends to the new rows. The pivot table source definition also extends.

2. Go to the pivot table. Click the Refresh button on the Options tab. The shape of the pivot table changes, but you do not care.

3. Go to the shell report. In real life, you are done, but to test it, enter a date in cell B2 such as **8/30/2015**.

> **NOTE** Every month, these three steps are the payoff to this chapter. As shown in Figure 15.21, the data for July changed from Budget to Actuals. Formulas throughout recalculated. You do not have to worry about re-creating formats, formulas, and so on.

This process is so simple that you will probably forget about the pain that you used to endure to create these monthly reports. The one risk is that a company reorg will add new regions to the pivot table. To be sure that your formulas are still working, add a small check section outside of the print range of the report. This formula in cell A22 checks to see if the budget total calculated in cell O19 matches the budget total back in the pivot table. Here is the formula:

```
=IF(GETPIVOTDATA("Revenue",UglyPivotTable!$A$3,"Measure","Budget")=$O$19,"", _
   "Caution!!! It appears that new regions have been added to the pivot table.
You might have to add new rows to this report for those regions."
```

In case the new region comes from a misspelling in the actuals, this formula checks the YTD actuals against the pivot table. Enter the following formula in cell A23:

```
=IF(SUMIF(B5:M5,"Actuals",B19:M19)=GETPIVOTDATA("Revenue",UglyPivotTable!$A$3, _
   "Measure","Actuals"),"","Caution!!! It appears that new regions have been _
   added to the pivot table. You might have to add new rows to this report for _
   those regions.")
```

Change the font color of both these cells to red. You do not even notice them down there until something goes wrong.

I thought that I would never write these words: GetPivotData is the greatest thing ever. How could we ever live without it?

Index

B

C

S

W

X-Y-Z